The Little
FIELD MARSHAL

The Little
FIELD MARSHAL

A LIFE OF SIR JOHN FRENCH

RICHARD
HOLMES

WEIDENFELD & NICOLSON

To all ranks of
A company
5th (Volunteer) Battalion
The Queen's Regiment

Weidenfeld & Nicolson
Wellington House
125 Strand
London WC2R 0BB

ISBN 0-297-84614-0

Printed and bound in Great Britain by
Clays Ltd, St Ives plc.

Contents

Foreword to the 2004 Edition

It is strange to look at a book that one wrote half a lifetime ago. Simply flicking through it triggers memories: its subject's excruciating handwriting; the delight at finding a tin trunk full of documents which had not seen daylight since 1925; generous welcomes in country houses with private papers; and the beginning of an uneasy relationship with the First World War which continues to haunt me. As I look at the references I am struck by the fact that I had more time for wading through primary sources then than has often been the case subsequently. If my CV has become grander than it was in 1981, one of its costs is that my diary no longer allows two days a week burrowing away at the Imperial War Museum.

A torrent of literature has poured over the First World War in the past twenty years. Indeed, I do not know a single area of history which continues to arouse so much controversy, or to induce so many to describe it in terms of stereotype forged in prejudice. When I wrote about Sir John French there were already two well-established approaches to First World War generalship. The 'Donkeys' school, reflecting, in part, the anti-authoritarianism of the 1960s, declared that senior British officers were mindless and inarticulate butchers. The Revisionists (with John Terraine at the head of their column) suggested that 'external factors' (like the transformation of weapons in the pre-war years, and the problems caused by the creation of a 'locked front') were at least as significant as 'internal factors' (specifically British military issues) in explaining what happened on the Western Front in 1914–18.

Since then many books have fitted comfortably into these two models. John Laffin's *British Butchers and Bunglers of World War One* (1988) is a classic assault on donkeydom. Its author fought as an infantryman in the Second World War, and I forgive him much on that count alone, but for bias winged with bitterness his book is hard to beat. On the other flank is Gordon Corrigan's

Forward to the 2004 Edition

Mud, Blood and Poppycock (London 2003), a piece of determined revisionism which, though a necessary corrective to works like Laffin's, cannot exonerate British generalship from the most serious charge still laid against it. This is that it fought a campaign for which there may indeed have been no real strategic alternative by using tactical methods which were frequently and predictably flawed.

Nowhere is this more true than in the case of the Somme in 1916. The offensive reflected coalition politics from which no British commander-in-chief could have stood aside. It was commenced earlier than Haig wished, and with less French participation than had been intended, because of the German attack on Verdun. But its initial concept, a steady advance to capitalise on a lengthy bombardment, was an uneasy compromise between the views of Haig and those of Rawlinson, whose army spearheaded the offensive. Failure on the first day was foreseen by some, and the bankruptcy of the piecemeal attacks which characterised Rawlinson's methods for much of July and August was widely identified at the time. In the strategic logic of 1916 the Somme was a necessary battle and an Allied victory on points. Yet if the British Army that emerged from it was better trained than that which began the battle four months before, it had paid a shockingly high price for the learning.

Indeed, it was this price – paid not simply on the Somme – that induced so many historians to focus primarily on the issue of generalship. But there is now an infinitely broader range of historiography than was the case when I wrote. Historians like Brian Bond, David French, Ian Beckett, Paddy Griffith, Robin Prior, Peter Simkins, Edward Spiers, Gary Sheffield, Tim Travers and Trevor Wilson weave happily between the poles. And the steady expansion of the 'Everyman at War' school – exemplified by writers like Martin Middlebrook and Lyn Macdonald in Britain, Bill Gammage and Patsy Adam-Smith in Australia, Pierre Berton in Canada and Stéphane Audoin-Rousseau in France – has given the more junior combatant his voice. As Peter Simkins has observed, this sort of history is 'just one skein in the tapestry,' and there are moments when the embroidered memories of later years obscure the real picture. Yet it is too important a thread to have been snapped off by A.J.P. Taylor as 'old men drooling over their youth.'

Forward to the 2004 Edition

In one sense the publication of the first volume of Hew Strachan's *The First World War* in 2001 drew a line under what had gone before. Here was an author touched by the war (the volume was dedicated to his grandfather) but who saw it as a global conflict, not simply as the Western Front with appendages. And at last the question of generalship emerged as just one aspect of what Trevor Wilson had termed a war with a myriad faces. The book embraces politics, diplomacy and economics, as well as conflict on land, at sea and in the air from Flanders to the Falklands and from Amiens to Anatolia, and points the path ahead in many useful ways. Such is the war's legacy that aspects still provoke an angry reaction – anyone suggesting on television that Haig had some merits must brace themselves for furious correspondence – but we are far better able to see the war in the round than was the case when I wrote this book.

Were I writing today I could scarcely fail to be influenced by all this. For instance, two of the volumes published by the Army Records Society, Ian Beckett's *The Army and the Curragh Incident, 1914* (1995) and André Wessels' *Lord Roberts and the War in South Africa* (2000) would have given greater breadth to these areas, and David French's *British Strategy and War Aims* (1986) would have assisted me with parts of Chapters 4 and 7. I wish that I had reflected more upon John French's views on the way that the army would have to change to win the war, and Peter Simkins' work on Kitchener's armies would have helped me do so. French had a low opinion of Rawlinson, and Robin Prior and Trevor Wilson's *Command on the Western Front* (1992) would have sustained my belief that he was right.

My overall judgement on French would, though, remain much the same. He was a brave Victorian general, and, on the evidence of the Boer War, the most distinguished cavalry officer since Cromwell. His mercurial personality and undisciplined intellect made him ill-suited to dealing with the problems posed by the Western Front in 1914–15. But however much we may look askance at his irregular private life or financial fecklessness, there is no denying that he possessed what Churchill called 'the sacred fire of leadership.' It was never enough to make him a great general, but it does begin to explain why many contemporaries, often folk of sound judgement, thought him the man of the hour in 1914. That they were wrong was their tragedy as well as his.

Richard Holmes
Ropley, 2003

Acknowledgments

For allowing me to include in this work material to which they hold the copyright, I gratefully acknowledge the gracious permission of Her Majesty the Queen (Royal Archives); Mr Mark Bonham-Carter (Asquith Papers); C & T Publications (some Churchill material); Lord Chetwode (letters of the 1st Lord Chetwode); Viscount Esher (letters and diaries of the 2nd Viscount Esher); Mr Adrian Fitzgerald (Fitzgerald Papers); Mr Jonathan Frewen (Moreton Frewen letters); Earl Haig (Haig Papers); William Heinemann Ltd, for quotations from Martin Gilbert's *Winston S. Churchill* volume III, Companion volume III and Companion volume IV; the Trustees of the Imperial War Museum (Wilson Diaries); the Trustees of the Liddell Hart Centre for Military Archives (Edmonds and Clive Papers); Viscount Long (Walter Long letters); Sir Nevil Macready (letters of General Sir Nevil Macready); Captain A. R. Murray (Murray Papers); Lord Mottistone (Mottistone Papers); Mr David Paget (letters of General Sir Arthur Paget); Lt-Col John Scott (Watt Papers) and Mr David Smith-Dorrien (Smith-Dorrien Papers). I should add that Lord Haig and Mr Smith-Dorrien were aware that their fathers enjoyed somewhat stormy relationships with French: lesser men might have denied me permission to use their copyright material in a biography of a man whom they may well regard with less than affection. For permission to reproduce photographs I would like to thank the following: The Army Museum Ogilby Trust, no. 2; BBC Hulton Picture Library, nos 3, 6, 7, 10, 20, 21; the Trustees of The Imperial War Museum, London, nos 9, 11, 12, 13, 14, 15, 16, 19; Lady Patricia Kingsbury, nos 1, 4, 5, 8, 17, 22, 23; the Watt Papers, no 18.

So many people have given me the benefit of their advice, assistance, and often hospitality, that it is no easy task to thank them all. I am, however, most grateful to the Marquess of Anglesey, Lady Diana Cooper, Dr Christopher Everett,

Acknowledgments

Dr Noble Frankland, Dr David French, the late Lady Essex French, Mr Peter Hippisley-Cox, Mr Edward Lydall, Major Antony Mallaby, Mrs Mollie Mallaby, Mrs Geraldine Scott, Lt-Col and Mrs John Scott, Mrs Joan Shivarg, Colonel H. E. Shortt, Lieutenant-Colonel Ben Winter-Goodwin and the Earl of Ypres. Their knowledge has saved me from numerous errors and solecisms, and for those that remain I am alone responsible.

All the museums and archives I visited were generous with their help, but I must draw particular attention to Sir Robin Mackworth-Young and his staff at the Royal Archives, undoubtedly the most civilised establishment to which my research has ever taken me, and Mr Roderick Suddaby and his staff in the Department of Documents at the Imperial War Museum. My unfortunate colleagues in the Department of War Studies at Sandhurst have had to contend with my incessant prattle on French for the last four years: churlish though it may seem to mention only two of them by name, Mr John Keegan and Mr Keith Simpson deserve my special thanks. My researches in Scotland were greatly eased by the vinous solace furnished by Mrs Charles Stott and Dr Hew Strachan.

This project would have been quite literally impossible without the advice and encouragement of French's granddaughter, Lady Patricia Kingsbury. She granted me unrestricted access to the French material in her possession, and she and her family have been the very soul of kindness. I can only regret that Mr Henry Kingsbury did not live to see the conclusion of a work in which he took such a lively interest.

Finally, I must thank my wife Lizzie, who has had to share me with the shade of the Little Field-Marshal for longer than she might have wished. She deserves my gratitude, and your sympathy.

R.H.

Alton
1981

Introduction

Johnnie French aroused anything but indifference amongst his contemporaries. His photographs, however, give little clue to a personality which moved men to extremes of loyalty and affection, enmity and disgust. He stares unblinking from the sepia page, heavy face dominated by a bushy white moustache, eyes giving, perhaps, the suggestion of a twinkle often submerged beneath the gold-braided peak of his cap or extinguished by a blighted landscape in the background. A quilt of medal ribbons lends colour to a tunic cut unfashionably long by the standards of modern military tailoring, its patch pockets reaching almost to the knee. Khaki barathea and glowing Sam Browne belt strive to conceal a thickening figure, and putty-coloured breeches, tucked into gleaming riding boots, complete the picture. We are all prisoners of our appearances, and French was condemned to the thraldom of an uninspiring physique and an expression which almost involuntarily provokes the adjective blimpish. He looks the archetypal First World War General, more familiar with the comfortable routine of a *château* than with the rigours of the trenches, cheerfully nailing British manhood to the cross of the Western Front.

Many of French's contemporaries, both soldiers and civilians, would have found this unpalatable image at variance with the facts, while others would have considered it a reasonable reflection of a man they despised. French's opponents were certainly vocal enough. Sir James Edmonds, the official historian of the war, thought him 'only *un beau sabreur* of the old-fashioned sort', and went on to call him 'a vain, ignorant and vindictive old man with an unsavoury society backing', noting that 'no-one regretted his departure' from command in France.[1] General Sir Hubert Gough described him as an 'ignorant little fool', and was likewise delighted when French was replaced as Commander-in-Chief.[2] But perhaps the most bitter of French's military critics was Sir Douglas Haig. In this case Haig's resentment was lent extra poignancy by the fact that French and Haig had once been close friends: their relationship became imbued with all the venom of a friendship which had turned sour. Haig wrote of his 'very jealous disposition' and 'unreasoning brain'.[3] Later, after their relationship had been scarred by the aftermath of Loos, Haig told an ADC 'that I would not receive Viscount French in my house. I despise him too much personally for that.'[4]

But soldiers were far from unanimous in their opinion. Field-Marshal Lord Chetwode was astonished to learn of Haig's feelings:

> He owed everything to French, who brought him out of nothing to prominence in South Africa, and was behind him in all his subsequent big appointments. I grant you that the two men were poles apart in their temperaments. French was a man who loved life, laughter and women, whereas Haig was a dour Scotsman and the dullest dog I ever had the happiness to meet ... French was full of imagination, and to my mind a man who might have done big things in open warfare. He was a lucky general, and inspired the greatest confidence in his troops. Haig never got anywhere near his troops or officers during the war, with the exception of his immediate and personal entourage ... [5]

General Sir Nevil Macready first met French on the rainy kopjes of Elandslaagte, served under him as Adjutant-General in France and was Commander-in-Chief in Ireland when French was Viceroy. In 1919 he congratulated Ian Macpherson on his appointment as Chief Secretary of Ireland. Macready, who had little affection for Ireland or the Irish, added that he did not envy Macpherson his task. But he felt that the job had one significant recompense, for 'you will be associated with one of the most lovable men I have ever met, my old Chief Lord French, and that alone to me would compensate for a very great deal, and I am sure you will find in him one of the most loyal and true-hearted individuals you are ever likely to come across'.[6] Even some unsuccessful claimants on French's patronage accepted his rejection with understanding. One such disappointed applicant wrote:

> I'm sure you are quite right, and that a man with my imperfect sight is not fit for active service ... No one ever had a better friend than you have been to me in all my troubles and at all times ... no words can express the affection and gratitude I feel and always shall feel to you ... I don't want any other billet, and shouldn't have asked for this except to be with you, I shouldn't care to serve with anyone else.[7]

Politicians were similarly divided in their opinions of French. The flamboyant J. E. B. Seely, whose career as soldier and politician was intimately entwined with that of French, planned to conclude his memoirs with the statement: 'to Sir John French England owes a debt that she can never repay. I know that it is true,' he added, 'and I suppose it is true to say that no public man knows more about it than I do.'[8] Lord Haldane, architect of the British army of 1914, believed that French had 'been a great Commander-in-Chief, a soldier of the first order, who has held the army as no other could'.[9] Lord Esher, himself closely involved in army reform after the Boer War, felt that French was 'obviously a soldier with not only the instincts of a fighter, but also imbued with common sense, free from fads, and has thought seriously about his profession'.[10] He was struck by French's 'romantic earnestness and strength of purpose', and described him to Balfour as, quite simply, 'the best soldier we have got'.[11] Even after the events of 1914–15 had changed his verdict on French's military ability, Esher could still write that 'the little Field-Marshal has fulfilled the expectations of all those who have known and cared for him'.[12] Months after French's departure from France, Esher received a letter from him,

> very embittered, but rather noble in his simplicity. He is grievously disappointed. In our history there are many cases of embittered soldiers and sailors who have done wonderfully well but just failed to come up to the highest expectations. It is always a tragedy. The little man is a lovable fellow and I am very sorry for him. But war is ruthless.[13]

Politicians' views of French were inevitably as much coloured by French's impact upon their own political careers as by purely military considerations. In May 1915 the Prime Minister, Asquith, told him that 'as the months go on, my admiration for what you and your men are doing becomes more profound, and my confidence in your own leadership, and in your ultimate success, has never wavered for a moment'.[14] This confidence wavered very considerably as evidence of French's complicity in the shells scandal mounted, and by 1919 relations between the two men had deteriorated to outright hostility, partly as a result of what Asquith termed the 'attacks of a fierce and violent nature' contained in French's book *1914*.[15]

Lloyd George, Asquith's successor, was somewhat more consistent in his opinion of French. He considered the Field-Marshal 'a far bigger man' with a much broader view than Haig, whose 'review of a world war is limited by the Passchendaele Ridge a few hundred yards above his front line'. Moreover, he felt that French had been the victim of a military conspiracy, and 'had fallen by the daggers of his own colleagues just as great opportunity was opening out to him'.[16] Lloyd George's favourable judgements were, however, no more altruistic than Asquith's less favourable conclusions, for Lloyd George saw French as an ally in his own struggle against Haig.

Churchill's career was similarly bound up with that of French, but the personal relationship between them was warmer than between French and any other politician with the possible exception of Esher – if, indeed, Esher can properly be termed a politician. In January 1915 Churchill wrote that 'our friendship, though begun late, has grown strong and deep, and I feel sure it will stand with advantage all the tests of this remarkable time'.[17] Almost a year later, after serious differences of opinion over the Dardanelles expedition, Churchill could still write: 'More than I can say I grieve at the thought of this untimely and uncalled for change [of command in France]. Your kindness to me has made an ineffacable impression upon my mind, already prepared by a long and well-tried friendship.'[18] On French's return from Ireland in the spring of 1921, Churchill paid tribute to his 'dauntless courage, force of

4

character and physical and nervous strength'.[19] Churchill's final verdict on French, in *Great Contemporaries*, is a balanced one:

> French was a natural soldier. Although he had not the intellectual capacity of Haig, nor perhaps his underlying endurance, he had a deeper military insight. He was not equal to Haig in precision of detail; but he had more imagination and he would never have run the British army into the same long drawn-out slaughters.[20]

Controversies buzzed around French like wasps around a jam-pot. He was involved in vigorous and well-publicised disputes with Roberts and Kitchener, two of the greatest military figures of the Edwardian army; with his subordinates Smith-Dorrien and Haig, and with his own civil superior, Asquith. During the lifetimes of the protagonists, the flames of these quarrels were fanned by the activities of supporters and publicists, who often pushed their principals into positions which, left to their own devices, they might have avoided. French's book *1914*, roundly condemned by one reviewer as 'one of the most unfortunate books that was ever written', was, in part at least, the work of French's propagandist Lovat Fraser.[21] It was unashamedly partisan, wrong on a number of points of fact, and simply lent fuel to the flames.

Nor did these controversies end with French's death. The major military figures of the period have attracted biographers, many of whom have taken at least a passing swipe at French. Some have hit a good deal harder. A. J. Smithers, in *The Man who Disobeyed: Sir Horace Smith-Dorrien and His Enemies* makes no secret of his disapproval of French, 'the wild beast'.[22] French's treatment of Smith-Dorrien was, as we shall see, far from generous. It is nevertheless unfortunate that Smith-Dorrien's biographer has failed to point out that Sir Horace had been rejected as unsuitable, because of his wild outbursts of rage, for the post of Commander-in-Chief of the Indian Army, and that he attributes Smith-Dorrien's misfortunes primarily to the enmity of French.[23] George Cassar's encyclopaedic study of Kitchener brushes French aside as an obstructive lightweight, while John Terraine's biography of

Haig stresses that it was only Haig's deeply-held conviction that French was manifestly unsuited for high command that persuaded him to indulge in what some would regard as double-dealing.[24] French's son Gerald took up the cudgels on his father's behalf with more gallantry than good sense: his studies of the French–Haig and French–Kitchener disputes demonstrate that passionate conviction is no substitute for reasoned argument.

If French has suffered from the attentions of other people's biographers, he has also, like the remainder of his military generation, fallen into the slough of popular history which portrays First World War Generals at best as refugees from a comic opera, and at worst as mindless and inarticulate butchers, churning away at the mincing-machine of the Western Front. Alan Clark's grimly evocative *The Donkeys* summarises French as 'a weak-willed man of medium height', and speaks contemptuously of a 'popular tradition of heroic infallibility ... which was to mate disastrously with the amateurish good humour and ignorance of contemporary military theory that was reality.'[25] The historiographical school of which *The Donkeys* is perhaps the *chef d'oeuvre* depicts most Generals as incompetent has-beens, hopelessly out of touch with the conditions into which they consigned hundreds of thousands of young men to suffering and death. The assertion is always that most of the carnage was produced primarily by bad generalship, and that narrow-minded and unimaginative commanders were incapable of seeing the truths which, in retrospect, seem self-evident.

It is eminently understandable that a conflict which produced suffering on the scale of that engendered by the First World War should be followed by the widespread questioning of many aspects of the struggle, particularly military leadership. It is equally natural that military leaders should be blamed for failing to solve the tactical and the strategic problems of the war. They, after all, were the professionals, whose careers should have prepared them for the supreme test. Many contemporaries certainly felt that they had been let down by their commanders – characters like Siegfried Sassoon's General, the 'cheery old card' whose plan of attack massacred his unfortunate subordinates.

Introduction

The tendency for suspicion and distrust to cloud relations between commanders and staff officers on the one hand and their subordinates on the other is a well-polished facet of military history. But it is far from certain that most combatants in the First World War shared Sassoon's view of Generals: indeed, a recent survey carried out among surviving First World War officers suggests that exactly the reverse may be true.[26] Furthermore, the life of a General or a staff officer was by no means as comfortable or secure as is sometimes imagined. Work at GHQ was hard, and the burden of responsibility crushed many. Generals were as mortal as their soldiers: some sixty British Generals were killed, or died of wounds received, on the Western Front. In statistical terms some Generals' appointments – notably that of brigade commander – were anything but safe. Many Generals certainly did live in elegant *châteaux* well behind the lines, out of range of anything but the heaviest guns. Could they have done their jobs better from the squalour of a dug-out close to the front line?

A historian who attempted a totally revisionist reappraisal of First World War Generals would be forced to wrestle with weighty evidence. Nevertheless, it seems clear that much of the criticism of British generalship during the conflict is based on false conceptions of the nature of war. War is a tissue of uncertainty, its theory often displaying conviction and confidence not reflected in its practice. Far-reaching changes are brought about by developments in weapons, transport and communications: at times this change is frighteningly rapid, and is much more clearly comprehensible in the heady clarity of hindsight than at the military coal-face at which commanders often hew in darkness and confusion. The fact that history abounds with contradictory military theories, many of them hopelessly wrong, does not necessarily prove the inflexibility of the military mind, but rather the sheer and staggering difficulty of many of the problems it is called upon to solve.

Although a number of strategists, notably Clausewitz and von Moltke the elder, stress the uncertain nature of war, and although a General's practical experience of conflict may lead him to recognise that combat is riddled with imponderables, the elimination of doubt and uncertainty from the minds of subordinates is a crucial function of military command. A

General who admitted that his knowledge of the enemy's strength was sketchy and his plan was based largely on educated guesswork would be unlikely to get the best out of his subordinates.

The fact that battles produce casualties, even for the victors, only worsens the problems. There is ample evidence that First World War Generals were painfully conscious of the consequences of their decisions in terms of human agony. But a constant preoccupation with the risks involved in military operations is itself an obstruction to effective high command. Generals therefore tend to attempt to distance themselves from the bloody results of their activities in order to retain an overview and, indeed, simply to preserve their own mental stability. The need to radiate a confidence which they often do not feel, allied to the casualty-producing effects of even the best of plans, often produces a psychological process of self-deception, by which commanders convince themselves that a plan will work because they cannot bear to embark upon it knowing that the chance of failure is great.

The changing nature of war came as a cruel surprise to most of the Generals of 1914: errors and misconceptions were not confined to the British army alone, and to suggest that these mistakes were the result of idleness or sheer stupidity is to ignore a vast corpus of intelligent and perceptive military literature written before the war, often by the very Generals who failed to meet the challenge of the war itself. There is, admittedly, a good deal of truth in many of the assertions made by Dr Norman Dixon in his seminal *On the Psychology of Military Incompetence*. Armies did not necessarily attract the best brains of Europe; they exhibited a 'web of rules, restrictions and constraints'; emphasised 'bullshit' of little real relevance, and were insensitive to criticism.[27] Generals were sometimes authoritarian, even obsessive, and had often been selected as 'social specialists' rather than 'task specialists'. These factors were common to all the contending armies of 1914–18: they were not an exclusive preserve of Britain. But military incompetence is, as Dr Dixon himself suggests, by no means more frequent than other sorts of incompetence, and to attribute the carnage of the First World War to this single factor is to distort history. However attractive and appealing the 'donkey' thesis may be, it is at best part of the truth, not the whole truth.

A biography of French needs, therefore, no excuse. He was a significant and controversial figure in his own right, holding a number of key appointments — Chief of the Imperial General Staff before the war, Commander-in-Chief in France 1914–15, and Lord-Lieutenant of Ireland 1918–21, to name but the three most important. His performance as a military commander and his influence as a theorist both merit examination. He has not received serious biographical attention, but has been splashed by the debris of other biographies, and has proved an attractive target for those who interpret the First World War primarily in terms of the incompetence of commanders. Moreover, recent revelations about the Field-Marshal's irregular private life have reduced him to the status of a lecherous old Irishman, pursuing an illicit love-affair to the detriment of his generalship. French is not altogether a great and good man who has been hideously misunderstood: Brian Bond's verdict in *The Victorian Army and the Staff College* — 'a brave fighting general who proved to be out of his professional depths' — is by no means wide of the mark.[28] Nevertheless, he is far too important a figure to be left on the periphery of military history, at best half-understood. And if we owe Johnnie French anything, it is surely to get behind those firm blue eyes and to try to discover reality, not myth.

Prologue

The Kopjes of Elandslaagte
21 October 1899

A hint of dusk was already creeping across the veldt, shrouding the glimmer of the Natal Railway in the deepening shadows of Jonono's Kop and Intintanyone, when a trooper of the Imperial Light Horse reined up in a hollow near Elandslaagte Station. Two squadrons of British cavalry, one of the 5th Dragoon Guards and one of the 5th Lancers, were drawn up in the dead ground, troopers dismounted, their officers forward on the edge of the depression, looking south-eastwards through their field glasses. They could make out, about a mile away, three kopjes which formed the end of a horseshoe-shaped ridge curling away from them before swinging back towards the railway to the south-west. White puffs of shrapnel snatched at the sky above the kopjes while shells coughed up clouds of smoke and debris on the hills themselves. To the south the officers could see the source of this mischief, the gun-line of the 21st and 42nd Field Batteries, their 15-pounders making good practice against the Boer riflemen who thickly garnished the boulder-strewn slopes. Between the officers and the guns, on the inner curve of the horseshoe, nine hundred men of the Devons sought cover behind rocks and ant-heaps, firing — rather optimistically, for the range was nearly a thousand yards — in reply to the Mauser bullets which cracked around them.

The main strength of the British force was, for the most part, hidden from cavalry commander, Major St J. C. Gore, and his two squadron leaders, Captain Oakes of the Lancers and Captain Darbyshire of the Dragoon Guards. Two more battalions, the Gordon Highlanders and the Manchesters, pressed forward along the toe of the horseshoe, their advance providentially shielded by a sudden thunderstorm which had swept the veldt at about 4.30, just before the trooper reached Elandslaagte. The trooper may have saluted, but he was a colonial, and these bronzed and independently-minded men were not unduly encumbered by regard for military protocol. He handed Gore a message, written in indelible pencil on a thin sheet of paper torn from a field-service message book. It was from the force commander, Major-General J. D. P. French, and was in the upright hand of his chief staff officer, Major Douglas Haig. 'Pursue with vigour,' read Gore, Haig's sharp underlining leaving no room for doubt, 'when you see the Boers beginning to fall back. Take command of all cavalry in your vicinity and press the enemy with the lance if you can.'[1]

Gore soon realised that he was being presented with the sort of opportunity which was usually confined to the darkest fantasies of cavalry officers. Shortly after 5 p.m., as the growing volume of rifle fire announced that the infantry were pressing home their assault on the Boer position, scattered parties of the enemy began to drift back, crossing the railway east of Elandslaagte and making for the Dundee road. They were in no semblance of order, and their numbers grew by the minute. The nearest were only 500 yards from Gore's position, trotting northwards on their solid little ponies, relieved no doubt, to have got off the kopjes before the arrival of the British infantry. Indeed, it was already clear that some of their comrades had stayed too long, for fresh bursts of firing, interlaced with the thin notes of the bugle and the shriek of the pipes, announced that the infantry were amongst the Boer rearguard with the bayonet.

It was about 5.30, with darkness closing in rapidly, when Gore ordered his squadrons to advance. The troopers picked their way forward for the first few hundred yards, across ground littered with boulders and lacerated by gullies. When at last the squadrons, moving side by side in extended order, emerged into full view of their quarry they were only 300 yards from the retreating Boers. The big cavalry Walers were fresh and recently watered, and their riders were eager to get to grips with an enemy who had, so rumour had it, abused the white flag. Swords rasped out of scabbards, and lances, nearly nine feet of steel-tipped bamboo, came down to the engage.

Many of the Boers never knew what hit them. Even those who saw the cavalry bearing down upon them had little enough time to escape. Gore's men crashed into the Boers with the sickening crunch of Waler against pony and steel against bone. Some Boers fired their Mausers from the saddle, bringing down a few unlucky troopers: some tried to make off, while others flung themselves from their horses and cried for quarter. Few were fortunate. The troopers' blood was up, and their momentum was irresistible. The charge shredded out into vignettes of sheer horror. One lancer caught up with two Boers making off on a single pony. His thrust transfixed them both, but he was shot moments later. Screaming Boers were riddled with lance thrusts – one received sixteen and survived. Others were punched with sword hilts as Dragoon Guards discovered that it was damnably difficult to do much damage with the blade. Officers snapped off their pistols at close-range fleeting targets, while all around the lance-butts flicked up as troopers wrenched them out of prostrate Boers.

Once through the Boers, the squadrons rallied, re-formed, and charged again, the fresh ebb of retreating horsemen riven by their impact. The same awful scenes repeated themselves. An officer called it 'most excellent pig-sticking', but it was by now pitch dark, and many of the troopers had lost some of their enthusiasm for the bloody and very personal work of the *arme blanche*. A number of prisoners were rounded up, and the cavalry bivouacked where they stood, the wreckage of their charge around them.[2]

With night came the rain. A persistent drizzle set in, drenching victor and vanquished alike, and adding immeasurably to the miseries of the wounded of both sides, lying out on the veldt. Some of the infantry bivouacked on the Boer position, while others coalesced around the station, finding what cover they could from the cold and rain. Captain Nevil Macready of the Gordons, returning from bringing in wounded, met General French touring the bivouacs and talking to the soldiers as they sat round their fires trying to keep warm. Macready had managed to loot some coffee from a Boer's kit, and he gave a cup of it to the General.[3] They chatted briefly before French moved on, going from bivouac to bivouac in the damp darkness.

Elandslaagte was his first victory. It was, perhaps, as his critics would point out, a lucky one: Colonel Ian Hamilton, the infantry brigadier, had handled his men uncommonly well, the storm had helped the Gordons and Manchesters get forward, and Gore's cavalry had caught the Boers in the half-light. But to French, a young Major-General for whom the future glowed rosily, Elandslaagte was more than a scrambling victory over an incautious enemy. It demonstrated the value of cavalry as a shock weapon: the huddled corpses that marked the Boer retreat seemed abundant proof of the efficacy of cold steel. It also taught him something about command. 'My personal experiences,' he wrote that morning, 'have showed me the great necessity for a General in command during an extensive engagement to keep in the most commanding position and in one place, if possible.'[4] French never forgot Elandslaagte. Sixteen years later, in the aftermath of Loos, where the lessons of Elandslaagte had seemed so terribly misleading, he wrote reflectively to his mistress, Mrs Winifred Bennett: 'This is the anniversary of the Battle of Elandslaagte. It was the first battle in which I commanded – fought on the 21 October 1899. How well I remember it – it seems like yesterday.'[5]

One

Light Cavalry
1852–99

John Denton Pinkstone French was born on 28 September 1852, at Ripple Vale, near Deal, Kent, the only son of Captain John Tracey French, a retired naval officer. Although it was a long way from the very English surroundings of French's early childhood to the green vortex of Ireland, the shadow of Ireland nevertheless lay heavily upon the family, and John French himself was never to escape from it. French was proud of his Irish ancestry. His branch of the family had lived in England since the eighteenth century, but French always considered himself an Irishman, tracing his lineage from fourteenth-century Norman settlers in Wexford, through his great-grandfather, John French of High Lake, Roscommon, to his grandfather, Fleming French, who had moved to Ripple and died there in 1818.[1]

John French's Irish ancestry is of more than merely genealogical significance. It gave him two portentous legacies; firstly, an intense interest in the problems of Ireland, and the conviction that his own background gave him a special understanding of them, and secondly, a character which exhibited all the passionate traits usually ascribed to the Irish temperament — warmth, generosity, physical courage, fierce temper, and the inclination to nurse a sense of injustice. But French was to be less fortunate as far as more tangible legacies were concerned. His was a cadet branch of the family, and the little estate at Ripple was a far cry indeed from the broad acres of Frenchpark, Roscommon. Although his parents were by no means poor, John had six sisters, and the family finances were

15

never particularly robust. Captain French, who in the course of an active and strenuous career had fought the Turks at Navarino and lost an eye serving under Sir Charles Napier in support of Dom Pedro during the Portuguese Civil War, died in 1854, leaving his widow with the task of bringing up their large family. She soon found the strain too much for her. In 1861 she began to show signs of what French discreetly referred to as 'incurable incapacity'. She was removed from the house the following year, and died, quite mad, in 1867.

The disappearance of John's mother left his upbringing in the hands of his sisters. They were an interesting brood. The eldest, Mary Ramsay French, married a solicitor, John Hawthorn Lydall, in 1867, and Eleanora — always known as Nellie — married his brother Wykeham. The forceful and strong-minded Margaret became the wife of an equally spirited individual, Gavin Sibbald Jones, who, as a young industrialist in India, had been wounded during the Mutiny, escaping from a massacre at Fatehgarh. Caroline moved to Hemingford Grey in Huntingdonshire, as wife of Augustine Whiteway, while Catherine — Katie to her brother — married Ernest Harley, of Condover Hall, Shropshire. By far the most remarkable of French's sisters was Charlotte, who married a wealthy businessman, Maximilian Despard. Her married life was reasonably conventional, but after her husband's death in 1890 she emerged as an important figure in her own right, becoming a socialist, pacifist, fervent Irish nationalist and well-known campaigner for women's rights.[2]

The lives of several of French's sisters and their husbands bore significantly upon John's own career. John Lydall's legal connections proved invaluable in extracting him from the morass of a hasty and ill-considered marriage, and Gavin Sibbald Jones boosted the flagging French finances on at least one occasion. Caroline's daughter Georgina, given away by French at her wedding in 1903, married Fitzgerald Watt, a young officer of the Yorkshire Hussars who became a trusted member of French's staff before, during, and after the First World War. Catherine Harley, by then a widow, led a group of British nurses in Serbia during the war, and was killed by shellfire at Monastir in March 1917.[3]

Lottie Despard, however, stands head and shoulders above

her sisters. French regarded her as, at best, a mixed blessing. Her husband left her comfortably off, and she was a useful source of funds for her perennially impecunious brother. Socially, she became more and more of an embarrassment to him as his career progressed. Her taste in dress was scarcely suitable for the sister of an aspiring general; in later life she invariably sported a black lace mantilla and sandals, and her sharp features gave her the air of a benevolent witch. It was bad enough that she was a pacifist and a socialist – French, perhaps predictably, abhorred both these tendencies – but she also campaigned vigorously for Sinn Fein when her brother was Viceroy of Ireland. On one occasion he had the mortification of driving past a crowd of Sinn Fein sympathisers which was being vigorously harangued by two striking women. One was his own sister, and the other the beautiful Maud Gonne, with whom, it was alleged, he had had an affair.[4]

French believed that his father's death and his mother's removal so early in his life had marked his character, writing that 'the absence of any powerful directing mind brought to bear on my childhood and upbringing has had a certain influence on all my after life'.[5] It is, though, hard to say how French would have reacted to such a 'powerful directing mind', for he struggled hard against his sisters' efforts to organise his education. They realised that the atmosphere at Ripple Vale – no parents, no brothers, only a bevy of older sisters fully preoccupied with the domestic affairs of their small estate or in preparations for their marriages – was an unnatural one for the boy. He had a governess for a time, and was then sent to preparatory school at Harrow, with a view to entering Harrow School later.

Although he was a quiet, rather retiring boy, French resisted stubbornly, giving some invigorating previews of a temper which was to be remarkable even in an army of short-fused generals. 'My ambition', he wrote 'was always to join one of the two fighting professions.'[6] He had no particular penchant for the sea, but realised that he could enter the navy four or five years earlier than the army. After a prolonged battle, his sisters gave way, and in the spring of 1866 he went to Eastman's Naval Academy at Portsmouth, where he came under the tutelage of the principal, Dr Spickernall, a disciplinarian of almost Dickensian aspect. Spickernall was the first male influence in French's life, and the boy reacted well: his few months at Portsmouth were happy, and he passed the qualifying examinations for entry into Dartmouth.

In August 1866 French exchanged one ferocious disciplinarian for another. He travelled down to Dartmouth to join HMS *Britannia*, an elderly three-decker, badly knocked about in the Crimea. She was commanded by the formidable Captain Randolph, who, as French noted with all the approval of retrospect, 'was a tremendous disciplinarian and believed thoroughly in the old fashioned drastic kinds of punishment, for he ordered frequent floggings ... He was a typical naval commander of the mid-Victorian era.'[7] The discipline at Dartmouth was harsh, but, perhaps surprisingly in view of his petticoat-haunted upbringing, French thrived on it. 'It was', he said, 'really the public school spirit and system working under the extra pressure of naval discipline and customs.'[8] French spent fifteen months at Dartmouth. He enjoyed his stay, and particularly welcomed the companionship of other boys, making many life-long friends among his contemporaries. His studies, alas, did not progress conspicuously well, and he emerged with only an 'average' certificate, which meant that he had to do six months further training at another establishment before becoming a midshipman.

It was a bitterly cold day in January 1868 when French, in company with some forty other cadets, joined the old frigate HMS *Bristol* at Sheerness. She was not a happy ship; her captain was punctilious and quarrelsome, and the depressing atmosphere aboard soon infected the newly-joined cadets who, as French observed, 'did very little and learned less'.[9] After a voyage which took him to the Azores, Madeira, Tenerife, Lisbon and Gibraltar, French emerged, six months later, as a midshipman. He was then appointed to the ironclad HMS *Warrior*, commanded by an old friend of his father's, Captain Boys. French served in *Warrior* for two years. The ship was part of the Channel squadron for most of this time, and was based in Lisbon. She nevertheless made a number of voyages, on one of which French was on watch when the recently-built HMS *Captain* capsized only a few hundred yards away. It was blowing hard, and *Captain*, made top-heavy by her new-fangled turrets and the heavy ordnance they contained, turned turtle and sank within five minutes.

Much as French enjoyed serving under the capable and benevolent Boys, he gradually realised that life in the navy left much to be desired. He was really at his happiest when ashore at Lisbon, for it was there that he could indulge his passion for horses and riding. He would hire Lisbon hacks, usually intractable and iron-mouthed nags, and spend long days riding over Wellington's battlefields. He was far more at home in the saddle than on the quarter-deck; moreover, he had a bad head for heights, which made ascents of the rigging a nightmare. He therefore decided to leave the navy, and when the fleet returned to Portland in November 1870, he resigned in order to seek entry to the army.

French's sisters were far from delighted by his decision. Not only did it seem irrational to them for their brother to quit the navy when a promising career seemed to be opening up before him, but it also cannot have escaped their notice that, while the navy was a cheap service, whose officers lived on their pay, the army was expensive. Private means were essential, and French's love of horses prompted him to join the most costly arm of all – the cavalry. But it was no easy matter to make the transition from the white tabs of a midshipman to the spurred boots of a cavalry subaltern. Many officers – among them French's friend and *éminence grise,* Henry Wilson, whose lanky figure and scarred visage will figure prominently in these pages – slipped into the regular army by way of the militia back door. A militia officer could obtain a regular commission provided he was nominated by his commanding officer and passed an examination: the drudgery of Sandhurst could be neatly side-stepped.

Duly discharged from the navy, French joined the Suffolk Artillery Militia, then under the genial leadership of Sir Shafto Adair of Hinxton Hall. He spent two years in the regiment, but wrote later:

> I cannot say that I look back upon this period of my youth with much pride or satisfaction ... I managed to put in about two months a year with my regiment and the remainder of the time was passed in the

establishments of 'Militia Tutors', a race that I believe has quite died out ... It was a ruinously expensive process. My nomination to a commission in the army came quite suddenly and being ordered for immediate examination I was totally unprepared for the educational side of it. Although I passed a good military test I failed the latter.[10]

This failure led French to change his tutor, and soon afterwards he abandoned another tutor, losing, in the process, all the fees he had paid in advance. He worked hard on his own with the occasional assistance of mathematics and language teachers, passed his second examination, and was duly gazetted to the 8th (Queen's Royal Irish) Hussars on 28 February 1874.

It was natural for French, who prized his Irish connections so highly, to join the 8th Hussars. It was a popular, efficient, and, unfortunately, expensive regiment. There is no evidence that he ever donned the red-and-white plume of the 8th, for almost at once another Gazette saw him translated to the 19th Hussars. The reasons for the change are not clear. It may have been simply a matter of bureaucratic convenience, but it is more likely that it reflected the desire of French's family, if not of French himself, to seek something less expensive. The 19th were to the 8th what a flinty provincial wine is to a fine Burgundy. Transferred to the Crown's service on the disappearance of the East India Company in 1858, the 19th had come to England in 1870. They were nicknamed the 'dumpies', either because of their elephant cap-badge, or because they accepted shorter recruits than other cavalry regiments, and consequently attracted a large number of rather hammered-down troopers.[11]

In the spring of 1874 the 19th gained a stocky addition to their officers' mess when French joined them at Aldershot. A young officer's first experience of regimental duty is an important formative influence, and it was certainly so with French. He entered a bustling garrison town which had grown rapidly over the previous twenty years. Aldershot had burgeoned from a village of merely 900 souls in 1851 to a town of 8,000 civilians and 25,000 soldiers in 1861.[12] In 1874 it housed a division under the bewhiskered Sir Hope Grant; a cavalry brigade, three infantry brigades and assorted divisional troops vied for space in the new barracks with their elegant gateways and rather less elegant barrack-rooms.

It was a world of rigid distinctions: between soldier and civilian, officer and private, and between the soldiers of different regiments. For private soldiers it was an all-absorbing life of serge and pipe-clay, leather and saddle-soap, brick-dust bringing a shine to metal-work, all overlaid with the aura of stables, latrines and honest sweat. Regiments marched to church in full dress on Sundays, and in the evenings soldiers, tricked out in all the tightly-tailored glory of walking-out uniforms, admired their passing reflection in shop windows, contributed to the well-being of local publicans and, soldiers being soldiers, became involved in spectacular inter-regimental brawls.

The life of a cavalry officer was not unduly exacting. During the drill season, which ran from April to late August or early September, brigade or divisional field-days took place in the sand and pine-trees of Long Valley about once or twice a month. Within the regiment, there were one commanding officer's parade and two adjutant's parades each week: the latter were attended only by officers junior to the adjutant. Good horsemanship, smart turn-out and efficient stable-management were all-important. 'Sleek, fat horses' were, as French observed, very much in vogue, and with the limited forage available this condition could not be attained or preserved if there was too much field training. The infantry took their training slightly more seriously, and French found the artillery and engineers commendably proficient. It nevertheless struck him that all arms were inward-looking, far more concerned with their own training than with 'progressing in the general science of war. They lacked the constant combination with other arms which is such an essential feature of all real war preparation.'[13] If training was hardly vigorous during the drill season, it was almost non-existent during the September–March leave season. Officers changed scarlet for pink and disappeared to the shires, and many private soldiers went home on furlough. The 19th was something of an exception in that its adjutant, Lieutenant Percy Barrow, an officer French greatly admired, had some success in getting training under way in the leave season.

French settled well enough into the mess of the 19th. Most of the officers came from the same sort of background, country gentlemen brought up in the tradition of imperial service, thinking much alike on most subjects, keen on hunting and polo, and with a paternalistic devotion to the welfare of their men. The regiment was not particularly rich. There was, no doubt, a good deal of drinking and betting, but things were not on quite the same scale as in the 9th Lancers, whose officers drank Claret for breakfast as a matter of course.[14] Pay had not risen significantly since the reign of William III, and a cavalry officer needed a private income of about £500–£600 a year if he was to make ends meet.[15] French should have coped well enough in this respect. Ripple Vale had been sold, and with an annual income of perhaps £1,000, he was much better off than many of his brother officers in the 19th.

The rigorous control of his personal economy was never French's strong suit. Throughout his life he found it difficult to keep expenditure below income, and he was fortunate, on more than one occasion, not to be forced to leave the army. As a subaltern he discovered that his income was barely adequate to meet the growing demands of his sporting and social life. He was a keen horseman, although even his most enthusiastic biographer was forced to admit that 'his short, square figure did not look well on horseback'.[16] Despite appearances French rode light, had a strong seat and a total disregard for danger. He was a great success at steeple-chases and in the hunting field, and seems to have preferred such individualistic scrambles to the teamwork of the polo-field. He trained his own horses, and won a number of races on his favourite mare, Mrs Gamp, a horse whose steadiness was almost legendary. But even Mrs Gamp was not perfect: she gave him a bad toss at Sandown, and he broke his right hand. The injury healed badly: his little finger remained crooked thereafter – his family called it 'the crochet hook' – and the damage at least partially accounts for his notoriously bad handwriting.

Horses were an occupational hazard of the life of a cavalry officer. Women were another. Most photographs of French show him in later life, and it is hard to imagine the wintry-faced old man as a dashing and attentive lover. Furthermore, he was very far from being the archetypal tall, languid cavalry-man. Nevertheless, his jet black hair, bushy black moustache, and piercing blue eyes were by no means unattractive. But the key to French's very considerable success with women lay in his personality rather than his looks. He had a pervasive and compelling charm, and a generous and warm-hearted nature. His letters to colleagues display an affectionate tone quite at odds with the conventional view of Victorian military correspondence. Friends are 'dear old boy'; it is always 'a perfect joy to see you again'; and sometimes nothing could be better than 'being shot when serving under you'.[17] With women he was even warmer, his letters positively burning with affection. He tended to see them as romantic heroines, and, very much in the tradition of late Victorian and Edwardian *affaires*, he was as much interested in the pursuit as in the eventual kill. Tall, dark-haired ladies were his particular favourite, and in later life he worshipped the Tsarina Alexandra. In this instance, alas, there was no suggestion that he was able to do more than admire from a respectful distance.

Freed from the restraints of naval discipline, and stationed within easy travelling distance of London, French gave free rein to his amorous and sporting inclinations. Although women and horses speedily made inroads into his capital, in the summer of 1874 he felt able to indulge in a commercial venture. Gavin Sibbald Jones, married to his sister Margaret, was a man of action who had settled in Cawnpore after his hair-raising adventures during the Indian Mutiny. He invited French to participate in one of his schemes, the Muir Mills, and the young man invested £4,000 for the promise of a healthy interest. It was one of French's few successful speculations: the business prospered and he made a handsome profit.

The success of the Muir Mills gave French only a temporary respite from financial difficulties, and he was forced to turn to his family for help. John Lydall, who had married Mary French, was a well-to-do solicitor, ensconced in the comfortable respectability of Ladbroke Grove. He seems to have been very much in the mould of Mr Barrett of Wimpole Street, stiflingly holy on Sundays but not averse to a little solicitorial jiggery-pokery during the week. For his wife's sake he paid off

French's debts, and was soon to turn his legal connections to the young man's advantage.

The 19th moved to Hounslow at the end of June and a year later French took a step that might have been almost deliberately designed to ruin his career. He married. A married subaltern was a rarity in the 1870s, and the union would probably have been damaging to French's prospects as a regimental officer even if his bride had been well-connected. In the event, Isabella Ireland Soundy was anything but eligible. The marriage certificate euphemistically describes her father as a merchant, and neither of the witnesses at the ceremony, which took place at Richmond Parish Church on 23 June 1875, was an officer in the 19th. Furthermore, owing, perhaps, to a slip of someone's pen, the bridegroom was described as 'Lieutenant, 12th Hussars' — a regiment which did not figure in the Army List at the time. It is likely that the marriage was kept secret from French's brother officers: it appeared in no military records or subsequent biographies. His second wife almost certainly did not know of the affair, and French's daughter Essex died in 1979 ignorant of her father's youthful *mésalliance*.

Why, then, did French marry Isabella Soundy? He was always an impetuous lover, disinclined to take 'no' for an answer: perhaps marriage was the price. Whatever the reason, it proved an unsatisfactory alliance, and within two years French was eager to be rid of his wife. Once again John Lydall came to the rescue. Divorce was, at the time, a serious matter, and French's career would have been imperilled if news of it had leaked out. Lydall managed to arrange matters so that Isabella appeared as the guilty party and one George Wilson figured as co-respondent. The decree became absolute in June 1878. A century later, and with no firm evidence to the contrary, the official version of Mrs French's misconduct cannot be refuted, but tradition — admittedly not always a reliable guide — within the Lydall family stresses that Isabella and George Wilson were brought together by John Lydall's money rather than by any mutual attraction.

The incident soured relations between French and Lydall, and when, soon afterwards, French visited Ladbroke Grove in search of cash, he was politely shown to the door and invited never to darken it again. Lydall thereafter lost interest in his scapegrace brother-in-law. Years later, when French was a Field-Marshal, Lydall read of his involvement in some major event – probably the Curragh affair – at a news-stand, and stumped off down the street, muttering 'sorry fellow, Jack French'.[18]

So far, perhaps, there seems little to distinguish French from any other hard-riding, spendthrift, roué subaltern of light cavalry. Nevertheless, French did strike his comrades as unusual in at least one respect. True, it was not enough of an anomaly to arouse more than mild amusement. French's equestrian prowess – and probably a discreet hint of his activities in the courts of Venus – made him a well-liked figure in the mess, where his naval background had earned him the nickname 'Captain Crosstrees', usually shortened to 'Trees'. But by the unexacting standards of a cavalry regiment of the period, in which, as French himself wrote, 'a highly proficient knowledge of the art of war was not deemed a necessary qualification', he was exceptional in that he tried hard to take his profession seriously.[19]

A fellow-subaltern wrote later that when travelling by rail with him, 'after observing the country for some time, he broke out: "There is where I should put my artillery." "That is where I should put my cavalry" and so on to the journey's end.' The same officer noted that French was 'continually studying military works, and often, when his brother subalterns were at polo or other afternoon amusements, he would remain in his room reading Von Schmidt, Jomini, or other books on Strategy'. A visiting Inspector-General, asking French's Colonel what use the young man was, received the lapidary response: 'always reading books'.[20]

It would be dangerous to over-stress French's early interest in military literature. A reputation for being studious and well-read was not a hard thing to acquire in the 19th Hussars of the 1870s. Furthermore, when French later rose to eminence authors looked for signs of promise in his early career, harder, perhaps, than the facts warranted. He seems to have been much more interested in campaign history than in heavier works of strategy, and was especially fond of the campaigns of Napoleon. He bought Napoleonic memorabilia when opportunity and funds permitted, and a bust of the Emperor habitually sat on his desk. This may have simply reflected a romantic affection for Napoleon's exploits, or have gone further, representing the sub-conscious appeal of one short, stocky soldier for another. French was heavily influenced by General Sir Edward Hamley's *Operations of War,* an encyclopaedic study of military operations from a historical viewpoint, solid enough on matters of fact but rather backward-looking in some of its interpretations. [21]

French was a voracious reader, and not merely of books connected with his profession. In mid-career he sat up late reading, and usually read in bed before going to sleep. Hunting stories were his favourites for lighter reading, and Surtees's characters Jorrocks and Soapy Sponge cavorted about the French book-case. For more serious reading French was addicted to the works of Charles Dickens. He had a remarkably retentive brain, and could recite great chunks of Dickens from memory. Later in his life his daughter Essex would amuse him by reading a sentence from any of Dickens's works and listening to him complete the paragraph. During his last illness French frequently recited Dickens to himself, stretching his mind to recall the words of his favourite author as his life slipped away. [22]

In June 1876 the 19th went to Ireland, taking French away from the temptation of London life. The regiment spent the drill season at the Curragh Camp, and was then split up in winter quarters, the same pattern being repeated for the next few years. All was not well in the 19th at this time. There were complaints amongst the men that the commanding officer, Lieutenant-Colonel H. C. Craigie, was giving the regiment more parades than any other, and in early September 1877, after being warned for an extra parade on a Saturday afternoon to inquire about a missing stable jacket, nearly 70 troopers disappeared. A party of military police found the men lying outside a pub, where they had been drinking porter out of a tub. The sergeant of military police begged them to return to barracks, but some of the troopers, who had by now armed themselves with sticks, warned the sergeant that if he sent the infantry pickets after them 'there would be murder'.

At this juncture Lieutenants Warde and French rode up. The men gave them a fair hearing, the two officers warning them that they were disgracing the regiment, and the sooner they got back to barracks the better it would be for all concerned. After telling Warde and French that they had mutinied only to get the Colonel cashiered, the men marched back to barracks, and were promptly arrested. Seven of the ringleaders received between five and eight years penal servitude: Craigie remained in command of the 19th for another sixteen months.[23]

In the autumn of 1880 the 19th moved by rail to Ballinrobe and Lough Mask to take part in the so-called Boycott campaign. Captain Boycott, Lord Erne's agent, had become embroiled in a bitter dispute with his tenants, and troops were called in to aid the civil power – a phrase which occurs with dismal frequency through so much of Irish history. The 19th helped by escorting a party of volunteers who were ricking Boycott's hay. French was supervising the work from horseback when an Irishman rushed at him and hamstrung his horse with a sickle. It was a grim initiation into the turbulent life of a country he loved so well.

Against this depressing backcloth of agrarian unrest, French's own career prospered. His success displayed the unique combination of luck and ability which was a vital feature of his early life. French's progress up the Army List was rapid, aided by the resignation of a senior subaltern and a very rapid turnover of the regiment's senior officers. The 19th had only three Majors in the period 1864–77: one officer, the unpopular Craigie, remained a Major for most of this time. In 1877 the establishment of Majors dropped to one, but there was a brisk turnover, with a different officer holding the appointment each year from 1877 to 1880. As Captains were promoted or resigned, so the Lieutenants progressed, and French found himself a Captain in October 1880, after only six years' service with the 19th.[24] So much for luck. His ability was recognised by his appointment as Adjutant at a time when the regiment's growing involvement in the preservation of peace in the troubled countryside made efficiency important. French was a coming man in the 19th, a close friend of its new Major, Kendall Coghill, and its other rising star, Captain Percy Barrow. His superiors were well aware of his professional commitment to the army, while French himself made no secret of his

27

admiration for the new generation of reformers, men like Garnet Wolseley, Henry Brackenbury and Redvers Buller.[25]

French's uncomfortable venture into matrimony had not altogether prejudiced him against the institution, and in 1880, at the age of 28, he married again. This time his bride could scarcely have been more suitable. Eleanora Selby-Lowndes was one of eight sisters known as the Belles of Bletchley. Her father Richard was a hard-riding, prosperous squire whose family had for generations held the mastership of the Whaddon Chase; a thrusting cavalry Captain must have seemed an ideal son-in-law. French bore his young wife off to Ireland, and his involvement in the Boycott campaign and subsequent Land League troubles did not prevent the customary round of visits to relatives, allied to the usual equestrian distractions of hunting and racing.

Eleanora brought more to her marriage than a pretty face and a useful legacy. She was slightly older than French, mature, steady and level-headed. In many ways the archetype of the woman he admired, Eleanora fired all the emotion latent in French's character: he was passionately devoted to her, and the first few years of their marriage were probably the happiest of his life. But as is often the case with love which burns with such intensity, the flames of French's passion soon burnt themselves out. Within ten years he was conducting spectacular affairs which inevitably aroused comment. Eleanora was hurt by her husband's unfaithfulness, but it was now that her courage and loyalty – the latter probably singularly strange to modern eyes – came to the fore. French gave her ample grounds for divorce on a number of occasions. He was himself cited as co-respondent in one action, and he later had what can only be termed a *maîtresse en titre*. Eleanora put up with it all. She provided a secure home for the children, and scrupulously refrained from blowing the whistle on her errant husband. French rode with light cavalry panache all over his own marriage vows and a number of other people's: he was fortunate indeed that his wife, motivated by a curious mixture of loyalty, affection and abhorrence of scandal, accepted her role with resignation.

The Frenches were, however, a devoted couple, in fact as well as in appearance, when, in 1881, they moved to a large and pleasant house near Morpeth in Northumberland. French had been seconded to the local yeomanry regiment, the Northumberland Hussars, as Adjutant. It was a welcome change from Ireland, where they had lived in a world of normality interlaced with alarming undercurrents of violence. French's finances were, for once, reasonably stable, and under Eleanora's steadying influence he settled into the comfortable routine of a yeomanry adjutancy. The regiment was commanded by the Earl of Ravensworth. Its officers were country gentlemen, 'all good sportsmen,' as French put it, 'and fine horsemen'.[26] French went down well with the regiment, whose history speaks of 'the keenness and enthusiasm with which this officer discharged his duties'.[27] The Frenches enjoyed a full social life, and made a number of lasting friendships in the county. Their first son, John Richard Lowndes, was born there in 1881, and a daughter followed soon afterwards.

Tragedy overtook the family the following year, when their daughter was accidentally suffocated by her nurse. Some measure of French's nature, and his feelings towards his wife at the time, may be gained from a letter he wrote shortly after the child's funeral.

> Our sweet little darling is in safer care than ours. Although so young she gave promise of being the exact counterpart of her dear mother in face and character ... for I never saw anything but a sweet little smile on her darling face ... and I think I have never seen anything so lovely as the dear child looked in her little coffin ... almost entirely covered with white flowers. She was carried to the grave by four little girls dressed in white.[28]

Although French enjoyed his time with the yeomanry – indeed, his subsequent regard for the Territorial Force owed a great deal to the Northumberland Hussars – the attractions of Morpeth began to pall when French heard that the 19th had been ordered on active service. An Egyptian army officer, Arabi Pasha, had, by the spring of 1882, usurped much of the authority of the Khedive, Mohammed Tewfik. On 11 July a British fleet bombarded the fortifications of Alexandria, and a force was landed to protect the European population and

29

safeguard the person of the Khedive. Later the same month the British government decided to send a force to suppress Arabi, and some 25,000 men, under the command of Lieutenant-General Sir Garnet Wolseley, were dispatched to Egypt. The 19th formed part of Wolseley's force, and assisted in the defeat of Arabi, who was beaten at Tel-el-Kebir on 12 September 1882, and surrendered soon afterwards.

French raged at his enforced inactivity, but his efforts to rejoin the 19th met with stern rebuffs from the War Office. Unlucky in this respect, French was more fortunate in another: promotions and an increase in the establishment of Majors brought French his Majority in April 1883, only nine years after joining the 19th. In December the same year his second son, Edward Gerald, was born.

The defeat of Arabi Pasha seemed to have brought the war in Egypt to an end. The 19th returned to Cairo in March 1883, and in November were ordered to prepare to return to England. It therefore seemed likely that when French rejoined his regiment, on the expiry of his secondment, he would have the morbid satisfaction of meeting it as it returned from Egypt. An attractive wife, a reputation as a hard man to hounds, and a fresh Majority, would all carry little clout in a mess full of campaign medals and Khedive's Stars.

Disturbing news from the Sudan brought a change of plans. The rise of Arabi had obscured another, potentially more dangerous, movement, which sprang up in Kordofan in the spring of 1881. Mohammed Ahmed, son of a boatbuilder from a village near Khartoum, proclaimed himself Mahdi, 'the divinely guided one', and preached a religious war. His army grew rapidly, and in December 1881 and May 1882 annihilated Egyptian columns sent against it. The town of El Obeid fell in January 1883. The Khedive's government responded by raising a force under Major-General William Hicks, assisted by a number of British officers. Hicks advanced from the White Nile in an attempt to retake El Obeid, but in early November he met the Mahdi's army at Kashgil and was utterly overwhelmed. The deteriorating situation in the Sudan came as an unwelcome shock to the Liberal government of W. E. Gladstone. Gladstone was reluctant to embark upon a campaign on the scale of that required to recapture Kordofan and suppress the Mahdi. Accordingly, he decided to evacuate the Western Sudan and to buy off the Mahdi, and Major-General Charles Gordon was sent off to Khartoum to effect this.

Events in the Eastern Sudan, meanwhile, took a turn for the worse. In mid-1883 an Arab slave trader, Osman Digna, raised the tribesmen in support of the Mahdi. His men laid siege to Sinkat and Tokar and in February 1884 routed an Egyptian relief column under Major-General Valentine Baker. Sinkat fell and its garrison was butchered; Tokar still held out, but only the presence of British warships saved the Red Sea port of Suakin.

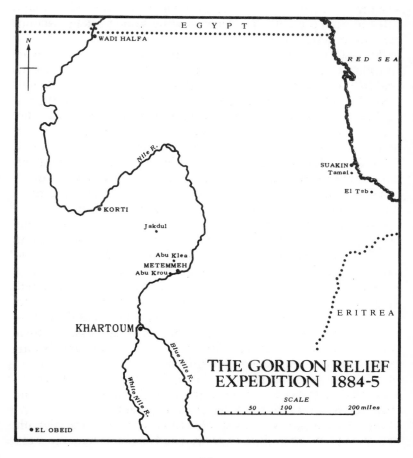

THE GORDON RELIEF
EXPEDITION 1884-5

Gordon reached Khartoum in February 1884, and failed to appease the Mahdi by offering him an independent Kordofan. In the same month, a British force, which included the 19th Hussars, left Cairo, and sailed from Suez for the Eastern Sudan under the command of Major-General Graham. Although he arrived too late to relieve Tokar, Graham defeated Osman Digna's men in two pitched battles. In the first of these, fought at El Teb on 29 February, the 19th were hotly engaged, and French's friend and mentor Lieutenant-Colonel Percy Barrow was desperately wounded. His life was saved by Quartermaster-Sergeant William Marshall, whose bravery earned him the Victoria Cross. The regiment was also at Tamai on 13 March, but was not seriously engaged in this action. Having burned Osman Digna's camp, the British force withdrew to Suakin, whence it was evacuated to Cairo in April.[29] Graham's successes in the Eastern Sudan were set against a picture of gathering gloom in the West. Khartoum was cut off in May, and Gordon's peril jolted Gladstone's government into sending a relief expedition. It was in this ill-fated endeavour that French was to receive his baptism of fire.

French, his tour of duty with the yeomanry over at last, arrived in Cairo in October 1884. He was thirty-two, young, by the standards of the day for a Major who had not received promotion for services in the field. He was well versed in the theory of war in general, and light cavalry operations in particular. Percy Barrow, the most formative influence on French as a junior officer, had emphasised that the real task of light cavalry lay in screening, scouting and reconnaissance, in methodical and painstaking observation of the enemy, and in manoeuvring as part of a combined-arms team.

But whatever French's virtues, he was undeniably deficient in two respects. He had, firstly, never been on active service. And however hazardous it may be to life or professional reputation, active service is the quintessential element of a soldier's career. Without it he shares the attributes of the unpublished author, the narrowly unsuccessful parliamentary candidate, and the policeman who looks forward expectantly to his first arrest. Peacetime reputations wilt under the thunder of the guns, and in the last analysis it is battle that bestows the

iron accolade on military leaders and tactical systems alike.
Circumstances were about to remedy French's lack of practical
experience of war. His second deficiency, the absence of Staff
College training, was destined to remain uncorrected. Nor is
there any evidence that French would have wished it otherwise.

Before discarding French as a thoughtless hearty who rejected opportunities to drink from the fount of military knowledge, it is worth examining the status of the Staff College in
the mid-Victorian army generally. It was, in the first place, a
comparatively new institution, given its present title in late
1857. There were few places each year – 15 in 1858, and 23–34
each year thereafter.[30] Many regiments, not only the cavalry,
shunned the establishment as a pedagogical talking-shop. 'It
was the proud boast of the Gordons,' wrote Ian Hamilton, 'that
none of their officers had ever entered the Staff College or ever
would.'[31] Between February 1856 and February 1881 only 38
cavalry officers went there. Nor were those who attended
always the rising stars of their military generations. In Brian
Bond's words:

> regiments were likely to shunt the idle, overtly
> ambitious or otherwise unwanted officer to Camber-
> ley – or at least would not stand in his way – until
> the Staff College attained such a high reputation
> that it became rather an honour to have an officer
> accepted.[32]

A miasma of suspicion and doubt hung around the Staff College throughout French's time as a regimental officer. It is not
surprising that he did not seek entry: it would have been
astonishing if he had.

However understandable French's failure to attend the Staff
College may be, it had unfortunate long-term consequences.
Although French valued some of the College's graduates
highly, he always retained an essentially Victorian view of the
relative duties and responsibilities of commanders and their
staff officers. He struggled hard against the growing weight of
military opinion which sought to make graduation from Staff
College the prerequisite for staff appointments. French believed, throughout his career, that the experienced regimental

officer could make as good a staff officer as a man who had spent two years at Camberley, and he always retained at least a trace of prejudice against staff officers as a breed. Yet at the same time he relied upon first-rate staff backing. French was never a commander who, like Kitchener, could act as his own chief of staff. He believed that a commander must have his hands free to make decisions and fight the battle; codifying and transmitting his decisions was a matter for the staff. Many officers of French's generation, and, no doubt, a significant proportion of officers of later generations, had more than a little sympathy with this view. But whatever its attractions as an abstract theory, its practical limitations were potentially serious. A commander without Staff College training often lacked the factual grounding in administration and logistics common to staff officers; he could not speak their *lingua franca*, and, as the redoubtable Wully Robertson pointed out, had, whatever his brilliance, to overcome 'numerous drawbacks'.[33]

Lack of staff training cannot have bulked large in French's mind when, at the head of a squadron of the 19th, he left Cairo on 25 October. Three squadrons of the regiment, under Percy Barrow, moved from Cairo to Wadi Halfa by rail and steamer, arriving on 12 November. The regiment was in good heart. Its men had an average of seven years' service, and most of them had fought in the Tel-el-Kebir and Suakin campaigns. Some were reluctant to be left behind at Cairo. One trooper waited, in full kit, to take the place of any man who, at the last minute, could not leave with the sabre squadrons. He was lucky, for one of his comrades had an accident, and the expectant trooper took his place. On the second day of the journey a stowaway bandboy was unearthed, complaining bitterly that 'he was the only *man* in the band without a medal, and he could not stand it'.[34] Experience had shown that the big English troop horses were ill-suited for desert work, and at Wadi Halfa the 19th took over hardy little Syrian Arab horses used by the Egyptian cavalry. The regiment marched, by squadrons, to Korti, where it was assembled on 20 December.

Korti was the base of the force which was being concentrated, under Lord Wolseley, to march to the relief of Khartoum. The 19th was the only cavalry with the force, which also

34

included nine battalions of infantry, four camel corps, a naval brigade and some guns. Wolseley's men had ascended the Nile in a flotilla built in England, manned by an engagingly polyglot crew of Canadian '*voyageurs*' and Kroomen from West Africa.

Wolseley had originally planned to carry out a methodical advance up the river to Khartoum, but a letter from Gordon, dated 4 November, warned that supplies within the town were running low, and forced him to think again. He eventually decided upon a two-pronged advance. The Desert column, under Brigadier-General Sir Herbert Stewart, was to make quickly for Metemmeh, whence it was to open up communications with Khartoum. Major-General Earle's River column was to advance methodically up the Nile, clearing it of enemy and eventually recapturing Berber. A detachment of the 19th was to accompany each of the columns.

Percy Barrow commanded the detachment with the Desert column, with French as his second-in-command. The 19th mustered only 135 officers and men in a total force of 1,607 fighting men and 2,228 camels. There was considerable speculation as to the steadiness of the camels when faced by the onslaught of the Mahdi's hordes, and Lieutenant Count Gleichen, who accompanied the column, describes how:

> in order to test the steadiness of our camels as regarded noise and firing, the 19th Hussars one day, at brigade drill, charged on the unprotected mass of camels cheering and yelling. Everybody expected to see them break their ropes and career wildly over the desert. The only result was that one solitary camel struggled to its feet, looked round and knelt down again: the others never moved an eyelid. The general opinion was that they would stand charging niggers or anything else with equanimity.[35]

There was less certainty that the soldiers themselves would stand the rush with equal coolness. This was the first confrontation between European troops and the Mahdi's main army, but Osman Digna's men had shown their mettle at El Teb and Tamai, and the wild onslaught of mahdists had already swamped the European-led Egyptian forces.

The difficulties facing Stewart were considerable. His

starting-point, Korti, and his objective, Metemmeh, were separated by 176 miles of barren desert. The only two substantial sources of water along the route were at Jakdul, nearly 100 miles from Korti, and at Abu Klea, 53 miles further on. Stewart's first move was to secure the wells at Jakdul prior to the advance of his main body. Jakdul was garrisoned on 2 January 1885 and on the 8th Stewart's main body marched out of Korti. The early part of the journey was uneventful, and the column left Jakdul on 14 January, having encountered only a few enemy stragglers.

Stewart's force was camel-mounted, and marched closed up around the guns, camels striding out across the stony desert floor. The 19th, the only horsemen with the column, were deployed well forward, scouting. Count Gleichen, riding with Stewart amongst the bobbing pith-helmets of the main body, describes how:

> On coming to a plain with hills in the distance, you'd see specks on the tops of the furthest hills, and with the help of your glasses discover them to be the 19th. Sir Herbert was immensely pleased with them and pointed them out to me as being the very acme of light cavalry.[36]

So far the advance had been uneventful enough. From the 19th's point of view it had involved the practical application of the drills practised on the rolling greensward of the Curragh, and the points, flankers and patrols so beloved of *Cavalry Drill* and Colonel Clery's *Minor Tactics* spread like a glittering web in front of the column. On 16 January French was sent forward with a patrol to make contact with the enemy in front of the Abu Klea wells. French and his men galloped into the gorge leading to the wells, in pursuit of a body of mahdists, and seized a straggler. The enemy response was brisk and unwelcome, as large numbers of hostile cavalry threatened French's retreat. Relinquishing its prisoner, the patrol hurtled back to the end of the gorge, where Barrow had brought the remainder of the detachment which kept the enemy cavalry off with carbine fire.

Stewart led the rest of the column forward to join the 19th, and the force made a zariba—a hasty breastwork, usually made of thorn bushes, but built of rocks in this instance — inside which it camped for the night. The enemy grew bolder as darkness fell, and kept up a hot fire into the zariba all night, causing few casualties but keeping the men awake. The bullets began to do more damage after dawn: men were hit, and the 19th lost some horses. Stewart had little choice but to press on towards the much-needed water, some three-and-a-half miles away. At about 9 a.m. he formed his command into a huge square, detaching the 19th Hussars to keep off a party of about 500 dervishes who threatened the square's rear.

It was nearly 10.00 when the square moved off, its advance impeded by the ravines and hollows which scarred the desert. There were frequent halts to maintain alignment, and to permit the camels carrying water and ammunition to keep up. The square had not gone far when the worst happened. A mass of swordsmen and spearmen, about 5,000 strong, surged up out of a fold in the ground and hurled themselves upon it. The British force, with the superior firepower of its Martini-Henry rifles and one Gardner machine-gun, should, on paper at least, have won easily. But the dervishes were a formidable foe, fanatically brave, and murderously expert with the broad-bladed *kaskara* and what Kipling called the 'coffin 'eaded shield and shovel spear'. In five minutes of desperate hand-to-hand fighting the British suffered cruelly. The Gardner gun jammed, as Gardner guns tended to, at the crucial moment, and its bluejacket crew was cut down. The flamboyant Lord Charles Beresford, attempting to clear the jam, was knocked senseless and left for dead. Perhaps the most distinguished casualty was Captain Fred Burnaby of the Blues, traveller and author of *Ride to Khiva*, who was speared in an unequal contest outside the square, and bled to death on the sand as the debris of the charge rolled back. Seventy-four of Stewart's men were killed, and another 94 wounded, many of them seriously. Of the total enemy force engaged that day, of perhaps 9,000, over 1,000 lay dead in and around the square.

The 19th had dismounted to support the square with their carbines when the dervishes attacked. As the tide of the charge eddied back, they mounted and followed up the retreating enemy. It was no storybook charge with flashing steel and serried ranks of galloping steeds. The horses could scarcely move out of a walk, having been without water for thirty hours, and the broken ground in any case rendered rapid movement difficult. Nevertheless, the 19th cut down a number of the enemy, and pushed on to the wells, prising out the dervish rearguard with carbine-fire. The square had shuddered its way to the wells by nightfall, and on the following morning a small fort was built to secure the vital water supply. The 19th, meanwhile, had the grisly task of returning to the battlefield to bury the British dead.

The column resumed its advance late on the afternoon of 18 January. Stewart hoped to cover the 25 miles separating him from the Nile without another battle, and determined to press on during the hours of darkness. It was a black, moonless night, and the column stumbled forward in growing disorder. Men got lost, fell asleep in the saddle and crashed from their camels to the ground as tiredness overcame them. The advance guard lost direction, and the whole force swung round in a great circle before, as dawn broke over the weary column, the vegetation and villages marking the line of the Nile came into view about six miles away.

Between the British force and the river was a low gravel ridge, and from this thronged swarms of dervishes. The column halted, made a hasty zariba, and checked the attack with fire. The first attacks ground to a halt some distance from the zariba, but those dervishes with firearms then began to shoot into the half-completed defences. Stewart himself was one of the first to be hit: he was mortally wounded, and died a few days later.

Command devolved on Colonel Sir Charles Wilson, and under his leadership the zariba was at last completed. The 19th Hussars, their horses quite exhausted, were left to guard the zariba while the rest of the force formed square outside it and marched off towards the Nile. As it neared the ridge the square came under heavy fire, but this stopped as dervishes rushed forward to attack. The ground was flatter than Abu Klea, and this time there were no skirmishes to mask the fire. The odds were all in favour of technology, for the dervishes had to cross a bullet-swept stretch of desert before they could come to hand-strokes. Not one of the mahdists reached the square: although their attack was pressed with bravery, the rifle-fire swept them away. The way to the Nile lay open, and the square reached the river near Abu Krou just after dark.

The Hussars did not reach the river until the afternoon of the 20th. By this time half their horses had been without water for 72 hours, and the remainder for 56: it is astonishing that only three of them died. Sir Charles Wilson was painfully aware of the state of his cavalry.

> The cavalry horses were quite done up. The way in which Barrow managed to bring the 19th Hussars across the desert is one of the best things of the expedition; but the horses had only a short drink at Abu Klea, and then barely enough to wash their mouths out until they got to the Nile on the 20th. The scouting of the Hussars on the march was admirably done: they were ubiquitous. But want of food and water no horses can fight against, and they were but a sorry spectacle as they moved out of the zariba to go down to the river. They reached the Nile almost useless as cavalry, and could only be employed for scouting purposes, at short distances from the camp.[37]

The 19th were sent forward to reconnoitre Metemmeh, and the column had begun to attack the place when four small steamers from Khartoum brought news that enemy reinforcements were on the way. Wilson suspended the attack in order to husband lives and ammunition, and three days later set off for Khartoum with 200 men in two of the vessels. He reached the town on the 28th, and learned that it had fallen two days before: Gordon was dead. The death of Gordon removed the expedition's *raison d'être*, and the fall of Khartoum released large numbers of dervishes whose advance rendered the column's position increasingly perilous. Wilson and his party rejoined the main force on 4 February, after a harrowing journey down a river whose banks teemed with dervishes. A week later Major-General Sir Redvers Buller arrived to take command, and ordered a retreat on Abu Klea.

Redvers Buller has gone down as one of the bad jokes of Victorian military history. He has been described as an admirable Captain, an adequate Major, a barely satisfactory Colonel and a disastrous General; his campaign in South Africa in 1899 is often regarded as the very epitome of bull-headed stupidity.[38] Taking up the cudgels on behalf of one imperfectly-understood General is enough for a single biography, but while Buller was probably, in Esher's words, 'a gallant fellow but no strategist', the picture of Buller as a clownish incompetent is drawn rather larger than life.[39] He was a member of the Wolseley Ring — a fact which cannot have endeared him to the members of that other charmed circle, presided over by Lord Roberts. Wolseley himself vividly describes Buller as:

> one whose stern determination of character nothing could ruffle, whose resource in difficulty was not surpassed by anyone I knew ... Had a thunderbolt burst at his feet he would merely have brushed from his rifle jacket the earth it had thrown upon him without any break in the sentence he happened to be uttering at the moment.[40]

Whatever Buller's merits or limitations, two facts are relevant to our understanding of French and his career. The first is that French, in common with the overwhelming majority of the army, idolised Buller. Years later, when Buller was living in discredited retirement, and could be of no use to anyone's career, French wrote to him:

> You have the heartfelt love of every soldier who has ever served with you and any of them would go anywhere for you tomorrow. I have constantly told my great pals and friends that I would like to end my life by being shot when serving under you. Lots of others think the same.[41]

Buller also cherished a high opinion of French. The mutual esteem of French and Buller was of pivotal importance as far as French's career was concerned. Buller became a powerful man in the 1890s. From 1890 to 1897 he held the important post of Adjutant-General at the War Office, at the very time when French, his military future hanging by a thread following an ill-considered burst of sexual tactlessness, urgently needed a friend in high places. He then went on to command at Aldershot, when French was a cavalry Brigadier under him, and his recommendation was crucial in securing for French the command of the cavalry in South Africa. French's star rose as Buller's fell, but French never forgot his old mentor who had smoothed the rocky road between half-pay Colonel and substantive Major-General.[42]

French's feet were still on the bottom rung of the ladder of success when, on 16 February, his chance came. Buller sent most of the 19th on to Jakdul, and retained only a small detachment, under the command of French. Threatened by a strong, aggressive enemy, Buller took the controversial step of filling in the wells before falling back on Jakdul. The tiny detachment of the 19th formed the rearguard, and it covered Buller's withdrawal throughout that most difficult of military operations, retreat across inhospitable terrain in contact with a cunning and merciless enemy.

Sir Evelyn Wood, whose service, like that of French, had started in the navy, was sent out from Korti to meet Buller's column on its way back from Jakdul. He found the retreating force in good order, but with the dervishes at its heels. It was here that he met French. He wrote:

> I saw him when our people were coming back across the desert after our failure, the whole force depressed by the death of Gordon. I came on him about a hundred miles from the river — the last man in the last section of the rear guard! We were followed by bands of Arabs. They came into our bivouac on the night of which I am speaking, and carried off some of our cattle.[43]

Buller, in a dispatch written at Jakdul on 26 February, paid handsome tribute to French's little band.

> I wish expressly to remark on the very excellent work done by the small detachment of the 19th Hussars, both during our occupation of Abu Klea and during our retirement. Each man had done the work of ten and it is not too much to say that the force owes much to Major French and his 13 troopers.[44]

The 19th Hussars were reunited in August 1885, when the

squadron which had formed part of the River column rejoined the regiment in Cairo. As the 19th recovered from the rigours of the campaign, French found himself rewarded with promotion to Lieutenant-Colonel and appointment as second-in-command. He was remarkably young for the rank, but he had, by any standards, distinguished himself during the operations of the Desert column: his Majority may have come by lucky seniority, but his Lieutenant-Colonelcy was well-earned. French had done more than win accelerated promotion and the golden opinions of his superiors. He had gained experience and self-confidence. The lessons he learned in Egypt in 1885 were to stand him in good stead in South Africa fifteen years later. Particularly valuable was his experience of horse-management in the field. It has become almost obligatory to chuckle at the equine preoccupations of cavalry officers, but in the period before 1914 a sound knowledge of horseflesh, and its campaigning requirements in terms of fodder and water, was as essential an attribute for a cavalry leader as an understanding of a tank's characteristics and petrol consumption is to the armoured specialist of the 1980s.

The 19th returned to England in the spring of 1886. French's homecoming was overshadowed by the death of Percy Barrow. Barrow had never fully recovered from the terrible wound he had received at El Teb in February 1884. He had gone through the Desert column's campaign without flinching, but, by a supreme irony, the wound opened up again while he was tent-pegging in preparation for the regimental sports in January 1886. He was dead thirty hours later. French took temporary command of the 19th, but was considered too young to command on a permanent basis, and Barrow's brother-in-law, Colonel Boyce Combe, was transferred from the 10th Hussars to take his place.

Between June 1886 and April 1888 French was stationed with the 19th at Norwich. During the Egyptian campaign, Eleanora and the children had moved to Hanslope Farm, near Stony Stratford in Buckinghamshire, on the estate of Eleanora's brother-in-law, Edward Hanslope Watts. French left his family there when he went to Norwich. Although they were probaby more comfortable in the rural surroundings of Buckinghamshire than they would have been in a quarter in

Norwich, Eleanora and the boys saw French comparatively rarely, and the ties of the marriage began to weaken. But all seemed well enough on the face of things, and French's daughter, Essex Eleanora, was born late in 1886.

French spent two fruitful years as second-in-command of the 19th. He was not content to take a back seat and wait for his turn at command, but he set about ensuring that the lessons learned in Egypt should be hammered home in peacetime. He had no use for what he called 'drawing-room soldiers', and pushed the regiment's young officers along at exercises and field-days. He took command of the regiment in the spring of 1888, in time for its move to Hounslow, which was then an attractive country village, as yet innocent of the urban sprawl which has now engulfed it. French brought his family to Hounslow, where they lived in what Gerald French remembered as 'a fair-sized yellowish building' just inside the barrack gate.[45]

Aldershot beckoned in the summer of 1888, and the regiment marched into East Cavalry Barracks, forming part of 1st Cavalry Brigade, commanded first by Sir Drury Lowe and later by Sir Baker Russell. The French family moved into the commanding officer's house, part of a grey stone block which included the officers' mess. A thin wall separated the nursery from the mess: Gerald recalled that this arrangement ensured that the children had numerous sleepless nights as the mess buzzed and roared next door. Part of the din was caused by a black bear which the subalterns had brought back from the Sudan. The beast lived in the mess, no doubt causing a good deal of far-from-innocent merriment as it set upon choleric Majors, but eventually it became so dangerous that it had to be put down.[46]

Evelyn Wood, himself a cavalryman, was commanding at Aldershot, striving hard to make training more practical and realistic. He had been impressed by what he had seen of French in the Sudan, and his respect deepened as he watched the young Colonel — for French was only 36 — hard at work perfecting the 19th. French continued to steer the regiment along the course he had helped to set as second-in-command, emphasising brisk and vigorous manoeuvres. French's methods stood out in sharp contrast to the rigid formalism of brigade manoeuvres, in which smart execution of 'change position by fours half left back' was the apogee of tactical excellence.[47] It was perhaps not too difficult for French to shine in such surroundings, and shine he did.

He was also well to the fore in implementing an important administrative change. Cavalry regiments had traditionally been composed of eight troops, each commanded by a Captain. Squadrons were formed on a more or less *ad hoc* basis for active service, and in 1868 there had been a short-lived attempt to introduce them as a peacetime administrative unit. The troop system had numerous disadvantages: when a regiment's strength fell below establishment, as it often did, a troop leader would finish up with a handful of men, and proper training became impossible. Captains varied greatly in terms of age and experience: some troops were commanded by veterans in their forties, while others were in the hands of young men in their early twenties.

French was a warm advocate of the squadron system, as he was later of the double-company organisation of infantry battalions, believing that it contributed to increased efficiency in both peace and war. Wood had tried, without success, to get the War Office to sanction the formation of permanent squadrons, and he noted with approval that French introduced the system into the 19th without formal permission, appointing squadron leaders on the basis of ability rather than seniority.[48] The War Office ordered all regiments to form squadrons in 1892, and the system has remained in use ever since.

In the summer of 1891 the 19th was detailed for service in India, and on 1 September it embarked at Portsmouth on the *Euphrates*. French – by now a brevet Colonel – had decided not to take his family to India. The boys would be educated in England in any case, and Eleanora felt that the Indian climate might prove dangerous. However rational this decision, it was to have unfortunate results. French seems to have felt that his wife let him down by her failure to go to India with him and her absence gave him both reason and opportunity for infidelity, and he was never one to let chances slip.

The 19th disembarked at Bombay on 28 September and proceeded by train to Secunderabad, where it remained for only two months before moving down to Bangalore. The regiment's reputation had gone before it, and French found himself working hand-in-glove with Sir George Luck, Inspector-General of Cavalry in India. French's relationship with Luck is every bit as significant as his connection with Buller and Wood. Wully Robertson, recently commissioned from the ranks, and serving in India at the time, wrote that Luck was:

> considered by officers of the old school to be more of a drill-sergeant than a cavalry commander in that he required regimental officers to know far more about their men and horses and the details of drill than was either reasonable or necessary. To my mind, he only asked of officers what it was their duty to give: he expected them to know their work and be able to instruct their men, and that is what many officers in India and elsewhere did not know and could not do.[49]

George Barrow, like many other Indian cavalry officers, thought Luck a martinet with an unnatural interest in drill, but felt that, all things considered, he had a beneficial effect.[50] Lieutenant Hubert Gough, whose regiment had also gone from Aldershot to India, believed that 'rapid mounted manoeuvres in close order' were considered the objective of cavalry training: this goal had been established by Luck, whose own manoeuvres always consisted of 'rapid drill movements which raised clouds of dust'.[51]

It is important to note the close affinity of ideas that sprang up between French and Luck. Luck admired French and the 19th because French had trained the regiment to exactly the pitch that Luck required: it swirled across the *maidan* at high speed, perfectly responsive to the orders of Colonel and squadron leaders. It was modern training by the standards of the 1890s, far removed from the stylised clatterings of the Aldershot Cavalry Brigade.

But as Gough and the younger generation of thinking cavalry officers were already beginning to suspect, Luck's ideas themselves, however beneficial in rousing Indian cavalry from its lethargy, were becoming outdated. French's time in India left him with a lasting affection for Luck-style manoeuvres, an affection which was to influence him when he later became Inspector-General of the forces.

Luck allowed French to try his hand at commanding a brigade on manoeuvres. In January 1893, at the camp of instruction at Muridki near Lahore, French's brigade comprised two regiments of Bengal Lancers and a composite regiment of Jhind and Nabha Lancers. French did well in exercises which included far-ranging reconnaissance and scouting drills. Most of the enemy were, however, 'flagged' or 'skeleton', with no capacity for independent action, and seriously though the manoeuvres were taken, even the hard-driving Luck had a truce at breakfast-time.[52] The manoeuvres also revealed the scanty extent of French's 'indianisation'. Many officers who served with British regiments in India picked up at least a little of the language and gained a lasting affection for the country. There is no evidence that French did either: the future Lord Birdwood, commanding the Jhind and Nabha Lancers at Muridki, pointed out that even these simple names were too much for French, who invariably garbled them as 'Jubber Lancers'.[53] In his official pronouncements as Commander-in-Chief in France French always paid handsome tribute to the work of the Indian Corps, but his letters and diaries reveal no trace of the deep emotional appeal which the Indian Army exercised on so many British officers, even those whose acquaintance with it was no deeper than French's.

A photograph of French as commanding officer of the 19th shows a firm, self-confident face, garnished with a thick black moustache. French was at his most successful and attractive, and he knew it. He was not one to survive long without feminine company, and while in India he embarked upon at least one affair, with the wife of another senior officer. He disappeared to the hills with her during a spell of leave, which some officers unkindly quipped at as 'French leave', and the infuriated husband promptly riposted by suing his wife for divorce, citing our saturnine hero as co-respondent. In his capacity as Luck's unofficial assistant French had made a number of enemies, and they lost no opportunity to spread the good news.

The business cast ripples far and wide. As late as 1907, when French succeeded the Duke of Connaught as Inspector-

General of the forces, Moreton Frewen, man-about-town, sportsman, adventurer and Irish Nationalist MP, raised the matter with R. B. Haldane, Secretary of State for War. He sought to persuade Haldane to convene a court of inquiry to investigate the case of his brother, Lieutenant-Colonel Stephen Frewen, peremptorily dismissed by French from command of the 16th Lancers during the Boer War. Thundered Frewen:

> Are you aware that he is an adulterer convicted in a court of law? Why did your late chief [Gladstone] drum my late chief Parnell out of public life while you advance French to the position lately occupied by the King's brother? Why am I to spare French? ... The debates of the next session will turn agreeably on the 7th commandment.[54]

Haldane did not grant Stephen Frewen his court of inquiry, but he managed, somehow, to pacify Moreton: in any event, the scandal failed to materialise.[55]

There was, however, scandal enough in the summer of 1893, when French, his tenure of command of the 19th providentially completed, returned home to England. Despite his undoubted success with his regiment, and the favourable impression he had made on Luck, he did not slip smoothly into another appointment. He was instead consigned to the half-pay list, by no means an unusual repository for ex-commanding officers, but one rendered uncomfortable by two alarming facts. Firstly, his pay was halved at a stroke, and he had already had to borrow money from Muir Mills against future profits. Secondly, time spent on half-pay was time out of his career: moreover, if he was to remain on half-pay for more than two years, compulsory retirement would automatically follow. French's biographers have been at a loss to explain his long sojourn in outer darkness at a time when all signs appeared, officially at least, to be so favourable. The scandal of the Indian divorce is a possible explanation.[56]

Eleanora and the children had moved, just before French's departure for India, to Lottie Despard's house, 'Courtlands', near Esher. Here French joined them. It was perhaps the most gloomy period of his career: he was desperately short of money, and the news from India cannot have made the French *ménage* notably cheerful. Lottie spent most of her time in London, but she paid occasional visits to the house, often accompanied by the members of a working men's club at Nine Elms, her project of the moment.

French's time was spent in long walks, accompanied only by his two mongrel dogs, Daphne and Tatters. He kept no horses, probably as a result of his acute financial embarrassment, so took up cycling as an alternative to riding. He was too self-conscious to be seen practising on a road, so he would march his sons to a secluded spot and then enlist their aid. He never mastered the process of mounting, and would disappear into the distance hopping wildly alongside his machine, but failing to get astride it.[57]

Light flickered through the gloom in the autumn of 1894. French was temporarily re-employed to command a brigade in the cavalry manoeuvres, which took place in the Vale of the White Horse under the command of Lieutenant-General James Keith-Fraser. A newspaper correspondent noted that French 'had rather the better of his opponent'. He favoured attacking with his regiments deployed in a number of lines, giving far greater flexibility than the single heavy line favoured by the other brigade commander.[58] French emerged from the manoeuvres with credit, and an officer who was present re-called his comments on their conclusion:

> there is no subject upon which more misconception exists, even among service men, than as regards the real role of cavalry in warfare. My conception of the duties and functions of the mounted arm is not to cut and hack and thrust at your enemy wherever and however he may be found. The real business of cavalry is so to manoeuvre your enemy as to bring him within effective range of the corps artillery of your own side for which a position suitable for battle would previously have been selected.[59]

The Berkshire manoeuvres showed that French was more than merely another hack-and-gallop merchant. He was well aware of the importance of that element whose influence was already profoundly affecting warfare: firepower.

French's performance was the only bright spot in the

manoeuvres. They were seen, by reformers within the army and by newspaper correspondents outside it, as glaring evidence of the desperate traits of British cavalry. Sir George Luck was accordingly brought to England to replace Keith-Fraser as Inspector-General of Cavalry. The first thing Luck wanted was a new Cavalry Drill Book, and he knew just the man to write it: Colonel French. French was brought off the half-pay list, just in time, for his two years were nearly up, and the spectre of early retirement beckoned. He was appointed Assistant Adjutant-General at the Horse Guards: Redvers Buller was Adjutant-General, and there is little doubt that his influence also helped bring French back from the brink of disaster. [60]

French took up his new appointment in August 1895, and was granted the substantive rank of Colonel. He spent nearly two years at Horse Guards, and during this time he carried through two major reforms. The first was the production of the new *Cavalry Drill*, which was both a clear and concise code of regulations for the organisation of mounted troops, and a complete tactical manual. Many of the book's merits were inevitably obscured by the fresh experience of the South African War. Nevertheless, it was a lucid and forward-looking manual, which stressed that 'all cavalry exercises have for object the training of leaders, men and horse for war'. It paid careful attention to scouting and reconnaissance, and did not neglect the dismounted duties of cavalry. Indeed, one authority has suggested that, 'If our cavalry had really learned all that this drill-book had to teach, it would have attained a fully adequate standard of efficiency.' [61]

The second reform concerned the introduction of permanent cavalry brigades. Brigades were, of course, nothing new: they were organised for war and for manoeuvres, and existed in peacetime at Aldershot. The formation of permanent brigades was, however, a much-debated point, for it involved numerous separate considerations, not least the cavalry's wartime deployment and peacetime posting schedule. French believed that all cavalry regiments stationed in the United Kingdom should be combined in brigades of three regiments, each brigade under a commander responsible for its administration and training. A sound start was made on this while French was at Horse Guards, although the system did not become universal until after the Boer War.

In May 1897 French was sent to Canterbury, as a Colonel on the staff, to take command of the newly-formed 2nd Cavalry Brigade. He moved his family from 'The Hut', opposite Sandown Park, to a house he had taken when his appointment to Horse Guards had been announced, in Canterbury itself, and settled down to knock his new command into shape. His return to favour had not diminished his unpopularity in some circles. Some traditionalists accused him of being a dangerous innovator, and the machinations which had brought him from semi-retirement, through an influential post at Horse Guards, to command of an active brigade, were seen as arrant jobbery. Major-General Reginald Talbot was one of his most vocal opponents. In the autumn manoeuvres of 1898 French surprised and over-ran several batteries of Talbot's artillery near Yarnbury Castle, and although the anti-French lobby gloomily predicted that such rashness would prove disastrous in war, the incident confirmed French's reputation as a rising man.

Early the following year French moved from Canterbury to take over the 1st Cavalry Brigade at Aldershot with the temporary rank of Major-General. It was a highly desirable post. Aldershot Command, under the genial Buller, would be certain to form the nucleus of an expeditionary force in the event of war, and thunder-clouds were gathering over South Africa. The Frenches took up residence in Anglesey House, their most luxurious accommodation to date, on the Farnham Road outside Aldershot, with Hungry Hill and the training area rising away behind it. It was a comfortable house, with a large garden, but Major-General French was anything but comfortable in it. He had run up substantial debts while on half-pay, and he had not managed to pay them off during his time at Canterbury. In the spring of 1899, therefore, it seemed by no means improbable that disaster would strike and that French, dunned by his creditors, would be hounded out of the army.

Help came from an unexpected quarter. Captain Douglas Haig, a dour and hardworking officer of the 7th Hussars, had been ADC to the luckless Keith-Fraser at the 1894 manoeuvres, and was probably on nodding terms with French at their conclusion. The first formal meeting between the two men came a year later, when Haig acted as French's staff officer on a staff ride organised by Evelyn Wood. He had also given French some translations of German papers on cavalry staff tours, and seems to have helped with the 1898 *Cavalry Drill.*[62] Haig then went off to Staff College, served with distinction in the Egyptian campaign of 1898–9, and appeared at Aldershot as French's Brigade-Major in the spring of the latter year. It is hard to look at the relationship between French and Haig without the bitterness of 1915–18 obscuring the issues. Nevertheless, for most of their professional association the French–Haig combination was a happy and successful one. Their abilities were complementary: French was always an ideas man, better in speech than on paper, while Haig was notoriously taciturn, but capable of writing concise and lucid prose, and giving form to French's conceptions.

Major Haig was a frequent visitor to Anglesey House. He talked freely enough to French on military topics, particularly on the situation in South Africa, which both men thought would lead to war. He was less than forthcoming to French's daughter Essex: she remembered him as being 'desperately dull'. Sometimes he would break a painful silence by saying, 'very nice tea today, Essex' while on other occasions he would gaze at the mongrel Daphne and mutter, 'Daphne, poor old dog.'[63] Whatever Haig's failings as a conversationalist, he was certainly far more astute than his brigade commander in the management of money. Haig was more likely to ride naked down the Mall than to get into debt: his letters and diaries reveal a pronounced preoccupation with money, and in the spring of 1899 Haig had disposable cash at the very moment when French urgently required it. He borrowed the sum of £2,000 from Haig, and although this appeared to be a loan, it seems that it was never repaid: it was certainly outstanding four years later.[64]

The transaction may be interpreted in a number of ways. It is perhaps simplest to see it as an act of kindness on Haig's part to an officer he admired. Duff Cooper believed that the loan was made 'not only out of friendship to the officer concerned but also in belief that his retirement would be a loss to the army'.[65] Less generous souls might suggest that it was hardly ethical for a junior officer to make what was in fact, if not in theory, a substantial gift — worth say £30,000 at today's prices — to a senior, knowing that the senior was responsible for initiating the reports which would determine his immediate military future. The propriety of receiving such a sum, and making no effort to pay it back, may also be challenged.

Haig's money solved French's immediate financial problems, but the respite was short-lived. French had invested a considerable sum in Transvaal Golds. It was not a wise investment, in view of the increasingly disturbed state of South Africa, and the shares eventually crashed on the London market. French lost a good deal of money, but his annoyance at the blow was soon assuaged by more momentous developments. As relations with the Boer republics worsened, the government toyed with the idea — it toyed with a lot of ideas in those hectic days — of sending out an army corps under Buller. On 22 September the Cabinet at last determined to send the corps. Buller had been making his own plans for some weeks, and had already made some crucial decisions: one of the first was to select French to command his cavalry. On 23 September 1899, just a few days before his forty-eighth birthday, French embarked at Southampton on the steamer *Norman* and set off for a war which was to ruin many reputations, but to make his own.

Two

Carving a Reputation
South Africa, 1899

Major-General French's khaki service-dress hat, a low-crowned masterpiece which had only recently emerged, like a butterfly from its chrysalis, from the Bond Street shop of Messrs Herbert Johnson, was in some peril from a wind which tugged at the shipping in Southampton harbour and pummelled the Solent to a lively chop. It was about 4.30 on the afternoon of Saturday 23 September 1899 when French and Haig boarded the *Norman*, crammed full of officers, men and their kit, all bound for the Cape. French took over a cabin normally used by the ship's second officer, and, finding that no accommodation had been allotted to Haig, he invited him to share the cramped quarters.[1]

As he surveyed the far from luxurious conditions aboard the *Norman*, French may have mused over the curious situation in which he found himself. All that was certain was that he was bound for South Africa. His rank was temporary, his precise destination uncertain and his mission gloriously vague. He had been appointed to command the cavalry under Lieutenant-General Sir George White, a sixty-four-year-old Irishman snatched from the Quartermaster-General's desk at the War Office to command the forces in Natal. White was himself at sea, a week ahead of French, and his troops were scattered over three continents and as many oceans. And if all this was strange enough, one thing was stranger still: there was as yet no war for them to fight.[2]

Whatever the official state of relations between Britain and the Boer Republics of the Orange Free State and the Transvaal

53

in September 1899, it was clear – and had been for some time
– that war was probable. It was the dull gleam of gold that
germinated the seeds of conflict long dormant in South Africa.
A Dutch colony at the Cape had been taken over by the British,
for strategic reasons, during the Napoleonic Wars. The settlers, mainly Dutch Calvinists, with an admixture of French
Huguenots and German Protestants, were at best resigned to
British hegemony. Many found the situation intolerable, particularly after the emancipation of slaves throughout the British
Empire in 1834. The Great Trek of 1835–7 saw those Boers
who were no longer prepared to submit to British rule spill out
across the Vaal and Orange Rivers. The British government
pursued an inconsistent policy: in 1843 it annexed Natal, one of
the newly-occupied areas, but in 1852 and 1854 it recognised
the independence of the Transvaal and the Orange Free State.
In 1877, in yet another shift of policy, Britain annexed the
Transvaal, only to relinquish it in 1881 after a brief but disastrous war in which General Piet Joubert's Boers had routed a
British force at Majuba Hill.

Majuba seemed ample proof of the British army's inability
to adapt to South African conditions, just as the Convention of
London, which ended the war, appeared to show the reluctance of British governments to become embroiled in a long-
drawn-out struggle. The discovery of gold in the Wit-
watersrand in the Transvaal, and the gold-rush this generated
in the late 1880s, dramatically altered the situation. The gold
was mined by foreigners, known as Uitlanders, a tough, self-
reliant crew, many of them of British extraction. There was
little in common between the Uitlanders and the dour Boers,
who ensured, by way of restrictive franchise laws, that the
Uitlanders were excluded from political power.

But the Uitlanders had their allies. The diamond-rich Cecil
Rhodes, Prime Minister of Cape Colony, in collusion with
Alfred Beit, another diamond millionaire, organised an expedition into the Transvaal: the raid was intended to coincide
with a rising of Uitlanders, and the whole affair would, so its
architects hoped, finish with the Transvaal, and its gold, once
again in British hands. The raid was a fiasco. Led by Rhodes's
trusted assistant, Dr L. S. Jameson, the invaders were brought
to bay at Doornkop, just short of Johannesburg. After a battle

scarcely less humiliating than Majuba, they were rounded up. Boer fatalities were half those of Majuba: only one man.[3] Although Joseph Chamberlain, the British Colonial Secretary, would have welcomed an Uitlander victory, there was no truth in Boer allegations that he had actively encouraged Rhodes. Nevertheless, the incident had serious consequences. It gave the Boers widespread foreign support, and encouraged them to re-arm with modern weapons which their rejuvenated economy could so easily afford. It also cemented the ties between the Orange Free State and the Transvaal, and triggered off a wave of anti-British sentiment amongst Cape Colony Boers. War between Britain and the Transvaal was now a decided possibility.

Tragedy might still have been averted had it not been for a sharp clash of personalities between two of the leading actors in the drama. The aged Paul Kruger – he was 74 in 1899 – had been President of the Transvaal for sixteen years. His hirsute countenance gave him the air of an Old Testament prophet, although his baggy black suits and huge pipe were more reminiscent of a prosperous rag-and-bone-man. Kruger's concept of politics was patriarchal rather than democratic, and it was primarily his intransigence which had kept the Uitlanders in the political shadows.

Sir Alfred Milner was 45 when, in 1897, he was appointed High Commissioner in South Africa. He was brilliant and urbane, an ardent Imperialist whose ultimate goal was 'mastery in South Africa': and squarely in front of this goal stood the untidy figure of Paul Kruger.[4] Milner at first hoped to persuade Kruger to grant concessions to the Uitlanders, stressing that Britain had no designs on the Transvaal's independence. Kruger feared that giving the vote to Uitlanders would open the floodgates: it would be political suicide for the Boers. In the late spring of 1899 the two men met at Bloemfontein, at a conference chaired by President Steyn of the Orange Free State. The meeting brought compromise no nearer. It confirmed Kruger in his suspicions that Milner wanted the Transvaal, and convinced Milner that only military pressure would force the Boers to give way.

Milner suggested to the government that 'overwhelming' force should be sent to South Africa. This led to considerable bickering along the labyrinthine corridors of the War Office as to what 'overwhelming' actually meant in this context, and whether the same effect might not be produced at less expense by sending the force to Salisbury Plain, whence it could over-awe Kruger at long range. Several obstacles impeded the smooth formulation of military plans. There was, in the first place, no love lost between Field-Marshal Lord Wolseley, Commander-in-Chief of the Army, and Lord Lansdowne, Secretary of State for War. Wolseley also perceived a threat from within the army, suspecting, rightly enough, that Lord Roberts and his adherents would strive to ingratiate them-selves with Lansdowne, imperilling Wolseley and his protégé, Buller. The intelligence available to Wolseley and Lansdowne was contradictory and vague, and plans for the defence of Natal and Cape Colony conspicuous by their absence. Finally, the political climate remained decidedly changeable, presenting military planners with new vistas of uncertainty littered with half-calculated risks and profitless expense.

The wind did indeed change during the summer of 1899. For a time it seemed, much to Milner's horror, that Kruger might grant acceptable concessions, and even when the cabinet de-cided, on 8 September, to strengthen the Natal garrison with ten thousand men, it still seemed that war could be avoided. Sir George White was sent off to command these reinforcements on 16 September. Buller, meanwhile, earmarked to command the army corps which might – or there again might not – follow White, was having serious misgivings about his role. He had originally been optimistic, remarking, 'Well, if I can't win with these, I ought to be kicked,' when shown a list of the troops making up his corps. But Buller knew the Boers better than any other general, and by early September he had serious doubts. The Boers might not be browbeaten by a show of force, and in that case White's men would be in for some unpleasant surprises if they pushed too far forward.[5]

The gradual dispatch of British troops, far from cowing Kruger, had almost exactly the reverse effect. By early Sep-tember he had decided that war was inevitable. This being the case, there was everything to be gained by attacking Natal before the arrival of British reinforcements. It might be poss-ible to swamp Natal and capture Durban before fresh troops arrived. This could spark off an anti-British revolt in Cape Colony, and would certainly damage Britain's international standing. President Steyn was unconvinced, and Kruger and his State Attorney, J. C. Smuts, lost valuable time in trying to convince him of the need for swift action.

Time was already short: on 22 September the Boers heard that Buller's corps was, after all, to be sent out. Of more immediate importance was the news that the first of the British reinforcements had already begun to arrive at Durban. On 28 September the Transvaal mobilised, and the Free State at last followed suit on 2 October. Seven days later the Transvaal presented an ultimatum: unless the British government agreed, within 48 hours, to accept arbitration on points under dispute, to withdraw its forces from the Transvaal's borders, to evacuate those troops who had arrived since 1 June, and not to land the troops currently at sea anywhere in South Africa, a state of war would exist between the Transvaal and Britain.

To many Englishmen, soldiers and civilians, it seemed nothing short of impertinent folly for the Boers to threaten war. Britain was a major world power, a nation of phenomenal economic and military strength, centre of an Empire which spanned the globe. In practical terms, however, the odds against the Boers were by no means as great as they seemed. The Boer military system was the epitome of simplicity. Most adult males were liable for military service, and were expected to report for duty with pony, rations for ten days, rifle and ammunition. Each electoral district, and there were 22 in the Transvaal and 18 in the Orange Free State, furnished a commando under an elected commandant, assisted by field-cornets, elected from each of the district's wards. Both Republics had small contingents of artillery, well-equipped with modern Krupp and Creusot guns, and commanded by professional foreign officers. The Transvaal also had its own police, the ZARPs, a uniformed para-military organisation. Between them the two Republics put about 48,000 burghers into the field on mobilisation, together with some 2,700 gunners and police. As the war went on, the grand total of Boers, including foreign volunteers and Cape Colony rebels, rose to perhaps 87,000 men.[6]

The Boers were, it is true, strange-looking soldiers by the

57

standards of the age. Most went off to war in their everyday clothes: formal discipline was unknown, and their leaders, with the exception of Commandant-General Piet Joubert and his gunner and police officers, were elected civilians. But beneath an unmilitary exterior, the Boer forces were dangerous adversaries. Many Boers, particularly the farmers from the backveldt, were natural shots, perfectly accustomed to living out on the veldt and comfortably mobile on their untidy little ponies. Nor were they unaccustomed to war. Some of them had followed Joubert to Majuba eighteen years before, while others had more recent experience against native uprisings. Their tactics were those of mounted frontiersmen based upon the long-range killing-power of their rifles and the mobility conferred by their ponies. Whatever their idiosyncracies in terms of dress or discipline, the Boers were, quite simply, the best mounted riflemen in the world.

Against them was pitted the creaking might of the British army. Although it seemed large – 227,000 regulars, swollen, with the addition of volunteers, colonial and native units to an overall total of over a million men, it was widely dispersed. There were less than 10,000 troops in South Africa in June 1899, and on 1 October, including those at sea, there were still only 22,000.[7] Moreover, despite the proud claim of the *Official History* that, 'the British army has had more, and more varied, service during the nineteenth century than any other in the world', much of this experience had been gained in conflicts like the Kaffir War of 1877, the Zulu War of 1878–9 and the Egyptian campaigns of the 1880s and 1890s.[8] It was all 'the small change of war', and however impressive it looked in the popular press of the day it had produced no common fund of shared experience and no unified military system.

Nevertheless, one must guard against uncritical acceptance of the pleasing image of a redcoated giant wallowing in a sea of bureaucratic inefficiency and archaic doctrine. Cardwell's reforms in the 1870s had seen the abolition of the purchase of commissions, the introduction of short service enlistment, creating a regular army reserve, and the organisation of the linked battalion system, with one battalion of the pair serving at home and the other abroad. The auxiliary forces – militia, yeomanry and volunteers – remained questionable assets, but were being subjected to increasing centralised control. The central authority had itself been reorganised by the War Office Act of 1870, and serious work had been done on mobilisation schemes from 1886 onwards.[9]

True, the system was far from perfect. By the 1890s the home battalions were little more than empty husks, scoured clean by the need to send frequent drafts abroad. The army reserve — 81,000 men in 1899 — was too small to keep the regular army up to strength in a major war.[10] The growth of the general staff was impeded as much by civilian suspicion of military planners as it was by opposition from within the army, and reductions in defence expenditure, the perennial hobby-horse of politicians in peacetime, prevented thoroughgoing reorganisations and forced reductions in establishment.[11] In 1891 the Stanhope Memorandum had defined the army's roles. Foremost was the support of the civil power within the United Kingdom closely followed by the demands of India. Fortresses and coaling stations at home and abroad were to be garrisoned, and, after all these requirements had been catered for, two regular army corps, and one partly composed of militia, were to be maintained. A final requirement, which the document stressed was improbable, was the ability to send two corps abroad if required.[12]

The British army of 1899 was, therefore, an institution intended primarily to keep the peace at home and to garrison India. It could fight small wars and, indeed, had gained considerable expertise in such operations. But it was not an army which mirrored Britain's status as a world power. The navy had pride of place in popular imagination as well as in governmental policy, and the army, stretched tautly to garrison an Empire, was ill-suited for fighting anything more than a small war. And, as so few British soldiers realised, a conflict with the Boers would be long, bitter and costly.

French had arrived at Cape Town by the time the Boer ultimatum expired on 11 October. Although there was now a war to fight, his specific role still seemed uncertain. On 10 October he had received two telegrams from the War Office. One, to be shown to White on French's arrival in Natal, directed White to form his troops into an infantry division and a cavalry brigade, using any spare units for duties on the lines of communication. A second telegram announced that Colonel Brocklehurst was to command the cavalry brigade, with Major Wyndham as his brigade-major. French appeared to have lost his command, and the undoubted comforts of the Mount Nelson Hotel were small consolation.[13] The following day he received orders to go to Natal 'for the present'. French and Haig presumed that this meant that they would return to the Cape, to form the cavalry division, after the army corps had at last arrived.[14] They re-embarked on the *Norman* on 14 October, and landed at Durban five days later. On arrival at Durban they entrained for Ladysmith, which they reached at 5.40 in the morning of the 20th.

The Major-General and his staff — Major Haig, Lieutenant Milbanke of the 10th Hussars and Captain Laycock of the Nottinghamshire Yeomanry — stepped from the train into a crisis of major proportions. For it was upon Natal that the major Boer offensive had fallen, and, at the precise moment of French's arrival, the first Boer shell splashed — for it was a dud — into Major-General Sir William Penn Symons's camp at Dundee, nearly forty miles to the north-east.[15] Symons was White's predecessor in the Natal command, and his decisions and advice were to affect profoundly the opening battles of the war. White had landed at Durban on 7 October. He met Symons there two days later, and heard that Symons had already come up with his own solution to a problem which had been exercising White during his voyage: how best to hold Natal? There were two alternatives. One, which Buller himself favoured, was to abandon the northern point of the Natal triangle — the hilly area north of Estcourt — and to concentrate on holding the line of the Tugela River. Symons favoured the other alternative, forward defence, and had already taken 4,000 men to Dundee, midway between the Tugela and the point of the triangle. The town was near the railway line from Durban to Johannesburg, and it lay squarely in the path of the Boer invasion: Majuba Hill and Laing's Nek, of evil memory, were on the Transvaal border to its north.

White and his staff did not share Symons's breezy confidence, but a visit to the governor of Natal convinced White that it was politically unacceptable to relinquish northern Natal without a fight. Despite his own reservations, White

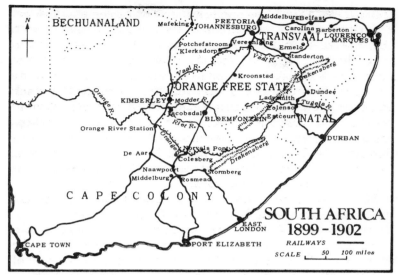

therefore let Symons stay put, but he compromised by concentrating the bulk of his force on Ladysmith. White may have started with two possible solutions, but he had now created a third, with most of the risks of forward defence and few of its advantages.

The Boer offensive unrolled in mid-October. Joubert's men moved off on 12 October: about 14,000 strong, they crossed the border and occupied Newcastle three days later. The 6,000 Free Staters of General Marthinius Prinsloo set off on 18 October, entering Natal across the Drakensberg, at right-angles to Joubert's advance. Both forces converged on Ladysmith. A detachment of Transvaalers under Lukas Meyer, hooking east of the main line of advance along the railway, shelled Symons's position at Dundee early on the morning of the 20th. The British artillery replied, and Symons then sent his infantry against Meyer's position on Talana Hill. The attack succeeded, but at a price: Symons was mortally wounded, and a high proportion of the casualties were officers. Moreover, the third act of Symons's three-part drama, the cavalry pursuit, went badly wrong, and Lieutenant-Colonel Möller, with more than 200 men of the 18th Hussars, was captured by the Boers.

News of Talana had not yet reached Ladysmith when French met White on the morning of the 20th. There were, however, reports that the enemy had cut the railway and seized a supply train at Elandslaagte, just outside Ladysmith, and French was ordered to investigate, taking with him the 5th Lancers, six squadrons of the Natal Carabineers and Natal Mounted Rifles, a battery of field artillery and an infantry brigade under Colonel Ian Hamilton. The column moved out of Ladysmith at 11.00, and two hours later French telegraphed that he had encountered 300 Boers at Elandslaagte. His infantry and guns would form a firm base, while he pushed on with the cavalry to reconnoitre the Boer position.[16] White immediately confirmed that the infantry were on no account to move more than four miles from Ladysmith. He was worried by reports of the activities of Prinsloo's Free Staters to the west, and shortly afterwards French was recalled to Ladysmith.[17]

The Boers at Elandslaagte were, in fact, about 1,000 strong. Under the overall command of General Kock, they included Ben Viljoen's Johannesburg Commando, about 200 German and Dutch volunteers, and three 75mm guns. Kock's men had seized Elandslaagte station and a train on the evening of the 19th, and the Boer force was concentrated there by dawn the next morning. French's reconnaissance apparently came into contact with the German volunteers, screening the main Boer position.[18] Kock had far outstripped the cautious Joubert, and his unsupported force offered an easy target to an enterprising British commander. And by the evening of the 20th, White was feeling decidedly more enterprising than he had in the afternoon: news of the victory at Talana had just come in, undimmed as yet by the bad news of Möller's capture. He accordingly felt confident enough to order French to return to Elandslaagte: he was to 'clear the neighbourhood of Elandslaagte of the enemy and cover the reconstruction of the railway and telegraphic lines.'[19]

French's advance guard, a squadron of the Imperial Light Horse, rode out of Ladysmith at 4.00 on the morning of the 21st. The ILH was recruited mainly from Uitlanders, some of whom had taken part in the Jameson raid. The British regular may have been unsure of what he was fighting for, and may have cloaked it beneath a phrase like 'Queen and Country' or even 'because we're 'ere'. The officers and men of the ILH had no such doubts. To them the quarrel was a personal one, and as they rode along the Dundee road as dawn came up, many of them must have looked forward with pleasurable anticipation to meeting the Boers and settling old scores. The point squadron's flankers shook out at daylight, and at 5.00 French ordered a ten-minute halt. Four more squadrons of the ILH, and a battery of the Natal Field Artillery, made up the remainder of the mounted force: along the railway to its rear clanked an armoured train, manned by a company of the Manchesters, with four more companies of the same regiment escorting a detachment of Royal Engineers in another train.[20]

It was shortly after 7.00 when the first Mauser bullets hummed over the point squadron. French telegraphed to Ladysmith that Elandslaagte was strongly held, and he had heard reports of three guns. 'I am advancing', he concluded, 'to clear them out.'[21] And clear them out he did. The antiquated 7-pounder muzzle-loaders tended by the Natal Field Artillery found the penetration of the corrugated iron station outbuildings within their limited competence, and a crowd of Boers scattered for the kopjes as the first two shells burst near the station. The ILH galloped into Elandslaagte, capturing a few Boers and releasing some colliery and railway officials. The Natal gunners had little opportunity to congratulate themselves before the first 75mm shell slammed into their position. The Boers found the range quickly, and French ordered the 7-pounders, hopelessly outranged, to fall back. He then withdrew his whole force at right angles to the railway, and at 9.00 sent word to White announcing that he was on the railway due south of Woodcote farm. The Boers held the hills south-east of the station in strength — French initially estimated 400 men and three guns — and his own guns could do nothing against them. He had detrained the Manchesters in the hope of tempting the enemy forward, but asked urgently for more artillery, and for any other support that was available.[22]

Information from the released prisoners, together with French's own observations, soon told him that there were between 800 and 1,000 Boers in the area. Some of them had now appeared on Jonono's Kop, to the north-west, and he decided to fall back on to the Modder Spruit to await reinforcements. Shortly after midday French asked White for firm orders: he pointed out that the decision to offer battle would have far-reaching consequences, and therefore should be White's, not his own.[23] The latter replied at 1.00 that reinforcements were on their way, and he ordered French to attack when they arrived.[24] French's own movement order went out fifteen minutes later, thanks, no doubt, to good pre-planning and deft staff-work on the part of Haig, and the advance began at 1.30, before most of the reinforcements had arrived. In all, French eventually received two batteries of field artillery, rushed out from Ladysmith with double teams, with a squadron of the 5th Lancers in escort, the remainder of the Manchesters, and two fresh battalions, the Devons and the Gordons. He had already met up with a squadron of the 5th Dragoon Guards, and had sent it off to probe the Boers' strength on Jonono's Kop, while the ILH drove in the outposts on the Boer left.

The ILH were already in action when the infantry detrained. White had apparently considered sending his Chief of Staff, Major-General Sir Archibald Hunter, to take command of the whole force — French was, after all, an unknown quantity as far as infantry work was concerned — but Hunter suggested that the job was French's by right, and White wisely let things be. He decided to take no chances with the infantry, and sent his Assistant Adjutant-General, Ian Hamilton, to command the three battalions.[25] French and Hamilton met down by the railway as the infantry detrained, and discussed the plan of attack. The railway ran across the open end of a horseshoe-shaped ridge. French and Hamilton conferred near the southwestern point of the horseshoe, looking across the open ground between the ridges to the three kopjes at the other end of the horseshoe, littered with the tents and wagons of Kock's position.

There was nothing revolutionary about French's plan for the battle. It was to be, like Symons's attack on Talana, a set-piece in the best traditions of Long Valley: artillery preparation, infantry assault and cavalry pursuit. French had already secured his start-line — the southern curve of the horseshoe — by the time Hamilton arrived. He had also ensured that the

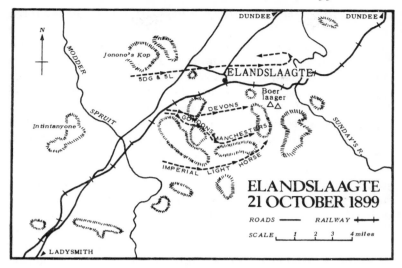

cavalry had watered their horses – an important consideration in view of the work he expected of them. French outlined the plan to Hamilton, and Hamilton then expounded the details to his battalion commanders. The Devons were to launch a frontal attack, in very open order, a point which Hamilton took care to emphasise. The Manchesters and the Gordons, with the ILH screening their right flank, would work round the toe of the horseshoe and attack the Boer left.

The guns had come into action on the ridge, the white puffs of their shrapnel standing out clearly against a huge black thunder-cloud behind the Boer position, by the time the last of the infantry finished detraining. The battalions moved off at about 3.30, and shortly afterwards French dispatched the Lancers to help the Dragoon Guards, who were under sharp fire from Jonono's Kop. The infantry attack was pressed with vigour. The Devons were pinned down well short of the Boer position, but their extended lines spared them heavy casualties. The Manchesters and Gordons, assisted by the ILH, most of whom had now dismounted, fought their way along the ridge under a galling fire, their advance providentially aided as the thunderstorm, threatened for so long, swept over the battlefield.

The final battle for the Boer position was desperate. Heavy

losses, particularly amongst officers, had taken the edge off the infantry's ardour, and Hamilton himself ran forward amongst them, cheering them on. Old General Kock, resplendent in top hat and frock coat, led a counter-attack as the infantry seized the crest, and there was a frenzied battle at point-blank range as the infantry, urged on by Hamilton, staff officers and French himself, wavered briefly before finally securing the ridge. By about 5.45 the position was in British hands, and a line of khaki figures topped the crest, waving their helmets and cheering 'Majuba, Majuba!'[26]

French had watched the battle progress from his right rear, just behind the Gordons. White had joined him before the infantry battle grew serious, but made it clear that he had come only as a spectator, not to take command: it was, he said, French's show.[27] Shortly after 5.00 French heard from Major Gore, senior officer of the two squadrons sent forward earlier to push round Jonono's Kop and turn the Boer right, that the squadrons were in position north-east of the station. French immediately ordered them to charge as soon as the Boers began to fall back.[28] Having sent off the order by galloper, French then followed the path of the infantry assault, and dismounted to lend a hand himself at the moment of crisis.[29]

The battle was over by 6.30. The cavalry had charged through the retreating Boers, reformed and charged again, turning the Boer retreat into a shambles. Boer losses were heavy: at least 60 were killed, over 120 wounded and nearly 200 captured. General Kock had been mortally wounded, and was taken off to die in Ladysmith. The Johannesburg Commando had been badly cut up, much to the delight of the ILH, and there had been heavy losses amongst the German and Hollander volunteers. The British had lost 50 killed and 213 wounded, which was by no means an excessive price to pay for the crippling of Kock's force and the capture of its three guns.[30]

The affair at Elandslaagte was a mere bagatelle even by the standards of the Boer War. Fewer than 5,000 men were engaged on both sides, and the main part of the action was over in three hours. Indeed, it may perhaps be thought that to deal with the battle at such length is to arrogate to it disproportionate importance. But whatever its significance for the campaign as a whole, Elandslaagte was crucial in the development of

French's career. England needed good news, and war correspondents lost no time in making of Elandslaagte something it was not—a major victory. French began his rise to the niche reserved for popular heroes: the daily press paid handsome tribute to his courage and good judgement, and the sketches of Melton Prior brought French's stocky, bulldog figure to life for the readers of the *Illustrated London News*.

French certainly felt that Elandslaagte was a decisive moment in his own life, and always noted its anniversary in his diary, an honour he never accorded to any other battle. There is no doubt that he had been lucky in some respects. Hamilton was a first-rate infantry Brigadier, whose insistence on open order, and reckless personal leadership, contributed greatly to the success of the infantry attack. The thunderstorm was opportune, and the final cavalry charge was shielded by failing light. Erskine Childers rightly called it 'a rare combination of ideal conditions'.[31] But there was more than luck. French undoubtedly fought the battle deftly, making a sound plan into which the reinforcements could be fitted with the minimum of fuss, and unleashing a two-pronged attack with plenty of gunfire to support it. Having set the wheels in motion, he let his subordinates fight their own battles, but was on hand at the critical point when the crisis came. It was, in all, a handy tactical victory, brought off by French's unique mixture of good luck and sound professional competence.

White realised that there was nothing to be gained by holding Elandslaagte, and French accordingly issued orders, at about 11 p.m. for a withdrawal early the following morning. Most of the troops went back by rail, the last of them leaving in mid-afternoon. On the same day Major-General James Yule, now commanding at Dundee in place of Symons, decided to fall back on Ladysmith, as his position was threatened by Joubert's main force. White endorsed Yule's decision and the bedraggled force began to fall back that evening, reaching Ladysmith on 26 October. The arrival of the exhausted Dundee garrison gave White about 13,000 troops in all. Although the military logic of the situation shrieked out that it was folly to remain in Ladysmith in the hope of fighting a pitched battle against the now combined Free State and Transvaal forces, this is exactly what he planned to do.

French was busy on the 26th and 27th, patrolling out towards the Elandslaagte battlefield and reporting the approach, in very considerable numbers, of the Boers. White toyed with the idea of a night attack, led by the intrepid Hamilton, on the Boer laagers, but eventually decided against it. On the 29th, however, he felt that his opportunity had at last come: French's scouts brought news of Boer positions on Long Hill, Pepworth Hill and Nicholson's Nek, across the railway line to Elandslaagte. White planned a three-pronged attack, a far from simple manoeuvre in view of the distances to be covered and the strength of Boer opposition. On the left, two battalions and a battery were to make for Nicholson's Nek. French, with two regiments of regular cavalry and Colonel Royston's colonials, was to secure the right flank, taking Lombard's Kop, and finally pursuing the retreating Boers. In the centre, five battalions were to attack Long Hill.

The day of 30 October was one of disasters. The left-hand column ran into trouble early on, and was eventually swamped at about 2 p.m. losing nearly a thousand prisoners. French, feeling for the Boer right flank, was heavily engaged from the hills around Lombard's Kop: his brigade was drawn into a fierce dismounted firefight, and was quite unable, even with the assistance of fresh cavalry, to make any progress. French's inability to secure the British right increased the difficulties of the centre column. This had already become divided by accident, and was soon in the sort of position which became grimly familiar to British troops in the first few months of the war. Its men were pinned down in untenable positions, subjected to merciless rifle and artillery fire to which they could make no adequate response. By late morning White realised that the attack was utterly fruitless: he was, moreover, disturbed for the safety of Ladysmith itself. He ordered his force to fall back on the town, and the centre column retired in what the *Official History* gently called 'extreme confusion', but which looked uncomfortably like panic to eye-witnesses.[32] French began to withdraw at about 1.00, and was in Ladysmith an hour and a half later, his retreat, like that of the centre column, greatly assisted by the disciplined shooting of the Royal Artillery, whose performance was the only bright spot on what was soon nicknamed Mournful Monday.

The bloody fiascos of Lombard's Kop and Nicholson's Nek ended White's attempt to meet the Boers in a decisive battle. He resigned himself to standing siege in Ladysmith, a town remarkably ill-suited to such an operation. It was a measure of Joubert's extreme caution and lack of enterprise that he permitted his forces to become involved in besieging Ladysmith, rather than pressing on towards Durban. For the next four months the fighting in Natal was to be dominated by Boer attempts to capture the town, and costly British efforts to relieve it.

French was reluctant to be caught up in a siege. He urged White to let him break out with the mounted troops while there was still time, pointing out that cavalry were likely to be of little use in a besieged town. White, however, would not countenance the plan. On the morning of 2 November French led a successful raid on a Boer laager, and returned to Ladysmith at about 1 p.m. to find that a telegram had arrived from Buller at the Cape, ordering him to leave Ladysmith at once and proceed to Cape Town to take command of the Cavalry Division. Haig was to accompany him. Being ordered to leave was one thing: getting out was quite another. Jack Milbanke set off for the station, and persuaded the railway officials to hazard a train. French, his staff, some servants and horses, left early in the afternoon. They had to run the gauntlet, for the Boer encirclement was nearly complete, and the line was in easy range of Boer riflemen and gunners. French and Haig spent part of the journey lying on the floor of their carriage as the shots crackled around them. Duff Cooper wrote:

> It is odd in the light of subsequent events, to picture the two Commanders-in-Chief of the British Expeditionary Force crouching on the floor of the little railway carriage in positions which could hardly be assumed with dignity and wondering, while the train staggered along under a hail of rifle and shell fire, whether at any moment they might not find themselves at the mercy of their enemy and condemned to spend the rest of the war in inglorious captivity at Pretoria. It was a close thing.[33]

Just how close a thing was revealed at the end of the journey, when a 3 inch shell was found lodged in Haig's kitbag. It was the last train out of Ladysmith: the Boers tore up the track minutes after it had passed. French's luck had held once more.

Tintagel Castle, with French aboard, left Durban on 3 November and dropped anchor in Table Bay on the 8th. French at once went ashore, with Haig in attendance, to visit Buller at his headquarters, a modest rented house in Grave Street. The General into whose presence the two officers were ushered was a worried man. On his arrival at the Cape on 31 October Buller had visited Milner at Government House, and had listened with sinking heart to a tale of woe. Not only had the Boers invaded Natal – and the depressing news of Mournful Monday was still coming in – but they were also threatening Cape Colony, whose population might, Milner feared, rise to join them. Kimberley, with the troublesome Cecil Rhodes inside it, was under siege, and far to the north, on the Bechuanaland border, the little town of Mafeking was also beleaguered. Milner's self-confidence wavered: instead of a short, sharp, victorious war, he seemed to have instigated a long and bitter conflict which might result in spectacular disasters.

Buller's original plan had been to push straight up to Bloemfontein, capital of the Orange Free State, with his whole corps, ending the war with a single mighty blow. But in view of the wide-ranging Boer threats he soon decided that this scheme was no longer viable: he would have to split the corps, dealing with the various problems simultaneously. The information brought by French and Haig served to confirm him in this view. They warned him that Ladysmith had supplies of food and fodder for only two months; there was a shortage of artillery ammunition, and the events of Mournful Monday had lowered morale. Haig went on to castigate White, condemning his oscillation between rashness and over-caution. The interview ended with Buller ordering French to concentrate the Cavalry Division at the Cape before proceeding to the front.[34]

The army corps began to arrive at the Cape on 9 November, and by 18 November over a third of its 47,000 men had landed there or gone on to Durban. To call it a corps at all is, perhaps, over-generous. Few of its component units had trained together in peacetime, and its four divisional headquarters contained few trained and experienced staff officers. Nevertheless, Buller's strategy, although it was later to attract much criticism, was by no means an unreasonable response to a difficult situation. Lieutenant-General Sir Francis Clery, commanding 2nd Division, was sent to Natal, with about a third of the whole force. Buller followed soon afterwards, to take command in what he regarded as the most important sector. Lieutenant-General Lord Methuen was to remain at the Cape, with orders to press forward and take Kimberley as soon as possible. The jaunty peer had his own 1st Division, considerably reinforced, and expected this task to take a few days. The troublesome north-eastern corner of Cape Colony was to be secured by Lieutenant-General Sir William Gatacre, divested of most of his troops of 3rd Division. He was also to guard against any Boer attack in the Stormberg area.[35]

Between Methuen, concentrating near Orange River Station, on the Cape Town–Kimberley–Mafeking railway, and Gatacre, on the right flank at Stormberg, lay about 150 miles of open country. Towards the centre of this area the main Bloemfontein–Port Elizabeth railway crossed the Orange River at Norval's Pont, a few miles north-east of Colesberg. At Naawpoort, south of Colesberg, a branch line ran north-west to join the Cape Town–Mafeking railway at de Aar. The Colesberg area lay bare and inviting before a Boer thrust. A Boer offensive from the southern border of the Orange Free State, aimed at Naawpoort, would outflank Methuen, sever lateral lines of communication and throw Cape Colony into a turmoil. Colesberg was the pit of Buller's capacious stomach.

French and Haig set to work laying out a camp for the Cavalry Division at Maitland, near Cape Town, on 9 November. But long before the Division's concentration was complete, French, now a local Lieutenant-General like the other divisional commanders, was ordered to proceed to the Colesberg sector.

On 18 November he left by train for de Aar, where he conferred with the craggy-visaged Major-General Andy Wauchope, commanding the lines of communication. He also received a telegram from Buller, ordering him to prepare a flying column of some 3,000 men, based on Hanover, in readiness to attack the Boers at Colesberg. French at once replied that Naawpoort was, in his opinion, a better base than Hanover, and he had accordingly ordered that 30 days' supplies for 3,000 men and 11,000 animals should be collected there as soon as possible.[36]

French reached Naawpoort on the afternoon of 20 November. His force consisted of two half-battalions of infantry, a mixed detachment of the 5th Lancers and New South Wales Lancers, some Cape Police, and two 9-pounder muzzleloaders. No sooner had he arrived than French issued orders for a reconnaissance the following morning, and he accompanied the patrol which left early on the 21st. He went as far as Arundel, 17 miles from Naawpoort on the Colesberg railway. Between Arundel and Colesberg the line passed between a number of rocky kopjes, and French decided to occupy Arundel, before working his way forward towards Colesberg through the kopjes, threatening the Boers in Colesberg and at the same time screening the rail junctions at de Aar to the north-west and Rosmead to the south-east. French telegraphed his plan to Buller the same afternoon, and urgently requested more troops. Reinforcements that evening brought the total strength of his force to 1,600 men.[37]

French's adversary was the Transvaaler, Commandant Schoeman, who had crossed the frontier at Norval's Pont on 1 November and occupied Colesberg on the 14th. Schoeman initially had some 700 men, but the local inhabitants responded with enthusiasm to his call to arms, and local Boers and reinforcements had soon more than doubled his force. Fortunately for French, Schoeman moved slowly, for the Naawpoort garrison had been withdrawn altogether for the first fortnight of November. It was not until the 22nd that he decided to advance to Arundel, but this move, albeit late, thwarted French's attempt to occupy the place on the 23rd.

Finding Arundel in Boer hands, French decided against direct attack, and wired to Buller that he was unable to get on for the time being, but that he did not think that the Boers intended to attack Naawpoort.[38] French remained convinced, however, that a passive defence was, with the small force at his disposal, likely to encourage the Boers. He therefore determined to keep them on their guard by a policy of aggressive patrolling. Buller approved of this, telling his Chief of Staff:

> French should attack Arundel as soon as he feels strong enough, but not before, and he should be sure that he is strong enough ... suggest to French that a policy of worry, without risking men, might have a good effect on the enemy at Colesberg and keep him occupied.[39]

Reinforcements, meanwhile, continued to trickle in, but on the 28th French was informed that his responsibilities had been extended to include the line to Port Elizabeth. He immediately occupied Rosmead Junction, but no sooner had he done so than Buller countermanded the move. This interference almost led to disaster, for a Boer force approached Rosmead the following day, 1 December, and the junction was saved only by the timely arrival of French's mounted infantry. Not until 14 December was French freed of responsibility for guarding the railway to his rear.

In early December French felt strong enough to threaten Arundel with the newly-arrived 12th Lancers, but they were soon off to join Methuen by an order from Buller's Chief of Staff. Further reinforcements, notably the New Zealand Mounted Rifles and the Carabineers, gave French enough mounted men for another thrust at Arundel, and on 7 December Colonel T. C. Porter of the Carabineers occupied it, and went on to take up good positions in the hills to the north of the station.

French arrived in Arundel the following morning, bringing with him two companies of infantry, which he left to hold the junction while his cavalry felt for the Boer flanks and mounted infantry masked their centre. By nightfall the Boer outposts had withdrawn to disclose the full extent of their main position, which lay among the hills athwart the railway at Rensburg. It appeared to be held by at least 2,000 men and three or four guns, and a Boer prisoner brought the unwelcome news that Schoeman's force now totalled no less than 4,000 men — over twice as many as French had. French warned Buller that, in view of the enemy's strength, he did not anticipate making much progress. He nevertheless retained confidence in his policy of vigorous aggressive defence, and noted in his diary on the 8th:

> We have heard a great deal in books and from lecturers of 'moral effect'. It was never better exemplified than in this action! The Boers had regularly 'established a funk'. ... To establish a 'moral superiority' over the enemy is an object of the *'first importance'*.[40]

For the next few days Porter's force at Arundel continued to harass the Boers, pinning them to their position and, on 11 December, pinching out Vaal Kop, an advanced post on the Boer right. This jolted Schoeman into activity. He had not moved his headquarters forward to the Rensburg position until Porter had captured Arundel and it took the setback at Vaal Kop to goad him into another advance. He decided to outflank Porter's detachment, cut its communications with Naawpoort, and, if all went well, to capture it. French had, however, anticipated that Schoeman might attempt such a move, and had ordered Porter to patrol widely to the east and north-east. Porter's men detected the Boer move as soon as it had started, and on the morning of the 13th his cavalry and mounted infantry, with the able assistance of R Battery, Royal Horse Artillery (RHA), mauled the advancing Boers in an action which cost the British only eight wounded. British fortunes elsewhere in South Africa were at a low ebb. Methuen had met with a bloody repulse at Magersfontein, and Gatacre had been defeated at Stormberg. Porter's useful little victory was the only spark of light on an otherwise gloomy horizon, and Buller, whose own defeat at Colenso was only a day away, sent French a fulsome telegram of congratulations.[41]

Major-General J. P. Brabazon arrived at Naawpoort on 14 December. French sent him forward to command the outpost line at Arundel, ordering him to cover Naawpoort and the Naawpoort–Arundel railway. He suggested that Brabazon could best accomplish this task by using Arundel as a pivot of manoeuvre, and holding a number of key points, such as Vaal Kop, from which he could harass the Boers by threatening their line of retreat on Colesberg.[42] Two days later the Boers attacked Vaal Kop, and its garrison fell back in some disorder.

French was particularly vexed by the incident, for he had reinforced the post after a personal reconnaissance only the day before. He decided that he could not risk further mistakes, and went forward to Arundel to take personal command, organising the forces there into a division of two brigades: one, under Porter, covered the area east of the railway, and the other, under Lieutenant-Colonel R. B. W. Fisher, the sector west of the line. Brabazon became second-in-command.

Before moving up to Arundel, French, taking stock of the depressing situation elsewhere in South Africa, had decided that, outnumbered though he was, he was nevertheless in a better state than other commanders. He accordingly offered to send all his cavalry off to help Methuen, even though this would mean shelving his plans for an advance on Colesberg. French's offer was declined on the grounds that there was too little water for the cavalry horses in Methuen's position on the Modder River.[43] The incident does, though, illustrate that French felt that he had the situation well in hand: his offer was remarkably unselfish, and must go some way towards countering assertions that French was a glory-hunter who coveted publicity.

Less altruistic motives were at work elsewhere. Lord Roberts, languishing as Commander-in-Chief in Ireland, received news of Colenso on the morning of Saturday, 16 December, and at once sent a long, forthright cable to Lansdowne at the War Office. Roberts warned that unless a 'radical change' was made in South Africa, an inglorious peace would follow. This change could, he suggested helpfully, best be accomplished by appointing him Commander-in-Chief in South Africa. Although Roberts, the 'Bobs' of Kipling's ballads, was a well-loved and highly-respected figure, he was nevertheless an astute politician, who resented the ascendancy of the Wolseley Ring and was determined to oust Buller.[44] Lansdowne, alerted by Roberts's earlier promptings, had decided that Roberts should replace Buller as soon as the news of Colenso arrived. Lansdowne got the appointment past Lord Salisbury and the Cabinet, and the urbane A. J. Balfour managed to persuade the Queen of the need for a change. So Roberts had his appointment at last, but his victory was flawed by tragedy. His only son, Freddy, a Lieutenant serving with

Buller in Natal, had been wounded in a daredevil attempt to save some guns at Colenso: when Roberts called on Lansdowne for official confirmation of his appointment, Lansdowne had to tell him that Freddy was dead. It nearly broke the old man, and he set off for South Africa riven by private anguish.

Between Roberts's appointment as Commander-in-Chief on 17 December 1899 and his arrival at Cape Town on 10 January 1900, French was the only senior British officer to pursue active operations against the Boers. Nor had the events of Black Week made his task any easier: Boer confidence was at its height, and he had every reason to expect that Schoeman, vigorously reinforced, might try to emulate his victorious colleagues elsewhere.

Even a slight advance into Cape Colony could have dangerous consequences: 'disloyalty', admitted the *Official History*, 'might largely increase his [Schoeman's] numbers in a night'.[45] Schoeman's force had, in fact, risen to 4,500 men, and was thus superior to French's, particularly as far as mounted men were concerned. But Schoeman himself had lost the confidence of his subordinates, and a gloomy Boer council of war decided, on 27 December, to evacuate the Rensburg position and fall back on Colesberg. The withdrawal took place two days later, and came just in time to pre-empt a plan, which French had already drawn up and was about to execute, for manoeuvring the Boers out of their position by turning their right flank.

French clung to the heels of the retreating Boers, and came into contact with their new position, covering Colesberg itself, on the morning of the 30th. The town enjoyed superb natural defences. It lay in a hollow, surrounded by a rough square of hills which rose sharply from the surrounding plain. The northern end of the square was fairly open, but, apart from this, the only point from which Colesberg could be seen from outside its surrounding hills was from the west, where the lofty detached Coles Kop, three miles from the town and a mile from the edge of the hills, offered a view of the tin roofs and dusty streets of Colesberg.

Away to the west and north-west a long chain of hills was broken at Rietfontein, where the old wagon road from Colesberg crossed the hills, and at Bastard's Nek, further to the west. Another crop of hills sprang up to the east and north-east of Colesberg, and the railway ran on through them to cross the Orange River at Norval's Pont, some twenty miles north.[46]

Schoeman's position was formidable. His Transvaalers, with most of his guns, were strongly posted in the hills on the southern side of the square, firmly blocking the direct route from Arundel. Commandos from Heilbron and Bethlehem held the western face of the square, with outposts extending along the north-western hills as far as Bastard's Nek. Other Free Staters covered the left flank and the railway, and small detachments held both the crossings of the Orange River, at Norval's Pont and Colesberg Wagon Bridge. French made a close personal reconnaissance of the position at dawn on the 31st. He was eager to turn the Boers out of Colesberg, and although he was still inferior in strength to Schoeman, he had just received another infantry battalion and some more cavalry, and the Boer withdrawal seemed ample evidence that he retained moral superiority. An unenterprising frontal assault would achieve little beyond enabling French to share with Buller, Methuen and Gatacre the comradeship of defeat. A wide hook round the Boer left, with the railway as its target, had obvious attractions, but it would stretch French's lines of communication round the south-east angle of the Colesberg hills, leaving it open to counter-attack. The Boer right undoubtedly offered the best prospects. French was already in possession of some high ground, Porter's Hill, which dominated the open ground south-west of the position. A flanking attack against the Boer right would threaten the Colesberg Wagon Road, an alternative Boer line of retreat, and might well induce the cautious Schoeman to fall back to safeguard his communications.

French's plan was clear in his mind by mid-morning, and he was eager to execute it as soon as possible, before Boer morale recovered from the retreat. Here he was fortunate that his Chief of Staff, Douglas Haig, and his intelligence officer, Captain Hubert Lawrence, were staff officers of marked ability, who lost no time in translating French's pungent comments and sharp gestures into formal orders. These were on their way by midday and the preliminary phases of the operation began four hours later. The main part of the attacking force moved off in the early hours of New Year's Day. Two regiments of cavalry, some infantry, and ten guns, all under Lieutenant-Colonel Fisher of the 10th Hussars, marched out to Maeder's Farm, five miles south-west of Colesberg. Fisher was to work his way round the outer ring of kopjes running along the western edge of the Boer position, while Porter, swinging down from Porter's Hill, threatened the Boer centre, and two detached squadrons masked the Boer left.

Shortly before dawn Fisher's infantry, led forward with panache by Major McCracken of the Berkshires, surprised the Boer picket on an outlying kopje, soon christened McCracken's Hill, on the western edge of the enemy position. French, controlling the battle from the dominant feature of Coles Kop, at once ordered Fisher to advance towards the north-west corner of the Colesberg Hills, and to command the northern exit from the town. As it became light his artillery doused the western hills with shrapnel covering Fisher's advance and taking some of the pressure off the Berkshires. McCracken's position was, however, precarious in the extreme, and French had ordered him to evacuate the hill when the appearance of Fisher's cavalry on the hills to the north-west made the Boers stop their attempts to retake the hill. In the late afternoon Schoeman emerged with a strong column and threatened the British right, but he was soon detected and forced to desist.

The results of New Year's Day seemed satisfactory enough. The Boer right had been turned at a cost of less than thirty British casualties, McCracken's Hill was firmly secured and Schoeman's counter-attack had been beaten off. French was, though, irritated by Fisher's failure to get across the Boer communications, believing that this had robbed him of a conclusive victory. He at once asked for reinforcements with a view to continuing the attack, and set about strengthening the newly-won positions on the British left in preparation for their arrival. Schoeman too, asked for help, and was soon reinforced with the Johannesburg Police and another commando. On 4 January he struck hard at the British left, but, after some initial success, was driven back with the loss of nearly 100 killed and wounded and no less than forty prisoners.

French's reinforcements, a battalion, a battery, and some

cavalry, arrived on the 4th and 5th, enabling him to set about the next phase of the operation. He had decided that the key to the Boer position was Grassy Hill, an eminence which lay at the junction of the roads from Colesberg to Norval's Pont and Colesberg Wagon Bridge, dominating these routes and the whole western side of the Boer position. French looked hard at the feature on 5 January, and issued orders for an attack early the following day. The assault, under Lieutenant-Colonel F. J. W. Eustace, French's artillery commander, was to be supported by demonstrations against the Boer centre and left.

Lieutenant-Colonel A. J. Watson, commanding the Suffolks on the British left, was convinced that he could take Grassy Hill without assistance in a night attack, and he persuaded Eustace to ask French for permission to try. At about 8.00 on the evening of the 5th French sent word that he agreed to an attempt being made if a favourable opportunity presented itself: Watson was, however, to notify him before proceeding. We may therefore picture French's surprise when, at 3.00 on the morning of 6 January, he was riding round to watch the opening of Eustace's attack when a burst of firing announced that the Suffolks were on Grassy Hill. They did not stay on it for long. An alert Boer sentry fired a warning shot, and the Suffolks were soon under heavy fire from the hill's defenders. Watson and many of his officers were killed, and the battalion was repulsed with the loss of over 150 officers and men. This rebuff convinced French that the Boers were now too much on their guard for any further attempts to be made against Grassy Hill, and on the following day he turned his attention to the Boer left. On the 11th his cavalry and mounted infantry began probing the Boer defences in the Bastard's Nek area but ran into strongly-held positions all along the chain of hills.

The fact that both his flanks seemed to have stuck fast did not deter French from continuing to keep up the pressure on Schoeman. At daybreak on 12 January a 15-pounder gun, hauled, with considerable difficulty, to the top of Coles Kop, began to drop shells into the Boer position, causing consternation amongst Schoeman's men. Two days later a flying column under Major E. H. H. Allenby threatened the Wagon Bridge, dissuading the Boers from using it thereafter, but elsewhere French's probes met with little success. On 25 January he struck at Plessis Poort, a pass five miles east of Bastard's Nek, but sensed that all was not well and pulled his advance guard back from the neck of the pass shortly before a concealed Boer force, lurking in ambush, opened fire.

French's hopes for the capture of Colesberg were destined to remain unfulfilled. On 29 January he was summoned to Cape Town to confer with Roberts, and two days later he returned to break up his command, leaving Major-General R. A. P. Clements, with a mixed force, to cover the Colesberg area.

The Colesberg operations are more than merely another of the blind alleys of military history. They are of prime importance in two respects: for their strategic consequences, and in terms of the development of French's own career. French had checked the invasion of Cape Colony, safeguarded the Midland line of communication, and covered the yawning gap between Methuen and Gatacre. His thrusts attracted Boer reinforcements which might have been used, with damaging effect, elsewhere. Even the *Times History*, generally critical of British commanders, spoke of 'an almost unbroken series of successes'. It went on to commend the moral ascendancy established by French at this critical time, his quick and practical grasp of tactics, and his readiness to throw every available man into the firing line at the vital moment. His achievement was all the more remarkable in view of the fact that his mounted troops never made up more than half his total strength, and were always outnumbered by the Boers by at least three to one.[47] Colesberg shows French at his best: energetic, tireless, with an instinct for the decisive point and a keen eye for the ground. The fighting established him as one of the leading generals of his generation, and the popular press, at a time when heroes were in short supply, found much to admire in the bluff Lieutenant-General with the whitening moustache and tight, high-collared tunic. A little ballad caught the mood of the moment:

There's a General of 'orse which is French,
You've 'eard of 'im o' course, fightin' French,

Carving a Reputation: South Africa, 1899

'E's a daisy, 'e's a brick,
An 'e's up to every trick,
And 'e moves amazin' quick,
Don't yer, French?

'Es so tough and terse,
'E don't want no bloomin' nurse,
And 'e ain't 'ad one reverse,
'Ave yer, French?[48]

Three

Cavalry Division
South Africa, 1900–2

'The cavalry must relieve Kimberley at all costs ... If it fails neither I nor the Field-Marshal can tell what the result on the Empire may be.' The unblinking gaze of Major-General Lord Kitchener of Khartoum, chief of staff to Lord Roberts, bored into French as he sat with Haig amongst the forest of tents south of Methuen's position on the Modder River.[1]

It was 10 February, and Roberts had been in South Africa for exactly a month. Even before arriving he had decided that his main effort would be directed against the Free State: by thrusting towards Bloemfontein he would end the threat to Cape Colony, and probably draw the Boers back from Kimberley and Natal. The precarious state of Kimberley induced him to modify this plan, and by early February Roberts and Kitchener had evolved a scheme for breaking through to the threatened town.[2]

Roberts, unlike his unfortunate predecessor, had adequate means at his disposal. A Colonial Division was raised, composed of local loyalists, and regular infantry were hastily converted into mounted troops. More guns arrived, including heavy pieces which would enable the Royal Artillery to take on the long-range Boer Creusots: field artillery shells were improved, and short-range firepower was increased with the addition of 49 Vickers-Maxim pom-poms. Roberts thoroughly recast the transport system, withdrawing regimental transport to form centralised transport companies. He also set about improving the running of the railways, which played a vital part in his concentration on the borders of the Free State.[3]

French spent 29 January discussing the situation with Roberts at Cape Town. News of Buller's defeat at Spion Kop four days before had convinced Roberts that he had to relieve Kimberley in order to win a recognisable victory to set against the catalogue of disasters. Moreover, disturbing messages from Kimberley, pointing to friction between Cecil Rhodes and the garrison commander, gave rise to fears that the town might fall. Roberts's plan had three phases. Firstly, the army would concentrate in absolute secrecy behind Methuen's position on the Modder River, but British activity elsewhere – Clements's arrival at Colesberg, for example – would induce the Boers to strengthen other areas. The army would then outflank the strongly posted General Cronje, who had so effectively blocked Methuen's advance. Finally, the cavalry would dash for Kimberley, while the rest of the force swung eastwards to take Bloemfontein.[4]

Roberts had not summoned French to Cape Town primarily to tell him of the plan: he was more concerned with the expenditure of horses and ammunition around Colesberg. The plan was, as the *Official History* puts it, 'only incidentally disclosed' to French during his visit, and the misunderstandings concerning French's role were to have significant long-term consequences. Although there is no evidence that Roberts and Kitchener planned to use anyone else to command his cavalry, French formed the impression that 'he only with difficulty persuaded them on January 29th to send the cavalry division and himself in command of it'. That this was manifestly not the case may be deduced from the fact that the details of the scheme were already laid down: indeed, French himself was given written orders on the 30th.[5]

It is not hard to find possible explanations for this misunderstanding. French, in the first place, undoubtedly viewed Roberts and Kitchener with some suspicion. He was, after all, a Buller man, and the apparent triumph of the Roberts Ring brooked ill for his old protector. It was Buller who had summoned him to the Cape to command the cavalry: the new Commander-in-Chief might well take a very different view. Moreover, he was doing very nicely before Colesberg, and hoped to manoeuvre Schoeman out of the place. Being summoned to Cape Town to be told, with seeming reluctance, of a new plan, was profoundly unsettling. Insecurity always brought out the worst in French and the events of October 1899 to January 1900 conspired to make him feel very insecure indeed. He had been sent out to command White's cavalry, only to discover that Brocklehurst had been given the job. Brought back to the Cape to command the Cavalry Division, he had been sent, with a scratch force, to plug the gap at Colesberg. Now another change of plan was mooted by officers he neither knew nor trusted.

French's career was to be inextricably entwined with those of Roberts and Kitchener. His bitter hostility towards Kitchener is well known, and will loom large in the pages that follow. There can be no doubt that there was a sharp clash of temperament between the ascetic, almost monkish Kitchener and the ebullient, mercurial French. Perhaps the only trait they held in common was a disinclination to give ground on major issues; a classic instance of the juxtaposition of irresistible force and immovable object.

Both men made occasional efforts to overcome their mutual dislike, but their disparate characters could never remain in harmony for long. French's feelings for Roberts are more ambivalent. At times he fell completely under the spell of 'dear old Bobs'. But it was far from the unconditional hero-worship which so many officers lavished on Roberts. French had serious doubts about Roberts's military ability: on 22 March 1900 he confided to his diary that the situation 'would be a grand opportunity for a great strategist at the head of affairs!'[6]

The relationship between the two men was to be strained by their disagreement over cavalry tactics after the war, and the Curragh incident of 1914 led, for a time, to a complete breakdown. As early as January 1900 there were serious differences of opinion between French on the one hand and Roberts and his Chief of Staff on the other. French objected violently to the scheme to centralise transport: he predicted, correctly, that it would lead to a collapse of supply arrangements, and managed to get his division excluded from the reorganisation.[7] A hairline fissure warned of the future split between Roberts and French with regard to cavalry tactics. French had already noted with disapproval that the New Zealand Mounted Rifles carried no swords, and had made them fix bayonets in their carbines and use them as lances.[8] Roberts had little time for the *arme blanche*, and French and Haig looked with suspicion at the steel-less 'Skallywag Corps' which Roberts raised with such enthusiasm. They appreciated the value of good colonial troops, like Rimington's Scouts, as they did of trained Mounted Infantry (MI), but complained that the hastily-raised colonials disappeared when action loomed, and the new MI lacked the ability to remain mounted for long.[9] Nor was this all. Buller had promised Haig the post of Assistant Adjutant-General of the cavalry division with the local rank of Lieutenant-Colonel. Roberts gave the post to Colonel the Earl of Erroll and French's vigorous protest met with no response. Haig served on as deputy Assistant Adjutant-General, and French, with characteristic obstinacy, worked through him, rather than Erroll, wherever possible.[10]

Whatever French's suspicions of Roberts and Kitchener, it was clear that the pair did not intend to do things by halves. Roberts had five divisions under his hand for the operation, no less than 40,000 men and a hundred guns. French commanded the Cavalry Division, which comprised three cavalry brigades, under Brigadier-Generals Porter, Broadwood and Gordon, and two brigades of MI under Colonels Hannay and Ridley. It was intended that the MI should join during the march, but in fact they did not succeed in doing so, and the division took the field with a provisional brigade of MI under Colonel Alderson.[11] Methuen's 1st Division was to pin Cronje to the Magersfontein position, while the 6th (Kelly-Kenny), 7th (Tucker) and 9th (Colville) Divisions followed the cavalry round the Boer flank.

The cavalry rode out of the crowded camps south of the Modder at 3.00 on the morning of Sunday 11 February. Roberts and Kitchener had visited the division on the previous day: Kitchener had emphasised the importance of French's task, and Roberts spoke to the Brigadiers and regimental commanders:

> I want to tell you that I am going to give you some very hard work to do, but at the same time you are going to get the greatest chance cavalry ever had ... You will remember what you are going to do all your

85

lives, and when you have grown to be old men you
will tell the story of the relief of Kimberley ... The
enemy are afraid of the British Cavalry, and I hope
when you get them out into the open you will make
an example of them.[12]

The division's advance guard, the sun-tanned, slouch-
hatted troopers of Rimington's Tigers, entered Ramdam towards mid-morning on the 11th, and the division had come up
by late afternoon. Ramdam was the jumping-off point for the
flank march. The concentration on the Modder had persuaded
Cronje that Roberts intended to continue Methuen's unsubtle
shoves along the line of the railway: on the 11th, however,
most of the troops on the Modder had fallen back southwards
to Enslin and Ramdam.

The march to Ramdam was the easiest part of the operation.
From there French was to strike for the crossings of the Riet
River, some 15 miles away, and secure them until the infantry

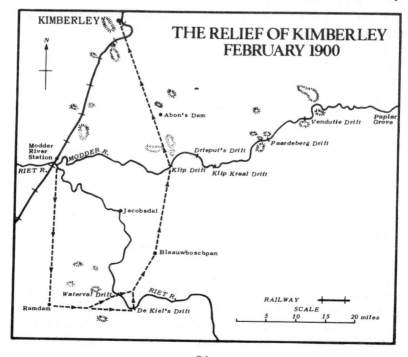

arrived. The second leg would take the cavalry over 25 water-less miles to the Modder drifts east of Magersfontein, where they would again pause for the infantry to catch up. French would then push on for Kimberley, 20 miles to the north-west. All this had to be accomplished at the hottest time of the year, and in less than five days: French took only six days' rations for the men and five days' forage for the horses. There was little room for error, but French felt supremely confident, and promised Kitchener that he would relieve Kimberley on 15 February. [13]

Haig called the division 'rather a scratch pack', and well he might: the Brigadiers joined the column only after the march had started, and the brigades' staffs were all new. Moreover, although French had been told to expect to have 8,500 horse-men under his command by the time he left Ramdam, in the event his force totalled less than 4,000 men and seven batteries of RHA. [14] French nevertheless decided to press on without waiting for stray units to catch up, and at 2.00 on the morning of the 12th he left Ramdam. The division rode on as long as there was moonlight, and when the moon went down it halted until dawn.

A weak Boer force under Christiaan de Wet managed to reach Waterval Drift just before the cavalry, but French left a brigade to engage de Wet and took his main force to De Kiel's Drift. As soon as French saw that the Drift was clear, he ordered his men to gallop for it, and by early afternoon, after a brisk fight, the crossing had been secured. [15]

The cavalry's baggage mules had been left at Ramdam, and were called forward as soon as the passage of the Riet was safe. French then discovered, to his intense annoyance, that Roberts had not given priority to the cavalry's transport, and it had become jammed behind the wagons of the leading infantry division. De Kiel's Drift soon got into what Haig called 'an indescribable state of confusion' as a medley of wagons and baggage-mules struggled for access. [16] Kitchener rode up early in the evening, decided that the Drift was thoroughly blocked, and told French to sieze Waterval, but not without acid com-ments about the errors of the Commander-in-Chief. [17]

The chaos at the crossings and the late arrival of the trans-port meant that the advance could not resume before 10.30 on the morning of the 13th, with the sun high in the sky and valuable hours lost. French's movement order, issued by Haig at 7 a.m., decreed that the division was to cross the Modder that day: it would march with Porter's Brigade in the centre, Broadwood's on the right and Gordon's on the left. Alderson's MI were to follow the cavalry as closely as possible, escorting the ambulance and ammunition wagons. Porter, leaving his brigade under its senior regimental officer, had the unenviable task of bringing up the remainder of the transport once it had been disentangled from the turmoil at De Kiel's.[18] In the event, only five wagons were extracted from the mêlée in time to accompany the division.

The division left the Riet in line of brigade masses, but soon shook out into the loose formation of line of squadron columns, moving steadily across the parched veldt on a five-mile front. The left brigade shrugged off a light attack just before midday, and at 12.30 the division halted while the ambulances were watered at a well at Blaauwboschpan, where French left a squadron of colonials to secure the well for the infantry. The advance was resumed at about 1.00 but the brief delay had enabled a party of de Wet's men, probably only about 300 strong, to occupy some kopjes between French and the Modder Drifts, which lay about twelve miles northwards. The Western Drift, Rondeval, was French's objective. To its east lay Klip Drift, Drieput's Drift and Klip Kraal Drift. The horse artillery drove the Boers from the kopjes, but the enemy continued to threaten French's right, leading him to suspect that de Wet's main body might soon arrive and interpose itself between the division and the river, or, worse still, attack his flank while the crossing was in progress.

His experiences at the Riet crossings had convinced French that 'it is advisable, if possible, to *threaten* or *feint* on several points'.[19] He decided, at about 2 p.m., to wheel the right and centre brigades half-right, as if they were making for Klip Kraal Drift, while the left brigade held its course for Rondeval. The Boers conformed to the movement, and soon French could make out the bushes marking the course of the Modder, and the Boers hurrying across the river at Klip Kraal Drift, ready to dispute his passage.

He then ordered Broadwood and Gordon to make for Klip

and Rondeval Drifts respectively, 'as rapidly as the state of their horses would permit', with Porter's Brigade following Gordon's.[20] The small parties of Boers holding the fords were taken by surprise, and the flanking Boer force was hopelessly out of touch, north of Klip Kraal Drift. French took the crossings with the loss of only three men wounded. On a grimmer note, however, over 40 horses had died from exhaustion in the heat and dust: over 500 were incapable of further work, and the cracks of the farriers' pistols provided an unsettling background to the ransacking of abandoned Boer laagers.[21]

At 5 p.m. French sent a galloper to tell Roberts that he was safely across the river. Roberts responded by urging on the infantry from the chaos of the Riet crossings. Kelly-Kenny left Waterval at 1.00 on the morning of the 14th, and after a crippling march, rendered particularly trying by rainstorms at night and searing heat during the day, reached the Modder exactly 24 hours later. French had already been chafing at the bit, begging Kitchener to send the infantry up as soon as possible so that he could resume the march on Kimberley before the Boers to his front grew too strong.[22] Porter brought the supply convoy into French's position on the night of the 14th–15th, and three days' supplies were distributed the following morning. By 8 a.m. Kelly-Kenny's men were north of the Modder, and French was at last free to resume his advance.

Wednesday 14 February had been a wasted day as far as French was concerned, and the poor staff-work which had led to the confusion on the line of march would have had serious consequences if Cronje had reacted swiftly and correctly to the changing situation. In the event, Cronje moved slowly. Initial reports which came in to his laager at Magersfontein were confusing and contradictory, but when refugees from the Modder drifts arrived on the 13th he concluded that French's advance was a feint, and sent Commandants Froneman and De Beer with about 800 men and two guns to attack the cavalry. Cronje's decision not to buttress the position north of Klip Drift was a fatal error: it gave French one of the greatest opportunities of his career.

French had spent much of the 14th peering through his field-glasses at the ground north of the Modder, assessing the Boer strength and formulating a plan. The river looped northwards between Klip Drift and Klip Kraal Drift. The Boers held a line of kopjes on the eastern side of the bend, while the country to the west was dominated by a long ridge which ran off towards Cronje's main position, about eight miles to the west. Between the end of the ridge and the first of the kopjes a long valley nudged up northwards towards Abon's Dam. French concluded that the valley was the weakest part of the Boer position. Its shoulders were a mile apart, and the riflemen on them could only engage troops in the valley at extreme range. There were some Boers in the valley itself, but they were probably too few to do any serious damage, especially as the valley seemed to be good galloping country for cavalry. French's objective was not to defeat the Boers but to relieve Kimberley: he therefore decided that he would capitalise upon the speed and mobility of his cavalry by striking hard at the Boer centre and tearing a hole through which the whole division would gallop on its way to the besieged town.

The division moved off at 9.30 p.m. on the 15th. French had conferred briefly with Kitchener, who had promised to support him with all available troops the following day. He then positioned himself with his staff at the head of Broadwood's Brigade, and rode north-eastwards following the course of the river, towards the neck of the valley. About a mile ahead of him was Gordon's Brigade, making good use of the cover provided by small kopjes which rippled down from the ridge-end. As Gordon's men came out into the open between the river and the valley Boer riflemen and gunners opened fire on them from the high ground on both sides. It was long range for musketry, but the Boer gunners made good practice, and French immediately unlimbered his horse artillery in reply. Kelly-Kenny's divisional artillery and two naval 12-pounders joined in, and soon no less than 56 guns were pounding the Boers, their fire evenly divided between the enemy riflemen to French's right front and the guns on the ridge to his left.

French now had a clear view of the neck, and premature Boer reaction to Gordon's appearance had also revealed the enemy positions. The sight confirmed the results of the previous day's reconnaissance: it was impossible to be sure that there was no wire in the valley, but in all other respects it appeared to be the weak spot in the Boer line. French spoke briefly to his Brigadiers. The ridge at the end of the valley was, he believed, not strongly held, and the fire from the flanks should not stop determined horsemen. He ordered Gordon to take the far ridge 'at a fast gallop',[23] Broadwood was to follow, while Porter and Alderson brought up the rear. The RHA was to keep up its fire until the last possible moment, then it too was to gallop for the ridge.

Gordon deployed his regiments, the 9th and 16th Lancers, in extended order, with between five and eight yards between each man and a twenty-yard gap between their two ranks.[24] Then they were off, hooves drumming on the hard and dusty ground, and the sun twinkling on lance-points. They were soon wreathed in dust, and from French's position, at the head of Broadwood's Brigade, riding towards the neck 800 yards behind Gordon, the picture looked confused. For an awful moment it seemed that some of the lancers were coming back, but then it became clear that they were simply extending to the flanks. The Boers in the valley tried to make off: some were successful, but others were ridden down, speared or taken prisoner. Their comrades on the high ground to the flanks could do little to help them. Perhaps 600 riflemen could engage the charging cavalry, but the range was long – 1,000 yards in many cases – and it was hard to pick targets from the fast-moving horsemen shrouded by dust. The weight of artillery fire made matters even more difficult, and did not encourage cool and deliberate shooting.

Gordon's men were at the head of the valley before 11.00. Their loss was trifling: two men had been killed and 17 wounded. They swung to the left in an effort to cut off the Boer guns, but the wily Major Albrecht had already got them away. The division was concentrated around Abon's Dam at 11.50, and enough water was found for the men, but not, alas, for the horses. French rode amongst his men congratulating them, telling them that Kimberley lay only a stone's throw ahead.

If Elandslaagte had initiated French's rise to eminence, and Colesberg had accelerated it, it was Klip Drift that really made his reputation. The *Times History* was lavish with its praise, saying:

The charge at Klip Drift marks an epoch in the history of cavalry. With other cavalry charges of former wars it has little in common, save the 'cavalry spirit' ... the quick insight that prompted it, the instantaneous decision that launched it against the enemy, the reckless, dare-devil confidence that carried it through. In its form it was something wholly new ... The thin line of unseen riflemen, with its wide gaps covered by converging fire, which had proved so unapproachable to the slow, short-winded foot soldier, availed nothing against the rushing speed and sustained impetus of the wave of horsemen ... This was the secret French had divined.[25]

Even Erskine Childers commended French's 'sensible resolve, promptly made and admirably executed'.[26] The German official account of the war called the charge 'one of the most remarkable phenomena of the war', and cited it as evidence that cavalry still had a future, even when faced by an enemy armed with magazine rifles.[27] The *Official History* described the charge as, quite simply, 'the most brilliant stroke of the whole war'.[28]

The very brilliance of French's exploit dazzled many commentators and cavalry theorists, who lost no time in making of Klip Drift something it was not, and extrapolating from it to reach dangerous conclusions. It was certainly not a cavalry charge in the generally-accepted sense of the term. French did not hurl his men at a resolute enemy with the intention of destroying him: he attacked a thinly-held sector of the enemy line with the intention of breaking through it. Nor was the episode conclusive evidence of the successful use of the *arme blanche*. The two regiments of lancers killed perhaps twenty Boers, certainly far fewer than Gore's two squadrons at Elandslaagte. The speed and dash of the attack undoubtedly contributed to French's victory, but the heavy weight of supporting artillery fire, and the cover produced by the dust, were also significant. It was, therefore, taking matters altogether too far to claim that Klip Drift was a classic instance of the successful use of shock action by the mounted arm.[29] French regarded

the affair as an example of the establishment of moral ascendancy over an enemy, and of the cavalry spirit at its best. It was,
in his view, powerful evidence in favour of the *arme blanche*,
because the troopers' confidence in their steel weapons imbued
them with exactly the panache that the attack required.
The threat of the cold steel was, French thought, almost as
important as its use, and it was this that had induced the
Boers to Gordon's front to recall an urgent appointment
elsewhere.[30]

French had a clear ride from Abon's Dam to Kimberley: the
Boer forces investing the town offered no serious resistance,
and at 6 p.m. on the evening of the 15th French rode into
Kimberley to a delirious welcome. He was lavishly entertained
by Cecil Rhodes at the Sanatorium, and seems to have fallen
completely under the spell of the persuasive Rhodes, who
convinced him that the garrison commander, Colonel Kekewich, had been overbearing and tyrannical during the siege.
There was an uncomfortable interview between French and
Kekewich, and when the division left two days later Kekewich
discovered that Porter of the 1st Cavalry Brigade had replaced
him as garrison commander.[31]

The incident is a vivid illustration of one of the weakest
points of French's character. He often judged people on super-
ficial evidence, but was reluctant to change his mind once the
decision was made. It was a habit which gave rise to lasting
and unnecessary enmities, and to injustices, like that suffered
by Kekewich, and at the other extreme to misplaced confidence
in the ability of men he trusted. It was a trait which partially
accounts for the divergence of contemporary opinion regarding
French. He could be a good friend, but could be an equally
good hater, and the motives for friendship or dislike were not
always clearly comprehensible.

The relief of Kimberley brought French the grateful thanks
of Lord Roberts, coupled with an expression of the Queen's
satisfaction at the cavalry's 'brilliant success'.[32] The aura of
victory tended to obscure other, less encouraging facts. De Wet
attacked Roberts's supply convoy at Waterval, and the Field-
Marshal decided to abandon it, losing 170 wagons in the
process. Secondly, Cronje had managed to slip across the front
of Kelly-Kenny, and was making off up the Modder. Roberts's

first impulse, on hearing this news, was to order French to set off in pursuit, but the Boers had cut the telegraph line to Kimberley and the message did not get through.

Even if French had received Roberts's order to pursue Cronje on the 16th, there was relatively little that he could have done about it. The gallop at Klip Drift had exacted a fearful toll of the cavalry division's horses, many of which had scarcely recovered from the galling advance from the Riet. French's line of march was marked by fly-blown carcasses, and his mobility, the very quality which had made the flank march possible, was seriously impaired. An abortive scramble after the Boer gun 'Long Tom' on the 16th killed still more horses: Gordon's brigade alone lost 68 that day.[33] On the 17th one of French's commanding officers noted in his diary: 'I had a horse parade, and there were only 28 horses that could raise a trot. A week ago I commanded the best mounted regiment in the British Army, and it is now absolutely ruined.'[34]

French was subsequently criticised for attacking the Boers around Kimberley on the 16th, rather than setting off at once in pursuit of Cronje. The cutting of the telegraph cable to Klip Drift meant, however, that French had no idea that Cronje was on the move. Moreover, there is no evidence that Roberts or Kitchener, on receiving no reply by telegraph, tried to send the order by heliograph or by another telegraph line. French, on the other hand, heliographed for orders at midday on the 16th and took good care that the message got through, using the Enslin heliograph station, which was available to Roberts's staff, had they cared to use it.[35]

The order to pursue Cronje reached French at 10 p.m. on the 16th, in the perspiring hand of Captain Chester Master of Rimington's Tigers. French acted swiftly. He ordered Broadwood to leave for Koedoesrand at 3 a.m., with two squadrons of the Carabineers following, under French himself, an hour later. The rest of the division was left to recuperate in Kimberley. The exertions of the previous days meant that French had only 1,500 mounted men and twelve guns fit for duty, but he realised that unless he moved very quickly indeed, literally twice as fast as the Boers, Cronje would escape. Kitchener's message admitted that French was his only hope: 'Our mounted infantry and field artillery are too sticky for words and the Boers fight an excellent rearguard action ... I fear we can do nothing really serious unless you can come we are too slow.'(*sic*)[36]

It was a close-run thing. French approached the Modder drifts shortly after 10 a.m. on the 17th, after a gruelling march from Kimberley. Cronje's burghers were preparing to cross the river to safety, confident that Kelly-Kenny's men were still miles behind them and the cavalry were still engaged around Kimberley. The first wagons were on their way across Ven-dutie Drift when the 12-pounders of French's horse gunners burst shrapnel over the leading teams. There was a brief panic, during which many of the Boer oxen and horses, outspanned to rest before the crossing, bolted. Most of the Boers took cover in the river bed, but Albrecht's guns soon snarled back and parties of the enemy tried to dislodge French from his blocking position. A determined attack would probably have suc-ceeded, for the cavalry were outnumbered by at least three to one, and another large Boer force, about 2,000 strong, was also in the area.[37]

The opportunity passed, and by the morning of the 18th Roberts's leading infantry divisions, 6th and 9th, were within striking distance of Cronje's force, which was by now entren-ched in the river banks near Paardeberg Drift. Kitchener had accompanied Kelly-Kenny's division to hurry on its rather cautious commander, and relations between Kitchener and Kelly-Kenny had become somewhat strained, with each man behaving as if he commanded the force.[38] The whole question of command was, indeed, somewhat complicated. Kitchener was a substantive Major-General, and was senior as such to Kelly-Kenny and Colville of 9th Division. But both the latter officers held local ranks as Lieutenant-Generals, and were therefore superior to Kitchener as far as operations in South Africa were concerned.

French, who was still only a substantive Colonel, was actually the senior local Lieutenant-General, but was in no position to interfere, being separated from the main force. Roberts was laid up at Jacobsdal with a severe chill, but intervened to settle the matter by telling Kelly-Kenny that Kitchener's orders were to be regarded as the orders of Roberts himself.[39] But the friction boded ill, and was a fitting opening for what Sir Philip Magnus called 'the most controversial episode in Kitchener's career'.[40]

Kitchener rode forward to examine the Boer position before dawn on the 18th. He had no doubt what should be done: the answer lay in frontal assault. 'Gentlemen!' he told the officers who had accompanied him on the reconnaissance, 'It is now six-thirty. By ten-thirty we shall be in possession of that laager; I shall then load up French and push him on to Bloemfontein with the cavalry.'[41] Kelly-Kenny would have preferred to shell Cronje into submission, but Kitchener's new authority gave him no choice in the matter. French agreed with Kelly-Kenny, and sent a message to Kitchener urging caution.[42]

Kitchener's attack was a disaster, costing the British over 1,200 casualties, the heaviest loss in any single day's fighting during the entire war. Kitchener himself, handicapped by a lack of staff officers, spent the day galloping about, issuing verbal orders which launched a series of disjointed assaults. A particularly misleading order to Colonel Hannay of the MI resulted in that officer, who felt that his personal courage had been called into question, attacking the laager in circumstances that were tantamount to suicide. Kitchener's nickname 'K of Chaos' was well earned that day; he became dangerously close to snatching defeat from the jaws of victory.[43]

French, unlike his fellow-Wolseleyite Kelly-Kenny, had a relatively quiet day. He had signalled to Kitchener that his horses were too exhausted to permit him to do anything but remain on the defensive, and held off Boers who tried to break into Cronje's position from the east.[44] Gordon's brigade, nearly 800 strong, came up late in the afternoon, but did not manage to establish contact with divisional headquarters until the 19th.

Roberts arrived on the battlefield at mid-morning on the 19th, and soon decided against renewing the attack. A properly co-ordinated attack on the laager, which really had very little natural strength, might very easily have worked, but Roberts, the memory of poor young Freddy fresh in his mind, was understandably anxious to avoid more casualties, and he found the divisional commanders sickened by the butchery of the 18th and similarly reluctant to launch another major attack. He therefore contented himself with keeping Cronje encircled, and bombarding the Boer position as heavily as his limited supplies of ammunition would allow. De Wet, who was rapidly establishing himself as one of the most capable Boer leaders, seized a kopje behind the British lines and did some damage until French drove him off on the 21st. This exploit encouraged Roberts to send the cavalry on to Bloemfontein: the division was reorganised into two brigades, under Gordon and Broadwood, but the continuation of Boer attacks on the British perimeter prevented the division's early departure.

Cronje surrendered with 3,919 men and four guns on 27 February.[45] The capitulation was a heavy blow to the Boers, removing as it did about one tenth of their fighting strength. It also did great damage to Boer morale, leading, amongst other things, to the withdrawal of the enemy forces from the Colesberg area in order to defend their homes and the Free State capital, Bloemfontein. Fortune at last smiled on Buller in Natal, and on the evening of 28 February his advance guard entered Ladysmith, ending the 118-day siege in which French had so nearly been involved.

Having duly disposed of Cronje, Roberts intended to march on to Bloemfontein. On 6 March he expounded his plan to a meeting of senior officers. The Boers had, he believed, 14,000 men and 20 guns at the very most, blocking the British advance in an improvised defensive position astride the Modder around Poplar Grove, nearly forty miles east of Kimberley. Roberts's plan was simple and robust: it was designed to reproduce, on a greater scale, the gratifying results of Paardeberg without, of course, the carnage which had resulted from Kitchener's intervention. French was to take his division and two brigades of MI round the Boer left flank in a wide hook which would enable him to sever communications with Bloemfontein. The infantry would then attack the main Boer position along both banks of the river, Kelly-Kenny, Tucker and the Guards on the south bank and Colville on the north. The Boers, Roberts hoped, would be encircled in the area of Poplar Grove Drift and would share Cronje's fate.[46]

The plan had one major weakness. It relied upon the cavalry carrying out a 17-mile march, undetected, around the Boer flank. Unless French was in position by the time the infantry attack went in, the net would close on thin air. And even on

March, before the first trooper had saddled up for the march to Poplar Grove, it was clear that there were insurmountable obstacles confronting the cavalry division.

French had left the Modder on the morning of Klip Drift with 5,027 horses, and by 28 February, the day before Cronje's surrender, he was down to 3,553, having lost about 1,500, almost all from exhaustion.[47] The arrival of remounts had brought his strength back up to 5,655 horses before the start of the Poplar Grove operation. Many of the remounts were, however, of poor quality, and a large number of the division's horses were on the sick list. French described his strength as 'quite inadequate for the purpose'. He added that the state of the horses was worsened by a serious shortage of fodder. 'Horses cannot possibly be kept alive on very hard work like that unless they are fed, and it was impossible to feed them.'[48]

The fodder question led to any ugly scene between French and Roberts, which was, in all probability, a decisive point of departure in their relationship. The cavalry horses were, at the time, entitled to an issue of 3lbs of fodder a day — itself a ludicrously inadequate amount, and less than half the quantity they had been receiving earlier in the month. Colonel W. D. Richardson, Roberts's Director of Supplies, complained to Roberts that the division was drawing well over its fodder ration. Roberts sent for French and his Brigadiers, and laid into them in no uncertain terms. L. S. Amery describes the scene, not, one suspects, without a hint of pleasure: 'the Little Chief this time let himself go and gave the cavalry a real dressing down'.[49] French left the interview hurt and embittered, feeling that he had been unjustly reprimanded, in intemperate language, in front of his subordinates.

Richardson shortly afterwards told Roberts that it had all been a mistake. He had forgotten that sick horses were also entitled to fodder, and had not taken account of them in his calculations: the cavalry division had not, in fact, been cheating. 'It seems,' wrote Roberts's biographer, 'that this unfair rebuff upset, no doubt unconsciously, that poise of mind so essential when difficulties and discouragements have to be overcome.'[50]

Another, rather more important, point upset the poise of British commanders' minds. Roberts's verbal orders had been amplified by a short written brief, but neither this, nor Roberts's speech, mentioned timings or orders of march. Timings were discussed in an informal huddle after the conference, with the result that French thought he was to start at 3.00 the following morning, and issued his orders accordingly, while Kelly-Kenny, whose division was to follow the cavalry, planned on starting an hour earlier. The confusion was made more serious because Roberts had omitted to mention the packing of baggage, and the early-morning scramble dented even the sturdy Scots humour of the officer responsible for the army's baggage, Lieutenant-Colonel Jimmy Grierson.[51]

French picked his way out of camp, at the head of his leading brigade, at 3 a.m. on 7 March. The moon had long since set, and the stars gave little light: by 5 a.m. French had had enough of 'struggling with emaciated horses in the darkness', and halted to await daylight.[52] He was on the move again forty-five minutes later, and by 7.00 had reached Kalkfontein, having covered twelve miles in a little under four hours. It was certainly not the speedy outflanking movement that Roberts had envisaged, but, bearing in mind the difficulties of a night move and the collision with Kelly-Kenny's men, there was every reason for the slowness. It soon became clear that the Boers had no intention of participating in an action replay of Paardeberg. At about 7.30 they began to abandon the position, streaming away towards Bloemfontein, taking with them the unmilitary figure of Oom Paul Kruger, driving his Cape Cart among the retreating burghers.

The events of the next few hours were to imprint themselves vividly on the memories of French, Roberts and a score of others. From Roberts's position it seemed that French was in a position to attack the Boer flank, or to interpose his division between the retreating enemy and safety. If ever an opportunity had been offered to cavalry, this, so it appeared to Roberts, was it. French saw things rather differently. The exhausted state of his horses caused him constant worry. He spent three quarters of an hour watering them at Kalkfontein dam, but this was a mere palliative, and many of them could not raise a trot: scarcely the material for a cavalry charge. Moreover, although the Boers moving across his front were clearly shaken, they were by no means routed. Kelly-Kenny's men were slow in coming up, largely as a result of the early-morning chaos, and French soon decided that it was simply too dangerous to attempt to cut off the retreating Boers. He concentrated his division in order to pursue, but was soon brought to a halt by a well-handled Boer rearguard.

Roberts was anything but pleased with the day's results, and his disappointment became intense when he discovered that Kruger had slipped past him. He had no doubt where the blame lay: French and Kelly-Kenny had been sickeningly over-cautious, and it was their pussyfooting around the Boer flank which had robbed him of his prize. If the horses of the cavalry division were in bad condition, it was because of bad horsemastership. If French had not been able, in what Roberts regarded as ideal conditions, to shatter the Boers with lance and sabre, it must be because of a long-standing defect in cavalry tactics and armament. If the *arme blanche* had any real advantages, this, surely, was the moment to show them.[53]

The *Official History* dealt kindly with French over Poplar Grove, saying that no living authority in the world could pronounce against his decision to halt to await daylight and his refusal to get across the Boer line of retreat.[54] Not all living authorities agreed with the *Official History*, and Poplar Grove was destined to become a *cause célèbre* in the debate on cavalry tactics. Two aspects of the battle merit emphasis. Firstly, although complaints about tired horses and scarce fodder sound somewhat trivial to the modern ear, they reflected defects which were every bit as serious as mechanical unreliability coupled with shortage of petrol and lubricants would be in a present-day armoured unit. There is, moreover, no room to doubt the truth of French's assertions concerning the shattered state of the division's horseflesh: subsequent courts of inquiry into the supply of remounts, and the authoritative veterinary history of the war, all testify to the prodigious waste of horses, brought about mainly by shortages of food and water.[55] Secondly, the painful scene between Roberts and the cavalry commanders on the 6th led some authorities to suggest that French, if not actually 'working to rule', was certainly giving less than wholehearted co-operation.[56] There is probably a measure of truth in this accusation. French appears to have believed that his task was impossible, and he was naturally disinclined to get his division lacerated in what he regarded as a fruitless battle.

Why, then, did he not tell Roberts that he believed his mission to be beyond him? Roberts had not consulted French when planning the operation, and the first French heard of it was at the conference on the 6th. It would have required quite remarkable moral courage for French, still only a substantive Colonel, to have publicly stated that the Commander-in-Chief's master-plan was not feasible. Roberts was ruthless with opponents, failures and weaklings: there is little doubt that French's exposure of the flaw in Roberts's plan would have been rewarded by a prompt posting to outer darkness.

The bitter taste of Poplar Grove soured even the army's victorious entry into Bloemfontein on 13 March. The jollifications which followed the city's occupation could not conceal growing differences within the British high command. Roberts thought that the fall of Bloemfontein brought victory within measurable distance: the burghers would now, he believed, see the futility of continued resistance and accept the amnesty he offered. Once he had reorganised his army, he would march on to Pretoria and demolish the Transvaal with the same sort of hammer-blow he had just administered to the Free State. Buller, on the other hand, prophesied that the Boers, almost indifferent to the fate of their capitals, would take to the veldt as guerrillas: Roberts's problems had, he warned, only just begun. At a lower level, the embers of distrust glowed brightly. French and Kelly-Kenny resented what they saw as Roberts's attempts to make them scapegoats for Poplar Grove, and Douglas Haig, a local Lieutenant-Colonel at last, wrote bitterly to his sister of the horses that Roberts squandered on the newly-raised 'Colonial Skallywag Corps'.[57] They united in attributing their misfortunes to the failings of Roberts and his staff, who had so cleverly contrived to lose the supply convoy at Waterval Drift, to massacre the horses by putting them on inadequate rations, and make a difficult task worse by abolishing regimental transport. Supplies, to be sure, trickled up the army's long line of communication, but they trickled up too slowly. And one of the most unwelcome consequences of the scarcity of balanced rations and the lack of medical supplies was the resurgence of typhoid: Bloemfontein had become Bobsfontein in March, but by April it was Bloomingtyphoidfontein.[58]

French was hard at work refitting his division. He made a couple of fighting excursions, to Thabanchu on the 20th and Karee Siding nine days later, but his main preoccupation was with getting his remounts into shape. His diary for early April reads more like a horse-coper's journal than the notes of a divisional commander: 'Went out at 6.00 and looked round sick and lame horses – looked at another lot of remounts – a fair lot on the whole – mostly Argentinian – rather small and underbred.'[59] By the middle of the month he felt confident enough to write that 'we may soon have a good division together again'.[60]

The question of the roles and importance of cavalry and mounted infantry also came to the fore. Early in April Roberts sent for French, who recorded the conversation in his diary:

> I asked him what he thought of MI. He said he was a great advocate for their use but that he was sure they could never in any sense replace cavalry. He has a strong idea that the value of their fire is much greater than that of cavalry. I think we ought to combat this idea very strongly. The Boer's Mauser Carbine is our strong argument.[61]

French's suspicions of the MI were deepened when he discovered that Major-General Edward Hutton, their commander, had tried to get his men relieved on outpost duty by the cavalry. French, whose rather paternalistic interest in the welfare of his subordinates came, at times, dangerously close to over-identification with his men, wrote crossly: 'Hutton has been behaving like an ass as usual! I had to go and see him and get his little game stopped ... My cavalry must have complete rest.'[62]

The rest stopped soon enough. There was considerable activity around Bloemfontein even before Roberts began the next phase of his campaign, the advance to Pretoria. On 31 March Christiaan de Wet cut up Broadwood's weak brigade at Sannah's Post, destroying the Bloemfontein water-works for good measure. On 4 April he swamped a detachment of regulars at the appropriately-named Dewetsdorp, but had less luck at

Wepener, where the Colonials of Brabant's Horse held him off until help arrived. Late April saw French thrashing fruitlessly around Thabanchu in pursuit of his will-o'-the-wisp adversary, and in early May he was summoned to join Roberts on the march to Pretoria.

Roberts had left Bloemfontein on 3 May. His advance followed the line of the railway. French, when he came up, was to take the left flank, while Tucker's 7th Division and Pole-Carew's 11th, with a dusting of MI, marched to the east of the line. It was a measure of Roberts's diminished confidence in French and the cavalry that pride of place, a semi-independent command out on the British right, went to Ian Hamilton, brought back from Natal, granted the local rank of Lieutenant-General, and given a mixed force of some 14,000 men, which included Broadwood's cavalry brigade. Roberts's great central thrust was paralleled by advances by Buller in Natal, and by Mahon and Hunter over on the Bechuanaland border.

French concentrated his three remaining brigades around Bloemfontein on 4 May, striving to bring them up to strength before joining Roberts. Despite the earlier refit the brigades were still below strength, and although they moved out of Bloemfontein on 7 May with a full complement of horses, many of them had only joined their regiments over the previous few days and were still 'raw and soft'.[63] French proposed to advance in easy stages to acclimatise the horses, but Roberts was already feeling the want of cavalry, and ordered him to rendezvous on the Vet River by 8 May. French arrived on time, but the forced march cost him 184 horses.[64] A few miles north of Vet, where Roberts's engineers were already hard at work on the bridges, the railway crossed another river, the Zand. It was along this obstacle that General Louis Botha proposed to make a stand, covering the Free State's temporary capital of Kroonstad.

A number of choices were open to Roberts. The simplest — frontal assault — was easily dismissed. Attacks round the Boer flanks seemed to offer the best prospects of success. The great question, however, was just how wide these hooks should be. Roberts eventually plumped for a modest solution. French, with Hutton's MI and his own cavalry, would strike from the British left, linking up, behind the Boer position, with

Broadwood, who was to strike from the right. But, as C. S. Goldman was to point out, 'the experience of Poplar Grove ... went to show that strong positions were abandoned by the Boers at the first sign of danger threatening their flanks or lines of retirement'.[65] French apparently favoured a longer hook, which would enable him to get behind the Boers unobserved.

In the event, Botha reacted quickly, and, perhaps, predictably, to French's presence to his right rear. He pulled back his forces opposite Roberts in the centre and reinforced his flank as French struck into it on 10 May. Porter's brigade met with a sharp reverse, and when Dickson's Brigade attempted to charge the Boers it discovered that its horse were far too tired to charge home with much effect. At 7.00 that evening Roberts ordered French to disengage his brigades from the fighting just west of the railway, and to swing wide round Kroonstad to cut the railway north of it. This plan might have worked had it been employed from the start, but the cavalry horses were by now exhausted by a fighting advance of forty miles.[66]

The action on the Zand river — the last occasion in which the Orange Free State and Transvaal armies fought as formed bodies under unified command — was the only major battle on the advance to Pretoria. It was, naturally enough, a disappointment to the British, for although Botha had been manoeuvred out of a strong position, he had got his army away in good order. The *Times History* admitted that French 'showed great rapidity in his movements', but suggested that he could have done more if he had kept his division more concentrated.[67] It is, though, hard to see how this could have been achieved while groping through broken country in the face of strongly-posted rearguards. But there was no doubt about Broadwood's performance: it had been lamentable. He had made little effort to turn the Boer left, and his unenterprising performance was a decisive factor in prejudicing Ian Hamilton against conventional cavalry thereafter.[68]

Roberts halted in Kroonstad from 12 May to 22 May, while the railway was repaired and supplies were brought up. Remounts arrived for the cavalry, but about one-third of them were unfit for service, and when the advance was resumed French and Hutton could, between them, put only 2,330 men into the field.[69] The Boers made little effort to hold the line of the Vaal, and on 24 May Gordon's men crossed the river by the dangerous Parys Drift while the remainder of his force found an easier passage upstream. Roberts had by now moved Hamilton round on to his left flank, and proposed to take Johannesburg, forty miles on, by sending Hamilton and French to outflank the town from the west. French bit at the Boer centre on the 28th, and the following day he elbowed his way round the enemy flank. Hamilton had, however, taken the bull by the horns, and his infantry, in a brave but unenterprising frontal assault, stormed the main Boer position at Doornkop before the flanking movement was complete. Some observers found Hamilton's decision puzzling, but the fact that this was *the* Doornkop, where Jameson's men had surrendered five years before, probably struck a chord in his emotional character.[70]

The army entered Johannesburg on 31 May. Roberts had decided not to press an attack on the city, and Botha's men flowed out of the place, taking their guns and bullion with them, the day before. Pretoria fell on 5 June, and although it was another useful propaganda victory for the British, it did not bring the victorious peace that Roberts hoped for. The loss of Johannesburg and Pretoria undoubtedly shook the Boers, and many were prepared to negotiate for peace. But the glimmer of peace flickered out in early June. A new generation of military leaders – Koots De La Rey and Christiaan de Wet amongst them – began to force the pace. Three sharp raps at British complacency: Piet de Wet's swamping of a battalion of MI at Lindley on 31 May, his brother's capture of a convoy at Heilbron on 4 June, and finally the seizure of Roodewal station, replete with supplies, on the 6th, went a long way towards restoring Boer morale and persuading the Boer Presidents that guerrilla warfare was a practical possibility. Hurt as they were by the loss of their cities, many of the Boer leaders realised that it was on the boundless veldt, not in the towns, that the conflict would be decided. Zand River and Doornkop were the last battles of the conventional war which had begun at Talana Hill, seven months before. The new war which began with the fall of Johannesburg had a different character born of determination and resentment: it was to lurch on for nearly two years.

Some things did not change. French, correctly dismissing talk of peace as premature, was once more stumping round his horse lines soon after daybreak, wrestling with the omnipresent problem of remounts. 'These are quite the worst lot I have ever seen', he wrote in late May. 'Half of them unfit for service – the Remount department at home has not done well by any means.'[71] And it was not merely the performance of the remount department at home that caused anxiety. The key post of director of remounts at Stellenbosch had been entrusted to a manic-depressive officer, unfit for any other duty, who did untold damage before eventually shooting himself.[72]

As the guerrilla war gained momentum, the hitherto logical and formalised deployment of troops became increasingly complex, with growing numbers of British garrisons guarding key points along the lines of communication, and flying columns chasing across the veldt in pursuit of the Boers. For French, the war initially focused on the North-Eastern Transvaal. On 11–12 June he co-operated in a major attack on Louis Botha's position at Diamond Hill, sixteen miles from Pretoria. The usual outflanking movement went badly wrong, and French, at the head of the leading Brigade, came under the close-range rifle fire of De La Rey's burghers. A medical officer, Major Hathaway, was shot in the stomach at his side, but French, with that coolness under fire which even his bitterest enemies acknowledged, ordered the leading troopers to dismount and fire. He held his ground that night, although Roberts had granted him permission to retire. Though he had failed to turn the Boer flank, French's dogged dismounted action still played a vital part in a hard-fought victory.[73]

The battle of Diamond Hill induced Botha to fall back to Balmoral, sitting squarely across the Delagoa Bay railway, which ran through Komati Poort on the Transvaal Border to the port of Lourenço Marques in Portuguese East Africa. The railway was the Boers' lifeline, and if Botha realised this so too did Roberts. But before Roberts could turn to the railway, the increasingly aggressive activities of the commandos around the weakly-garrisoned Pretoria diverted his attention. In mid-July French was busy south-east of Pretoria on the Standerton road, but was recalled, with much of his force, when Roberts heard of the successes of De La Rey and Grobler against isolated garrisons to the west. French believed that Roberts was allowing the activities of the guerrillas to distract him from his real target. He wired that he would come back at once, 'but suggested an alternative plan – advance at once on Balmoral – I pointed out that we should thus sever the enemy's main line of communication at once and force him to draw back his right flank in some haste'.[74]

Roberts, however, took a more serious view of the activities of De La Rey than French did. And although French's plan offered a reasonable prospect of success as far as Botha's army was concerned, it reflected a misunderstanding of the nature of the war. De La Rey was not Botha's right flank: he was a semi-independent guerrilla leader living largely off the country. French's mind was still locked within the confines of conventional warfare. The true nature of the guerrillas and their real sources of support were, as yet, a mystery to him.

Roberts decided against an immediate attack on Botha. He strengthened the defences of Pretoria and organised columns to clear the country to the north and west. He sent French back to the east to prepare for a general advance against Botha, which began on 23 July. French again disagreed with Roberts's plan for the attack. He initially hoped to make 'a very wide turning movement', cutting the road and railway well to the rear of Botha's army. But no sooner had he finished briefing his commanders than Roberts vetoed the move in favour of a far less ambitious outflanking movement. 'I fear,' French wrote crossly, 'all this entirely does away with the sweeping and decisive character of the great turning movement I had designed.'[75]

There is no doubt that Roberts's caution was ill-advised. Botha's army was too heavily laden to have escaped rapidly. It would, in all probability, have been trapped by the wide right hook planned by French. 'Here, as on more than one occasion,' admits the *Times History*. 'Lord Roberts thought more of gaining ground than of striking a vital blow at his adversary's army.'[76] At sunset on 25 July French stood beside Hutton at Naawpoort Drift over the Olifant's River, watching 'a very wonderful sight'; Botha's force retreating, 'in much disorder', to the east.[77] It was too dark for pursuit, and the horses were tired by a long march. But the real opportunity, of surrounding and destroying Botha, had already been missed.

Roberts halted at Middelburg on the Delagoa Bay railway on the 27th, telling French that he would remain there for a fortnight. French, in company with other commanders, was becoming increasingly exasperated by the errors of Roberts's staff. Kitchener was a conspicuous failure as Chief of Staff. He behaved more like a deputy commander, flitting around South Africa, reinforcing a garrison here and inspecting a railway bridge there. Roberts's own ability to exercise centralised control was naturally restricted by his presence with the field force in the North-Eastern Transvaal. There was, in consequence, an empty office rather than a nerve centre in Pretoria, and the absence of a co-ordinating authority led to misunderstandings. In late July, for example, there was a serious disagreement between French and Pole-Carew, commander of the 11th Division, over areas of responsibility. When Pole-Carew declined to accept French's orders, French retorted by asking to be relieved of responsibility for Pole-Carew's area. He was particularly nettled by the affair, writing: 'I fear the discipline of our army is very indifferent – this shows itself more in the higher ranks than anywhere else.' He was not impressed by Roberts's reply that 'I should find things all right', complaining: 'I suppose I must leave the matter in this way, but such accidents as this have brought armies to grief many times in the world's history!' Relations between French and Pole-Carew were eventually patched up after what French delicately called a 'somewhat stormy' interview.[78]

By the middle of August French held an outpost line well beyond Middelburg. Despite Roberts's orders to remain on the defensive, he had behaved very much in the same spirit as at Colesberg, probing at the Boer outposts and striving to establish a moral ascendancy. He hoped that Roberts would allow him to concentrate the cavalry division in order to take the offensive against the Boers to the south, or preferably, to effect another wide outflanking movement by marching on Barberton, which lay on a spur of the Delagoa Bay railway, near the Swaziland border. Roberts replied that Barberton lay 'beyond the sphere of our proposed operations', which were to consist of a drive eastwards along the railway. Buller, his methodical advance through Natal completed, was to swing north and join French, and they would then press forward against Botha's position across the railway. French was dissatisfied with this pedestrian scheme. A bold attack on Barberton, or even a more modest outflanking movement, seemed to offer better prospects than a shoving match against a dogged opponent. But whatever the differences of opinion between Buller and Roberts, they were at least united on one point: the cavalry would remain hitched firmly to Buller's apron string.[79]

The result was eminently predictable. The British advance ground on, slow and laborious, with French chafing at the constant changes of plan, total lack of enterprise and absence of a firm directing hand. On 24 August he noted: 'We sadly want someone in Chief Command here.'[80] By the end of the month French was at Waterval Onder, almost two-thirds of the way to Komati Poort, and it was only now that Roberts at last authorised a thrust to Barberton. Such a move carried out a fortnight before could have led to the encirclement of Botha's force, but the advance had now progressed so far that this enticing prospect no longer beckoned. Nevertheless, Barberton remained an important strategic objective: it was a major Boer commissariat depot, packed with stores and rolling stock.

The natural defences of Barberton made those of Colesberg look like ant-hills in comparison. Barberton lay in a cleft in rugged 3,000 ft hills. The best approach was along the railway, following the De Kaap valley from the north, but this was too well guarded. The other roads in were difficult and dangerous, crossing hard and inhospitable country. French's approach to the problem was characteristic. He chose a difficult route to maximise the chance of surprise, and concentrated on travelling light and moving fast. He left the Delagoa Bay line at Machadodorp, and rode south to Carolina. On 9 September his two brigades left Carolina, carrying only eight days' supplies with them. The local commandos, misled as to his intentions, went off to look for him on the Ermelo road. Recalled in haste, they reached the Nelhoogte Pass before him but were brushed aside. By dawn on the 13th French was within striking distance of Barberton, although a sharp ridge separated him from the town. He decided 'to get across the mountains by bridle path and take Barberton by surprise'. His guns and wagons went by road, while French himself led the 1st Cavalry Brigade along the 'rugged and precipitous' track. The two squadrons of the Greys under Harry Scobell scrambled off northeastwards, and when their heliograph announced that the railway from Barberton had been cut, French dropped down on the town from the heights to the west.

Most of the Boers had managed to get away, but French met the area commandant, Van den Post, in a carriage driven by a local banker. Van den Post was anything but pleased: 'he was in a violent state of excitement and complained that he had been led into a trap—he seemed altogether off his head'.[81] There were captures of greater importance. Scobell's men had secured £10,000 in gold and notes, and over 40 locomotives were seized, with a good deal of rolling stock and a vast quantity of supplies. French's telegram announcing the capture caused a good deal of mirth at Roberts's headquarters. 'Have captured forty engines,' it ran, 'seventy wagons of stores, eighty women all in good working order.'[82]

The inhabitants of Barberton were not altogether overjoyed by the arrival of their visitors, and some of them indulged in a little sniping from the hills. French had already encountered this sort of threat and was convinced that severe measures were appropriate. He immediately issued a proclamation warning that unless the sniping ceased forthwith he would withdraw his troops and shell the town without further notice. The firing stopped.[83]

The capture of Barberton seemed to herald the end in the Eastern Transvaal. Buller pressed Botha's army up against the border. Kruger left the country on 11 September. He sailed for Holland from Lourenço Marques on 19 October, never to return. President Steyn got away to join de Wet, and the more determined members of Botha's army slipped off into the trackless country north of the Delgoa Bay railway. But to the British it seemed very much as if the war was nearly over. French found his Colonials replaced by regular MI, and sent down the line for repatriation. It seemed that the cavalry division was being broken up: on 31 October Roberts told French that it would cease to exist as a unit, and that he would take command of the Johannesburg area. On 10 November French was informed that he would retain 'nominal command' of the division: his new area of responsibility was defined, lying roughly within the triangle Johannesburg–Klerksdorp–Vereeniging.[84] Roberts himself left for England on 10 December to be rewarded by an earldom, a cash grant, and Wolseley's post as Commander-in-Chief of the British army. Buller had already gone home, though with rather less lustre, to take over his old command at Aldershot.

The year 1900 lumbered into 1901 with a number of depressing portents, indicating that optimism was premature. On 13 December Smuts and De la Rey cut up a British force at Nooitgedacht, and four days later news came in of an invasion of Cape Colony by a strong force under General Kritzinger and Judge Herzog. Surprising though it may seem, it is likely that French welcomed Roberts's replacement by Kitchener. Despite the damage done to their relationship at Paardeberg, and their temperamental incompatibility, French and Kitchener could at times work well together, and in the winter of 1900–1 they were almost friends. Perhaps it was that, as far as French was concerned, Kitchener was the lesser of two evils. Roberts's view of the cavalry had been discoloured by the action – or rather lack of it – at Poplar Grove. On 11 November Roberts had summoned French to discuss the question of cavalry armament. 'I fear', wrote French, 'he is somewhat inclined to take the MI view and regard the *rifle* as the principal cavalry arm.'[85] At least Kitchener seemed to display no predilection for turning the cavalry into little more than up-market MI.

Moreover, despite the respectful tone of his correspondence with Roberts, and the relative moderation of his diary entries, French had disagreed with Roberts on a number of operational issues, and did not share the popular view of Roberts's military genius. French's confidence in Kitchener seemed to be reciprocated. In August Kitchener 'spoke in the highest terms' of French to the future King George V, and at about the same time he wrote to Roberts that French was 'quite first-rate, and has the absolute confidence of all serving under him, as well as mine'.[86]

Kitchener wanted to end the war as quickly as possible. A laudable enough desire, certainly, although his motives were anything but disinterested: he was anxious for the post of Commander-in-Chief in India, and feared that the continuation of the war would deprive him of this prize. At the end of February, he negotiated with Botha at Middelburg in the hope of reaching a settlement, but Milner tightened the terms and nothing came of it. At the same time Kitchener applied his dynamo-like energy to the prosecution of the war. He began to implement a systematic policy of 'drives', and it was these that were to dominate the remainder of French's time in South Africa. Drives brought the tactics of the grouse-moor to the veldt. Converging columns tried to trap the guerrillas between them, or to sweep them up against a defended line. The ground covered by the columns was swept bare of anything that might possibly aid the guerrillas. Farms were burnt, and their occupants herded together in the enclosures whose name gives a bitter tone to this phase of the war — concentration camps. Kitchener also set about the fortification of railway lines by means of barbed wire and blockhouses, although this system was, in the spring of 1901, still in its infancy.

French spent the early part of the year on a drive in the Eastern Transvaal. The drive displayed most of the characteristics of such operations, features which were to become painfully familiar as the year went on. Intelligence was of crucial importance, but the information which reached French's headquarters was all too often out of date. It was difficult to control the various columns under French's command: heliograph, dispatch rider and telegraph were all used, but rapid and secure communication could never be guaranteed. On 4 February, for example, French wrote hopefully: 'I think now if we can only secure Smith-Dorrien's co-operation we should have a fair chance of surrounding the enemy in or near Ermelo.' A dispatch was sent ordering Smith-Dorrien to link up with Allenby's column to the rear of Ermelo, blocking the Boer retreat, and French advanced eagerly into Ermelo itself. On arrival he discovered that Smith-Dorrien had only just received his message: the pincers bit on thin air. The Boers made off in the direction of Amsterdam, and the whole wretched process had to begin again.[87]

On 1 June French received a wire from Kitchener ordering him to take command of field operations in Cape Colony. A further telegram emphasised 'the necessity of *severity* in dealing with captured rebels'.[88] Draconian treatment of Cape Colony

Boers taken in arms was an essential part of Kitchener's stick-and-carrot policy, and was intended to accompany lenient treatment for those who surrendered voluntarily.[89] It must be remembered that the inhabitants of Cape Colony had been British subjects throughout the war. The question of their loyalty had no light and shade as far as Kitchener was concerned. If they took arms against the Crown, they were rebels. And rebels swung. French and his staff received Kitchener's instructions with rather more than mere compliance, and French lost no time in telling the president of the Standing Court Martial to proceed against captured rebels 'with the utmost rigour'.[90] There is an understandable, if undesirable, tendency for the military mind to abhor uncertainty and to see things in black and white, not in tones of grey. Politicians usually find such rigidity unappealing, and so it was with the question of Cape Colony rebels. St John Brodrick, Secretary of State for War after the Conservative victory in the 'khaki election' of the autumn 1900, soon warned Kitchener that only rebels whose conduct had been markedly 'mutinous' should be executed. French had already had a lengthy letter from Milner warning him that the army was there to protect the people, not to carry out vigorous policing. 'Whatever we may think of our Dutch friends,' he wrote, 'it won't pay to treat every Dutch speaking man as a rebel, unless he proves the contrary.'[91]

Neither Milner's practical advice nor Brodrick's long-range mediation had a great deal of effect upon French. He was fighting a war in which a number of his close friends had already been killed, or died of disease. French never acquired that stoic indifference to casualties which so easily passes for callousness, and his diary is full of mournful references to the deaths of subordinates. Moreover, juggling columns around the Cape in pursuit of the elusive commando leader Kritzinger seemed unlikely to bring the war to a speedy conclusion. Boer intransigence was prolonging a fruitless conflict, and if harsh measures would end the war, they were, in French's view, justified. French, in common with most other soldiers, took a practical and short-term view of the problem in Cape Colony: he was not concerned with more than ending the war.

The Standing Court Martial did its work with deadly speed. On 8 July French saw a deputation which sought clemency for some Boers condemned by the court. 'I heard their arguments,' wrote French, 'which were very vague and weak and told them I could not accede to their wishes.'[92] Kitchener had already confirmed two death sentences, and one of the prisoners, Marais, was hanged in the main square of Middelburg: French ordered some of the inhabitants to attend the execution, and noted that the incident 'made a great impression on the Dutch'.[93] He was clearly surprised when, at the end of the month, Brodrick complained about the hanging: 'The S of S for War has asked my reason for compelling the attendance of the disloyal Dutch at the executions. I have replied. There appears to be a fuss about it at home.'[94]

Brodrick's intervention produced no dramatic change of policy. Kitchener continued to confirm death sentences, and French went on with the executions. Haig felt that Kitchener's stick and carrot policy was by no means firm enough. In October 1901 he complained to Brinsley Fitzgerald, French's stockbroker, now thinly disguised as a Lieutenant of Imperial Yeomanry, that Kitchener's approach was not nearly strong enough. 'However,' he added, 'I suppose it is better to start late than never to start at all ... I hope several will be tried by court martial and shot.'[95]

Military operations in Cape Colony followed the now familiar pattern. French, usually on the move, on horseback or by train, co-ordinated the activities of numerous flying columns, each of them usually a mixture of cavalry and MI, often with a couple of guns. Military reputations were quickly made and as quickly lost. Lieutenant-Colonel Crabbe, for example, was one of the many who came unstuck. 'Crabbe has let Kritzinger slip by him,' French wrote angrily. 'This is entirely because of his failure to obey orders and move on Spitzkopf in time.'[96] Kitchener ordered Crabbe's replacement a few days later: he was lucky to finish his career as a Brigadier-General. Charles Callwell, who left the army as a Colonel in 1909 but returned to serve as Director of Military Operations during the First World War, also fell into disrepute: French accused him of letting a commando slip through his fingers and sending in exaggerated reports of Boer strength.[97]

For successful column commanders the future was bright. On 22 September French sent Roberts the names of officers who had done well at the heads of columns, or in command of groups of columns. Of the eighteen listed by French, few ended their careers below the rank of Lieutenant-General, and two – Allenby and Haig – became Field-Marshals. Horace Smith-Dorrien's name headed the list, an interesting fact in view of the subsequent French–Smith-Dorrien relationship. Douglas Haig's name was well up in the order of merit. Highly dependent though he was upon Haig's services as a staff officer, French had recommended him for command of what amounted to a brigade, believing that it would be unfair on Haig to deny him the opportunity.[98]

The war dragged on. Kritzinger was driven out of Cape Colony in mid-August, and on 5 September Harry Scobell surprised and captured Lotter's commando. This led Kitchener to write approvingly to Roberts that French deserved success: 'he has been working very hard for it and has had very little or no help from Cape Colony officials – I feel sure he will cope with the great difficulties in time'.[99] It was, alas, a case of taking two steps forward and one step back, for only two days after Scobell's victory Smuts lacerated a squadron of Haig's 17th Lancers at Elands River Poort. Another notable guerrilla leader, Gideon Scheepers, was captured on 11 October, and Kritzinger himself was at last captured just over a month later.

But still the war dragged on, and in early 1902, with commandos active in Cape Colony, Kitchener was less patient. 'French has not done much lately in the colony,' he told Roberts on 17 January. 'I cannot make out why, the country is no doubt difficult but I certainly expected more.'[100] He met French at Naawpoort in February, and reported: 'He was quite cheerful and happy about progress made, though it appears to me slow.'[101]

French had by now come to the conclusion that it was fruitless to expect quick victory in this sort of war: good intelligence—his Field Intelligence Department was first-rate – and methodical operations alone produced real results. In March he summed up the situation in a letter to Brinsley Fitzgerald, concluding: 'About September I fancy the job will be finished.'[102]

Slow or not, French was making progress. Smuts managed

to take his commando across the colony in the autumn of 1901, but he produced no practical results: the inhabitants did not flock to join him, and his tiny force narrowly escaped disaster on a score of occasions. French's columns, and the ever-increasing lines of wire and blockhouses, made it impossible for guerrillas to operate anywhere in Cape Colony except for the dreary and almost unpopulated wastelands of the west. And if Kitchener was disappointed, he gave little sign of it to French. Ian Hamilton, now acting as Kitchener's Chief of Staff, observed that French was 'very much left to his own devices ... he was one of the few men that Kitchener had trusted to do a job on his own'.[103]

By the late spring of 1902 many of the Boers who had been prepared to fight to the bitter end believed that the bitter end had indeed come. A delegation arrived in Pretoria on 12 April, and, although negotiations were complicated by friction between Milner and Kitchener, agreement was at last reached. On the morning of Sunday 1 June French received a telegram from Kitchener announcing that terms had been signed the previous night. Instructions to the surviving commandos were sent out under white flag, and British columns were ordered to cease offensive operations.[104] Four days later French was ordered to return to England once the surrenders were complete, but on the 20th he was ordered to hand over at once, so that he could sail on the same ship as Kitchener.[105]

Uncertainty had shrouded French's arrival in South Africa, but no such clouds surrounded his departure. He already knew what his next post was to be, for on 23 October 1901 Kitchener had telegraphed that the King had appointed him to command the 1st Army Corps at Aldershot in place of Buller. French had correctly discerned the hand of Roberts behind the appointment, and wrote to thank him in the warmest terms.[106] But his delight at receiving the appointment was tinged with guilt at replacing his old chief, Buller. On 23 November he wrote to Buller, stressing that he had not been offered the post, but had been appointed to it by the King, and adding: 'I can never hope to fill your place, but you may be sure I shall leave no stone unturned to profit by your lessons and follow in your footsteps.'[107] Nevertheless, he was delighted with the appointment. He told a personal friend: 'This is certainly a great piece of luck for me. I think it insures my participating in the next war, which is bound to come in a year or two.'[108]

He was a successful General, sailing home with a grateful Commander-in-Chief to what promised to be an enthusiastic welcome. It was a measure of his new sense of self-importance that he closed his diary for the war with the not unpretentious phrase, 'this concludes my campaign in South Africa'.[109]

Four

The Dangerous Years
1902–13

Lord Kitchener's sense of humour, never one of his more
notable characteristics, was conspicuous by its absence as he
descended the gangway of the *Orotava* at Southampton on 12
July 1902. He was not at all pleased to see the cheering crowd
on the quayside, and turned to mutter 'what's all this fuss
about?' to one of his staff. He found his tumultuous reception
in London later that day every bit as unsettling. Driving
through flag-decked streets past crammed pavements in an
open carriage with French beside him, Kitchener looked bale-
fully to his front, and maintained a stony silence except when,
on passing the colours of a regiment lining the route, he drew
French's attention to them by digging him in the ribs and
grunting 'Colours!'[1]

French's emotional character was far more susceptible to
praise and pageantry, and he was gratified by his enthusiastic
welcome in England, and by the honours which flowed in thick
and fast. The fall of Pretoria had already brought him a KCB,
and a KCMG, an unusual reward for a soldier, followed with
peace. French liked decorations – George V later complained
about his fondness for wearing 'stars in khaki' – and two
knighthoods in as many years was a pleasing achievement.[2]
Civic and academic recognition abounded: he received honorary degrees from Oxford and Cambridge, Kimberley presented
him with 'a very handsome and costly sword of honour', and he
became a freeman of a number of cities and livery companies.[3]

Sir John was very much in the public eye. For while
Kitchener shunned the limelight, French courted it. Kitchener

was deeply suspicious of the press, and on one occasion greeted a group of expectant journalists with the unhelpful bellow: 'Get out of my way, you drunken swabs.'[4] French, on the other hand, was always ready to chat to correspondents. Indeed, at times he was too eager to unburden himself to the press, and was to talk his way into trouble in more than one instance. His frank and breezy manner had already made him a favourite with war correspondents whose stories about 'the shirt-sleeved general' and 'Uncle French' reflected something of the affection which French aroused in his men, an affection which Kitchener had reported to Roberts:

> French is the most thoroughly loyal, energetic soldier I have, and all under him are devoted to him – not because he is lenient, but because they admire his soldier-like qualities.[5]

It is difficult to imagine the staid and slightly pompous French of the First World War smoking a disreputable briar pipe and enjoying being mistaken for a private soldier.[6] But such was the picture the press painted of French, the Boer War general: energetic, fearless, and with a lively and direct appeal to officers and men alike.

Between 1902 and 1914 French held a series of increasingly important appointments, and moved ever closer to the centre of the stage. His rise went on against a background of feverish activity in almost all branches of the defence establishment, and simply to chart his progress on a chronological basis could scarcely fail to present a mish-mash of strategy and tactics, personal crises and professional turning-points. In examining French's role in the dangerous years separating the Boer War from the First World War the strictly chronological approach will, therefore, be foresaken for a more thematic exploration, albeit at the risk of imposing more cohesion upon events than they may have possessed to those who lived through them.

Reform and Reaction: The Professional and Political Background

The Boer War had shown up flaws in almost every aspect of

Britain's military systems. Organisation, recruitment, equipment, training, tactics: all had been tried and found wanting. And the Boer War, important though it had been, was not as vital to British interests as, say, the defence of India. If a possible national catastrophe was to be averted, the problems posed by the South African experience had to be solved, and solved quickly.

St John Brodrick, who had become Secretary of State for War in the autumn of 1900, had grasped the essence of Britain's strategic problem. The army had to provide forces for three essential tasks: the defence of the United Kingdom, land operations in a European War and the defence of India. In the spring of 1901 Brodrick suggested that Britain should be able to send abroad a force of three corps and a cavalry division, some 120,000 men, while at the same time defending the United Kingdom and certain key garrisons overseas. The solution lay, he believed, in the formation of six army corps, organised on a regional basis. Two would be all regular, one mainly regular, and three would contain large non-regular elements. The scheme had many attractions, not least because it sought to make proper use of the militia and volunteers. But it was never really feasible in view of the poor state of recruiting and the inevitable demands for financial retrenchment.

But the Brodrick period was not altogether sterile. New barracks arose at Tidworth as Salisbury Plain began to threaten Aldershot's status as home of the British army, and new weapons and equipment were accepted into service. A. J. Balfour, who had succeeded his uncle Salisbury as Prime Minister in July 1902, took a marked interest in defence, and it was owing largely to his efforts that the decrepit Defence Committee of the cabinet was reorganised into the Committee of Imperial Defence (CID). A useful start was made on analysing the lessons of the Boer War, and the Elgin Commission, before which French gave impressive evidence, reported in July 1903.

Brodrick had serious disagreements with Roberts, and also got on badly with the King, and these frictions helped bring about his resignation in September 1903. He was replaced by H. O. Arnold-Forster, who immediately floated an ambitious project of his own. He envisaged the creation of two armies, a General Service Army to serve abroad and a Home Service Army for home defence. This scheme encountered hostility every bit as fierce as that which had greeted Brodrick's plan, and was a dead duck by the time the Conservative government fell in December 1905.

Arnold-Forster had, however, made at least one useful contribution to reform, for it was he who offered the post of chairman of a committee which was to study the organisation of the War Office to Reginald Brett, Viscount Esher. Esher is a character of pivotal importance. 'The spider in his web', he exercised power without responsibility, and shunned public office but wielded vast influence. Esher had met French during the sessions of the Elgin Commission, and had reported to the King that he believed French to be the outstanding general of his generation, not only a brilliant commander in the field, but also a man who had thought deeply about his profession.[7] Esher also praised French to Balfour, but the latter was not entirely convinced, and it was his opposition which prevented French's appointment to the Esher Committee.[8]

The Esher Committee got to work with phenomenal rapidity, and between February and March 1904 it recommended sweeping changes in the organisation of the War Office, changes which were implemented with a speed which horrified some observers. Colonel Henry Wilson, a rising staff officer and a Roberts protégé, wrote, with characteristic virulence: 'This is most scandalous work – destroying and constructing at a pace and with a lack of knowledge which quite takes one's breath away.'[9] It is nevertheless clear that Esher was supported not only by the King and the Prime Minister, but also by many serving officers. Wilson objected partly because the reorganisation abolished the post of Commander-in-Chief, stripping Roberts of his job in less than dignified circumstances.[10]

R. B. Haldane, a Lowland Scots lawyer of formidable intellectual attributes, took the War Office in the new Liberal government of 1906, largely because nobody else would touch it with a bargepole.[11] He was careful to avoid the headlong plunge into reorganisation which had marred the efforts of his predecessors, and was in any case fortunate that most of the

Esher recommendations had been adopted; the tide of reform was already running strongly when he came to office.

Haldane made wide use of the younger generation of professionally-minded officers, and between 1906 and 1909 carried out a series of reforms which did more than merely correct the defects revealed by the Boer War: they created an army capable of taking the field, promptly and effectively, in a European conflict. The efficiency of the new General Staff and the reorganised War Office steadily improved, and new Field Service Regulations gave the army a solid framework of military doctrine. But Haldane's most difficult task was to break through the obstacles which had blunted the efforts of Brodrick and Arnold-Forster, and thoroughly to recast the field army and the reserve system.

Powerful undercurrents within the defence establishment helped shape Haldane's course. The General Staff had gradually concluded that France was no longer Britain's most probable continental enemy. Hard-hitting memoranda pointed to the threat posed by Germany, and serious planning for a war against Germany began in 1905. In 1907 the Anglo-Russian *entente* at last laid the spectre of a Russian descent upon India, and left the General Staff free to concentrate upon the German problem.

But not all the General Staff's enemies were foreign. There was mounting conflict between it and the Admiralty within the CID, conflict which revealed a profound difference of opinion on basic strategic issues. The traditional view of strategy relegated the army to a secondary role, which the increasingly effective General Staff not unnaturally resented. With the decline and subsequent disappearance of the Russian threat, the growth of the German menace, and the navy's insistence, in the 1903 invasion inquiry, that invasion was impossible as long as command of the sea was retained, the way was open for the General Staff to smash the restraints of Admiralty-dominated strategy and seize a European role for the army. The navy, dominated by the autocratic Sir John Fisher, was unwilling to see its time-honoured supremacy eroded by the machinations of the General Staff, and virtually boycotted the CID from 1905–6. There thus arose a serious divergence of policy which was not to be reconciled until the outbreak of war in 1914, and which persisted, to a more limited extent, into the war itself.[12]

The General Staff's growing preoccupation with the prospect of aiding France or Belgium in a war against Germany, coupled with the anxieties of the Foreign Secretary, Sir Edward Grey, provided vital ingredients for Haldane's plans for army reform. He was not presented with the multifarious hypotheses of 1902–5, but with an increasingly sharply-focused picture of a European war in which Britain would support France against an aggressive Germany. A Special Army Order dated 1 January 1907 laid down that the regular army at home would, in time of war, form an Expeditionary Force of one cavalry and six infantry divisions. Haldane experienced greater difficulties with the auxiliary forces, largely because of the intransigence of many influential militia officers, but he was soon able to institute an army and Special Reserve of 80,000 men, whose reinforcements would keep the Expeditionary Force in the field, and a Territorial Force of fourteen divisions for home defence.[13]

Although Haldane had taken great care to sample the best military opinion, his measures did not meet with universal approval. Many regular officers felt that the Territorials could never attain a sufficiently high standard of training, and a majority of senior officers, led by Roberts himself, felt that they were a shabby substitute for conscription which, they believed, was essential, at least for home defence.

Roberts and the National Service League managed to get the invasion issue re-opened at a second invasion inquiry in 1908, seeking to demonstrate that the Territorials would be unable to carry out their task, but the inquiry's conclusion was broadly similar to that of 1903.[14] And whatever the military pressure, conscription, as Haldane realised only too readily, was never a practical political possibility at the time.

The Ladder of Success: Professional Advancement and Private Tribulations

Sir John French took up residence in Government House at Farnborough, two miles up the road from his old home,

Anglesey House, in September 1902. His appointment to Aldershot had given him the substantive rank of Lieutenant-General, and his finances were already solid enough for him to tell his stockbroker friend, Brinsley Fitzgerald, with that cheery insouciance which always made French such a disaster where money was concerned:

> I am sure you will take me at my word dear old boy and ask me for money whenever it is required for anything you may do for me ... as regards other shares I would far rather you would act exactly as you think best.[15]

The splendour of Government House was short-lived, for on 16 January 1903 the place was gutted by fire, and French, in London for the night, returned to find the garden 'strewn with every conceivable article of household equipment, everything was white with frost, and the skeleton of the house was bespangled with icicles'.[16] The family moved into the Royal Pavilion while Government House was being rebuilt. It was a wooden building, sparsely furnished and decorated, on Queen Victoria's instructions, with striped wallpaper to give the impression of the inside of a tent. Designed only for summer occupation, it was bitterly cold in winter.

French's main preoccupation at Aldershot was with increasing the efficiency of I Corps. He identified himself with the corps in the same way that he had identified with the cavalry in South Africa, and strained every fibre in his efforts to stave off what he perceived as threats to its well-being. French believed that, whatever the merits of the Brodrick or Arnold-Forster schemes, I Corps should form the army's main striking force, and as such should be kept fully up to strength, with a division ready to move at short notice, whether as a small force in its own right or as the advance guard of the remainder of the corps.[17] In August 1904 he attended a meeting of all the available members of the Army Council, and reported happily to Esher:

> They have fully consented to the principle that the First Army Corps should be organised on quite a different footing to [sic] the other Commands, and

that the staff I work with in peace shall be the staff which I take to war.

He nevertheless regretted that the Army Council had decided not to bring his second division fully up to strength.[18] Lieutenant Maurice Brett, Esher's son, who was serving as French's aide-de-camp, replied that his father had pressed upon Sir Neville Lyttelton, Chief of the General Staff, the necessity of giving French as free a hand as possible. Esher was confident that French would lick the corps into the shape he wanted. Brett added:

> There is no doubt that you will be hampered in details as you say in your letter but as the A[rmy] C[ouncil] never know their own minds two days running and you know yours perfectly, my father thinks if you stand firm you are sure to get your own way.[19]

French saw the threat to I Corps as twofold. On the one hand, he suspected other commanders of empire-building, and in September 1904 complained that they were 'trying to lay violent hands on the troops of the First Army Corps'.[20] On the other, the War Office exhibited a worrying tendency to interfere with the Aldershot command. French accused the Army Council of meddling in matters that did not concern it, complaining to Esher: 'They'll go on in the same kind of halting, stupid, small-minded way as long as they hold their appointments.'[21]

Sir John was generally on good terms with Haldane, who valued his advice on the restructuring plan.[22] Nevertheless, when Haldane attempted to reduce the Guards by two battalions, thereby effectively destroying one of the Aldershot brigades, French put his opinion, as usual, in unvarnished terms. Esher reported the matter to the King, who was far from pleased at the prospect of losing two Guards battalions. 'So strong was the impression made upon the mind of Mr. Haldane by the arguments used by Sir John French,' he wrote confidently, 'that Viscount Esher feels satisfied that the proposals will not be proceeded with.'[23]

French's desire to weld the Aldershot corps into a

homogeneous fighting formation was anything but discreditable. It reveals, however, a single-minded determination bordering on the obsessive, and it brought Sir John into open conflict with the Army Council, giving rise to a number of spectacular rows which throw useful light on to his character and convictions.

French had never made any secret of his opposition to the 'Blue Ribbon' concept of a General Staff open only to officers who had passed Staff College. It is therefore surprising to discover that he allowed his supporters to press his candidacy for the post of Chief of the General Staff in the winter of 1903–4.

Both Esher and Fisher recommended French for the job. 'He has never failed', claimed Esher, while Fisher urged: 'Plump for French and efficiency.' Fisher suggested that French was young and energetic; he had a brilliant record in South Africa: he was a first-rate corps commander and a good judge of men. But he also had another attribute which, so Fisher believed, made him unique amongst his colleagues: he was an enthusiastic believer in joint military and naval operations. 'In his belief', wrote Fisher, 'he is almost solitary amongst all the Generals, who want to play at the German army.'[24]

There was more than a little truth in this assertion. Sir John remained sympathetic to his old service, and in 1903 he summed up a lecture given by a naval officer with a forthright declaration of the navy's importance, and the hope that combined manoeuvres would soon be carried out.[25] Fisher regarded French as a potential ally in the growing conflict between the naval and military views of strategy: with French as CGS, perhaps the army's demands for an independent European role would be muted.

French's candidature ended when Edward VII, who considered him too junior for the post, refused to sanction his appointment. French looked upon this with undisguised relief. He told Esher:

> To go to London now would be the very last thing I desire and agree with you that N[eville] L[yttelton] should certainly remain where he is. I expect any

CGS would have trouble with A[rnold]-F[orster] for a time![26]

French soon found himself locked in conflict with the Army Council over the question of staff appointments. He recommended one of his aides-de-camp, Major Algy Lawson, for the vacant post of Brigade-Major of the 1st Cavalry Brigade. The appointment was not approved: Lawson had not passed Staff College, and a significant minority of the General Staff refused to countenance the entry of an unqualified outsider into the charmed circle. French was furious. Algy Lawson was a personal friend, and Sir John had formed a very high opinion of his ability. He agreed with Esher that it was absurd to require the qualification of Passed Staff College (psc) for many staff appointments, which could perfectly well be held by selected regimental officers.[27]

Worse still, French suspected a General Staff conspiracy, master-minded by Wilson and Brigadier-General Henry Rawlinson, commandant of the source of all this iniquity, the Staff College. He warned Esher:

> Now *both those fellows* did much harm in Roberts' time. They are very clever and were R's special "Pets." They are now *trying it on again* and if the Army Council are to retain the confidence of the Army these two young gentlemen must have their wings clipped. Their chance is in the weakness of others and I am not alone in thinking they are getting round A-F.[28]

French made it clear to the CGS that he was not prepared to accept 'no' for an answer in the Lawson case, and Lyttelton referred the matter to a committee chaired by Lieutenant-General H. D. Hutchinson, Director of Staff Duties. The committee shrugged off pressure from Esher, and reported against waiving the rules, a view with which the Army Council concurred.

Esher suggested that French should take the matter up direct with Arnold-Forster, but warned him that it was not a serious enough issue to warrant a last-ditch struggle.[29] But French's blood was up. He thundered against 'the intolerable interference of Hutchinson and Co.', and threatened to play what he considered to be his trump card. 'I want to approach the King as our Commander-in-Chief and Military Head. If he approves I have nothing more to say, but if not, I will not stand it.'[30] This was a clearly-implied threat of resignation, but this extreme step proved unnecessary. On 23 December Esher informed him that Arnold-Forster had given way, and 'signed Lawson's appointment on the mere rumour of your indignation. So you have won all along the line'.[31] A similar dispute, this time involving Maurice Brett, was also resolved in French's favour, though not until Sir John had presented the case to Edward VII's private secretary for onward submission to the King.[32]

The squabble over Lawson's appointment is another graphic illustration of French's determination. He was prepared to take on the Secretary of State and the Army Council, formidable adversaries for a district commander who was still only a relatively junior Lieutenant-General. The fact that he went as far as to threaten resignation gives some indication of his ability to lose his sense of perspective over issues that were anything but crucial. The victory increased his sense of self-confidence and self-importance, and seemed comforting evidence of his ability to trade on his prestige and influence to do very much as he pleased.

The Lawson affair also demonstrates the importance French attached to the monarch. He had been deeply depressed by the death of Queen Victoria, but soon developed a high regard for her successor. He met Edward VII frequently, at the King's visits to Aldershot, and at dinners, audiences and garden parties. They corresponded on matters dear to the King's heart, such as the efficiency of the Household Cavalry, or the correct dress for inspecting the Corps of Commissionaires.[33] French shared with many of the leading figures of the day, Esher and Haldane for example, a deep devotion to the King. Years later he wrote wistfully to Esher: 'I do think of our old days in King Edward's time and what a difference he made in all our lives. I hope he *knows* how we think of him.'[34]

French left Aldershot at the end of November 1907 to become Inspector-General of the Forces in the place of the Duke of Connaught, who went, not entirely willingly, to be Commander-in-Chief and High Commissioner in the Mediterranean. The post of Inspector-General had been created in 1904 as a result of Esher's recommendations, and had initially been offered to, and declined by, Roberts. Esher had been grooming Sir John for it for some time, although there was one nasty moment when it seemed that Lieutenant-Colonel Repington, military correspondent of *The Times*, was suggesting that Kitchener should take the appointment on his return from India.[35] Esher believed that French would have a far-ranging influence as Inspector-General, and in September 1906 he wrote:

> For the sake of the army nothing could be more perfectly satisfactory than that you should be responsible for its supreme training. The Inspector-General of the future will be a very different functionary from the Duke of Connaught.[36]

French was well aware that he owed the appointment to Esher, and asked him for his views before he began to lay down principles of his own.[37] The King also backed French for the post, and his private secretary conveyed to Sir John the King's hope that he would be ruthless and searching in his new duties.[38]

French needed no urging. He made it abundantly clear that he regarded the post as anything but a sinecure, and at once drew up a memorandum on the department's duties, a document which Esher considered 'quite excellent in composition and ... very well expressed. The General's term of office should leave the army in a different state to [sic] that in which it is found today.'[39] Sir John saw the inspectorate as 'the eyes and ears' of the Army Council: its prime concern was the 'immediate efficiency of the troops for war'. The department's annual routine was laid down, going from the preparation of memoranda and instructions, to observation and inspection, and culminating in the annual manoeuvres in August–September.[40]

The reorganised inspectorate soon showed its teeth. Harry Scobell, whose column had done so well in Cape Colony, commanded the cavalry division in the August 1908 manoeuvres. He was a well-connected officer and a close friend of

Sir John's, but his staff had soon discovered that London figured more prominently in his itinerary than did the less fashionable Aldershot training areas.[41] The manoeuvres gave clear evidence of his languid approach to his profession. He cantered on to the field on a magnificent thoroughbred, and surveyed the four brigades drawn up before him. After a long pause for thought, he unveiled his master-stroke: the division would advance in column of troops.[42]

French watched the exercise with disgust, and at once reported that Scobell was 'quite unfit' for his post, and had no excuse for his failure, because the raw material of the division was superb. Despite his personal regard for Scobell, French considered himself duty bound to report on his dismal performance, though he was well aware that it would finish Scobell's career.[43]

The fate of Scobell gave a broad hint as to French's policy as Inspector-General. Whatever his failings in other respects, French's work with the inspectorate leaves no doubt of his zeal and perception in the spheres of organisation, tactics and training. Divisions were inspected during detailed and searching exercises, and thorough inspection reports listed the inspectors' conclusions. French paid attention to numerous topics which lay outside his immediate experience and service background. Such things as the target allocation of heavy artillery, the use of howitzers for indirect fire, the need for better infantry trenches and the use of machine-guns as a substitute for an infantry firing-line, all received attention in his reports.[44]

Some significant strands emerge from French's painstaking reports. There can be no doubt that the influence of Sir George Luck lingered on. In 1908 French complained that the cavalry needed more practice in 'rapid mass movement', and the following year he reiterated the complaint, adding: 'too much time was given up to "manoeuvres" and to the working out of extensive "schemes." Very little, if any, "drill" in large masses was practised.'[45] French believed that drill and discipline were important because of their morale-producing qualities. The battlefield was a dangerous place, and 'moral ascendancy' was vital. 'The discipline that keeps men steady on parade is the same discipline that is required to keep them quiet and attentive in the excitement that precedes an assault.'[46] French's belief in the need for moral ascendancy echoed the writings of some continental strategic thinkers, and it undoubtedly originated in his forays into military literature, and had been confirmed by his experience in South Africa.

Sir John was generally dissatisfied with the performance of the infantry, and his last report, in 1911, concluded that: 'We appear to have got into a groove, and that a deep one, and some great shake-up is necessary to give freshness and originality to the work.' Some of the difficulties originated, in his opinion, in the existing company organisation. He advocated double companies, that is, the formation of four large companies instead of eight small ones.[47] The reorganisation, which he later forced through when CIGS, made him less than popular with many infantry officers, who complained about cavalrymen tinkering with things they did not understand.

Until August 1910 French's responsibilities included British troops serving abroad under the control of the War Office, and in the winter of 1909–10 he carried out a tour of inspection in the Far East. In the summer of 1910 he visited Canada, at the request of the Canadian Government. He reported that there were some organisational defects in the Canadian system, but he found it generally satisfactory. He declined to comment on demands for 'universal service' in Canada, arguing that the existing voluntary system had not had a fair trial.[48] This confidence in voluntary part-time service rather than short-term conscription was also reflected in Sir John's support of the Territorials in Britain. He shared the doubts of many senior officers about the effectiveness of Territorial artillery, but he saw the TF as a generally satisfactory alternative to conscription for home defence, and formally denied that he supported conscription.[49]

French had been succeeded at Aldershot by Lieutenant-General Sir Horace Smith-Dorrien, a forward-looking infantryman with liberal views on discipline and man-management. French had worked with Smith-Dorrien in South Africa, and the two men were on reasonably cordial terms when French left Aldershot. Thereafter their relationship deteriorated rapidly: the friction flared into a blaze in 1914–15, and its embers glowed on long after French's death. Smith-Dorrien's biographer understandably casts French as the villain of the piece, and on balance Smith-Dorrien was probably more sinned against than sinning. History would be ill-served by an attempt to denigrate Smith-Dorrien, a capable and popular General, in order to exonerate French. Nevertheless, the quarrel is important, and deserves more than the simplistic mud-slinging it usually receives.

There were a number of reasons for the clash. Both men attracted firm friends and obdurate enemies: Sir Tom Bridges believed that both were self-opinionated, and Hubert Gough suggested that personality differences had always prevented them from getting on well together.[50] Smith-Dorrien was happily married to a young and pretty wife: on at least one occasion he commented on French's lax sexual morality.[51] They also disagreed on some fundamental points concerning discipline. On taking over at Aldershot Smith-Dorrien had abolished the pickets which had roamed the streets in search of drunken soldiers – rarely a fruitless mission then or now – and later he rescinded the order which had prohibited soldiers from entering public houses when on manoeuvres. He also transformed the physical appearance of Aldershot by more than doubling the amount of playing fields available to the troops, by cutting down large numbers of trees between Government House and the town, and by building better barrack facilities.[52]

French was singularly unimpressed by this burst of activity. At the emotional level, he regretted that his Aldershot, the garrison-town he had known as subaltern, colonel, brigadier and corps commander, was gone forever. He felt that Smith-Dorrien's reforms reflected badly on his own tour of command at Aldershot: he had opened a number of soldiers' institutes, and felt that Smith-Dorrien was getting all the credit. French believed that he had left the Aldershot corps in excellent order: why, then, did Smith-Dorrien want to interfere with it? There can be no doubt that Smith-Dorrien did a great deal for Aldershot, but French may be forgiven for feeling nettled. He was in much the same position as someone who sells a house he has built and decorated, and which he regards as perfect, only to find that the purchaser changes the colour-schemes and builds an extension. The architectural merits of the case are almost irrelevant: the vendor is likely to feel hurt and annoyed.

But French's mounting suspicion of Smith-Dorrien had

other, more practical causes. Sir John was a confirmed believer in old-style discipline, a quality which, he argued, was one of the main links binding armies together at moments of crisis. Weakening the ties of discipline in garrison would, he feared, have damaging consequences in the field. The storm-clouds thickened when Smith-Dorrien turned his attention to a subject at the very core of French's heart: the cavalry. Smith-Dorrien was dissatisfied with the musketry of the cavalry under his command, and was vexed to observe that they spent more time mounted than dismounted. On 21 August 1909 he saw all his cavalry officers in the 16th Lancers' mess, and forcefully told them the error of their ways.[53] French was as affronted by what he perceived as an insult to his own arm as Smith-Dorrien was by French's preference for double companies in the infantry.

A final element in the quarrel was Smith-Dorrien's temper. Worse, far worse even than French's, Smith-Dorrien's wild rages were a by-word in the Edwardian army. There were suggestions that they were more than just bad temper caused by neuralgia. Esher once dined with Smith-Dorrien to find out if he had indeed 'changed and weakened' as the rumour had it, but found him perfectly normal.[54] The victims of Smith-Dorrien's spectacular bursts of rage found them utterly astonishing, and, in the nature of things, it was natural that some of French's friends should be the unwilling recipients of Smith-Dorrien's frenzy.[55] Lord Crewe, a school friend of Smith-Dorrien's, turned him down for the post of Commander-in-Chief in India on the grounds that his health and temper were not equal to the task. 'When unwell,' wrote Crewe, 'the unlucky result is loss of temper and self-command, to an extent which might be serious in such a position.'[56] By 1910 the battle-lines were drawn, and the mutual hostility between French and Smith-Dorrien was, as Charles Callwell put it, 'almost a matter of common knowledge in the service'.[57]

There was no official residence attached to the post of Inspector-General, and Lady French and the family were soon installed in the Manor House at Waltham Cross in Hertfordshire, rented from Lady Meux, widow of the brewery owner Sir Henry Meux. But the Manor House, despite Gerald French's implications, was never really the French family home, because Sir John was rarely there.[58] Indeed, while several hundred of his letters survive, the author has encountered only two addressed from Waltham Cross. The truth is sad, if predictable. French's popularity on his return to England from the Boer War had not diminished his desirability as a lover, and by 1907 he was regularly involved in the discreet affairs which bubbled away beneath the outwardly placid surface of Edwardian society.

In October 1903 French had given away his niece, Georgina Whiteway, at her marriage with Fitzgerald Watt, who had served as a yeomanry officer in South Africa. Fitz Watt fell under French's spell, and was soon spending the manoeuvre season as his aide-de-camp. He was an official ADC when French was Inspector-General, and later acted as Private Secretary when Sir John was appointed CIGS. In 1904 French often borrowed Watt's London flat at 20 Park Mansions, and in 1905 he purchased it, although the negotiations seem to have clouded their relationship for some months.[59] The flat was a useful spring-board for French's extra-marital activities, and when Lady French and the children moved to Hertfordshire, French stayed in London.

Fitz Watt was by no means the only man who felt the magnetic appeal of the thick-set and cheerful cavalry General. George Gordon Moore was an American who had made a fortune out of building railways. His love for extravagant parties and loud music, and his jet-black hair and flat, dark face gave him the air of a Red Indian, and made him an unmistakable, if not entirely well liked, figure on the London scene. French met him in about 1909, and the two men soon struck up a warm friendship. Moore hero-worshipped French, and Sir John had a high opinion of Moore's judgement and enjoyed his lively and stimulating company, so different from that of the men he met in the course of his professional life. In the summer of 1910 French told Brinsley Fitzgerald that George Moore had asked him to join him in taking a house at Lancaster Gate, but he had kept the flat for the time being.[60] Before long, however, French was established at 94 Lancaster Gate, a large house with a pleasant view over the park. It was a fashionable area at the time, and within easy striking distance of French's London haunts. The move did not go unnoticed: it was a big house for two men living on their own, and in 1913 Henry Wilson noted: 'Dined Johnnie French at 94 Lancaster Gate. An enormous house and what he is doing there I can't think.'[61] Wilson was being uncharacteristically naive. French and Moore were ardent ladies' men – Moore was devoted to the beautiful Lady Diana Manners – and the house enabled them to entertain in the lavish style which Moore's income made so easy.

Lady French gave no sign of the pain that her husband's infidelity caused. Her children sided with her, and it was not until French's last days that he was reconciled with them, and even then it was only Gerald who really re-established a proper relationship with his father. Regard for her husband's position was one of the motives which prevented her from making a fuss. But a close examination of her surviving ephemera suggests that there was another, more poignant, reason for her silence: she still loved him.[62]

In March 1912 Sir John followed Lyttelton's successor, Sir William Nicholson, as Chief of the Imperial General Staff. While French was obviously the front runner for the post, it was a not altogether satisfactory appointment. French had never expressed much confidence in the General Staff, and had little regard for either of his predecessors. These two factors were closely related, for French's suspicion of the General Staff as a body sprang in great measure from his dislike for several of its members. At one meeting of the CID he had become scarlet and speechless with rage while listening to Sir Neville Lyttelton expounding upon the wisdom of defending Egypt by means of naval vessels in the Suez canal.[63] While commanding at Aldershot he pursued a feud with Hutchinson, Director of Staff Duties. He strongly advised Arnold-Forster to put Haig in Hutchinson's place, suggesting that this would also compensate for the inadequacies of Lyttelton.[64] He had absolutely no time for Nicholson, who, he said, 'was born to be a damned nuisance to everyone'.[65]

French might have thought better of the General Staff had he known more about it. In January 1912 he attended the annual staff conference at the Staff College, and told Esher, with evident astonishment: 'I was surprised and delighted to hear the discussions which went on, and the concise and lucid manner in which they all expressed their views on the subjects raised.'[66] French's growing respect for staff officers did not, however, cause him to modify his view of their strictly subordinate nature. Later the same year he addressed Staff College students, pointing out that many difficulties could be overcome:

> if you endeavour to comprehend clearly the definite line of demarkation which exists between the function of the commander and the function of the Staff. It is the duty of the Staff to present all the facts of the situation to a commander with perfect accuracy and impartiality and then to take the necessary measures for carrying his decisions into effect.

He concluded by warning his audience that they must not set themselves apart from regimental officers and men by the 'affectation of superior knowledge'. Their role was largely 'one of self-effacement and unselfishness'.[67] Staff officers were tools in the hands of the commander, mere mechanicals who should do as they were told. French's desire to curb the pretensions of staff officers may have struck a chord in the hearts of regimental officers. But it was a strange attitude for one presiding over a General Staff which was in the process of establishing itself as an important policy-making institution.

Sir John had no doubt that his goal as CIGS was, as he told the heads of his three directorates on 16 March, 'to get the army ready for war'.[68] He soon discovered that having a clear sense of mission was no guarantee of success. Internal reforms were impeded by friction within the military establishment; budgetary constraints hindered attempts to improve pay or procure new equipment and, in the last analysis, French was ill-suited by temperament, experience or inclination for the business of piloting a desk amongst the shoals of the War Office.

He had at least one point in his favour. In June 1912 Haldane became Lord Chancellor, and was replaced as Secretary of State for War by Colonel Jack Seely. A yeomanry officer with a well-deserved reputation for personal bravery, Seely lacked political acumen, and someone cruelly quipped that if he had more brains he'd be half-witted. But he got on remarkably well with French, and their friendship was destined to survive the vicissitudes of 1914 and end only with French's death.

French nevertheless made heavy weather of his job. His preference for firm and conclusive action almost always produced a squall as disappointed parties protested at what they saw as high-handedness. In the autumn of 1913, for example, the selection board, over which French presided, passed over four Generals. There were accusations of partiality, and the King's private secretary wondered if selection was really such a good idea. He warned French that many officers were:

> animadverting in by no means favourable terms upon the decisions of the Board, and regretfully looking back to the days of the Duke of Cambridge. NB: HRH used to say that he did not believe in selection, as he always found that officers were 'much of a muchness'.[69]

A similar dispute attended the introduction of double companies into the infantry. French told Seely that a majority of district commanders, 'the great mass of brain power in the army', and wondrous to relate, the Kaiser himself, all favoured the change.[70] His opponents put in a brisk counter-attack, arguing that French and Haig, the scheme's leading advocates, were cavalrymen and therefore ignorant of the real issues at stake.[71] French replied sourly that the debate was only staggering on because the Quartermaster-General, who had changed his mind over the matter, had been nobbled by 'a few rabid riflemen'.[72] Sir John eventually won the day, but only after sweating copious quantities of ink.

The difficulty of recruiting sufficient officers and men had worried French for some time, and he was in favour of reducing officers' expenses and increasing their pay. In January 1913, in a persuasive memorandum to Seely, he pointed out that the duties of officers were becoming increasingly complex: there had been a steady rise in the officer establishment, and at the same time social changes had reduced the numbers of applicants. French was not in favour of sweeping innovations in officer recruitment, and always retained a sneaking affection for officers from the traditional sources, but he stressed that the army had to appeal to 'the wider classes from which our professions are recruited', if it was to obtain sufficient officers of the right calibre.[73] French's urgings played a great part in bringing about an increase in army pay and allowances with effect from 1 January 1914.[74]

Honours had continued to flow in since French's return from South Africa. He became GCVO in 1905 and GCB four years later, and in 1913 he succeeded Wolseley as Colonel-in-Chief of the Royal Irish Regiment. His relationship with George V was far less intimate than it had been with Edward VII, but it was the King who, in April 1913, told Seely that he proposed to make French a Field-Marshal in the next honours list.[75] French was delighted. He was sixty-one, and it was nearly forty years since he had joined the 19th Hussars at Aldershot: promotion to Field-Marshal seemed a fitting prelude to the end of a long and distinguished career. He had mixed feelings about the future. CIGS was, after all, the pinnacle of a peacetime career. He could hardly step down to another appointment, and in any case his age was now against him. But he had spent ten years being groomed for command of the British Expeditionary Force (BEF) in war, and he half hoped that his chance might come before he fell out of orbit. The dark beauty of war still held a curious fascination for him. He was later to write to his mistress, Winifred Bennett, of 'glory and her twin sister murder', and to admit that, although he felt war to be barbarous, 'in the campaigns I've been in during my life I've never felt satisfied at the end of any and have looked forward to the next.'[76]

The Road to Mons: War Planning

From the time of French's appointment to Aldershot it was clear that he would hold an important command in the event of a future war, and from 1906 onwards he was officially recognised as Commander-in-Chief designate of the BEF. In February 1906 he told Major-General J. M. Grierson that he would be Commander-in-Chief if war broke out, with Grierson as his Chief of Staff, and later that year Haldane told Esher that French would indeed command the striking force.[77] The arrangement was reiterated with each successive war scare, and even after French's resignation as CIGS in 1914 there seems to have remained an agreement that the command would still be his.[78]

Sir John's position as embryo Commander-in-Chief brought him into the forefront of strategic planning. This was something of a paradox. French had been given I Corps and the promise of the BEF primarily because of his performance as a tactician in South Africa. The fact that he would command BEF naturally provoked his involvement in the formulation of war plans. French thus became a planner by accident, and there is no evidence that he had any aptitude for the task. He certainly had ideas aplenty and could produce sound written appreciations of militiary problems. In October 1904, for example, he reported on the strategic importance of the Dardanelles in a paper whose conclusions Fisher warmly applauded.[79] But in the CID, of which he became a member in 1905, he usually addressed himself only to 'nuts and bolts' questions: the impossibility of keeping horses at sea for long periods with an embarked force, or the perils of reducing the strength of the Brigade of Guards.[80]

Part of French's problem lay in his inability to sustain a consistent attitude on major strategic issues. This is, perhaps, not totally surprising, for the whirlpools and rapids of inter-service politics and personal loyalties sometimes made it difficult for even the most astute to steer a straight course. But French found it particularly hard, torn as he was between regard for his old service and concern for the status of his current one. And if he could take a strong-minded stand on individual issues, such as the appointment of Algy Lawson, he remained equally capable of harbouring undercurrents of doubt which could surge up to produce a sudden change of direction.

In the autumn of 1905 Esher and Sir George Clarke, Secretary of the CID, were increasingly perturbed by the development of the Morocco crisis, and were concerned to find out how England might best assist France if the crisis led to a general European war. Clarke discovered that the navy had no co-ordinated plan for offensive operations, and there had been minimal consultation between the General Staff and the Admiralty on war plans. Esher chaired a four-man committee which met in December 1905 and January 1906 to consider Britain's role in a European war.

French was a natural choice for the committee, whose other members were Clarke and Captain Ottley, the Director of Naval Intelligence. Sir John would command the striking force if it was dispatched, he was highly regarded by Esher, and his reputation as an enthusiast for amphibious warfare gave him some inter-service appeal. Yet his enthusiasm for combined operations had already begun to cool. In the 1904 manoeuvres he had commanded an 'invasion' force which had landed at Clacton and advanced inland. Although the landing itself was unopposed and the disembarkation was carried out in peace-time conditions, there were serious difficulties with the horses and guns and some stores were lost.[81] The manoeuvres gave French first-hand experience of the difficulties which would attend even a small-scale raid on the British Isles, or, for that matter, a British landing on an enemy coast. Two years later French told the *Daily Mail*'s readers that, while a raid by 50,000 men would cause serious disruption to Britain, the presence of trained volunteers would dissuade an enemy from risking such a venture.[82]

The committee considered the options open to Britain when it met at the CID's offices at Whitehall Gardens on 19 December. There were three main possibilities: purely naval action; combined action, such as a landing on the Baltic coast; and purely military action in the form of direct aid to France or Belgium. The committee decided that the navy should investigate the possibilities of joint action with France, and should also examine a wide-ranging spectrum of contingencies from direct aid to France to amphibious operations in the Baltic. French was asked to produce his corps mobilisation scheme, together with details of timings, embarkation ports and reinforcement plans.[83]

At the next meeting on 6 January 1906, French unveiled the Aldershot mobilisation plan, which envisaged embarkation on the tenth day of mobilisation. There was also a scheme to save time by completing mobilisation on French territory. The meeting decided that no military forces would be sent to the Baltic until the situation there had become clear. French's force would go straight to Belgium if that country was invaded;

if not, it would go to France. It was, however, recognised that there were some suitable landing places in the Baltic, such as the island of Rugen.[84] The navy did not fall upon this crumb of comfort with alacrity. Ottley had not produced the information requested at the first meeting, and it appeared that the navy favoured gaining command of the sea before it did anything else.

It was not merely the navy's reluctance to co-operate in joint planning that led to the triumph of the General Staff. In late December 1905 Repington of *The Times* had been in contact with Colonel Huguet, the French military attaché in London. Grierson, the Director of Military Operations, told Repington over dinner of the General Staff's plans for sending troops to Namur and Antwerp. Huguet was very much in favour of military rather than naval assistance, and on 5 January, after seeing him again, Repington met Esher and Clarke at Whitehall Gardens. It was agreed that Repington should sound out the French General Staff on an unofficial basis: he visited Paris in mid-January with a list of questions, to which the French replied.[85] Grey and Haldane were busy electioneering at the time, but they met briefly in Scotland and agreed to continue these 'conversations' in a semi-official manner. On 14 January Haldane obtained the Prime Minister's approval for the General Staff to carry on negotiations with the French, on the strict precondition that none of the plans would be binding on the government.

By mid-January the General Staff's view of strategy was fast becoming dominant. On 12 January the committee discussed the Admiralty's plan for shipping troops to northern France, and the size of the force – two corps, four cavalry brigades and two mounted infantry brigades – was agreed upon. Grierson, who attended the meeting, was asked to prepare a plan for moving this army from the south coast ports to Le Havre.[86] The final meeting on 19 January again included Grierson, but Ottley was not present, indicating Fisher's disapproval of the way the debate was going. Grierson outlined the General Staff's detailed plans for sending the force, and, although the committee now had the answers to Repington's questionnaire, and knew that the French favoured unified command, with British supremacy at sea and French on land, it concluded that the British force would be 'an independent body under the general control of the French commander-in-chief'.[87] Seldom have so few words caused so much trouble.

French had attended all the committee's meetings, and had expounded the Aldershot mobilisation plan on 6 January. His own views on the matter are, however, remarkably difficult to gauge. The official reports of the meetings contain no suggestion that French was anything but enthusiastic about the General Staff plan, but Repington heard that Sir John favoured Fisher's preference for 'scratching about on the Baltic', and was opposed to a junction with French forces on French soil.[88] Repington's evidence has been seen as more proof that French still favoured an amphibious solution, but it is at best inconclusive.

Other sources indicate that French simply could not make up his mind. On Christmas Day 1905 he suggested to Esher they should lunch with Huguet to extract information from him. In the same letter, however, he said that the separation of forces brought about by the Baltic plan was not too dangerous.[89] By February he knew enough of France's war plan to write approvingly: 'It is the best disposition they could adopt, and if carefully and skilfully worked should go far to frustrate a German invasion.'[90] But he still gave no clear indication as to where he thought the British force should go.

On balance, it is probably true to say that French favoured sending direct aid to France or Belgium, but did not rule out the Baltic as totally impossible. Two points of importance, as far as French is concerned, emerge from the 1905–6 discussions. The first is the emphasis they placed on Antwerp. The weight of General Staff opinion and in particular the sustained urgings of Henry Wilson, eventually ensured French's complete conversion to the 'WF' (With France) plan for assistance to France, but the idea of landing at Antwerp never entirely left his mind. The question of command was also significant. Nothing, from 1906 to 1914, suggested to French that he would be anything less than an independent commander, in support, but not under command, of the French Commander-in-Chief.

Until the Morocco crisis was resolved in late March, French believed that war was likely, and had several meetings with Grierson to discuss appointments in the expeditionary force.[91]

In June he wrote to Brinsley Fitzgerald: 'All our "War" plans are over for the present, but one never knows how soon they will rise up again.'[92] The following month he visited the French manoeuvres in Champagne, and submitted an enthusiastic report on the French army's performance. The Belgians were altogether less inspiring.[93] French had travelled to the continent every year since his return from South Africa, usually to tour Napoleonic battlefields. His visit in an official capacity did not, however, pass unreported, and was seen as positive evidence of an Anglo-French military *rapprochement*. Once again his reluctance to send journalists away empty-handed got him into trouble. Grierson, who accompanied him, agreed that all he did was to 'utter a few platitudes to the correspondent of the *Figaro*', but it was enough for Sir John to be accused of giving unauthorised interviews to the French press.[94]

Sir John visited France again in November. This time the trip was unofficial, and he stayed at a country inn near the village of La Bouille in the north-west, in an effort to learn the language. He wrote that the place was delightful, and his linguistic ability was steadily improving,

> I haven't heard a word of English spoken since I landed at Dieppe. I have conversations twice a day. In the morning with the curé, to whose house it is an hour's walk, and that suits me well. In the afternoon or evening with a kind of village schoolmaster who is a very knowledgeable person. Then I read a lot of French — the paper etc.[95]

All this effort was, unfortunately, not conspicuously successful. His French remained extremely shaky, and always broke down under pressure. Fitz Watt told his daughter of one particular howler, the mistranslation of footman as *piedhomme*.[96]

The following summer, a few months before his time at Aldershot came to an end, Sir John entertained the French Commander-in-Chief designate, General Michel, at Government House, at last rebuilt after the fire. The visit was a brainchild of the Foreign Office, which had suggested that he should receive a group of French officers, ostensibly to repay the hospitality of autumn 1906. The fact that the visit was, officially, 'of a personal nature', did not prevent the French from watching the Aldershot divisions on manoeuvres and visiting London.[97] Sir John was most impressed by his visitors, and his daughter Essex found them 'far more polite, and nicer' than British officers.[98]

In the winter of 1908–9 French was a member of the 'Military Needs of the Empire' subcommittee of the CID. This body considered that the existing General Staff scheme was the best available at the moment, and recommended that work on it should be continued. It stressed, though, that the question of Britain's entry into the war was one which the government of the day alone could answer. During the discussion French toed the General Staff line, and even opposed a scheme of Esher's in order to do so.[99]

If French was increasingly convinced by the logic of the General Staff's case concerning strategy, he remained obdurate over conscription, regarding Robert's hypothesis of a 'Bolt from the Blue' — a sudden invasion which could best be met by a conscript home defence army — as 'absurd'.[100] He sat on the 1907–8 CID subcommittee which studied the invasion question, and as the case against the invasionists gathered momentum, he remarked to Slade, the Director of Naval Intelligence, 'I see the process of pulverisation has begun.'[101] The subcommittee rejected the 'Bolt from the Blue' theory, but concluded that the prospect of a surprise attack was not so remote that it could be totally ignored. The home defence force should be adequate to repulse small raids, and to force the enemy to invade with a force so large that it was unlikely to escape detection on the high seas. At least two regular divisions should be retained at home until the Territorials were fit to take the field.[102]

Keen though the General Staff was to carve out an independent role for itself, it was far from unanimous in its inclination for close collaboration with the French. Major-General Spencer Ewart, who followed Grierson as Director of Military Operations (DMO), never saw Huguet, and the work was carried on by subordinates.[103] Nor was Sir William Nicholson, who shared Ewart's fear that staff negotiations with France would be likely to bind Britain more tightly than the government might wish, more helpful. He took great care to have nothing to do with Huguet, and never even met him socially.

In August 1910 Brigadier-General Henry Wilson became DMO. He was an ardent francophile, passionately committed to the French cause. He threw himself wholeheartedly into the task of planning the BEF's arrival in France. Previous plans had been 'entirely academic', and 'not a single practical step had been taken to give effect to them'. Wilson changed all this, and was primarily responsible for the detailed plans of mobilisation, transport and concentration of the BEF.[104]

Wilson was a Roberts protégé and, indeed, remained on very close terms with Roberts until the latter's death in 1914. This in itself was enough to make French suspicious of him, but by 1906, when he supported Wilson's candidacy for command of the Staff College, French had begun to change his mind.[105] By 1912 the change was complete, and Wilson had become French's single most trusted adviser. Part of the attraction was, typically, emotional. French was captivated by Wilson's chatty persuasiveness, his humorous flattery and his burning sense of purpose. And whatever Wilson's defects — driving ambition and unscrupulous intrigue among them — he was a remarkably capable staff officer, expert at exactly that branch of the military craft which always remained a dark mystery to French.

In the summer of 1911 another crisis darkened the international horizon as the German gunboat *Panther* arrived at Agadir. The prospect of war revived all the old problems of a clash between the rival strategies of the General Staff and the Admiralty. There was a brief attempt to avoid confrontation. On 20 August Fisher wrote that French had been to see him to discuss continental strategy, 'as the tool of Sir William Nicholson. I told him to go to Hell.'[106] French was the obvious candidate for such a mission. His views on amphibious operations might have changed, but he was convinced of the need for close co-operation between the two services, and spoke on exactly that topic to the Navy Club that year.[107]

Compromise proved impossible, and the CID met on 23 August to resolve the matter. In the morning, Henry Wilson unfolded the General Staff plan with what Captain Maurice Hankey, the CID's Secretary, called 'remarkable brilliancy'. Nothing had been left to chance: so detailed were the plans that they included *'dix minutes pour une tasse de café'* at Amiens. The Admiralty plan stumbled on to the stage in the afternoon. It was simplistic, crude, and relied upon obsolescent tactical concepts. The meeting ended with the rout of the navy.[108]

The war scare was serious enough for the autumn manoeuvres to be cancelled, ostensibly because of a shortage of water in the exercise area, and Sir John departed for France with Grierson and Huguet. Grierson recorded how: 'Crossing the probable German lines of advance between the Belgian frontier and Verdun, French talked to me of war in which I should be his CGS and [Sir Charles] Douglas and [Sir Arthur] Paget command armies under him.' They conferred with the French War Minister and with General de Castelnau, Assistant Chief of the General Staff, and Grierson noted, on their return to London, that 'things look well for war'.[109] Henry Wilson had already been active, visiting Paris in late July to assure the French General Staff that, subject always to government approval, the 150,000 strong BEF would concentrate in northern France if war broke out.

His visit coincided with a significant shift in French strategy. General Michel, Vice-president of the *Conseil Supérieur de la Guerre* and earmarked for command of the French armies in war, favoured an essentially defensive project, Plan XVI, and called for the unusual step of merging regular and reserve units to increase front-line strength. Michel's plan was rejected in July, and a decree reduced the importance of his post. The CGS was henceforward to command the army on mobilisation, and on 28 July this post was entrusted to a compromise candidate, General Joseph Joffre, a large, well-fed sapper, whose benign features – he was nicknamed Papa Joffre or *le grand-père* – gave little clue of his remarkable determination and resolution.[110]

In the summer of 1911, with war likely and planning in a state of flux, Joffre was eager to get help wherever he could. General Dubail hurried off for talks with the Russians, who agreed to advance into East Prussia to take some of the weight off France. Joffre's immediate revisions of the existing project made provision for the inclusion of British troops on the French left, by no means an unimportant sector in the terms of Plan XVI. But over the next two years, as Joffre's staff drafted their final scheme, Plan XVIII, the balance of forces seemed to improve, and Joffre's hearty optimism encouraged him to plan for an offensive. 'Whatever the circumstances,' ran his orders, 'it is the Commander-in-Chief's intention to advance with all forces united to attack the German armies.'[111] To the authors of Plan XVIII, British co-operation was desirable rather than essential, and the BEF was allotted a relatively unimportant role, concentrating in the triangle Le Cateau–Hirson–Maubeuge, exactly where the French planners expected the Germans not to be. Bearing in mind the continued emphasis that the BEF's arrival 'remained doubtful', it would have been rash for Joffre to have planned to deploy it in a vital sector.[112] Involving Britain in the war was less a matter of obtaining immediate practical assistance than a guarantee of subsequent reinforcement, coupled with maritime and economic support.[113]

Shortly after returning from France, Sir John was again on the move. This time he visited the German manoeuvres in Mecklenburg as a guest of the Kaiser. The visit was less incongruous than it seems. French was, after all, an acknowledged cavalry expert, and was well-qualified to cast an eye over the top-boots and spiked helmets of the Guard Cavalry Division. There was no certainty that the planners would ever translate their schemes into reality, and the popular invasion literature and growing anti-German sentiment could not cut at a stroke the military ties which bound Britain and Germany. The Kaiser was a British Field-Marshal, and took a paternalistic interest in the regiment of which he was Colonel, the Royal Dragoons. French had a number of acquaintances in the German army, and until the outbreak of war he enjoyed friendly relations with the Kaiser himself, who features as 'the Emperor William' in French's diaries.

After a long day in the saddle during manoeuvres, French retired to his quarters for a bath. He was disturbed by persistent knocking at the door, and eventually opened it to discover a German officer bearing the insignia of the Order of the Red Eagle. French was duly given the order, clad only in his bath towel, in what Gerald French called the world's most informal investiture. He later received a signed photograph of the Kaiser from the hands of the monarch himself, who remarked, with a singular lack of tact: 'You may have just seen how long my sword is: you may find it just as sharp.' Sir John narrowly contained an understandable, if undiplomatic, burst of rage.[114]

In November 1912 the worsening situation in the Balkans persuaded Seely and French that war was, once again, likely to break out. On 8 November Wilson helped French draw up a list of the holders of key appointments, and four days later the Army Council finalised these details. The BEF's two armies were to be commanded by Haig and Smith-Dorrien, while Allenby led the cavalry division: Grierson was to be CGS.[115] On Sunday 17 November French, Haig, Grierson and Wilson met to discuss strategy. Smith-Dorrien, designated as an army commander less than a week previously, had unaccountably been replaced by Sir Arthur Paget, who attended the meeting in his new capacity. Wilson found the discussion depressing, and wrote crossly of 'some amazing contributions to strategy and a general want of knowledge and clear thinking which makes me hope we don't go to war just at present'.[116] There was the almost predictable conflict with the Admiralty over transport arrangements, and in this sphere at least Wilson approved of French's efforts. 'Johnnie French working well for us,' he wrote, 'and hitting out.'[117] But he remained convinced that Sir John really lacked the intellectual apparatus that was necessary for his job.[118]

The Balkan crisis was still fizzing away when, in February 1913, Repington's articles in *The Times* revived the invasion debate, demanding compulsion for home defence and attacking the Territorial Force's (TF's) low establishment. The resultant inquiry included the Prime Minister and leading naval and military men, among them French. The committee examined the matter in considerable detail, and did not report until the spring of 1914. Its conclusions were similar to those reached in the 1908 inquiry. French agreed with Roberts that the retention in the United Kingdom of one regular division would prevent an invasion by less than 70,000 men, but the committee believed that two divisions gave a better margin of safety. This was not the conclusion that the General Staff had hoped for, for it whittled away at the already small size of the BEF.[119]

In the summer of 1913, with the invasion inquiry still in progress, Sir John, accompanied by Grierson and Wilson, visited the French manoeuvres in Champagne. French was pleased enough with what he saw, and was received with the sort of pageantry which always delighted him.[120] But Wilson, committed though he was to the concept of coming to the aid of France, had nagging doubts about some of the strategic assumptions of the French General Staff. The French were certain that the main clash would take place along the Franco–German border, and that few, if any, Germans would be found north of the River Meuse. Wilson suspected that the Germans might also move north of the river, and he persuaded Sir John to re-open negotiations with the Belgians, through the British military attaché in Brussels, with a view to gaining permission for the Anglo–French forces to enter Belgium. The negotiations were a dismal failure: in 1914 the Belgians actually deployed a division to guard against a landing by British troops.[121]

Wilson's influence grew steadily. The autumn manoeuvres took place around Aylesbury in late September, with Haig and Paget as army commanders. The manoeuvres opened several eyes. Haig's performance in the 1912 manoeuvres had been far from masterly, and a staff officer noted: 'Haig was so completely outmanoeuvred that the operations were brought to a premature end.'[122] In 1913 he was equally unfortunate, and his dispositions left a three-mile gap in the British centre.[123] Yet Haig himself was dissatisfied with the way the manoeuvres had been conducted. French had acted both as Exercise Director and commander of the British Force, which manoeuvred against a skeleton enemy. Haig considered that the Field-Marshal's performance had been poor, and Sir John himself admitted that 'the manoeuvres taught *us all* many lessons'. He was thoroughly annoyed by one of Repington's *Times* articles, which implied that he had found it difficult to beat a skeleton enemy, and he castigated the journalist's remarks as 'childish, *stupid*, and inclined to be rancorous'.[124]

The manoeuvres did more than diminish Haig's confidence in French and Wilson's in Haig. They brought about a change in the post of CGS designate. On 26 September, before leaving the exercise area, Sir John told Wilson that, on the evidence of the past week, he was no longer happy with Grierson, and they discussed possible solutions. Wilson believed that French would have given him the job, but his lack of seniority – he was still only a Brigadier-General – prevented this.[125] The choice eventually fell on Major-General Sir Archibald Murray, an intelligent and cultivated man, who had made a bad recovery from a stomach wound received in South Africa. Sir James Edmonds described him as 'a complete nonentity'.[126] This is probably a harsher verdict than the evidence warrants, but he was certainly not the man for the job. A good staff officer in peacetime conditions, his health was not equal to the strains of campaigning, and his personality was ill-suited for dealing with a headstrong and mercurial Commander-in-Chief.

Early in 1914 a staff exercise took place in the gymnasium at the Royal Military College with the object of testing the workings of the BEF's headquarters. Major-General Sir William Robertson, commandant of the Staff College, acted as exercise director and Henry Wilson played the part of CGS. The exercise was a disaster, and Robertson drew attention to Wilson's ignorance of certain regulation procedures. He then turned to French, and said, in a stage whisper, easily audible to all around: 'If you go to war with that operations staff, you are as good as beaten.'[127]

Five

The Tactical Debate
1902–14

French was a cavalry general. The tribal markings of the mounted arm were heavy upon him, from his bow-legged strut to his hunting stock and Newmarket crop. His military perspectives widened as he clambered up the ladder of promotion, but cavalry – its equipment, organisation and tactics – always remained dear to his heart. And while his views on strategy were sometimes inconsistent and his knowledge of staff-work hazy, on the subject of cavalry his opinion was always crystal clear and forcefully expressed.

The technical innovations in weaponry which occurred, with increasing rapidity, from the mid-nineteenth century onwards, brought with them far-ranging changes in tactics. But although the relationship between weapons and tactics was always intimate, it was rarely simple and there was a tendency for tactical theory to lag behind the lethal realities glistening in the world's arsenals. The frightful consequences of faulty tactics should not blind us to several important facts. Evaluating the effects of untried weapons on an unfought battle is a hazardous business, and even the comparatively simpler task of transferring the lessons of one war to a slightly different scenario has yawning pitfalls. Tactical lessons seem clear in retrospect. For the French knights to charge English archers at Agincourt or for French columns to assail British lines in the Peninsula appears every bit as ill-advised as it was for British infantry to stride to destruction on the Somme. At the time, however, the gallop towards the taut longbows, the scramble up the slope, or the measured march across no-man's-land, all seemed feasible solutions to a tactical conundrum.

It is not only the difficulty of assessing the effects of new weapons that makes tactics such a fragile art. Politics within the defence community—the tissues of personal ambitions, friendships and enmities, together with competition between arms and services for status and cash—makes it all the more difficult for decisions regarding weapons and tactics to be made purely on the merits of the case. It is a truism to say that armies are generally unwilling to embark upon radical change. This reluctance is usually attributed to the bone-headed conservatism of the military establishment, and certainly the resistance of elderly senior officers to change, and their suspicions of novel views put forward by their subordinates or, worse still, by outsiders, have undoubtedly played their part. But not all the motives for reaction are discreditable. Soldiers tend to be preoccupied with facts rather than speculation, and with the evidence of their own experience rather than tendentious extrapolations from the theories of others.

Between the end of the Boer War and the beginning of the First World War European armies devoted a great deal of time and ink to scrutinising the tactical changes produced by the improvement of weapons, and in studying recent conflicts, notably the Boer War and the Russo–Japanese War, to see what lessons could be drawn from them. Books, periodicals and discussion groups examined the problem from all angles, and it was certainly a multi-faceted question: artillery, infantry and cavalry were all receiving new weapons whose probable effects were analysed in exhaustive detail.

French was most directly involved in one particular aspect of the tactical debate, the controversy over the role and armament of cavalry. The dispute was by no means a new one, and for years before the Boer War soldiers had argued about the real functions of cavalry. There were, broadly speaking, two schools of thought. Traditionalists stressed that improvements in firearms had not rendered impossible the cavalry's old battlefield role of shock action. Cavalry should therefore be equipped with sword or lance, and trained to charge home when the opportunity arose. The carbine or rifle could be carried as secondary weapons, but it was upon the *arme blanche* that the trooper should rely. Innovators attacked these views as conservative and outdated. While they were divided on the merits of the cold steel — some wished to discard it altogether, while others sought to retain it for use in emergencies — they agreed that the firearm, not the sword or lance, should be the trooper's main armament. Cavalry would produce the greatest effect by dismounting to employ fire, rather than by remaining mounted in an effort to apply shock. There was a general agreement that the increasing size of battlefields and the improvement in communications was likely to increase the cavalry's role in war, if the true essence of this role could only be grasped. [1]

Sir John's service as a regimental officer, and particularly his experiences in the Sudan, put him on the traditionalists' side of the fence. He placed great emphasis on scouting and reconnaissance, and believed that firearms were essential for these tasks. But the prime function of cavalry remained shock action, and for this an effective steel weapon, and extensive training in its use, was essential. South Africa did not significantly alter his views, but it brought him into the forefront of the debate, for he emerged as the country's most successful cavalry leader.

The innovators were not slow to point out that events in South Africa hardly conformed to the cavalryman's view of war. There had been very few charges with the *arme blanche*, and a Boer who was cut down by the sword or impaled by a lance was a very exceptional, as well as unlucky, man. Erskine Childers believed that there had been only four real cavalry charges, and the casualties inflicted by cold steel totalled perhaps 100. [2] To those traditionalists who claimed that South Africa was full of abnormalities which would be unlikely to recur elsewhere, Childers suggested that the real peculiarity of the war was that the Boers did not carry the *arme blanche*. With that single exception, all the other alleged peculiarities of the war — shortage of water, exhausted horses and difficult ground — would recur, in greater or lesser measure, elsewhere. [3]

But Childers was forced to grapple with a significant paradox. He acknowledged that French was the ablest cavalry officer of his age, and a weighty authority where cavalry matters were concerned:

Any critic who founds his criticism on that war, finds himself continually confronted by the seemingly unanswerable argument that our ablest cavalry officer believes in the *arme blanche*, and our ablest cavalry officer, himself endowed with long experience, must be right.[4]

Childers considered the facts to be self-evident: but the cavalry, to whom correct interpretation was of paramount importance, remained unconvinced. This failure to accept what now appears to be incontrovertible evidence and to persist in training for mounted action is often regarded with mirth and derision.[5] In the early part of this century, however, the facts seemed far less conclusive, and many other factors — personal and social, as well as purely military — influenced the debate.

The events leading up to the fall of Bloemfontein convinced French of the merits of traditionally-armed cavalry. They could charge, as Gore's squadrons had at Elandslaagte, or they could fight dismounted, as they had on so many occasions in the Colesberg operations. French was well aware that the protagonists of Mounted Infantry used the same campaign experience to prove the superiority of MI. He believed, though, that cavalry possessed several important advantages over MI. In the first place, their horsemanship and horse-mastership were better. And even if MI were so well trained as to neutralise these two points — and there were few such MI in South Africa in 1900 — the cavalry still had the edge. They alone carried the *arme blanche*, and it was this weapon which endowed them with the 'cavalry spirit', giving them all those qualities of dash and élan which the pedestrian-minded MI could never have. French never denied that there was a great need for MI in South Africa: horses gave infantry mobility without which they were of limited use. But for them the horse was a means of transport, nothing more.

Roberts drew different lessons from the experience of South Africa. He already entertained serious doubts about conventional cavalry by the time he arrived there, and the Poplar Grove fiasco confirmed his suspicions. On 5 April 1900 he spoke enthusiastically to French about MI, but French was not convinced.[6] A few days after this French wrote to Colonel Lonsdale Hale, sometime professor at the Staff College, thanking him for championing the cavalry against 'the chatter and cackle of our military opponents'. He warned Hale that the lessons of the campaign would not be properly understood: MI were undoubtedly useful, but they were no substitute for real cavalry. He quoted the opinion of the German gunner, Major Albrecht: 'Why don't you teach your cavalry to shoot instead of *trying* to teach your infantry to ride? They never saw us because they are always employed in trying to keep their hats on.'[7]

But the 'chatter and cackle' grew in volume. Roberts ordered French to convene a committee to investigate the organisation and equipment of cavalry. In September 1901 French told Roberts that he was collecting the views of regimental commanders, and would forward his conclusions as soon as possible. He suggested that cavalry, like other arms, would gain strength as their firearms improved, and agreed that dismounted action would become more frequent. He was, however, adamant that no changes should be made which would reduce the cavalry's 'power of offensive action *as cavalry*', and with this in view a better sword should replace the existing 'antiquated weapon'.[8] The subsequent formal report of French's committee roundly condemned the existing carbine and demanded an effective rifle, but did not suggest that this should be more than a secondary weapon.[9]

Roberts had made up his mind on the matter long before the report reached his headquarters, and the cavalry were ordered to relinquish their steel weapons for the duration of the campaign. Sir John complained that with swords had gone the cavalry's highly-prized moral ascendancy. The Boers, he told Roberts, 'never attempted to come ... on with the dash and vigour they display now when the cavalry being deprived of their weapons for mounted attack have always to get off their horses and resort to their fire arms'.[10]

French's case in the cavalry debate was firmly established by the time he left South Africa. He was sure that the cavalry required an effective rifle, not merely a carbine, and should be expert in its use. He agreed with Major-General Edward Hutton, the army's greatest MI expert, that it was 'the bullet that kills', but stressed that the preservation of 'the moral power of cavalry' was what the argument was really about.[11] French's evidence to the Elgin Commission hammered home these views. Although he was delighted that the cavalry were to receive a new rifle, he 'absolutely disagreed' with the suggestion that this should be their main weapon. Sword or lance would remain supreme, although he emphasised that he would take 'the greatest pains' to train cavalry in shooting.[12]

By this time the debate was gaining momentum, and it had become apparent that much more was at issue than the survival of the cold steel. The innovators broadened their attack to encompass the wider questions of officer recruitment and training. In the spring of 1903 Hutton told French that although he agreed that cavalry did indeed require some capacity for shock action, the real issue was not so much weaponry as attitudes. Only when officer recruitment was reformed and professional zeal developed would the cavalry 'become a professional service and be removed above the level of social, plutocratic and aristocratic control'.[13] French had high regard for Hutton, and the two remained friends throughout the controversy, but it was comments like this that persuaded French that if the innovators had their way, cavalry as he knew it would leave the British army for ever. Whatever his intellect told him about the officer recruit problem – and he was well aware that the expenses of joining the cavalry deterred many worthy young men and produced a chronic shortage of officers – his emotions swept him in another direction. Years later he summed up his admiration for the cavalry with the telling conclusion: 'I think *their officers* are better.'[14] He violently dissented from Hutton's view of cavalry officers, and attacked those who claimed that 'officers care about nothing but polo and hunting'.[15]

The clash of personalities lent bite to the debate. French always preserved a respectful tone when corresponding with Roberts, but growing mistrust festered beneath the polite phraseology. And while French suspected that Roberts was merely the stalking-horse for more dangerous innovators, Roberts believed that French was being hustled along by his own hot-heads, notably Haig.[16] Assurances of mutual respect, and protestations that the differences between them were trivial, characterised the correspondence between French and Roberts, but neither man was unaware that a pitched battle was under way.

Roberts won the first engagements. He complained to the Adjutant-General that the cavalry were disregarding the lessons of South Africa, and suggested that the sword should be replaced by an automatic pistol. In March 1903 the Adjutant-General circulated a memorandum embodying Roberts's views. The document marshalled impressive historical evidence to suggest that shock action was obsolete, and deduced from this that: 'our cavalry should be armed with the most effective firearm, viz the rifle'. The importance of swordsmanship was fully recognised, but the lance was no longer to be carried on active service.[17]

Six months later Roberts presided over a conference which examined cavalry tactics. Haig championed the conservative cause. 'I strongly maintain,' he wrote, 'that the chief method of action for cavalry is the mounted role. He [Roberts] hotly opposes me and the principles laid down by me in Part IV Cavalry Drill "Collective Training."'[18] Haig's *Cavalry Training*, which owed a good deal to French's 1898 *Drill Book*, emerged in 1904. It contained plenty of fodder for the traditionalists, but its conservative tone was muted by a powerful preface written by Roberts himself. He drew the attention of the cavalry to the arm's increased importance as a result of long-range guns and rifles. These new developments meant that 'instead of the firearm being an adjunct to the sword, the sword must be an adjunct to the rifle'. He believed that there was still a place for shock tactics, but emphasised that the charge would not be in close order, and must be carefully prepared by rifle and artillery fire.[19]

This preface was the high-water mark of Roberts's success, and the traditionalists' counter-attack led to a protracted and bitter struggle. French spearheaded the counter-thrust. In response to a request from Arnold-Forster, he submitted a memorandum to the Army Council which embodied his views on the subject:

> Having served in the cavalry nearly all my life, I have formed the strongest opinion that ... If it is laid

down by regulations that cavalry soldiers are to regard the rifle as their principal weapon, and that shock tactics are to be resorted to under very exceptional circumstances, we shall soon find that we have no cavalry in the British Army worthy of the name.

He then fastened upon an argument which had emerged since the Boer War and pointed out that it was in a European war, against powerful enemy cavalry trained for shock action, that the weaknesses of Roberts-style horsemen would be fully apparent. The war would begin with a 'great cavalry battle', and it was in this cavalry *versus* cavalry phase that shock action, or the threat of it, would be crucial. Without indoctrination in shock tactics, the cavalry spirit would evaporate.

> It is difficult to define what one means by the 'cavalry spirit', but it is a power which is *felt* and *realised* by those who have served much with that arm. Its attributes are 'dash', 'elan', a fixed determination always to take the offensive and secure the initiative. Such a spirit can never be created in a body of troops whose first idea is to abandon their horses and lie down under cover in the face of a swiftly-charging mass of horsemen.

He agreed that 'no stone should be left unturned to make cavalry soldiers the best possible shots and thoroughly adept in all dismounted duties'. Nevertheless, he concluded, it was the cavalry spirit that really mattered, and that could only be preserved if the *arme blanche* retained pride of place.[20]

Both sides drilled their forces for the next phase of the struggle. Kitchener expressed his support for Roberts, saying that cavalry should be able to seize and hold positions, 'instead of wandering about, sometimes aimlessly, seeking for the enemy's cavalry in order to charge them as their only role in war'.[21] Kitchener, however, was in India, and Roberts's power-base was crumbling. His departure as Commander-in-Chief of the Army weakened his position: amazingly influential though he remained, he had lost his grip on the reins of power, and his opponents knew it. French made sure that the King was kept well informed of the progress of the debate, and warned him that Roberts wanted to convert the cavalry into Mounted Rifles. Roberts denied that this was so, and told Sir John that he merely sought to give the cavalry soldier more confidence and make cavalry capable of acting independently of other arms, 'and this I think you must acknowledge it has never been able to do since the introduction of long-range rifles'. French remained obdurate, and scrawled in the margin: 'Relief of Kimberley – Capture of Bloemfontein – heading off Cronje at Paardeberg – capture of Barberton – were all the *independent* work of cavalry and Horse Artillery.'[22] He replied to Roberts:

> as I tried to explain to you the other evening I have only made the same representations on the subject to the army council as I have repeatedly made to you as Commander-in-Chief. Nothing can make me alter the views I hold on the subject of cavalry and I am sure they are nothing like so much at variance to yours as you appear to think.[23]

Roberts was well aware of the damage the traditionalists' royal contacts were doing his cause. He told Sir Charles Douglas that the King would give way if Roberts was supported by the younger officers who, he felt sure, recognised the wisdom of his argument.[24] There is no evidence that Roberts was correct in his supposition concerning younger officers, and it soon became evident that a majority of senior officers were opposed to him. Sir Robert Baden-Powell, the Inspector-General of Cavalry, was forthright: 'I fully agree with General Sir J. French's remarks as regards the role of the cavalry.'[25] Sir Francis Grenfell told the CGS that he agreed with French, and, moreover, added that he had not spoken to a single cavalry officer who supported Roberts.[26] His remarks were echoed by Sir Evelyn Wood, who was worried about the disappearance of the cavalry spirit, and who also believed that Roberts lacked real support.[27] Lyttelton himself felt that French was right. South Africa was something of an exceptional case, and Sir John's insistence upon careful musketry training proved that he had a balanced view of the subject.[28]

The Army Council eventually decided, in February 1905,

that *Cavalry Training* should be issued without its controversial preface, but offered a sop to Roberts and his supporters by confirming the abolition of the lance as a weapon of war.[29] French took no notice of the latter decision. His 1st Cavalry Brigade at Aldershot was composed of lancer regiments, and he let them carry their lances on field training. There was widespread sympathy for the lance within the cavalry, and in June 1909 it was at last reinstated as an official weapon.

The return of the lance showed the way the battle was going. In 1907 the new edition of *Cavalry Training* decreed that 'thorough efficiency in the use of the rifle and in dismounted tactics is an absolute necessity'. It nevertheless encapsulated the classic article of faith: 'It must be accepted as a principle that the rifle, effective as it is, cannot replace the effect produced by the speed of the horse, the magnetism of the charge, and the terror of cold steel.'[30]

The publication of the new *Cavalry Training* was not an isolated phenomenon, but an element of a general counterattack launched by the cavalry, a move in which French played an important part. In 1906 the first edition of the *Cavalry Journal* appeared, promoted by, amongst others, C. S. Goldman, who had already published an adulatory study of French's exploits in South Africa. The journal contained articles on weapons, tactics and organisation, and sought to awaken a professional spirit within the cavalry as a whole. In 1911 it was put on an official basis, and its editorship became one of the duties of the commandant of the Cavalry School.

1906 also saw the publication of an English translation of Lieutenant-General Frederick von Bernhardi's *Cavalry in Future Wars*. French's preface consisted of a summary of his own views on cavalry, together with his comments on the performance of the arm in the Russo-Japanese War. Although it was subsequently attacked by Erskine Childers in both *War and the Arme Blanche* and *The German Influence on British Cavalry*, it was by no means an extreme or illogical statement of the cavalry case. Sir John opened by suggesting that the cavalry spirit was not totally inimical to dismounted action:

I am absolutely convinced that the Cavalry spirit is

and may be encouraged to the utmost without in the least degree prejudicing either training in dismounted duties or the acquirement of such tactical knowledge on the part of leaders as will enable them to discern when and where to resort to dismounted methods.[31]

It was in the cavalry battle, which cavalry theorists agreed would open the next war, that shock tactics were likely to be essential. Once the enemy cavalry had been disposed of, friendly cavalry would find good opportunities for the use of fire. French was not suggesting that cavalry should be squandered in headlong charges against unshaken infantry. Although shock action could be used against infantry who were already in disorder, or were surprised on the march, its main use was in the opening cavalry battle, where quick and decisive action to take the initiative was essential. It was the old question of moral superiority, and French was convinced that this could only be seized by aggressive and confident troopers trained to charge home when the time came.

Not all Sir John's argument was this reasonable. He attempted to write off the failure of cavalry in the Russo–Japanese war by asserting that the Japanese were indifferently mounted and their riding was poor, and that the Russians 'thought of nothing but getting off their horses and shooting'.[32] French was certainly wrong as far as the Russians were concerned. Indeed, one of the official British observers pointed out that sketchy training in dismounted action was one of the major reasons for the ineffectiveness of Russian cavalry.[33] Sir John was arguing on the basis of inadequate facts. Balanced reports of the Russo–Japanese war did not emerge until at least a year after he had written the preface: he fell into the trap of twisting the available information to produce the conclusion he wanted.

On the whole, however, French's views, as expressed in his preface to von Bernhardi's book, were anything but unrealistic folly. Even Sir Ian Hamilton, an opponent of the *arme blanche*, was worried that an excessive emphasis on fire might sap the cavalry's offensive spirit, and Brigadier-General E. C. Bethune, an MI expert with wide experience in South Africa, agreed with French that the secret of the mounted arm was to combine fire and shock in the right proportions.[34] French put the case for the compromise when summing up a lecture given by Bethune. 'One amateur centaur,' he said, 'would dash the sword and lance entirely out of the cavalryman's hand. Another fanatic (Beau Sabreur) would throw the horseman's splendid fire-arm to the wind.' But he repeated his belief that before MI could be of any use, 'the enemy's cavalry must be absolutely overthrown': and this was where shock, and the moral superiority it engendered, really counted.[35]

The debate spluttered on until the outbreak of the First World War. The appearance of Erskine Childers's anti-*arme blanche* books in 1910–11 went some way towards weakening the cavalry case, as Roberts, who himself wrote the preface to *War and the Arme Blanche* hoped it would.[36] But despite the fact that Roberts was supported by a number of senior officers, including Smith-Dorrien, Ian Hamilton and Henry Wilson, he was unable to dislodge the cavalry from the position it had gained in 1906–7. Indeed, the only major change between 1907 and the outbreak of war favoured the conservatives: in September 1913 the Army Council decided that MI would not be used in a European War, and the two existing Mounted Brigades, a mixture of MI and cavalry, were broken up.[37]

It is ironic that French, who had done so much to champion the cause of conventional cavalry, eventually believed that the cavalry tended to go too far in training for shock at the expense of fire. At the conclusion of the 1908 manoeuvres he criticised the unsatisfactory performance of dismounted duties. Haig complained that he 'gave vent to some terrible heresies such as the chief use of Cavalry Division in battle is their rifle fire: led horses to be moved, and men need not be close to them'.[38] Sir John again criticised bad dismounted work in his 1909 Inspection Report. He warned that led horses must be better concealed, and pointed out forcefully that 'cavalry officers require also to familiarise themselves with the methods to be employed in a fire-fight'.[39]

French's demands that the cavalry should master dismounted tactics were not mere stratagems for countering the arguments of the reformers. He agreed that, in most circumstances, the rifle was mightier than the sword. But Childers was right when he said that belief in the sword was a matter of faith.[40] Moral superiority, French believed, was a key element in war, and the cavalry spirit animated men to capture this superiority. If the psychology of the sword was lost, whatever the weapon's practical value, the cavalry spirit was gone for ever. French might have argued his case less vigorously had he possessed a higher regard for his opponents, and had he not believed that the survival of the cavalry as an arm was at stake. Given his tendency to over-identify with his subordinates, his opposition to far-reaching reform within the cavalry is easily comprehensible. This opposition was by no means illogical or destructive, but it did facilitate the survival of some tactical concepts which French himself regarded as outdated.

Sir John's preoccupation with the cavalry did not blind him to the changes that improved weapons were bringing about in the tactics of other arms. He was one of those who pressed hard for the rapid adoption of the 18-pounder field gun in 1904, telling Esher that any reasonable increase in weight was a small price to pay for increased firepower. He emphasised that it was the first few rounds of gunfire that counted: 'A good target soon becomes an indifferent or bad one – hence the necessity for effective fire power QUICKLY.'[41] Sir John's inspection reports also contain abundant evidence of his belief in the need for effective artillery support. He recognised the value of howitzers, whose high-angle fire enabled them to operate from behind cover or large concentrations of friendly troops. While reiterating his confidence in the principles expressed in the current manual on the employment of artillery, he warned against slavish adhesion to the text. Training was, he pointed out, 'a preparation for war, and for war only': it was a waste of time to evolve tactics just for use at manoeuvres.[42]

Infantry officers often found French's forays into the tactics of their arm displeasing, but much of what he said about infantry was eminently sensible. In 1908, for example, he observed that the infantry were particularly poor during the latter stages of the attack, leading up to the assault itself. Here French had recognised the single most serious defect in infantry tactics. There was an abundance of advice in the manuals which would get the commander to within about 300 yards of his enemy. There, at precisely the most dangerous moment, practical suggestions were replaced by sweeping platitudes, and the lack of cohesive tactical theory tended to produce chaos in the final stages of the attack.[43]

Although Sir John's views on tactics were heavily based upon his own experience in South Africa, the annual manoeuvres in which he participated between 1903 and 1913 helped shape his opinions. These manoeuvres usually took place over large tracts of private land, in an area where special regulations had been imposed by Act of Parliament. Useful though they were, their value was limited by the difficulties of umpiring. In the so-called 'Battle of Chislebury Ring' attack and counter-attack followed in quick succession, and 'at the finale the embattled hosts resembled a Swiss roll', with lines and lines of infantry piled around one another.[44] A more serious limitation from French's standpoint was that he was soon too senior to be a 'player' in manoeuvres. They gave most of his 1914–15 subordinates the opportunity of commanding divisions in reasonably realistic conditions, but after 1904 French himself was never really put to the test. Even in 1913, when Sir John acted as army commander, he was also exercise director, and was more concerned with setting problems for his subordinates rather than putting himself under pressure. There can be no doubt that French's own ability to command in the field, and the workings of the BEF's headquarters, would have been greatly improved by manoeuvres which tested the army's command structure as well as its component divisions. Sir John commanded a divisional-sized force in 1904: his next experience of the responsibility and uncertainty of command was not to occur until 1914, and the Germans were less forgiving than umpires would have been.

By 1914 French was recognised, in both Britain and Europe, as a tactical theorist of some repute, although, naturally enough, it was his pronouncements on cavalry tactics that attracted the widest notice. The fact that the *arme blanche* school was apparently proved wrong by the events of 1914–15 should not be used as proof of the folly of its members. The British cavalry of 1914 had exactly the cavalry spirit which French had so often described. Tom Bridges, who went to war as a squadron leader in the 4th Dragoon Guards, described the cavalry motto as 'we'll do it: what is it?'[45] The battlefield performance of British cavalry was not always perfect, but it was head and shoulders above that of its German opponents or its French allies. Horses were kept fresh because British troopers walked as often as they rode, and the skilful combination of shock action and dismounted fire quickly established the moral superiority of British horsemen. When the Cavalry Corps was thrown into the line at Messines in October 1914 it fought on foot with a tenacity of which infantry regiments would have been justly proud.

Six

Irish Imbroglio
The Curragh, 1914

Sir John French was no stranger to 'the spirit of Irish distress'.[1] As a young man he had seen it vigorously manifested in a brawl in a Mayo rickyard, and by the autumn of 1913 it had again come to loom large in his mind. Successive Liberal governments, from 1886 onwards, had endeavoured to give Home Rule to Ireland, and in the summer of 1911 Asquith's government had at last pushed its Home Rule Bill through the Commons. The 1911 Parliament Act meant that the Lords, with their Conservative majority, could not block the bill indefinitely: it would become law, regardless of the Upper House's opposition, if it was passed by three successive sessions of the Commons.

The apparent imminence of Home Rule was a matter of direct concern to the CIGS. It had become uncomfortably clear that Ulster had no intention of becoming part of a united Roman Catholic Ireland. Unionist rallies attracted huge crowds, thousands signed the Ulster Covenant, and volunteers drilled and trained enthusiastically with imported rifles. In January 1913 the volunteers adopted the title Ulster Voluntary Force and Lord Roberts, markedly sympathetic to the Unionist cause, was asked to suggest an ex-regular officer to take command. He recommended Lieutenant-General Sir George Richardson, a retired Indian Army Officer, who established his headquarters in the Old Town Hall at Belfast, assisted by a staff which contained a number of ex-regulars, and soon included the brilliant Captain W. B. Spender, until recently the youngest staff officer in the British army.

By the late summer of 1913 it seemed that the government was in a cleft stick. If it persisted with Home Rule, without excluding Ulster on a permanent basis, civil war would flare up in the North. If, on the other hand, the cabinet dropped Home Rule altogether, agitation in the South would intensify, and the government, dependent for survival on the votes of Irish Nationalist MPs, would be swept from power. Passions ran at fever-pitch on both sides of St George's Channel. Unrest in the traditionally turbulent cities of Belfast and Londonderry was to be expected, but in July a crowd of 15,000 assembled in the sylvan surroundings of the grounds of Blenheim Palace to hear Andrew Bonar Law, Sir Edward Carson and F. E. Smith lavish a good deal of intemperate language on the Ulster question. The dour Bonar Law warned that the Ulster people would be entirely justified in opposing Home Rule by force of arms, and Carson, the eloquent Unionist firebrand, concluded grimly: 'We will shortly challenge the Government to interfere with us if they dare, and we will with equanimity await the result.'[2]

The army over which French presided from his desk at the War Office in Whitehall was, in theory, an apolitical institution, serving the government of the day without regard for the colour of its party ticket. This well-polished veneer will not stand close scrutiny. By the early part of the twentieth century the army's officer corps had become politically polarised. Most officers tended to sympathise with the Conservatives, impelled to do so, in part at least, by the anti-military overtones of Liberalism. There was also a degree of mutual suspicion between soldiers and politicians, based partly upon the army officer's high opinion of his own calling and corresponding low regard for what General Sir Arthur Paget was to call the 'dirty swine of politicians'. These factors must not, however, be over-emphasised. Although a few officers were in close contact with the Conservative inner circle – Kitchener and Henry Wilson are two good cases in point – the average officer shunned involvement in politics. Furthermore, the latent tension between soldier and politician was usually submerged beneath the quiet waters of the social round. It was only in times of crisis that attitudes hardened and suspicions deepened.

French took good care to remain politically colourless. Like most of his comrades, he considered himself to be the King's man above all, vesting his supreme allegiance in sovereign rather than government. But, unlike so many senior officers, he had good friends in the Liberal camp. He graced the house-parties of Liberal political hostesses with his bulldog swagger and roving eye, and he was on warm enough terms with Margot Asquith – who thought him 'a hot Liberal' – to send her the badges from his horse-cloth as a souvenir when he went off to war in 1914.[3] And Sir John's relationship with his political boss, Jack Seely, was more than merely conventionally polite. The two men were close friends and when Seely's first wife died in childbirth in August 1913 he found French's support a great consolation.[4]

If the government went ahead with Home Rule, as it seemed likely to, there was every chance of the army being used to coerce Ulster into a united Ireland. The dangers inherent in such a step were clearly apparent, not least to the King, who on 22 September 1913 asked Asquith if he intended to use the army to put down disorders in Ulster. In a statesmanlike letter he reminded the Prime Minister:

> that ours is a voluntary army; our soldiers are none
> the less citizens; by birth, religion and environment
> they may have strong feelings on the Irish question;
> outside influence may be brought to bear upon them;
> they see distinguished retired officers already or-
> ganising local forces in Ulster; they hear rumours of
> officers on the active list throwing up their commis-
> sions to join this force. Will it be wise, will it be fair
> to the sovereign as head of the army, to subject the
> discipline, and indeed the loyalty of his troops, to
> such a strain?[5]

The King had already asked French to give his views on the effect on the army of intervention in Ulster. Sir John replied that the army 'would as a body obey unflinchingly and without question the absolute commands of the King no matter what their personal opinion might be.' But he went on to add the caveat that discipline would be subjected to a very great strain, and 'I feel sure that there are a great many officers and men ... who would be led to think that they were best serving their

King and country either by refusing to march against the Ulstermen or openly joining their ranks.' He ended by stating his determination to act firmly against dissidents within the army, and to impress on all serving officers 'the necessity for abstaining from any political controversy'.[6]

Sir John took very much the same line in his advice to the government. In December he advocated acting harshly against waverers, and suggested that Captain Spender should be cashiered '*pour décourager les autres*'.[7] He and Seely had already taken the first tentative steps towards planning to deploy the army. General Sir Arthur Paget, the sixty-two-year-old guardsman who commanded in Ireland, was summoned to the War Office for discussions. He replied that he had prepared most of the information required for the meeting, but declared that he would have to raise 'the question of *partial mobilisation*'.[8] The death of Paget's brother caused the postponement of the conference, but a few days later Seely told the Prime Minister that Paget would be over on 4 November, 'and the Macready question can then be settled. I anticipate no difficulty.'[9] Paget's mention of partial mobilisation, together with the mention of Macready, gives an unmistakable clue to the way Seely and French were thinking as early as November 1913. Major-General Sir Nevil Macready was the army's leading expert on the use of troops in the aid of the civil power. He had been employed in South Wales during the miners' strike of 1910, and Augustine Birrell, Chief Secretary of Ireland, had consulted him on the use of troops in the Belfast riots of 1912. In October 1913 Seely hinted that he would be given a division in Ireland, and later sent him off to report on the state of the police in Dublin and Belfast.[10]

On 4 November Sir John had a long discussion on Ulster with Henry Wilson, DMO at the War Office. Throughout the crisis French took Wilson into his confidence: although he was well aware that Wilson's sympathies were with Ulster, he had no idea that Wilson was working closely with Bonar Law, and keeping the Unionists *au courant* with War Office policy and feeling within the army. Wilson found that French was:

> evidently nervous that we are coming to a civil war
> and his attitude appears to be that he will obey the

King's orders ... I was much struck by his seriousness. I *cannot* bring myself to believe that Asquith
will be so mad as to employ force.

Wilson told Sir John that he would not fire on Ulstermen at
the dictates, as he put it, of Irish Nationalists, and suggested
that French should put in writing the fact that he could not be
responsible for the actions of the whole of the army. French
replied that he had already told the King of this.[11] Three days
later Wilson assured Bonar Law that any attempt to coerce
Ulster would lead to serious trouble in the army, information
which can have done nothing to discourage Unionist
intransigence.[12]

By the end of November French had taken up the position
he was to retain throughout the crisis. He had no wish to see
the army involved in Ulster, and felt that any attempt to use
military force to coerce the North would, to a greater or lesser
degree, split the army. Nevertheless, if the government decided to embark upon this hazardous course, he would obey
orders and ensure that as many as possible of his subordinates
followed suit. And if this meant cashiering recalcitrant officers,
so be it. Firm action might at one and the same time prevent
the fragmentation of the army and deter the Ulstermen from
armed conflict: weakness, he believed, would worsen the army
split and encourage the Volunteers.

Sir John later became a Home Ruler, but it is unlikely that
his opinion on the Home Rule issue influenced him, one way or
the other, in 1913–14. He was simply not prepared to disobey
a legitimate order, however painful its consequences. His
friendship with Seely undoubtedly pushed him nearer the
government than might otherwise have been the case. The
unexpected arrival of his Field-Marshal's baton, a blessing for
which he held Seely at least partially responsible, placed him,
as Wilson feared, under something of an obligation to the
Secretary of State.[13]

French laboured under a number of disadvantages. In the
first place, his willingness to toe the government line brought
him into disfavour with elements of the army, who regarded
close collaboration with a Liberal government as a political act
in itself. Secondly, he was out of touch with feeling in the army.

Henry Wilson was, at best, an unreliable gauge of the climate of military opinion. French certainly paid heed to the advice of other officers – one Unionist politician thought enough of Fitz Watt's influence over the Field-Marshal to write him a personal letter of thanks – but he was isolated behind the florid facade of the War Office, wrestling with problems for which his training and temperament had not equipped him.

Sir John was also singularly unlucky as far as personalities were concerned. Liking Henry Wilson was one thing: trusting him, alas, was quite another. Nor was Sir Arthur Paget any more reliable. It is perhaps the kindest to call him gallant but impulsive, although one authority has gone as far as to brand him as a 'stupid, arrogant, quick-tempered man'.[14] Even Sir Harold Nicolson, deploying the accomplished charm of a royal biographer, felt compelled to comment that, even in his less excited moments, 'he was not a man of measured language or meek tact'.[15] French and Paget were on excellent terms. A few years earlier Paget had written to Sir John to say how much he had enjoyed serving under him at Aldershot.

> The reason that I have never spared myself in my endeavour to please you is not far to seek. Irrespective of my liking for you as a soldier and leader ... You were the only man in South Africa who was capable of commanding an army in the field and had you not taken me under your sheltering wing ... I should have retired from the army.[16]

Despite suggestion that the Curragh affair ended this friendship, French remained fond of the flamboyant guardsman, and in 1915 suggested – in the face of impressive evidence to the contrary – that he was fit to command an army.[17] As Commander-in-Chief in Ireland, Paget was exactly the wrong man for a post where tact and diplomacy were vital. Moreover, he had increasing doubts about the reliability of his officers, and his fears of a large-scale withdrawal of obedience fused with his natural impulsiveness to produce an inflammable combination.

The final ingredient in this explosive mixture was the commander of the 3rd Cavalry Brigade, based at the Curragh, just west of Dublin: Brigadier-General Hubert Gough. 'Goughie' was an experienced and popular cavalry officer, with an excellent record in South Africa. Like French and Wilson he was of Irish ancestry and had corresponded with another Irishman, Lord Roberts, on the subject of cavalry tactics. Roberts later played down his relationship with Gough, assuring the King that he had never served on his staff and they had not been in communication for 'years'. The latter point was, while technically true, something of an oversimplification. Gough was on first-name terms with Roberts's daughter, and when the Curragh affair was over he sent her copies of many of the relevant documents. This was hardly the act of a casual acquaintance, and it may be the tip of the iceberg: the army's senior Field-Marshal was a potent ally for a junior Brigadier engaged in a head-on clash with the Army Council.[18] Gough, with his well-deserved reputation as a 'thruster', was also known to enjoy French's confidence, although his memoirs make no secret of the fact that this esteem was by no means mutual.[19]

On 16 December 1913 Seely spoke to the assembled Commanders-in-Chief of all the army's regional commands at the War Office. Sir John and Sir Spencer Ewart, the Adjutant-General, were also present. The Secretary of State opened by telling his listeners something of which they were already well aware, namely that numerous officers would resign their commissions rather than fight the Ulstermen. He went on to state that if the army was to be employed in aid of the civil power, it was bound to use the minimum force necessary to preserve order. There was, therefore, no question of it being called upon to perform 'some outrageous action, for instance, to massacre a demonstration of Orangemen'. Nevertheless, he went on, the army was bound to obey lawful orders, and officers and men had no right to 'pick and choose' which orders they would obey. Seely concluded by telling the generals that he would hold them personally responsible for discipline within their commands. If any officer tendered his resignation, he was to be asked his reasons, and if he indicated that he wished to 'pick and choose which order he should obey', this fact was to be reported to Seely, who would 'submit to the King that the Officer should be removed'.[20]

The gist of Seely's speech was fully in accordance with French's recommendation, delivered only three days before, that a firm line should be taken with disaffected officers. But the speech itself was anything but a succinct summary of a conclusive argument. It asked as many questions as it answered. Seely had emphasised that soldiers were not bound to obey 'outrageous and illegal' orders. But was this not, after all, 'picking and choosing?' Might it not be outrageous to order the army to Ulster in the first place? Seely's audience may be forgiven for agreeing with Macready's gloomy prophesy that, where aid to the civil power was concerned: 'Whatever you do, you are sure to regret it.'[21]

Early in 1914 the situation worsened considerably. The Ulster Volunteers, some 100,000 strong, trained with a determination and efficiency that delighted Henry Wilson when he visited them in January. The government's intelligence agents produced alarming reports of their plans, leading Seely to suspect that an attack might be made upon the ammunition store at Carrickfergus Castle. On the political front, backstairs negotiations failed to produce a compromise that would satisfy Nationalists and Unionists. The former would agree only to the temporary exclusion of Ulster from a united Ireland, while the latter, in Carson's memorable words, found 'sentence of death with a stay of execution for six years' equally unacceptable.[22]

Shortly before the Home Rule Bill was debated in the Commons, Asquith, disturbed by the rumours emanating from Ulster, set up a five-man cabinet committee to consider the problem. On 12 March Lord Crewe, its most level-headed member, fell ill, leaving Seely, Birrell, Sir John Simon and the First Lord of the Admiralty, Winston Churchill, to discuss the matter without his moderating influence.

Birrel and Simon seem to have carried little weight, leaving Churchill and Seely in control. Churchill's standpoint was made crystal clear at Bradford on Saturday 14 March, when he declared that there were worse things than bloodshed, spoke darkly of a 'treasonable conspiracy' by Unionist leaders, and ended with the clarion call: 'Let us go forward together and put these grave matters to the proof.'[23]

Even as Churchill's persuasive oratory rolled over his audience at Bradford, a letter was on its way from the War Office to Paget's headquarters. Signed by the Secretary of the Army

Council, it warned Sir Arthur that 'evil-disposed persons' might attempt to seize arms and ammunition. Certain depots were specified as being 'specially liable to attack', and Paget was ordered to take the necessary steps to safeguard them. He was to inform all officers in command of barracks where weapons and ammunition were stored that they would be held personally responsible for the safety of the stores under their care. Finally, Paget was urged to omit no measures which might ensure the safety of all government stores throughout Ireland.[24]

On Monday 16 March Seely sent a telegram to Paget, asking what he had done to implement the precautions demanded in this letter, directing him to reply by 8.00 the following morning, and to report to the War Office on Wednesday 18 March, bringing his detailed plans with him. Paget duly wired that he had taken all available steps and issued general instructions, but on Tuesday 17th he pointed out that although he had taken special precautions in several places, he felt that large-scale troop movements would 'create intense excitement in Ulster and possibly precipitate a crisis'.[25]

French had initially been reluctant to summon Paget to London, but in early March Seely told him that the government possessed secret information that certain hotheads amongst the Ulster Volunteers intended to take matters into their own hands and strike for Dublin. It was only when Seely convinced Sir John that this intelligence was thoroughly reliable that he agreed that Paget should be sent for. On the morning of the 18th French was present in Seely's room at the War Office, where the Prime Minister opened a meeting which included the cabinet committee on Ireland, the Adjutant-General, Paget, and a few other officers, including Macready. Paget was informed that he might have to deal with a wide variety of situations on his return to Ireland. Six specific possibilities were mentioned, ranging from armed opposition to troops on their way to safeguard depots, to the 'organised, warlike movement of Ulster Volunteers under their responsible leaders'. The latter contingency would have to be met by concentrated military force, and reinforcements would be sent from England if Paget required them. Sir Arthur was also told that Macready would be appointed GOC Belfast District, with powers over the police which would, in effect, make him Military Governor of Ulster.

The politicians who attended the meeting, in their subsequent utterances on a subject which had by then become decidedly delicate, initially maintained that on 18 March they had merely given verbal amplification to the orders Paget had already received. But as Asquith himself eventually admitted, this was not strictly true, for on the 18th Paget was ordered to send troops to Newry and Dundalk, neither of which had been mentioned in the original War Office letter. Both towns were in Nationalist districts, and were therefore unlikely to be attacked by the Ulster Volunteers. Newry, moreover, contained no military stores whatever: merely an old, empty barracks. The towns were, however, strategically important points for any advance into Ulster from the South.[26]

The troop movements ordered on the 18th were opposed by all the soldiers present at the conference. Indeed, the real reason for them remains one of the most elusive unsolved questions of the whole Curragh affair. The dispatch of troops was almost certainly motivated by more than a legitimate desire to safeguard military property in the North. It may have been part of a Seely–Churchill 'plot' to stampede the Volunteers into premature military action, thereby forcing the army's hand, or the prelude to a full-scale drive into Ulster.

It was only Seely's repeated insistence on the reliability of the government's intelligence that had persuaded French that the meeting was necessary in the first place. Having accepted that there was a Volunteer threat, he did not oppose the move into Ulster on principle, although he believed that it was tactically unsound to spread troops around the North in penny packets. On the evening of the 18th he complained to Wilson: 'they are contemplating scattering troops all over Ulster as though it was a Pontypool coal strike. Sir John pointed out that this was opposed to all true strategy etc. but was told that the political situation necessitates this dispersion.'[27] Wilson, predictably enough, again warned French of the effect intervention would have upon the army, but did not feel that he had carried the point, for he regretted that he had not spoken more about the Field-Marshal's personal position and responsibilities as CIGS.[28]

Seely, as we have seen, had consulted French and Paget in the autumn of 1913 on the possible employment of troops in Ulster. It is, though, likely that these discussions did nothing more than sketch out possible courses of action in the broadest terms. No detailed plans for such a move existed at the War Office, and when the question of planning arose in mid-March a practical problem arose. The DMO was responsible for military operations outside the United Kingdom, the Director of Military Training for home defence, and the Adjutant-General for aid to the civil power. When the DMT, the blunt Major-General Sir William Robertson, was officially informed that the planning was to start, he at once inquired which branch of the General Staff would be responsible. There was a brief squabble during which DMO, DMT and Adjutant-General all passed the buck as deftly as they could, and on the 18th Wully Robertson received the unwelcome news that his own department was to undertake the thankless task.[29]

On the night of 18 March Paget wired his Major-General in charge of administration, Major-General L. B. Friend, ordering the planned movements to be executed by dawn on Sunday 31st.[30] Another meeting took place at the War Office on Thursday 19th. The Prime Minister was not present on this occasion, but the other members of Wednesday's conference were there, as was the First Sea Lord, Prince Louis of Battenberg. Seely began by acknowledging the seriousness of the situation, and told Paget that he had full authority to take whatever steps he considered necessary. The Secretary of State assured his listeners that the government was determined to persist with Home Rule. He hoped that bloodshed would be avoided if it was made clear to the Ulstermen and their supporters that the government 'had not the smallest intention of allowing... civil war to break out'. This presumably meant that the government intended to use overwhelming military force to crush the Volunteers if they offered armed resistance. The prospect was rather too much for Paget, who announced wildly: 'I shall lead my army to the Boyne.' French immediately told him not to be a 'a bloody fool'.[31] Prince Louis's presence at the meeting was significant, for on the 19th the 3rd Battle Squadron was ordered to steam to Lamlash on the Firth of Clyde, a short distance from Belfast, and other vessels were directed to assist with the movement of troops and the defence of key points.[32] A squadron of battleships is scarcely the embodiment of the principle of minimum force. Its dispatch was an index of the way Churchill thought about the crisis, and the following night he told French that if Belfast showed fight his fleet would have the town in flames in twenty-four hours.[33]

Following the conference, French had a long talk with Wilson and Robertson. Wilson did his best to persuade him that a large-scale move against the North was fraught with peril: it would necessitate general mobilisation, and would lead to widespread resignations and desertions. It was likely to have serious consequences not only in Glasgow, but as far afield as Egypt and India. Wilson made little headway. 'Sir John, I think,' he wrote, 'agreed with very little of what I said. He is absolutely "snaffled" by this cursed cabinet.'[34] Here Wilson was colouring events with the vivid hue of his own political convictions. French was only too well aware of the seriousness of the situation, but he remained convinced that he was duty bound to obey the government's instructions.

The Field-Marshal was dressing for dinner at Lancaster Gate early on the evening of the 19th when a telephone call summoned him to 10 Downing Street: he was particularly requested to use the garden entrance rather than the front door. He arrived at 7.30 p.m., and found that Asquith, Seely, Churchill, Birrell and Paget were already present. Sir John was told that Carson had left for Ireland after an angry scene in the Commons, and the cabinet expected him to proclaim a provisional government. Precautions were, therefore, more necessary than ever. Some specific measures were discussed: French suggested that the artillery at Dundalk should be withdrawn, but Asquith insisted that infantry should be sent to Dundalk to defend it.[35]

The Downing Street meeting had important results. It convinced French that there was a very real danger of an imminent Unionist *coup* in Ulster. Seely's repeated emphasis on the reliability of the government's intelligence, coupled with the Prime Minister's own insistence on the need for precautionary measures, all persuaded Sir John that there was no plot to coerce Ulster. The army was being employed in a perfectly legal manner, and his duty as CIGS was clear. Perhaps French was too gullible. The conclusive evidence of which Seely spoke has not survived to be evaluated by historians, and it is not improbable that Seely and Churchill were deliberately over-stating the danger. French was reluctant to challenge Seely, a man he liked and trusted, but he did ask the Secretary of State, probably at the Downing Street meeting, how the army should be used if a European crisis arose at the same time as the trouble in Ireland. Seely's reply stressed that 'large mobile forces of the Regular Army' would only be sent to Ireland as a reaction to a move by the UVF. He was sure that the Ulster-men and the opposition would support the government if the Germans took advantage of unrest in Ireland to launch an attack.[36] The meeting also compounded the confusion which already clouded Paget's mind. He had received no written orders at either of the War Office meetings, either because he claimed to understand his instructions so well that no written confirmation was required, or because the politicians were reluctant to put anything in writing. After the Downing Street conference he was in a state of high excitement, and a train journey and sea crossing that night did nothing to calm him.

On the morning of Friday 20 March Sir Arthur addressed his senior officers at his headquarters in Dublin. Three differing accounts of his speech exist, but there can be no doubt that, whatever the precise details of his address, his well-known im-pulsiveness turned a tinder-box into an inferno.[37] He rambled on about the precautions already taken, and the possibility of armed actions against the Ulstermen. Gough understood him to say that 'active operations were about to commence against Ulster', but he anticipated no trouble because the army would be too strong. Paget then looked at Gough and warned him that he could expect no mercy from 'your old friend at the War Office' – meaning Sir John – a remark which served only to put his hackles up. Sir Arthur then went on to say that he had, with French's assistance, obtained two 'concessions' from Seely. Firstly, officers who actually lived in Ulster would be allowed to 'disappear' for the duration of operations. Secondly, officers who were unwilling to serve against the North would not be permitted to resign, but would be dismissed from the service. Paget concluded by ordering the officers to speak to their subordinates without delay, and to notify him of the results as soon as they could.

The question of officers' loyalty had certainly been discussed on 19 March. French, Paget and Ewart had all agreed that officers who had 'direct family connections with Ulster' should be excluded from operations in the North. Sir John believed that other officers who refused to obey orders or threatened to resign should be court-martialled, but Ewart pointed out that this would be a lengthy process: the three officers eventually agreed that the simple 'removal' of such officers would be best.[38] But in issuing an ultimatum to his officers Paget was undoubtedly going beyond the instructions given him on the 19th. Had he issued direct orders for a march North, warning his commanders that officers who demurred would be dismissed, the evidence suggests that the great majority of officers would have obeyed. Asking a hypothetical question, however, introduced a dangerous element of choice into the question of obedience.

As the meeting broke up, Major-General Sir Charles Fergusson, commander of the 5th Division, cornered Gough and one of the infantry Brigadiers to discuss their dilemma. Fergusson, a level-headed General whose calm approach was to inject a much-needed element of sanity into the crisis, urged that the army should hold together whatever the cost, and said that he would march North if ordered. But Gough declared that he would not go, and set off to speak to the officers of one of his regiments, the 5th Lancers. He also sent a telegram to his brother Johnnie, Haig's Chief of Staff at Aldershot, telling him of the alternatives offered by Paget and his own decision. Paget held a second meeting in the afternoon, which Gough did not attend. Sir Arthur and his staff went into details of the proposed operation, emphasising that it was hoped that 'a big demonstration' would deter the Volunteers from armed resistance. The stress Paget placed upon overawing the Ulstermen rather than fighting them was fully in accordance with Seely's policy. But Paget could not confine himself to matters of fact, and went on to assure Fergusson that all the orders had the monarch's personal sanction.

Henry Wilson saw Roberts on the morning of the 20th, and helped the old Field-Marshal to draft a letter to the Prime

Minister, spelling out the dangers of splitting the army over Ulster. He then heard, from Johnnie Gough, the news of Hubert's resignation, and at once telephoned French. Sir John had heard nothing about it and, in Wilson's words, 'talked windy platitudes till I was nearly sick'.[39] The full force of the tempest hit the War Office that evening. At 7 p.m. a telegram from Paget announced that almost all the officers of the 5th Lancers – the first regiment Gough had visited – intended to resign, and much the same was probably true of the 16th Lancers.[40] Seely told the Prime Minister the ominous news at 11 p.m. He had certainly consulted French and Ewart before this, because he replied to Paget on behalf of the Army Council, telling him to suspend from duty any senior officers who had tendered their resignations: Gough and two of his Colonels – there was still doubt concerning the attitude of his third regimental commander – were to report to the War Office without delay.[41] Shortly before midnight, a second telegram brought worse tidings: 57 of Gough's officers would prefer to accept dismissal rather than be ordered North.[42]

On the morning of Saturday 21 March Fergusson began to visit his units, assuring them of his own Unionist sympathies, but pointing out the vital importance of maintaining the army's cohesion. He was generally successful in persuading his officers to subordinate their personal feelings to the demands of duty, and his performance gives some idea of the effect that Gough might have had upon the officers of his brigade had he tried to hold them together. Paget, who spoke to Gough's officers at the Curragh, had comparatively little influence: one officer described his rambling tirades as 'absolutely unconvincing and inconclusive'.[43] Nevertheless, Sir Arthur was able to report to the War Office that all the precautionary moves decided upon on the 18th and 19th had been carried out.

French spent a hectic Saturday at the War Office. Wilson, fresh from a visit to Bonar Law, suggested that only prodding the Prime Minister to take 'instant action' would prevent resignations among the General Staff. Sir John went off to consult Seely, who, in Wilson's words, 'asked what the army would agree to and I was asked to put it in writing. This I did as a promise on the part of the government not to employ the army to coerce Ulster.' French took the document to Seely, but, not surprisingly, it was 'not agreeable to Asquith and his crowd'. Wilson, warmly seconded by Robertson, kept impressing on Sir John the danger inherent in the situation , but was unable to persuade him to tell Seely that the army would not march.[44]

Roberts had contacted French when the crisis was still in its infancy, and had asked him down to Ascot to discuss it. French replied, on the 19th, that he was too busy to get away from London, but was in a 'most unfortunate and difficult position', and would be delighted to see Roberts if he was in London.[45] Roberts telephoned Sir John at the War Office on the morning of the 21st. He had read of the worsening crisis in the newspapers that morning, and was, in any case, being informed of the progress of events by Wilson and others. French recorded the conversation as follows:

> LORD ROBERTS. I am speaking from Ascot. What do you think of this terrible state of affairs?
> SIR J. FRENCH. It is very difficult to talk about such matters on the telephone.
> LORD ROBERTS. I hope you are not going to associate yourself with this band of (certain epithets were used which I could hardly catch). If you do you will cover yourself with infamy.
> SIR J. FRENCH. I must do my duty as a soldier like everyone else and put up with whatever consequences may ensue.
> LORD ROBERTS. Goodbye.[46]

Lord Roberts remembered the conversation rather differently. He admitted that he 'felt strongly and spoke strongly', and warned French that he would have to bear his share of the 'obloquy or calumny (I forget which word I used)', if he helped the cabinet to 'carry out their dastardly attempt to bring on Civil War'.[47] But whatever the precise details of their telephone call, it is clear that each Field-Marshal was striving to do his duty as he saw it. Roberts was doing his best to prevent a split in the army, and was convinced that the army could only be held together if the politicians were convinced of the calamitous consequences of using it in Ulster. French was equally horrified at the prospect of a split, and was eager to obtain reconciliation within the bounds of discipline. But, despite his personal misgivings, he was determined to remain loyal to the government, and was convinced that the sort of action suggested by Wilson and Roberts was utterly unconstitutional.

Shortly after his painful conversation with French, Roberts received a telegram from Hubert Gough, telling him of the situation at the Curragh and asking for advice. It was now a little late for Gough to request guidance, and it is hard to resist the conclusion that he sent the telegram largely in the hope of stirring Roberts into action. If this was indeed his intention, he was not disappointed, for Roberts immediately telephoned the King's Private Secretary, told him of the telegram, and requested an audience. Lord Stamfordham asked him to come at once. The King, who had read the news in the papers, had already spoken to Seely, and when Roberts arrived the King told him that the Secretary of State had maintained that he — Roberts — was 'at the bottom of all the trouble with the army'. Seely had complained that he had incited Gough, and had called the politicians 'swine and robbers' in the course of his conversation with French.[48]

Roberts indignantly denied these charges. He assured the King that he had not been in contact with Gough for years, and he had always advised officers not to resign over the Ulster question. He admitted that he was opposed to the coercion of Ulster, and he told the King that at least half the officers in the army would resign rather than participate in such an operation. The King found the old man 'in despair about it all, and said it would ruin the army'.[49] His audience at an end, Roberts went over to the War Office in search of Seely and French. He eventually ran the former to earth, but had a thoroughly unsatisfactory interview. Seely seemed 'distant and official': Roberts left for Ascot in low spirits, feeling that the Secretary of State was 'drunk with power'.[50] But the meeting had one important result. Roberts discovered that Paget had been acting without authority in offering the alternatives to his officers, and he left a note telling Gough of this.

Roberts had failed to find Sir John because the CIGS had already been called to the palace by the time he arrived. French had had another busy and frustrating day, with two meetings of the Army Council and a number of informal discussions with Robertson and Wilson. Early in the afternoon Major-

General Edmund Allenby, Inspector-General of Cavalry, arrived from the Curragh, and gave Sir John an up-to-date account of events. Allenby, his massive frame drawn up squarely in front of the fireplace, told of the goings-on in the 3rd Cavalry Brigade, while French stumped crossly up and down the room, swearing 'damn that Gough' and thumping Allenby in the chest to lend emphasis to his point.[51] In the early evening he was summoned to an audience with the King who, thoroughly alarmed by his talk with Roberts, impressed on French the gravity of the situation, warning 'that if great tact were not shown there would be no army left'.[52] After French had departed, the King wrote to Asquith, expressing his grief at the 'disastrous and irreparable catastrophe' which had over-taken the army, and asking that no further steps should be taken without his being consulted.[53]

The Gough brothers arrived at the War Office shortly before 10.00 on the morning of Sunday 22 March. They met at their mother's flat in Sloane Square, and Hubert discovered, by way of the note left at the War Office by Roberts, which Johnnie had accidentally opened and read, that Paget's ultimatum was not what the government had intended. Consequently, when he was ushered into the Adjutant-General's office at 10.15, Hubert felt that he had a reasonably strong case. Spencer Ewart introduced Gough to an officer he believed to be Mac-ready, asked him to sit down and said that it was a grave business. Gough replied sharply that he was well aware of that. Ewart then said that he merely wanted to obtain Gough's version of the facts, and proceeded to interview Gough while the other officer took notes. Ewart's final question was pivotal.

> Do you think an officer has any right to question when he should go or not go in support of the Civil Power to maintain law and order?
>
> None whatever, sir. If the GOC-in-C had ordered my brigade to go to Belfast, I should have gone without question.[54]

So much for the 'mutiny'. Gough's Colonels were subsequently called in to give their accounts, and were, like their Brigadier, ordered to remain in London, within reach of a telephone.

The War Office was a hive of activity that Sunday, with a number of meetings between Ministers and members of the Army Council. At some time during the day, or possibly on the previous one, Lord Haldane, the Lord Chancellor, advised French and Ewart to admit that a mistake had been made in asking officers what their action would be in 'hypothetical contingencies'.[55] This advice, together with Ewart's account of his conversation with Hubert Gough, seems to have persuaded French that, although Gough was behaving somewhat unreasonably, it was Paget's heavy-handedness which had precipitated the confrontation. Gough had indeed been placed in an impossible position, and when French saw the King that afternoon he declared that he would resign if Gough was not reinstated in his command.[56]

The politicians were now doing their best to pour water on the coals. Paget was ordered to report to London on the 23rd, to give his own version of the affair, and, although Macready was at last to be sent out to command Belfast District, there was to be no official announcement of this. Asquith told the King that Paget had been given no instructions which would justify his behaviour on the 20th or 21st, and assured him that the government had no intention of doing anything more than safeguarding the armouries and stores in the North.

He promised the King that no further troop movements would be carried out without his being consulted, and agreed to speak to the editor of *The Times* in order to ensure the publication of a reassuring statement. It seemed very much as if the genie could be coaxed back into the bottle. Asquith had already cancelled the naval deployment: all that remained was to get Gough safely back to the Curragh. With their Brigadier reinstated, the cavalry officers would probably withdraw their resignations, and the worst would then be over.

Monday 23 March began badly for French. His usual hearty breakfast was rather spoiled by Repington of *The Times*, who complained that 'the whole affair had been grossly mismanaged by Colonel Seely, Mr. Churchill and Sir John French, and these three men are mainly responsible for an episode without parallel in the history of the army'.[57] Hubert Gough, meanwhile, breakfasted with Henry Wilson, and it is likely that Wilson suggested that, as the cabinet was now eager for conciliation, Gough should refuse to be reinstated without a formal declaration that the army would not be used to coerce Ulster — a document similar to the one Wilson had drawn up on the 21st. Hubert then joined his brother at their mother's flat. Lieutenant-General Sir Douglas Haig, Johnnie's chief at Aldershot, arrived shortly afterwards, and suggested to Hubert that he could now climb down graciously, and the sooner he returned to the Curragh the better it would be for all concerned. Haig later called on Haldane at the House of Lords, and told him that the officers of his command were very much in favour of Gough. A clear statement of government policy was, he suggested, the only way to calm the army.[58]

Hubert Gough was shown into the CIGS's room at the War Office at about 11.15. French and Ewart were both cordial. 'I believe it's time we settled this unpleasant matter', said Sir John. 'As your old friend and chief, I want you to trust me and believe that it has all arisen from a great misunderstanding.' Gough was reluctant to clutch at passing olive branches: he had already had a short conference with his two Colonels, and had agreed not to accept any offer of reinstatement without a written undertaking that the army would not be called upon to impose Home Rule on the North. He denied that there had been a misunderstanding on his part, and declined French's suggestion that he and his Colonels should return to their commands as if nothing had happened. He required 'a definite assurance that we shall not be asked again to enforce on Ulster the present Home Rule Bill'. Sir John at once replied that he was willing to give such a guarantee. 'I must ask for an assurance in writing, sir,' responded Gough unhelpfully. French asked if his word was not good enough, and, when Gough replied that a written document was essential, retorted that it was quite impossible. 'I am very sorry sir,' said Gough , 'but I cannot go back unless I am given a written assurance.' There was a painful silence as French sighed and sat down heavily in his chair. After a long pause, Sir John spoke to Ewart. 'Well,' he said, 'we can't do anything more for him. You will bear me out that I have done my best for him — he will never know how much I have done. There is nothing for it but to take him to the Secretary of State.'

Sir John made a last attempt in the corridor outside his office. He took Gough's arm and begged him:

> For God's sake, go back and don't make any more difficulties, you don't know how serious all this is. If you don't go back, all the War Office will resign. I've done my best for you. If they had attempted to penalise you I would have resigned myself.

Gough refused to be drawn. 'I'm awfully grateful, sir,' was all he would say.

Seely was in his office with Paget and the officer Gough had mistaken for Macready the previous day—possibly the Quartermaster-General, Sir John Cowans.[59] They all sat down at the conference table, with Seely at its head. Seely immediately stared at Gough in an attempt to browbeat him, but Gough was as resistant to Seely's truculence as he had been to French's blandishments: he stared back, and eventually Seely lowered his gaze. The Secretary of State then embarked upon a lengthy harangue on civil-military relations, and ended by saying that Paget's speech had been the result of a misunderstanding. He asked Gough to return to his command, but Gough again demanded a written guarantee, and Seely replied that it was impossible to give one.

It was French who broke the deadlock:

> Perhaps General Gough has not made it quite clear that he feels he will not be able to return to his officers or regain their confidence unless he can show them the authority of the Army Council; and that he feels his own verbal assurances will not be sufficient now that feeling has been so greatly aroused.

Seely saw the chink of light. 'I see,' he said, 'I think that is only a reasonable request.' Ewart quickly drew up a document which Seely took across the road to Downing Street for cabinet approval.[60] Seely had to leave the cabinet meeting for an audience with the King before a decision had been made on the draft, and on his return the meeting was in process of breaking up. Asquith handed him an approved text, which Seely pocketed and remained in the cabinet room, chatting to John Morley, until all the other members had left.

At this juncture a message arrived from Gough, asking whether he might expect a reply. Seely then took from his pocket the paper passed him by the Prime Minister. It read as follows:

> You are authorised by the Army Council to inform the Officers of the 3rd Cavalry Brigade that the Army Council are satisfied that the incident which has arisen in regard to their resignations has been due to a misunderstanding.
>
> It is the duty of all soldiers to obey lawful commands given them through the proper channel by the Army Council, either for the protection of public property and the support of the Civil Power in the event of disturbances or for the protection of the lives and property of the inhabitants.
>
> This is the only point it was intended to be put to the officers in the questions of the General Officer Commanding, and the Army Council have been glad to learn that there never has been and never will be in the Brigade any question of disobeying lawful orders.[61]

Seely realised at once that Gough would never accept the document as it stood. He was perfectly correct in this assumption for Gough had, with Wilson's help, drawn up a note to Ewart in which he stipulated that the draft must specify that the army would not be used to impose Home Rule on Ulster.[62] This message had probably not been communicated to Seely, but he was by now all too well aware of Gough's attitude. With Morley's assistance, the Secretary of State therefore added two more paragraphs to the draft. Both men were experienced politicians, and it is strange that they felt able to alter a cabinet document without the cabinet's authority. Perhaps – and this is the 'official' version – the addition was simply an honest blunder on Seely's part. But the possibility exists that Seely genuinely acted in accordance with a cabinet decision which was subsequently withdrawn, leaving him as the scapegoat.

The 'peccant paragraphs', as they soon became known, ran thus:

His Majesty's government must retain their right
to use all the forces of the Crown in Ireland or
elsewhere to maintain law and order and to support
the Civil Power in the ordinary execution of its duty.

But they have no intention whatever of taking
advantage of this right to crush political opposition
to the policy or principles of the Home Rule Bill.[63]

These paragraphs conceded the very point demanded by
Wilson and the Unionists. They were a frank declaration that
the army would not be used to coerce Ulster, and, as they
stood, effectively killed Home Rule.

Haig called in to see French during the afternoon, while the
draft was still being drawn up in Downing Street. He told the
CIGS that all the officers of Aldershot Command were likely to
resign if Gough was punished. French was somewhat surprised by this information: he seems to have believed, on the
evidence of the relative calm in Fergusson's division, that the
unrest in the 3rd Cavalry Brigade was an isolated case. Haig's
news strengthened his conviction that the affair had to be
ended, and ended quickly.[64] Gough had been told to return to
the War Office at 4 p.m. By this time the document had been
copied and initialled by Seely, French and Ewart; it was
handed to Gough at about 4.15 p.m. He asked for an opportunity to discuss it with his Colonels, and French, beside
himself with impatience, gave him fifteen minutes. Hubert and
Johnnie discussed the document with the Colonels, and were
joined by a gleeful Wilson, who suggested that Gough should
add yet another paragraph to prevent any possible misunderstanding. 'I understand the meaning of the last paragraph,'
wrote Hubert, 'to be that the army will not be used under any
circumstances to enforce the present Home Rule Bill on
Ulster.' He then returned to French's room with his Colonels,
and read out his interpretation. 'That seems all right,' said Sir
John, who then added: 'Let me have a look at that paper.' He
took a couple of turns round the room, and then sat down at his
desk to write in his inimitable hand:

This is how I read it.

J.F.
CIGS[65]

The three officers thanked French politely, although in Gough's case the gratitude was more than a little tongue in cheek, and left to catch the night mail. Sir John went off to Buckingham Palace to assure the King that all was now well, while Henry Wilson strode jubilantly about the corridors of the War Office, announcing that the army had accomplished what the opposition had failed to do. Not all who heard Wilson shared his elation: the future Field-Marshal Earl Wavell, then a young captain in Wilson's directorate, wrote angrily that the army had no right to become embroiled in politics in this fashion.[66]

Asquith, who spent the afternoon in a well-measured defence of the government's action in the Commons, was alarmed when he heard of the peccant paragraphs. A telegram was sent to Gough, telling him that they were not to be regarded as operative, and he was, more discreetly, asked to return the document for amendment. Gough would have stood firm in any case, but Wilson took no chances and urged him not to give way, realising that 'as long as we hold the paper we got on Monday, we can afford to sit tight'.[67] He then spared a thought for French, whose career, he predicted confidently, would be ruined as a consequence of his having initialled Gough's interpretation of the document. He wrote:

> Later on I saw Sir John. I told him I thought he would be kicked out by the government when they found out what he had written for Hubert and in that case the army would go solid with him.[68]

French knew that his position was weak. His support of the government during the early stages of the crisis had brought him into disrepute with an element of the army: now his approval of what he took to be a cabinet document had made him an embarrassment to the government. He was deeply hurt by suggestions that he had betrayed the army. Roberts had written him a pained letter on the 22nd, denying the 'swine and robbers' comment, and regretting that they seemed unable to work together during the crisis.[69] Relations between the Field-Marshals had always been uncertain, but French was galled by this rebuke. 'I am bound to say,' he replied, 'it caused me great pain to hear you conceived it possible that I *could* adopt any course of action which might "cover me with infamy in the eyes of the army".[70]

His standing in the army already damaged, Sir John felt the political rug being tugged from beneath his feet. On Wednesday 25 March Asquith publicly repudiated Seely's additional paragraphs. French had initialled the document: the Prime Minister's rejection of it made, in effect, a liar out of him. On Thursday Asquith admitted that 'his position is very difficult, but he has been so loyal and behaved so well that I would stretch a great many points to keep him'.[71] Wilson, fearful that some last-minute compromise would relinquish the ground gained on Monday, was less eager to stretch points. On the 26th French called Wilson, Robertson and the Director of Staff Duties into his room, and told them he had offered his resignation, but Seely had refused to accept it. Shortly afterwards there was a meeting of Commanders-in-Chief of home commands. French and Ewart explained their actions, and said that they had offered to resign. Wilson believed that the meeting also revealed unanimous determination not to fight Ulster.[72]

In mid-afternoon Wilson was summoned by French, who told him that the cabinet was opposed to his departure and would try to find some way round the problem. Wilson maintained 'that he and Ewart must stick to their resignations unless they were in a position to justify their remaining on in the eyes of officers'.[73] Sir John then left to see the Lord Chancellor. On his return he again called for Wilson, and said that Haldane had obtained the Prime Minister's agreement for him to assure Gough that the army would not be used to coerce Ulster, in accordance with a statement made by Haldane in the Lords on the 23rd.

Sir John spent much of Friday 27 March closeted with politicians. With Haldane's help he drafted a statement which, he hoped, would prove an acceptable compromise.

> Sir John French has handed in his resignation and the Prime Minister has requested him to withdraw it. Sir John French is anxious to do this if he can do so consistently with his duties and his position. He holds most strongly that there can be no question of

conditions being made by officers as to obeying orders, and agrees that a definite army order should be made to that effect ...

[When agreeing to Gough's terms] he was simply acting in accordance with instructions corresponding to the statement made by the Lord Chancellor in the House of Lords on Monday, and did not conceive himself to be arranging conditions. He is ready to remain in his present position in the belief that the Lord Chancellor's statement of Monday still stands.[74]

This statement, initialled by French and Haldane, was sent to Asquith, and an Army Order dated that day decreed that officers and men should not be asked hypothetical questions about their attitude to orders, and reminded them of their duty to obey lawful commands.[75]

French's precarious stance on this narrow piece of middle ground was hotly assailed from both sides. Sir John told Wilson that he hoped for a compromise based on Haldane's speech, pointed out that the Quartermaster-General and Master-General of the Ordnance had both begged him not to resign, and asked for advice. If he was hoping for moderation he was grievously disappointed. 'I told him,' wrote Wilson, 'that he *must* go.'[76] He warned that the Army Council was out of touch with feeling in the army, and offered to test the climate of opinion at Staff College. He duly departed for the Staff College point-to-point at Arborfield, chatted with several of his cronies, and produced the 'almost unanimous verdict' that French should resign. He telephoned Sir John to give him these glad tidings, but the Field-Marshal was out. 'It seems to me,' wrote Wilson, whose own resignation had been singularly elusive, 'his course is quite clear, he must go and set us an example of what a gentleman should do.'[77]

Asquith was fast coming to the same decision, albeit for very different reasons. His Private Secretary brought him the French–Haldane statement on Sunday 28th, and he found it totally unacceptable: 'from their point of view it was a sophisticated evasion, and from ours a surrender of the whole position'.[78] Wilson told French the result of his excursion to

Arborfield the following morning, and then went off to lunch with Bonar Law, discussing French's anticipated resignation and gleefully foretelling that it would break the cabinet.[79] He called on Sir John at Lancaster Gate that evening, and discovered, to his chagrin, that yet another attempt at compromise was under way. With Haldane's assistance, French had drafted a letter to Asquith, assuring the Prime Minister that he had only given the document to Gough because he thought it 'represented the considered opinion of His Majesty's Government'. He believed that a statement made by Asquith that Friday was quite satisfactory and concluded that he and Ewart had not resigned from any desire to embarrass the government, but simply because: 'Nothing could be more unfortunate in the best interests of the army that the word of a member of the Army Council or indeed of an officer could be lightly set aside after it had served its immediate purpose.'[80]

Wilson told Sir John that the paragraph approving of Asquith's Friday speech 'would never do', and French duly deleted it.[81] Haldane hoped that Asquith would read the letter to the House, but the Prime Minister found even the unamended draft too much to swallow. On the following day, 30 March, he told Haldane that while he had 'the utmost disposition to make any terms with French, that are compatible with our Parliamentary position,' he was convinced that:

> we could not possibly survive any recognition, express or implied, of the Gough treaty, and it is equally clear that French will not remain except on that footing ... I see no way out of the imbroglio but for Seely to go also, and I propose myself, for a time to take his place.[82]

At 12.30 that day Wilson was called into Sir John's office to hear the news he had awaited for days: French and Ewart had resigned. 'This is good', he noted laconically.[83]

Wilson was not alone in believing that resignation was the only honourable alternative open to French. Lord Esher had called on French on 22 March, fearing 'that he is too much in the hands of the politicians. Of course this is very natural. Plausible devils.'[84] On the 30th he told Stamfordham that French was in honour bound to resign: 'From the point of view of the army and its solidarity, from the point of view of his position, and influence over soldiers in peace and war, French is inevitably lost if he remains at his post.'[85]

H. A. Gwynne of the *Morning Post*, who had corresponded with Sir John throughout the affair, pressing him to tell the cabinet that the army could not be relied upon to coerce Ulster, congratulated Fitz Watt in using his influence to save French from 'a disaster which would have ruined him forever'.[86] Godfrey Locker-Lampson, a Unionist MP, also paid tribute to Watt's 'unselfish devotion to higher interests' in helping persuade Sir John to resign.[87]

Bearing in mind its troubled antecedents, Sir John's resignation took place in remarkably restrained circumstances. Asquith observed that 'French behaved admirably, and when I told him privately that I thought of going to the War Office, he was delighted and promised all his help.'[88] French proposed that Sir Charles Douglas should take over as CIGS, at least for the three or four months that Asquith intended to remain Secretary of State. It is possible that Asquith gave French some promise of future employment, for Margot Asquith believed that he 'comes back to a high place in a very short time'.[89] This probably referred to her husband's intention to appoint Sir John to the post of Inspector-General, which he did on 26 July.[90]

Whatever Asquith may or may not have promised in March 1914, Sir John evidently believed that the Curragh affair had ended his career. Churchill asked him to join him for the trial mobilisation of the fleet in mid-July, and thought that the Field-Marshal, 'for all his composure, was a broken man'.[91] There is some evidence that French remained Commander-in-Chief designate, but Sir John was, as we shall see, far from convinced that he would in fact receive command of the BEF when it mobilised in early August.

A more lengthy assessment of the Curragh episode would be out of place in these pages: Sir James Fergusson's balanced verdict, which points to collusion between Seely and Churchill for a pre-emptive stroke against Ulster, is probably as near the truth as historians are likely to get.[92] But the affair's consequences were to have an important bearing on French's subsequent career. It left him very much in credit with Liberal politicians: 'French is a trump, and I love him', wrote Sir Edward Grey.[93] In terms of wider civil-military relations, however, the Curragh boded ill, and gave early warning of the split between soldiers and politicians which was to occur during the war. The affair also left enduring scars within the army; the Gough brothers thereafter cut Henry Wilson who, despite his manifest ability, was rightly mistrusted by many senior officers.

Sir John's behaviour was to lead to accusations that he was 'a political general'.[94] Yet it is precisely because he was politically naive that he got into such difficulties. He pursued what he regarded as an honest, if painful, course, carrying out the orders of his political masters in the belief that they were acting wisely and honestly. He was not the first or indeed the last General to discover that this course of action, whatever its attractions to a man brought up in a hierarchal environment where discipline and obedience are cardinal virtues, is itself fraught with peril. The affair also demonstrated his ability to misjudge men and fall prey to bad advice. And the next time he listened to Henry Wilson, it was lives, not reputations, that were at risk.

Seven

Mons and the Marne
August–September 1914

On the warm evening of Sunday 2 August 1914 Sir George
Riddell, an influential newspaper proprietor with ready access
to the corridors of power, held a dinner party at his London
home. The circumstances were far from cheerful: for the past
few days the European situation had been steadily deteriorating. Bismarck had predicted that 'some damned foolish thing
in the Balkans' would start the next war, and it seemed very
much as if the old fellow would be proved right. On 28 June the
Archduke Franz Ferdinand had been assassinated by Serbian
nationalists, and events thereafter took on the horrifying
tempo of a dance of death. Austria declared war on Serbia on
28 July, and mobilised on the 30th. Russia mobilised the same
day, and Germany followed suit on 1 August. Late that afternoon mobilisation posters speckled the walls of French towns
and villages: the race was on.

Riddell's guests were politicians, and their conversation
centred on England's attitude to the European conflict. The
issue had split Cabinet and Parliament, and caused Paul Cam-
bon, French ambassador in London, to ask if England understood what honour was. Ramsay MacDonald got up after
dinner to make a telephone call, but the phone rang as he
approached it. Riddell picked up the receiver: it was Sir John
French. 'Can you tell me, old chap,' asked Sir John, 'whether
we are going to be in this war? If so, are we going to put an
army on the continent, and, if we are, who is going to command it?' Riddell put his hand over the receiver, spoke briefly

to his guests, and replied: 'Fancy you not having heard. Yes, you are to command all right.'[1]

This news came as no real surprise to French. On Thursday 30 July he had been summoned by the CIGS, Sir Charles Douglas, and told that he would command the BEF if England went to war. The army had already begun its run-up to mobilisation: the Precautionary Period had commenced the previous day. Sir John spent much of Sunday closeted with the French military attaché, and his phone call to Riddell was probably part of his attempt to assure the French that Britain would 'remain true to our friendly understanding with the *Entente* Powers'.[2] France's fears that Britain would remain on the sidelines might have proved justified had the Germans not violated Belgian neutrality. But the invasion of Belgium was more than even a Liberal cabinet could tolerate, and at midnight on the 4th Britain found herself at war with Germany.

On the afternoon of Wednesday 5th, Sir John, looking, in his top hat and black jacket, not unlike a bemused walrus, arrived at 10 Downing Street for a Council of War. Asquith called it 'rather a motley gathering'.[3] It included most of the Cabinet; French with Lieutenant-General Sir Archibald Murray, his Chief of the General Staff; Douglas Haig and Jimmy Grierson, the corps commanders; Henry Wilson, sub-Chief of the General Staff; the CIGS and a number of his officials from the War Office. The new Secretary of State for War was also present. This was Lord Kitchener, snatched back from the boat-train at Dover to an appointment which Asquith admitted was a 'hazardous experiment'.[4]

The Council of War gave a dismal foretaste of the strategic talking-shops which were to govern British policy for the first two years of the war. A struggle against Germany had been envisaged for the previous decade, and plans to meet this contingency had been drawn up, but neither the government nor its professional advisers had fully grasped the implications of Britain's commitment to a continental war.[5] After a brief general statement by Asquith, French presented the War Office plan. Hankey, the committee's secretary, believed that: 'The general tenor of his opinion was that the Expeditionary Force should be sent to France: a safe place for concentration should be selected, and events should be awaited.'[6] French pointed out that the plan specified Maubeuge, south-west of Charleroi, as the BEF's concentration area, but, as the British mobilisation would now lag behind that of France, Amiens might be safer. But this was a detail: what mattered, stressed Sir John, was sending the BEF to France intact, and sending it as quickly as possible.

Having expounded the plan which Wilson's directorate had drawn up with such care, French then revealed a capacity for lateral thinking which horrified Wilson and made Haig tremble. It might, he suggested, be possible to operate from Antwerp against the German right flank. This project bore considerable similarity to the Antwerp schemes discussed in 1905–6, and it reflected Sir John's reluctant conversion to continental strategy. It was also an ample demonstration of his tendency to let attractive concepts obscure the sordid realities of staff-work and logistics. French had only recently given up the post of CIGS: he was well aware of the existence of Wilson's plan, and, indeed, had been involved in planning for war with Germany from an early stage. Yet he still remained capable of recommending the jettisoning of a carefully-devised project in favour of another, far more ambitious, scheme.

If the Antwerp operation was to have any chance of success – and, given the logistic and diplomatic constraints of August 1914, such chances were probably very slim – it could not be undertaken as a piece of inspired improvisation. The project foundered when Churchill refused to guarantee safe passage across the North Sea, but the idea of some sort of flanking assault lingered on in French's mind.

The discussion then stumbled on, with Haig asking a number of basic questions which, as the anguished Wilson complained, led 'to our discussing strategy like idiots'.[7] Churchill suggested that the BEF should concentrate well to the rear of the French army to form a strategic reserve and Ian Hamilton backed Kitchener in recommending Amiens as a concentration point. Lord Roberts, cast in the role of the elder statesman amongst the soldiers, spoke in favour of the original War Office plan, and there was general agreement that this was indeed the wisest course. Although Churchill was confident that the fleet's early mobilisation made invasion improbable, the question of home defence shook its hoary locks, and a definite decision on the number of divisions to be sent abroad was not taken. The question of the BEF's exact line of operations was also left open, and the French were to be asked to send a staff officer to consult with the General Staff.

The following morning the Cabinet agreed to the dispatch of an expeditionary force of four infantry divisions and a cavalry division, a decision hotly debated at another Council of War that afternoon. Kitchener, now formally installed as Secretary of State for War, foresaw a long conflict and advocated caution: Sir John, on the other hand, shared the view of the most senior officers that the war would be short, and clamoured for the immediate dispatch of five divisions. Sir John was overruled, and the suspicion that Kitchener was trying to starve him of troops was implanted in his receptive brain then, long before the first shot was fired.

For the next few days French divided his time between the Edwardian splendour of the Hotel Metropole, where GHQ was forming, the bustling corridors of the War Office, and his own house at Lancaster Gate. Huguet, formerly the French military attaché in London, paid a short visit to Wilson, but he had left France without an adequate briefing, and departed almost immediately. Kitchener was furious that Huguet had not been brought to see him, and was also annoyed with Wilson for telling the Frenchman of the BEF's embarkation schedule. Wilson, never easily cowed, answered back, and wrote: 'I have no intention of being bullied by him, especially when he talks such nonsense as he did today.'[8] The incident soured relations between Wilson and Kitchener: it is of crucial importance, for French's relationship with Kitchener, always unsteady, was significantly worsened by Wilson's goading.

Huguet was back again by the 12th, accompanied by two other French army officers. They had a long discussion with Sir John and Wilson at Lancaster Gate, and then proceeded to the War Office to persuade Kitchener that the BEF should, after all, concentrate at Maubeuge. After a three-hour haggle, during which Kitchener spoke perceptively of the danger north of the Meuse, concentration near Maubeuge was at last agreed upon, and French accompanied Kitchener to the Prime Minister to obtain his consent.[9]

While politicians and generals squabbled over the BEF's size and destination, the army clattered smoothly through the machinery of mobilisation. The mobilisation order went out at 4.00 on the afternoon of 4 August, and the embarkation programme began five days later. By the 20th the BEF was all but complete in its concentration zone, a pear-shaped area between Maubeuge and Le Cateau. Much has been written about the BEF of 1914, and although most of its members have long since faded away, it still marches on, moustachioed and pipe-smoking, down the tree-lined pavé of British folk-memory. A few points merit restatement here. Unlike its continental counterparts, the British army was recruited by voluntary enlistment rather than conscription. This fundamental fact influenced the BEF's size and quality. It was small: at around 100,000 men, a mere visiting-card by the standards of European war. And while continental armies were a mass of conscripts shored up by small regular cadres of officers and NCO's, about half the members of the BEF were regular soldiers, reinforced by reservists with several years service with the colours behind them. On average, the British soldier of 1914 marched better and shot straighter than his opponents, or, indeed, his allies. But not all British soldiers were laconic, bronzed Old Bills. There were a number of young soldiers in the ranks of the BEF, callow youths whose experience did not stretch beyond the parade-grounds of Aldershot or Catterick. Many of the reservists had settled comfortably into civilian occupations: readjusting to army life amidst the turmoil of a summer's battle was anything but easy.

French and Kitchener were both uncomfortably aware that the BEF was more than merely an expeditionary force. It was the cutting edge of the British army, and if anything untoward happened to it there was precious little left behind. True, there were the Territorials, but they were an unknown quantity, very much mistrusted by Kitchener, and might not be ready for war for months. The fact that there was no conscription in Britain meant that, alone amongst European powers, Britain had available large reserves of manpower. But volunteers, however enthusiastic they may be, are not necessarily soldiers, and the thousands of young men who responded so cheerfully to Kitchener's call to arms would not be trained and equipped for months and, in some cases, years. The BEF was a torpedo-boat amongst the battleships: deadly perhaps, but liable to be pounded into oblivion if its helmsman made a false move.

The formal instructions which Sir John received from the Secretary of State bore witness to the ambivalent feelings surrounding the dispatch of the BEF.

> The special motive of the Force under your control is to support and cooperate with the French army against our common enemies ...
> ... during the assembly of your troops you will have every opportunity for discussing with the Commander-in-Chief of the French Army, the military position in general and the special part which your Force is able and adapted to play. It must be recognised from the outset that the numerical strength of the British Force and its contingent reinforcement is strictly limited, and with this consideration kept

steadily in view it will be obvious that the greatest
care must be exercised towards a minimum of losses
and wastage.

Therefore, while every effort must be made to
coincide most sympathetically with the plans and
wishes of our Ally, the gravest consideration will
devolve upon you as to participation in forward
movements where large bodies of French troops are
not engaged and where your Force may be unduly
exposed to attack.

Should a contingency of this sort be contemplated, I look to you to inform me fully and give me
time to communicate to you any decision which His
Majesty's Government may come to in this matter.
In this connection I wish you distinctly to understand that your command is an entirely independent
one, and that you will in no case come under the
orders of any Allied General.

In minor operations you should be careful that
your subordinates understand that the risk of
serious losses should only be undertaken where such
risk is authoritatively considered to be commensurate with the object in view ... [10]

These instructions were an accurate summary of the BEF's
mission as Kitchener saw it, but because of the novelty and
uncertainty of the situation, 'their wording was in places necessarily vague and even contradictory. In them lay the germs of
controversies that would bedevil the British Command
throughout the war.'[11] Sir John was to co-operate with the
French, but to avoid heavy losses while doing so: he was to
'coincide most sympathetically' with French plans, but was not
to come under French command. Given the infinite imponderables of August 1914, it is difficult to see how Kitchener could
have worded the instructions differently. But their inherent
contradictions were to cause difficulties before the month was
up, and their equivocal tone implanted doubts in Sir John's
mind even before he landed in France.

It was not only what the instructions actually said that
caused trouble. Their very existence remained secret from the

French, with the almost incredible result that, for the first nine or so months of the war, there existed a fundamental misconception as to the nature of Sir John's command. The Repington questionnaire of 1906 had spoken of unified command on land and sea, and although subsequent negotiations had not resulted in a formal Anglo-French agreement on the subject, the French believed that the BEF was under the orders of the French Commander-in-Chief. In the spring of 1915 Esher told Sir John of a recent conversation with Millerand, the French War Minister, who was:

> thunderstruck to learn that you had received implicit instructions to act as Commander-in-Chief of an Allied Army.
>
> He had received *quite the contrary impression*! Joffre has been allowed to think, from the beginning, that you had been instructed to act under him, and that the refusal to do so came from you and that the *Government* were too weak to insist. [122]

French himself believed that the absence of a unified command was a serious source of weakness. In late September 1914 he complained: 'We suffer terribly from a lack of "unity of command". Allies must always suffer so.'[13] Yet if Sir John was ready to approve the principle of unified command, he was less prepared to accept its inevitable practical consequence – the subordination of the BEF to the French high command. This was due in part to his own desire to remain an independent commander. He had been grooming himself for command of the BEF for years. Not only was he, as a Field-Marshal, senior to Joffre, who was a General, but he felt, not unreasonably, that he was more experienced than any French commander; finally, his mercurial temperament made enforced subordination abhorrent to him.

The whole question of unified command was inextricably bound up with Sir John's feelings towards the French, and the issue is more than usually complex because these feelings, as was so often the case with his turbulent emotions, were frequently in a state of flux. He suspected that French officers were not quite gentlemen: '*Au fond*, they are a low lot, and one always has to remember the class these French generals mostly

come from.'[14] He could be driven into one of his spectacular
rages by a tactless communication from French headquarters,
and lamented that Joffre tended to treat him like a corporal.[15]
French leaders could, he complained, 'become absolutely
mulish to the point of obstinacy'.[16]

Yet his reverence for Napoleon and his visits to France in
the pre-war years gave Sir John a bittersweet affection for the
Gallic soul. He told Winifred Bennett:

> These Frenchmen are gloriously brave, and I love
> them, but their leaders try me very hard sometimes.
> They always look at things from their own point of
> view, and consequently expect me to do the impos-
> sible ... They've put me in the cart badly once or
> twice before and I don't mean to let them do it again.
> But I hate wrangling with friends.[17]

Sir John's amorous inclinations provided some common
ground. In May 1915 he wrote:

> My great friend is *Foch*. He's a regular Frenchman.
> The devils were dropping bombs all round here the
> other night and some of the women ran about the
> streets in their 'nighties.' I was telling Foch about
> it – he only said *'Mais mon général, un état tres jolie!*
> [*sic*][18]

The news of Sir John's appointment to command the BEF
was well received in England and France. *The Times*
announced blithely that: 'There was not a moment's hesitation
about the appointment of Sir John. There was no painful
canvassing of candidates, no acrimonious discussion, no
odious comparison of the merits of individual generals, no hint
of favouritism, of party intrigue.'[19] Huguet observed that the
appointment was a popular one in France: Sir John was warm
and generous, easily approached, had the well-being of his
men at heart and was loved by his soldiers.[20] The latter point
may sound out of place in a war where generals were, at least
as far as popular history is concerned, lofty and distant figures.
There can, however, be no doubt that French had an almost
Bullerish popularity with the rank and file. Wully Robertson,
an ex-ranker who crossed swords with Sir John on more than

one occasion, admitted that French's task was far harder than that faced by his successor:

> Sir John was exceedingly popular with the troops, and I doubt if any other general in the army could have sustained in them to the same extent the courage and resolution which they displayed during the trying circumstances of the first six months of the war.[211]

C. D. Baker-Carr, whose military career encompassed a meteoric rise from chauffeur to Brigadier-General, saw a good deal of French during the retreat from Mons:

> Sir John French may not have been a great soldier in the modern sense of the word, but he was a great leader of men. His unfailing cheerfulness and courage at that time were of inestimable benefit in keeping up the morale of the soldiers, and if he ever realised the desperate plight of the army under his command he showed no sign of it.

The sight of the Commander-in-Chief wandering about GHQ in a blue dressing-gown, whistling cheerfully, lifted the spirits of all who set eyes on this improbable vision.[22]

There were, it is true, those who had their doubts about the wisdom of Sir John's appointment. Douglas Haig felt unable to keep his suspicions to himself. In the course of a conversation with the King, he agreed that French would loyally carry out any orders he might be given, but:

> I had grave doubts, however, whether his temper was sufficiently even or his military knowledge sufficiently thorough to enable him to discharge properly the very difficult duties which will devolve upon him ... In my own heart, I know that French is quite unfit for this great command at a time of crisis in our nation's history.[23]

Haig considered it his duty to tell the King of his misgivings. Less than a week later he made similar observations to a junior officer on his staff, declaring that French was 'quite unfit for command in times of crisis'.[24] Haig valued loyalty highly, and once spoke sharply to the devoted Johnnie Gough when the latter ventured a mild criticism of his orders. But as far as loyalty to the Commander-in-Chief was concerned, a convenient double standard applied.[25]

On the afternoon of Friday 14 August Sir John, accompanied by a small group of staff officers, crossed the Channel in the cruiser *Sentinel.* After an enthusiastic reception at Boulogne, he set off for Amiens, though not before he had watched two infantry brigades arrive in camp, noting that the men looked 'well and cheery'.[26] He spent the night in Amiens, and the following morning inspected the nearby Royal Flying Corps base. French was particularly interested in aircraft, and soon developed a high regard for their usefulness in reconnaissance. 'I was', he wrote, 'much impressed with the general efficiency of the aircraft force. I saw the squadron commanders and told them so.'[27]

Sir John arrived in Paris the same afternoon, stepping from his train at the Gare du Nord to the thunderous applause of a delighted crowd. Accompanied by Sir Francis Bertie, the British Ambassador, he first paid an official call on President Poincaré. The President was not impressed. He found little military in Sir John's appearance, apart from his habit of looking one straight in the eye, and commented acidly that 'one would take him rather for a plodding engineer than a dashing soldier'. The interview was not auspicious. 'He speaks our tongue with great difficulty', observed the President, who went on to complain that the BEF, which was not likely to be ready for action until the 25th, would be late at the rendezvous.[28]

French then went off to the War Minister in the Rue Saint-Dominique with Messimy, the War Minister, who was soon to exchange the cares of office for the command of a battalion at the front. Messimy made arrangements for Sir John to meet Joffre the following day, and the Field-Marshal left for the British Embassy, where he was to spend the night. He dined quietly at the Ritz with Brinsley Fitzgerald, on his staff once more, his meal disturbed by: 'The usual silly reports of French "reverses" which hung about – all quite untrue.'[29]

Sir John reached Joffre's headquarters at Vitry-le-François south-east of Rheims at midday on the 16th. He found Joffre and his Assistant Chief of Staff, the well-upholstered General

Berthelot, jubilant over the capture of a German colour which had just been brought in. Joffre told him that information on the enemy was as yet so imprecise that it was difficult to issue firm instructions, but his general plan was to attack the German forces in the north-east. He expected the BEF to advance towards Nivelles, on the left of the French 5th Army. Sir John said that his army would not be ready to advance until the 24th, but promised to accelerate its movements if at all possible. The two Commanders-in-Chief formed a generally favourable opinion of one another. Joffre thought that French was 'a loyal comrade-in-arms, firmly attached to his own ideas and, while bringing us his full support, anxious not to compromise his army in any way'.[30] Sir John had never met Joffre before and his first impression, confirmed by their subsequent relationship, was of 'a man of strong will and determination, very courteous and considerate, but firm and steadfast of mind and purpose, and not easily turned or persuaded'.[31] The Field-Marshal was also impressed by the air of calm deliberation which prevailed at *Grand Quartier Général* (GQG).

There was less calm and deliberation at the British GHQ, temporarily established at the Lion d'Or in Paris. In the excitement of its departure from London, the code books had been left behind, and a new set was brought by Lieutenant E. L. Spears, liaison officer with the 5th Army. On arrival at the hotel Spears found Archie Murray, the Chief of the General Staff:

> worried not so much by the situation, which he was trying to unravel on all fours on the floor where enormous maps were laid out, as by the fact that chambermaids kept coming into the room, and he had only his pants on.[32]

And this was the nerve-centre of the first British force to venture on to the continent for a century.

Had Murray known what the situation really was, he might have been less preoccupied with the threat posed to his dignity by French chambermaids. For while the French planned to surge forward into the lost provinces of Alsace and Lorraine, their blind confidence in the offensive spirit enshrined in Joffre's directive that, whatever the circumstances, his concentrated forces would advance to the attack, the Germans had other ideas. Faced with the unappealing prospect of a war on two fronts, they had decided to destroy one enemy at a time, taking a calculated risk on one front and relying upon speed and efficiency on the other. The Schlieffen Plan, first devised in 1905 and considerably modified thereafter, was designed to reproduce Cannae, the classical battle of encirclement, on a vast scale. The bulk of the German armies would be concentrated in the west, leaving only a skeleton force to mask the Russians. The impossibility of gaining a rapid breakthrough in the heavily-fortified zone along the Franco–German border had persuaded the Germans to send no less than 54 divisions north of Metz, through Belgium, marching to the west of Paris before swinging east to snap the French back against their own fortress system in a great battle of encirclement that would smash the French armies and end the war in the west.

The combination of the Schlieffen Plan and Plan XVII boded ill for the Allies. For even if the French offensive, launched, let it be said, into country admirably suited for defence, proved successful, its very success would aid the Germans. The Schlieffen Plan was, as Sir Basil Liddell Hart put it, 'like a revolving door — if a man pressed heavily on one side the other side would swing round and strike him in the back'.[33] The German plan, despite its flaws, might have worked had its creator presided over its execution. But Schlieffen's successor as Chief of the German General Staff, the younger von Moltke, lacked his predecessor's iron nerve. He tinkered with the plan, narrowing the frontage of the German advance through Belgium, reacting to an apparently worsening situation in the east by shifting troops to the Russian front, and, most crucially, by permitting commanders in the path of the main French assault to strike back hard and prevent the French from putting their heads into the noose.

All this was of life-or-death importance to the BEF. The marching wing of the German armies would trundle through northern France like a field-grey steamroller, and the British concentration area lay directly in its path. Kitchener knew nothing about European armies, ran the War Office as a one-man show, and reduced the General Staff to the status of clerks. But his intuition rarely erred: he was right in planning for a long war when most authorities expected the conflict to be over by Christmas, and he was equally correct in opposing French and Wilson when they pressed him to be allowed to concentrate forward at Maubeuge rather than to the rear at Amiens. Sir John, his romanticism enflamed by Wilson's francophile urgings, and his confidence in Joffre's strategy boosted by his visit to French GQG, was embarking upon a plan which would not merely interpose the BEF between the sledgehammer and the nut, but would result in the nut leaping up to meet the descending hammer.

Joffre had warmly recommended to Sir John the commander of the 5th Army, General Lanrezac, described by Spears as the French army's star turn. This recommendation rang somewhat hollow when the two men met the following morning at Lanrezac's headquarters at Rethel on the Aisne. Lanrezac was a big, heavy man, with a brilliant peacetime reputation and a fondness for expounding plans to his subordinates, eyeglasses hooked over his right ear. The meeting got off to a bad start. Lanrezac's CGS, the dapper Hély d'Oissel, met Huguet with the cutting greeting: 'At last you're here: its not a moment too soon. If we are beaten we will owe it to you.'[34]

Accounts of the meeting vary, but it is clear that French and Lanrezac spent some time alone, and their inability to communicate only worsened the French general's already short temper. An attempt at discussing the situation with the aid of staff officers soon foundered. Sir John stepped forward to a wall map, put on his glasses, found a place with his finger, and asked Lanrezac:

> 'Mon Général, est-ce-que ... ?' His French then gave out, and turning to one of his staff, he asked 'How do you say "to cross the river" in French?' He was told, and proceeded; 'Est-ce-que les Allemands vont traverser la Meuse à------ à------?' Then he fumbled over the pronunciation of the name. 'Huy' was the place, unfortunately one of the most difficult words imaginable to pronounce, the 'u' having practically to be whistled. It was quite beyond Sir John. 'Hoy' he said at last, triumphantly. 'What does he say? What does he say?' exclaimed Lanrezac. Some-

body explained that the Marshal wanted to know whether in his opinion the Germans were going to cross the river at Huy? Lanrezac shrugged his shoulders impatiently. 'Tell the Marshal,' he said curtly, 'that in my opinion the Germans have merely gone to the Meuse to fish.'[35]

The conference ended soon afterwards, and French drove off to Le Cateau. The meeting was nothing short of disastrous from the point of view of Anglo–French relations. It left French with the impression that he was dealing with an ungrateful boor, a Staff College pedant of the worst kind, while Lanrezac, for his part, made no secret of his contempt for Sir John and his khaki-clad latecomers.[36] This would, in itself, have been bad enough, but worse was to follow. For whatever Sir John thought of Lanrezac as a man – and his opinion had deteriorated significantly by the time it came to preparing his memoirs – he took away from Rethel a favourable opinion of the general's military ability. 'General Lanrezac appears a very capable soldier', he wrote in his diary that night, 'and struck me very much by his nerve and decision of character. We fully discussed the situation and arrived at a mutual understanding.'[37] The vital point about the Rethel meeting was, therefore, not merely that French and Lanrezac struck up a brisk mutual dislike; it was that Sir John left the conference convinced that, churlish though he was, Lanrezac was about to take the offensive. By 17 August, however, taking the offensive was exactly what Lanrezac hoped to avoid.

Bad news was waiting at GHQ, now established at Le Cateau. Jimmy Grierson had often joked that the collection of medals on his ample chest commemorated many a hard-fought battle with the knife and fork, and a heart attack killed him in the train on the way to his corps headquarters. French was upset by Grierson's death; they had worked together, on and off, for the previous nine years, and Grierson was a well-liked, capable and fluent General. The immediate consequence of his death was scarcely less dispiriting. French wired Kitchener, asking for Sir Hubert Plumer to be sent out to command II Corps, for although Ian Hamilton asked for the post, Sir John felt unable to recommend him. Kitchener chose neither of them. He selected instead an officer whose bad relations with French were a matter of common knowledge in the army: Sir Horace Smith-Dorrien. This was Kitchenerism at its worst: he knew that French cherished 'great jealousy of and personal animosity towards' Smith-Dorrien, but nevertheless imposed the appointment on Sir John. French was already suspicious of Kitchener's intentions, and the news of Smith-Dorrien's appointment infuriated him. It was a singularly bad start.[38]

On the 18th Sir John saw his corps commanders and their staffs — though Smith-Dorrien had not yet arrived — and explained 'our probable and tentative plans'. He relied exclusively upon GQG's intelligence bulletins, which suggested that masses of German troops were moving north and west of the Meuse. At least five corps and two or three cavalry divisions were expected to advance south-west from the line Brussels–Givet. The BEF, as soon as its concentration was complete, would take up a position north of the Sambre, on the line Mons–Givry. 'Should the German attack develop in the manner expected,' concluded French, 'we shall advance on the line Mons–Dinant to meet it.'[39]

Both GQG and GHQ were guilty of tailoring the facts to fit their own preconceptions. The sinister nature of the German move north of the Meuse failed to penetrate Joffre's robust optimism, and Sir John, dominated during these breathless days by the enthusiastic francophilia of Henry Wilson, accepted GQG's appreciation of the situation without demur. Nor was he necessarily wrong to do so; his own means for gathering intelligence were far more slender than those available to Joffre, and there initially seemed little reason to doubt the accuracy of French estimates. But he did not neglect elementary precautions, and on the 19th two aircraft of the RFC made the corps' first reconnaissance on active service. On the 20th Sir John noted that German movement north of Sambre and Meuse had become more accentuated. This might have worried him had he not been confident that the French still held the line of the Sambre in strength. 'They are only waiting', he wrote, 'for our concentration to be complete, and it is said that General Lanrezac rather chaffs [*sic*] at the delay.'[40]

If Lanrezac was chafing at anything, it was not at the delay in advancing. He had already spoken gloomily of having to retire, and it was only a firm instruction from Joffre that seemingly restored his confidence in the offensive. Ironically, Lanrezac's depressing estimate of German intentions was far nearer the truth than were the blithe pronouncements of GQG. The three marching armies on the German right wing contained no less than sixteen corps, six *Landwehr* brigades, and five cavalry divisions, poised to fall, like the headsman's axe, on the BEF and the 5th Army.

The 20th was a bad day for Joffre. His hitherto victorious offensive into Alsace-Lorraine ran into a German counter-attack which mauled the 1st and 2nd Armies. Yet if the news from his right flank was discouraging, that from his left was distinctly better. Lanrezac seemed to have forgotten his pessimism, and was now up on the Sambre between Namur and Charleroi, while French had announced that the BEF should be able to begin its advance next day. Joffre still discounted the German threat to his left: indeed, the fact that the Germans had extended so far into Belgium encouraged him to issue orders for the 3rd and 4th Armies to attack the German centre in the Ardennes the following day.

Exhilaration still prevailed at GHQ. French spent a good deal of his time away from his headquarters, travelling on horseback or by car, looking at his troops as they came up. On the 18th he watched the Dorsets and the Suffolks on the march: 'The men looked rather tired but quite cheery. Some of the reservists are rather "soft" as yet and want more practice in marching.'[41] Two days later it was the turn of the 1st Division: 'I saw the 4th Brigade (Scott-Kerr) file by on the march – they looked splendid.'[42] Visits to units occupied a considerable amount of French's time during the concentration and, later, on the retreat. It was all very much the Johnnie French style of command: the chat to a South African veteran here, the congratulation on the third stripe there. It put the Field-Marshal firmly in contact with his soldiers, but kept him away from GHQ. There were to be several occasions when decisions could not be taken because the Commander-in-Chief was absent. The personal, ear-tweaking approach had sufficed in South Africa, where French enjoyed the support of a first-rate staff and where the problems of command and control were far smaller than they were in 1914. It is a curious paradox that

French might have fared better had he commanded in the more distant style adopted by Joffre. However encouraging and inspiring it was to chat to old friends on the line of march, it was not the way to fight a modern war.

There was one acquaintance Sir John was not pleased to renew. Smith-Dorrien arrived at GHQ on the 20th, and during the course of his conversation with the Commander-in-Chief mentioned that the King had asked him to report directly on the doings of II Corps. This would involve keeping a special diary, for which he formally requested permission from Sir John, knowing that this permission could only be withheld if French chose to defy his sovereign.[43] This invigorating piece of news can scarcely have increased French's affection for Smith-Dorrien: not only had he got the very corps commander he did not want, but the wretched man was in a position to criticise him to the King. It was not a situation calculated to bring out the best in French, and it would have been surprising if a breakdown had not, sooner or later, occurred.

The BEF advanced on the morning of 21 August, Allenby's cavalry pushing on well ahead and reaching the line of the Mons–Condé Canal. The Field-Marshal was away from GHQ on a visit to Allenby when Lieutenant Spears arrived from 5th Army headquarters with what should have been disturbing news. Lanrezac had declaimed at length on the folly of attack, and was reluctant to leave the security of his splendid positions. Spears warned Wilson of Lanrezac's attitude, but the information did little to dent Wilson's optimism, although he did agree that it would be no bad thing if French and Lanrezac were to meet the next day.

Reports from the RFC and the cavalry all brought ominous intelligence of great German strength to the north of the BEF, but the spell remained unbroken. In his reports to Kitchener, French was quietly confident, although he did admit that the fog of war had not yet lifted. His commitment to the concept of an offensive was total: indeed, even after the Battle of Mons he was able to write that a thrust deeper into Belgium at this time would have disrupted the German advance and 'secured many advantages'. This was also Wilson's view, and it was undoubtedly his infectious euphoria which encouraged Sir John's blind confidence in the French plan to triumph over the well-

1 Colonel French in full dress, 1892.

2   Colonel French with his brigade staff on manoeuvres in Berkshire, 1894. Major Robert Baden-Powell is second on the right.

3   Boer war. Infantry crossing the Modder River with the aid of life lines.

4   With Algy Lawson outside the Royal Pavilion, Aldershot, 1904.

5   Lady French at Government House, Aldershot, *c.* 1904.

6 General Sir Arthur Paget and the Hon. Mrs R. Grenville at the races, 1912.

7 French's sister, Mrs Lottie Despard (*centre, with white hair*), after a suffragette demonstration in Downing Street, 17 November 1911.

8 French and Fitz Watt leaving the War Office during the Curragh crisis, March 1914.

9 At Queensferry, Scotland, accompanying Winston Churchill on a tour of naval establishments, July 1914.

10 (*top left*) Field-Marshal Sir Henry Wilson; (*top right*) Field-Marshal Sir Douglas Haig; (*below left*) General Sir Horace Smith-Dorrien; (*below right*) Field-Marshal Lord Kitchener.

11 Arriving in France, August 1914. Colonel Victor Huguet follows French off HMS *Sentinel*.

12 Cavalry on the retreat from Mons, August 1914.

13   Royal Scots Fusiliers marching confidently to the Front in Flanders, autumn 1914.

14   First Battle of Ypres. Scots Guards dug in near the Menin Road, their trenches primitive by later standards.

15   Neuve Chapelle. Headquarters of the 21st Infantry Brigade, camouflaged in a haystack.

16   After Neuve Chapelle. The British front line strewn with bodies and debris.

17   Walking wounded at Vermelles, during the later stages of the Battle of Loos.

18   French with some of his personal staff (*left to right*) Fitz Watt, Kwajah Mohammed Khan and Major Jack Dawnay, August 1915.

19   French talking to Joffre, with Haig (*right*), spring 1915.

20   Al fresco lunch with Fitz Watt, summer 1915.

21 Farewell to Ireland. French with Sir Nevil Macready, May 1921.

22 French with Winifred Bennett, September 1920.

23 Last parade. (*Centre front*) Joffre. The pall-bearers behind him are Lord Horne, Sir Horace Smith-Dorrien, Sir Arthur Barrett, Lord Beatty and the Duke of Connaught. Those on the far side are Sir Hugh Trenchard, followed by Sir James Willcocks, Sir Ian Hamilton and Lord Methuen.

measured logic of GHQ's own intelligence branch. Sir John's disillusionment, when it came, was to be harsh indeed.[44]

Not all GHQ shared the Commander-in-Chief's confidence. Wully Robertson, the Quartermaster-General, was not given to Wilsonian enthusiasm, and had his doubts. On the 22nd he discussed with Major-General Robb, the Inspector-General of Lines of Communication, the measures which might have to be adopted if the BEF was forced to retreat and had to change its main bases of supply. It was a wise precaution.[45]

The BEF resumed its advance next morning, and, not long after dawn, Major Tom Bridges's squadron of the 4th Dragoon Guards drew the BEF's first blood in an encounter with German cavalry. Sir John, meanwhile, set off to see Lanrezac, and on the way, quite by chance, he met Spears near Avesnes. Spears told him that the 5th Army had been roughly handled on the 21st, and Lanrezac was in no position to launch the offensive upon which the British advance depended. Sir John was only partly convinced. He accepted that one of Lanrezac's corps had been 'knocked about a good deal', but felt that the French General was capable of attacking if he chose to do so. Hearing that Lanrezac was at a forward command post rather than his main headquarters, Sir John decided not to press on and see him. The Rethel meeting continued to bear its deadly fruit. French could see little point in undertaking a long drive with the probability of being insulted at his destination in a language he could not quite understand.[46]

Spears accompanied Sir John to GHQ, and saw the Director of Intelligence, the level-headed Colonel Macdonogh, who was now well aware of the scale of the German manoeuvre and the imminent threat to the BEF's left flank. For French, however, the penny dropped more slowly. After looking at some air reconnaissance reports he declared that: 'There still appears to be very little to our front except cavalry supported by small bodies of infantry.'[47] He was having a late dinner at his quarters, a small château not far from GHQ, when Spears returned. The results of the day's fighting had convinced Spears that the BEF was now about nine miles ahead of the main French line, and there was a gap of several miles between the BEF's right and the 5th Army's left. Lanrezac had no intention of attacking, and if the 5th Army continued to be driven back while the BEF advanced, the British force, isolated and exposed, would be cut to pieces.

Spears arrived at the château with Macdonogh, fortified by a half bottle of champagne which the latter had put by for emergencies. They were quickly ushered in to see French and Murray, and Spears reported on the situation of the 5th Army, warning that it was half a day's march behind the BEF. Macdonogh then chimed in, giving the Field-Marshal the latest batch of air reconnaissance reports, and stressing that the BEF was faced by at least three German corps, one of which was marching on the BEF's left flank. Spears, asked if he had anything to add, asserted that Lanrezac 'had no intention of attacking, even were he in a position to do so, which he was not'.[48]

French listened in silence, the grim-faced Murray beside him. Macdonogh and Spears were then asked to wait in the dining room, where they found staff officers from the corps and the cavalry division, maps spread out on the table, tying up details of the next day's advance. Murray entered twenty minutes later, and said to the officers around the table:

> You are to come in now and see the Chief. He is going to tell you that there will be no advance. But remember that there are to be no questions. Don't ask why. There is no time and it would be useless. You are to take your orders, that's all. Come in now.[49]

Not long after the officers had departed for their formations, Huguet brought an officer of Lanrezac's staff to see French. He requested that the BEF should, the next day, attack the flank of the German formations which were assailing the 5th Army. It was a strange demand in view of the fact that, at exactly the same time, Lanrezac was telling Joffre that the BEF was actually in echelon to the rear of the 5th Army, a position from which this flanking attack would, of course, have been quite impossible.

Later, in *1914*, Sir John complained:

> In view of the most probable situation of the German Army, as it was known to most of us, and

the palpable intention of its Commander to effect a
great turning movement around my left flank, and
having regard to the actual numbers of which I was
able to dispose, it is very difficult to realise what was
in Lanrezac's mind when he made such a request to
me.[50]

French's diary makes it clear that it was his realisation of
German strength, not his doubts about Lanrezac, that prompted him to abandon his advance. Even so, he agreed to remain
in his present position for twenty-four hours, impelled to do so
by a mixture of loyalty to Lanrezac and the shreds of the past
week's optimism. It was now 12.30 on the morning of the 23rd:
French decided to snatch a few hours sleep, and brief his corps
commanders later that morning.[51]

The orders group convened at Smith-Dorrien's headquarters at Sars-la-Bruyère at 5.30 a.m.[52] A few miles to the
north, the BEF was deployed across what was to become, in a
matter of hours, the battlefield of Mons. On the left, II Corps
held the line of the Condé Canal, with I Corps, on the right,
echeloned back from Mons towards Grand Reng. Both the
BEF's flanks were exposed. There was a clear gap between
Haig's right and Lanrezac's left, and on Smith-Dorrien's left
only three French territorial divisions stood between the BEF
and the coast. A French cavalry corps under General Sordet
was on its way to the British left, but its horses were exhausted
by a week of fruitless meanderings in front of the 5th Army,
and its orders were far from clear.

It is more than usually difficult to piece together what went
on at this key conference on the morning of Mons. French and
Smith-Dorrien have both left accounts of it, and these differ
significantly on points of fact. French's version in *1914*, which
agrees substantially with what he wrote at the time in his diary,
states that he told his commanders of the doubts which had
arisen in his mind over the previous twenty-four hours, and
warned them to be prepared for an advance or a retreat.[53]
Smith-Dorrien initially wrote that he found the Field-Marshal
'in excellent form', denied that French said anything about
being prepared to advance or to retire, and left the meeting
feeling that Sir John was full of optimism and intended to use

the canal position merely as a jumping-off place for a continuation of the advance.[54] By the time he came to write his memoirs, however, Sir Horace had changed his mind. He now agreed that French had warned the corps commanders that they might have to advance or retire. He also added that he had complained about the over-extended nature of his position, and suggested plans for a local retirement if enemy pressure became too great.[55] French, on the other hand, maintained that it was he who had warned Smith-Dorrien of the weakness of his position in the 'salient' in front of Mons itself.[56] It seemed safe to conclude that the position of II Corps was fully discussed, and to agree with the *Official History* that French did indeed order the corps commanders to be ready to move in either direction. The evidence also suggests that Sir John, buoyed up, perhaps, by Henry Wilson, was once again underestimating the strength of the enemy threat.[57]

When the conference broke up the sounds of battle could be heard to the north. French thought that nothing of importance was afoot, and the Germans were merely 'trying to "feel" our position all round'.[58] Accordingly, he drove off to Valenciennes to inspect a newly-constituted infantry brigade and talk to the local French commander. He left Murray at Sars-la-Bruyère, and did not return to GHQ until early afternoon. In the meantime, the fighting had swollen into a pitched battle, with the disciplined musketry of II Corps cutting swathes through attacking German infantry.

Sir John remained convinced that the attack was not serious. At about 3 p.m. he dictated a message to Macdonogh, for onward transmission to Spears, telling Lanrezac of his intentions:

> I am prepared to fulfil the role assigned to me when the Fifth Army advances to the attack. In the meantime I hold advanced defensive positions ...
> I am now much in advance of the line held by the Fifth Army, and feel my position to be as far forward as circumstances will allow, particularly in view of the fact that I am not properly prepared to take offensive action until tomorrow morning, as I have previously informed you.[59]

It is not hard to find the source of this false optimism. Wilson spent the afternoon making what he blithely called a 'careful calculation', which persuaded him that the BEF was faced by one corps and a cavalry division, or possibly two corps. As II Corps had already positively identified two German corps and a cavalry division early in the day, this says little for Wilson's calculating ability. Wilson then continued: 'I persuaded Murray and Sir John that this was so, with the result that I was allowed to draft orders for an attack tomorrow ... '[60] At 6 p.m. Macdonogh brought Sir John his appreciation of the situation, but the planned attack survived until a message arrived from Joffre about an hour later. It announced that the BEF was threatened by three German corps; this, in French's own words, 'rendered it necessary for me to radically change my dispositions for tomorrow'.[61]

Even now Sir John hoped to avoid a retreat. He spoke crossly of 'more or less pessimistic messages' from Smith-Dorrien, and at 8.40 sent him the following order: 'I will stand the attack on the ground now occupied by the troops. You will therefore strengthen your position by every possible means during the night.'[62]

It was midnight when Spears arrived at Le Cateau with news which made a continuation of the defensive battle impossible. He had discovered that Lanrezac had issued orders for a withdrawal, an action which threatened to expose the BEF to certain destruction. Sir John also deduced from Spears's report that the French 3rd and 4th Armies were retiring.[63] Although neither French nor Spears knew so for certain at the time, this was indeed the case. The two French armies had been badly cut up in encounter battles with two German armies around Virton and Neufchâteau, and had fallen back. The news of Lanrezac's decision stunned French. He had done his best, whatever his personal feelings, to give loyal support to Lanrezac, who now intended to retire without so much as a by-your-leave. The incident did more than confirm Sir John in his hatred of Lanrezac. It convinced him that the French were basically untrustworthy as Allies, and sowed seeds of distrust which, from time to time, bore bitter fruit.

The practical problems of extricating the BEF were bad enough, and they were worsened by the sort of fudged staff-work which amply bore out Wully Robertson's gloomy prognostications made in the Sandhurst gymnasium seven months before. Corps Chiefs of Staff were summoned to GHQ, to be told by Murray, at about 1.00 on the morning of the 24th, that the army would make a general retreat of some eight miles. No detailed instructions for the withdrawal were issued: the corps commanders were simply ordered to settle arrangements in consultation. The fact that II Corps made as good a withdrawal as it did was no thanks to Murray or the Operations Branch at GHQ. Indeed, it was to become clear over the next few days that Murray lacked the moral fibre or physical stamina for his post. His weakness was to prove particularly serious. Not only was French, to whom staff procedures remained shadowy mysteries, dependent upon the services of a first-rate CGS, but Murray's inability to assert himself left the field clear for Wilson.

French's disenchantment with Lanrezac was summed up in a terse message dictated to Spears early on the 24th. Should his left flank be seriously threatened, French warned, he would retire on his lines of communication, leaving Lanrezac to look after himself.[64] Lanrezac received this news with remarkable aplomb and passed the information on to Joffre. The French Commander-in-Chief was now preoccupied with the threat to his left, but realised that 'it was the British alone who could offset this menace and yet it was precisely this army to which I had no right to give orders'.[65] He contented himself with asking French to delay the enemy as best he could, and, if he had to retire, to do so in the direction of Cambrai rather than Amiens. The danger on the left did, however, induce Joffre to shift troops on to the threatened flank. Initially only two reserve divisions were sent to assist the over-extended Territorials on the British left. Sordet's cavalry was also on its way, but Joffre realised that it was by now too exhausted to be of much use. Nevertheless, this reinforcement was the forerunner of an important re-grouping of the French armies, which was to result, some days later, in the creation of a new formation, the 6th Army, between the BEF and the sea.

It was fortunate for the Allied cause that French's high regard for Joffre, a relic of their cordial interview just over a week before, had partly survived the strains and disappointments of the past few days. Sir John replied in mid-afternoon: 'I am falling back slowly to position Maubeuge, Valenciennes ... If driven from these positions I will act in accordance with your wishes.'[66] He had been out to see I Corps at midday, noting with satisfaction that Haig's men were 'very active and pushing', and sparing some admiration for the German gunners, whose 'shells seemed to burst very well'.[67] Smith-Dorrien's men were in rather less good order, which was only to be expected after a stiff defensive battle and a withdrawal in contact with the enemy. On his way back to Le Cateau Sir John met General Sordet, a quiet, regular-featured man who reminded the Field-Marshal of a piece of Dresden china. French renewed his request for assistance on his left, but Sordet pointed out that he had as yet received no orders for this move, although he promised to do all he could to help.[68]

Sir John stopped briefly at Le Cateau, where he was pleased to see the leading elements of the 4th Division, whose dispatch had been notified to GHQ on the 19th. Its arrival would bring the BEF's strength up to five infantry divisions and a cavalry division, though the 4th Division lacked some of its essential services and, moreover, would be detraining straight into battle. French then returned to his forward command-post at Bavai, where Murray and his staff were installed in the Mairie, working flat-out in the intense heat. The scene provoked French, never an admirer of staff officers, to write:

> Personally, I have always been far more a regimental than a Staff Officer ... but when I have witnessed scenes and gone through days such as I am now imperfectly describing ... it makes my blood boil to hear and read of the calumnies which are often heaped upon the head of the unfortunate 'Staff'.[69]

Murray was already feeling the strain badly, and his curt diary entry for the 24th speaks volumes: '24 hours without undressing, no sleep.'[70]

Early in the afternoon reports from GQG that the 3rd, 4th and 5th Armies were falling back convinced French that there was no chance of making a stand in the position to which the army was retiring: the BEF was still ahead of the 5th Army, and the RFC's reports were alarming. This being so, he had two alternatives: to continue to retreat, or to take refuge under the guns of the fortress of Maubeuge. It did not take him long to reject the seductive appeal of Maubeuge. The place 'loomed out of the fog of war like a safe and welcoming haven'. But two considerations impelled him to resist the siren call of the fortress. In the first place, he had an instinctive feeling that the Germans were trying to make him take refuge there, and, secondly, he remembered the passage from *Operations of War* in which Hamley wrote that the commander of a retiring army who throws himself into a fortress acts like one who, when the ship is foundering, lays hold of the anchor. The retreat must continue.[71]

French passed an anxious night, and was pleased to hear from Murray, on the morning of the 25th, that the retirement had begun and was proceeding well. His anxiety was well-founded. The large, thickly-wooded Forest of Mormal lay across the BEF's line of retreat, and Sir John, recognising that no roads ran north–south through this barrier, had reluctantly decided that II Corps should retire along its western side while I Corps moved to its east. I Corps had a quiet day, its withdrawal hampered more by sharing road-space with French units than by enemy action. II Corps was less fortunate, and the rearguards of the cavalry and 3rd Division spent a gruelling day warding off German hooks at the British left.

Major George Clive, British liaison officer with GQG, visited GHQ that morning. He met Sir John, out and about as usual, on the road: 'The one question was, "What is your old man (Joffre) going to do?" The general feeling was one of great dissatisfaction at the action of the French, in not supporting us on Sunday or Monday ... '[72] French had a lengthy discussion with Murray and Wilson on the desirability of holding a position around Le Cateau, just south of the Forest of Mormal. Wilson feared that the Germans were trying to turn the BEF's left and sever its line of communications. Sir John disagreed, but favoured retirement to conform with the French and 'if necessary to get behind the Oise to reorganise and refit'.[73]

This belief that the BEF could somehow return to its corner like a winded boxer and take a well-earned breather was to loom large in the Field-Marshal's mind over the next week. It was the product of a number of considerations. Firstly, Sir

19 French talking to Joffre, with Haig (*right*), spring 1915.

20 Al fresco lunch with Fitz Watt, summer 1915.

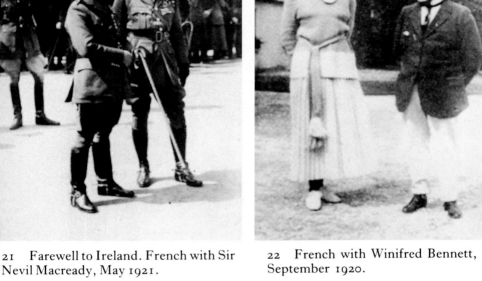

21   Farewell to Ireland. French with Sir Nevil Macready, May 1921.

22   French with Winifred Bennett, September 1920.

23   Last parade. (*Centre front*) Joffre. The pall-bearers behind him are Lord Horne, Sir Horace Smith-Dorrien, Sir Arthur Barrett, Lord Beatty and the Duke of Connaught. Those on the far side are Sir Hugh Trenchard, followed by Sir James Willcocks, Sir Ian Hamilton and Lord Methuen.

John was becoming convinced that his force was being hazarded to exactly that risk which Kitchener's instructions had warned him against. Furthermore, he felt that Lanrezac's 'desertion' had somehow discharged him of any moral responsibility towards the French: if he helped Joffre, it was out of the goodness of his heart and because of the affection of one bluff General for another. French's consideration for his men now bulked larger than his regard for his Allies. The rear area of a retreating army is a depressing place, and useful though it was for Sir John to see his troops on the march, he was profoundly disturbed by their condition, and felt certain that they required rest. This was more than the BEF: it was the old regular army he knew and loved, cap-badges he had seen twinkle for nearly half a century, men he had soldiered with since the days of pipe-clay and scarlet. The thought that this warm, rough body was being smashed to pieces around him was a powerful factor in French's decision-making.

There was also the problem of personalities. Poor Archie Murray was already desperately tired, and he dwelt too much in the Commander-in-Chief's shadow to chivvy Sir John into issuing formal orders as often as he might have done. Smith-Dorrien had visited Bavai on the evening of the 24th, requested detailed orders from French, and bullied Murray into issuing an army order for the withdrawal to the Le Cateau position. The incident served only to worsen the strain between the Field-Marshal and Sir Horace. French had seen far more of I Corps than he had of Smith-Dorrien's command, and the latter's attitude struck him – quite wrongly, in view of the pressure being sustained by II Corps – as unnecessarily agitated.

GHQ moved to St Quentin on the evening of the 25th, and orders for a continuation of the withdrawal went out at 7.30 p.m. Smith-Dorrien had already been told, in a hasty note from Henry Wilson, that it was the Commander-in-Chief's intention to retreat on the 26th.[74] French was awakened at 2.00 on the morning of the 26th with the alarming news that Haig's corps headquarters, at Landrecies, was under heavy attack. Sir John was fond of Haig: if the unflappable Douglas reported that he was in dire straits, such must indeed be the case. Wilson suggested that the Germans might be trying to exploit the gap between the corps, and at 3.50 a.m. II Corps was asked to march to Haig's assistance. Smith-Dorrien, however, 'professed himself unable to move a man'.[75] Haig's position was, in fact, far less serious than it seemed, but Smith-Dorrien's refusal to help, eminently justifiable though it was, did not endear him to the Commander-in-Chief.

'No sooner', wrote French, 'had anxiety on Haig's account ceased than trouble arose with Smith-Dorrien.'[76] Sir Horace was under orders to resume his retreat at daybreak, and had already issued preliminary orders to that effect. In the early hours of the morning, however, he decided, after consultation with Allenby and Major-General Hubert Hamilton of the 3rd Division, that the Germans would be upon him before he could get away. He therefore decided to stand and fight at Le Cateau, hoping that a brisk 'stopping action' would halt the Germans long enough for the withdrawal to proceed uninterrupted. Major-General Snow, whose 4th Division was not under Smith-Dorrien's command, agreed to co-operate.

Smith-Dorrien told French of his decision in a message which reached St Quentin at 5 a.m. The Commander-in-Chief's reply was not discouraging:

> If you can hold your ground the situation appears likely to improve ... Although you are given a free hand as to the method this telegram is not intended to convey the impression that I am not anxious for you to carry out the retirement, and you must make every endeavour to do so.[77]

Not only did Smith-Dorrien feel that his action was approved of by GHQ, but he also hoped for assistance from I Corps, as the Le Cateau position had originally been selected with a view to occupation by both corps once they had united after passing the Forest of Mormal.

French never admitted to sending the early morning telegram, either in his diary or in the less reliable *1914*. In both works he maintained that as soon as he heard what was afoot, he 'urged Smith-Dorrien to withdraw from the action and retire as soon as he possibly could'.[78] Wilson's diary illuminates the issue. He awoke French as soon as Smith-Dorrien's message arrived, and the Field-Marshal, without seeming to grasp the full import of the news, agreed to the proposal, but insisted that the exhausted Murray should not be woken up. The vital telegram, therefore, represented the first fragmentary thoughts of a man roused from sleep after an exhausting day. After a few more hours' sleep, and mature reflection, Sir John changed his mind, and ordered Wilson to speak to Smith-Dorrien on the telephone and urge him to break off the action as soon as he could. Smith-Dorrien's confidence was contagious, and the conversation ended with Wilson saying: 'Good luck to you; yours is the first cheerful voice I have heard for three days.'[79]

Smith-Dorrien's decision to fight at Le Cateau was to become a *cause célèbre* and a bone of contention between Sir Horace and Sir John. The argument was long and complex: both protagonists attracted supporters and opponents, and the dispute can only be summarised here. French's official dispatch on the battle, written in early September, stated that Smith-Dorrien had been ordered to retire 'at the earliest possible moment', but ended with a handsome tribute to Smith-Dorrien's 'rare and unusual coolness, intrepidity and determination'.[80] In *1914* French excused this fulsome praise by saying that the dispatch was written before the full facts were available. These facts, he maintained, showed that Smith-Dorrien had risked the destruction of his corps in an unnecessary battle which had cost it 14,000 men and 80 guns.[81]

Smith-Dorrien vigorously defended his decision to give battle, maintaining that 'an impartial Commander-in-Chief' would have considered that the circumstances warranted his action. He accused French of wilfully overstating the casualties sustained by II Corps – the *Official History* gives them as 7,812 men and 38 guns – and of failing to appreciate the exhausted state of the corps before the battle. He suggested that *1914* was 'mostly a work of fiction and a foolish one too ... '[82]

There can be no doubt that *1914* was, to a great extent, another shot in a propaganda campaign which had gone on since Smith-Dorrien wrote a newspaper article on the subject in 1917. But the inaccuracies of *1914* should not be allowed to conceal an important fact. French, in company with Murray, Haig, Wilson and Huguet, and through him GQG, all believed, genuinely enough, that Le Cateau spelled the end of

II Corps as a fighting formation. It was not until after the retreat, when stragglers came in and units reassembled, that the real cost of the battle could be established. In April 1915 French told Haig that he regretted not having tried Smith-Dorrien by court-martial after Le Cateau: he was preaching to the converted, for Haig had already written harshly about 'the ill-considered decision of the commander of the II Corps to give battle at Le Cateau'.[83] Murray, who was fond of Smith-Dorrien, calling him 'a straight honourable gentleman, most lovable, kind and generous', nevertheless felt that 'he did wrong to fight other than a strong rear-guard action'.[84]

Most historians would agree with Smith-Dorrien and his supporters that the stand at Le Cateau was justified. John Terraine describes the battle as 'not only the most brilliant exploit of the BEF during the retreat, but one of the most splendid feats of the British Army during the whole of the war'.[85] The battle checked the pressure on II Corps, which was thereafter allowed to continue its retreat more or less unmolested.

The reasons for French's opposition to Smith-Dorrien's decision to fight, and his subsequent attacks on the commander of II Corps, are not hard to discern. He had a poor opinion of Smith-Dorrien's military ability, an opinion worsened, however, wrongly, by the events of 23rd–25th August. He was convinced that delay would result in the annihilation of II Corps, and had no confidence in Smith-Dorrien's assertion that a stand was essential. Sir John was not alone in doubting Smith-Dorrien's judgement. Forrestier-Walker, II Corps's Chief of Staff, had attempted to resign his appointment during the battle of Mons, having had enough of his General's vile temper. Murray told him 'not to be an ass' and sent him back to his post, but the affair cannot have boosted GHQ's confidence in Smith-Dorrien.[86] It must nevertheless be recognised that Le Cateau and the debate it sparked off redound little to the Credit of the Commander-in-Chief or his staff. Sir John's account in *1914* is riddled with inaccuracies which the peculiar circumstances under which the book was written can only go a short way towards excusing. French never forgave Smith-Dorrien for Le Cateau. The Field-Marshal was, as even his most steadfast supporters admitted, 'as bad an enemy as he was a good friend', and from 26 August onwards he lavished the full force of his hatred upon Smith-Dorrien.[87]

While II Corps was fighting for its life at Le Cateau, French met Joffre and Lanrezac at St Quentin. The meeting was characterised by what Huguet termed 'extreme coolness' and 'lack of cordiality'.[88] French complained bitterly about Lanrezac's behaviour, and was, as he later admitted to Spears, profoundly galled by the French General's vague and academic reply. Things went from bad to worse when Joffre discussed his latest plan, for a fighting withdrawal to a new line and the formation of the 6th Army around Amiens. Sir John looked puzzled during Joffre's speech, and declared that he knew nothing of the scheme. It transpired that the relevant order — *Instruction Générale No. 2* — had been received at GHQ during the night, but had not yet been shown to the Commander-in-Chief. Joffre thereupon went over his plan again, but it struck his audience that he had already lost confidence in its success. In an atmosphere of growing hostility, Sir John insisted that he must continue his retreat, and even Joffre's promise to strengthen the Allied left failed to shake him.

Although Joffre left the conference with 'a serious impression as to the fragility of our extreme left', the meeting was not altogether disastrous. He believed that French agreed with him that the Allied left was indeed the crucial point, and would press Kitchener to send the remaining British division to France rather than to Belgium, where French suspected it might be sent. Some of the wounds inflicted at the conference were soon healed. Joffre, never a man to decline a good meal, accepted Sir John's invitation to lunch, during the course of which he partially appeased French by frankly admitting that his plans had failed, and expressing considerable dissatisfaction with Lanrezac.[89]

GHQ left for Noyon that afternoon. It was decidedly frayed. Murray had collapsed the previous night, when the news of the German attack on Landrecies arrived. He was helped through the 26th only by an injection given him by GHQ's medical officer. Henry Wilson, as sub-Chief of the General Staff, was Murray's deputy, and should have presided over the operations and intelligence branches during his superior's incapacity. The extent of his failure is demonstrated by the fact that he let Sir John attend the meeting with Joffre without informing him that *Instruction Générale No. 2* had arrived at GHQ. The smooth running of GHQ was Murray's responsibility, but French can justly be criticised for failing to appreciate the extent of Murray's inability to cope. Had Sir John been a trained and experienced staff officer he might have been able to have remedied some of GHQ's deficiencies. As it was, however, he continued to tug hopefully at the chain of command without realising how hopelessly tangled it had become.

So gloomy was the atmosphere at Noyon in the wake of what was generally seen as Smith-Dorrien's defeat that Huguet informed GQG that the BEF had 'lost all cohesion'.[90] Throughout the 27th Joffre's liaison officers painted a gloomy picture of a shattered BEF, stumbling back in confusion and uncovering the left flank of the 5th Army. Sir John warned Huguet that there would be a 'feeling of bitterness and regret' in England when news of the early battles arrived, and in response to Huguet's urging, Joffre sent Sir John a warm message of congratulation, expressing his gratitude at the BEF's energy and perseverance.[91] The pessimism at headquarters did not accurately reflect the events of the 26th: I Corps had retired in good order, and the strenuous efforts of Smith-Dorrien's staff had maintained the cohesion of the hard-pressed II Corps. Nevertheless, French believed that II Corps was crippled. Smith-Dorrien met him at 2.00 on the morning of the 27th and, in an interview made more than usually acrimonious by the fact that Sir Horace had not been told of GHQ's move and had only found its new location with difficulty, French accused him of being unrealistically optimistic.

The army resumed its retreat on the 28th. While GHQ moved back to Compiègne, French took the opportunity to see his men on the line of march. He had not seen much of the troops since the 25th, and contact with the marvellous raw material of the BEF soon went some way towards dispersing his depression. He wrote:

> I had a most agreeable surprise. I met the men and talked to them as they were lying about resting. I told them how much I appreciated their work and what the country thought of them. I told them also

of Joffre's telegram and its publication in England. The wonderful spirit and bearing they showed was beyond all praise $-\frac{1}{2}$ a million of them would walk over Europe![92]

But if French's own morale was recovering from the shocks of the 26th, GHQ remained profoundly pessimistic. Murray collapsed again, and Wilson ordered the corps to jettison all unnecessary impedimenta and 'hustle along'.[93]

Cheered though he was by the sight of the BEF's well-ordered retreat, Sir John remained reluctant to embark upon any manoeuvres which would put his force at risk. This was particularly unfortunate, for Joffre had given Lanrezac firm orders to counter-attack, but Haig's request to co-operate with the 5th Army in a thrust against the German flank was turned down by the Commander-in-Chief. Lanrezac was furious, and even Spears felt that Sir John was at fault.[94]

On the 29th encouraging news of a neat little victory won by Chetwode's 5th Cavalry Brigade at Cerizy prompted French to make in his diary a comment which throws interesting light upon his state of mind at the time. 'Perhaps,' he speculated, 'the charms of war lie in its glorious uncertainty.'[95] His army was in full retreat before a powerful enemy; relations with his allies were parlous, and he was seriously considering withdrawing from the fighting line to rest and reorganise. Yet he still believed that war had charms and that uncertainty – and the full extent of his uncertainty regarding French movements and intentions can only be grasped from reading his diary – was glorious. This highly emotional aspect of Sir John's character sat uneasily beside its more rational elements, and it lends a distinctive, and not always easily comprehensible, aura to his generalship.

Lanrezac's army fought the Battle of Guise on the 29th, advancing along 25 kilometres of front in an attack which gave the German 2nd Army a bloody nose and helped induce the commander of the German 1st Army to wheel to his left, turning in front of Paris, rather than behind it as Schlieffen had intended. The BEF scarcely budged. French's visit to his troops had convinced him that the men needed rest, and his over-identification with his tired soldiers, coupled with his reluctance to co-operate with a commander whose unreliability was, in his view, a matter of record, persuaded him to keep the BEF out of the battle.

Joffre spent the morning with Lanrezac, and then drove to Compiègne to see Sir John. The French Commander-in-Chief was worried by rumours that Sir John and his government were casting nervous glances towards the Channel ports. He emphasised the vital importance of the BEF's remaining in line with its flanking French formations. The Russian offensive in the east would soon produce an effect upon the Germans, and it would then be possible for the general offensive to be resumed. Joffre could see that he was making little impression on French. Murray stood behind the Field-Marshal, tugging at the skirts of his tunic as if to prevent him from yielding to Joffre's pleas. French insisted that his troops required forty-eight hours of absolute rest, and Murray reinforced his chief's argument with an intelligence report showing the strength of German forces concentrated against the BEF. Joffre left Compiègne in a very bad humour, certain that the project laid down in *Instruction Générale No. 2* was now impracticable.[96]

After Joffre had departed, Sir John received news, from a French staff officer, that the 5th Army had been pushed back behind the Oise. It seems likely that this information was the result of a misunderstanding, but it prompted Sir John, who always feared the worst where Lanrezac was concerned, to issue orders for a retirement on the line Rethondes–Soissons. No sooner had these orders been issued than another message arrived, announcing that the 5th Army was, in fact, doing remarkably well. French admitted that he was 'sorry to have ordered the retirement tomorrow but it can't be altered now'.[97]

By the 30th, French's gaze was fixed unblinkingly on the area south of Paris. Spears visited him in the morning, and found him 'one of the coolest and calmest people at GHQ'.[98] Cool he may have been, but it was the coolness of a man who had come to accept the worst. As soon as the Field-Marshal heard that the 5th and 6th Armies were continuing to fall back, he announced that he would resume his own withdrawal. He telegraphed Joffre:

I feel it very necessary to impress upon you that the British Army cannot under any circumstances take up a position in the front line for at least ten days. I require men and guns to make good casualties which have not been properly estimated owing to continual retirement behind fighting rearguards. You will thus understand that I cannot meet your wishes to fill the gap between the Fifth and Sixth Armies ...

Later that day Huguet wired that Sir John wished to withdraw behind the Seine, to the area Mantes–Poissy–St Germain, in order to rest and refit. He added, in a letter, that it was only the news of the continued French retirement that had persuaded Sir John to retreat. He intended to remain behind the Seine for as short a time as possible, and would advance as soon as the reorganisation was complete. The BEF's main base was to be changed to St Nazaire, and Le Mans was to replace Amiens as the forward base.[99]

Joffre had little choice but to agree to French's suggestion, although he did so with the proviso that the BEF should move east of Paris to avoid becoming embroiled in the lines of communication of the 6th Army. Kitchener heard of the plan by way of the BEF's Inspector-General of Communications, and in view of the fact that Sir John's recent messages had been reasonably hopeful, the news came as a rude shock. He asked French to elaborate on the meaning of his orders. Sir John replied by telegram that he was quite unable to remain in the fighting line in view of the continued French retirement. He proposed to retire behind the Seine to refit: 'This means marching for some eight days without fatiguing the troops at a considerable distance from the enemy.' He then went on to lambast the French high command.

> I do not like General Joffre's plan. I should have liked to have assumed a more vigorous offensive at once, and this has been represented to him, but he pleads in reply the present inability of the British Army to go forward as a reason for retirement and delay.

Sir John concluded by assuring Kitchener that he had no intention of making 'a prolonged or definite retreat'.[100]

A letter from Sir John, sent by King's Messenger from Compiègne on the same day, took much the same tone:

> I cannot say that I am happy in the outlook as to the further progress of the campaign in France. My confidence in the ability of the leaders of the French Army to carry this campaign to a successful conclusion is fast waning, and this is my real reason for the decision I have taken to move the British Forces so far back ... I have been pressed very hard to remain, even in my shattered condition, in the fighting line, but I have absolutely refused to do so and I hope you will approve of the course I have taken. Not only is it in accordance with the spirit and letter of your instructions, but it is dictated by common sense.

He believed that French soldiers were excellent fighting men, and attributed their failure 'to no other cause than defective higher leading'.[101]

Both these communications, and the telegram in particular, were badly-worded and, as historians have been swift to point out, bore evidence of the confused state of their author's mind. If, for example, Sir John felt too weak to remain in the line to fight a defensive battle, how could he suggest that a vigorous offensive would have suited him better? The messages do, however, give some insight into French's thinking, and should not be dismissed as the rambling excursions of a General who believed himself already beaten. Sir John had altogether lost confidence in the French leadership, and his disillusionment was all the greater in view of the confidence that he had previously entertained. Joffre emerges from the mists of history as a clear-headed General of remarkable fortitude, but in late August 1914 French may be forgiven for seeing him as the author of disaster on a grand scale. French's unfortunate experience with Lanrezac had permanently prejudiced him against that officer. So low was his regard for the 5th Army that he did not believe reports of the Battle of Guise until he had sent a trusted emissary — none other than Jack Seely, in khaki once again — to interview the corps commanders concerned.

Having once been put 'in the cart' by Lanrezac, he had no intention of repeating the experience.

Kitchener's instructions, and French's own long experience in a small army where to sustain heavy losses was exceptional, also played their part. He believed that the Kaiser, 'in his rancour and hate', was making a special effort to bring about the destruction of the BEF, and the losses his force had already incurred – losses which GHQ consistently overestimated at this period – were severe by the standards of his own military experience. Sir John, in short, still failed to grasp the true nature of the conflict in which he was involved. He saw it as the Boer War writ large, not as the death-grasp of two mighty alliances, a struggle in which the losses of Klip Drift or Paardeberg were utterly insignificant.

On the 31st French encountered the first gusts of reaction to his decision to withdraw. Joffre renewed his appeal, pointing out, through Huguet, that the Germans were already shifting troops to the east. Kitchener expressed surprise at his decision, and urged him to conform, if at all possible, to Joffre's plans.[102] Sir Francis Bertie, the British Ambassador, relayed a message from President Poincaré begging him to 'fill the gap'.[103] Sir John was adamant: 'I cannot do anything until I can refit', he wrote.[104] He wired to Kitchener:

> If the French go on with their present tactics which are practically to fall back right and left of me, usually without notice, and to abandon all idea of offensive operations, of course then the gap in the French line will remain and the consequence must be borne by them.

He thought that the BEF was in no condition to sustain an attack by even one German corps, and that II Corps was in a 'shattered condition'. He did, however, promise to remain north of a line running east–west through Nanteuil, as long as the French held their present positions. Sir John expected to reach that line the next day, and would try to refit there. He ended by saying 'I think you had better trust me to watch the situation and act according to circumstances ... '[105]

Kitchener was disinclined to take a back seat at a time of crisis. He decided to visit France to see the situation for himself, and a midnight meeting of such Cabinet members as could be found authorised his trip. In the early hours of 1 September he telegraphed to Sir John, warning of his imminent arrival and asking French to suggest a suitable meeting place. French had, meanwhile sent yet another telegram, in which he told Kitchener that:

> In its present condition the force under my command is unable to support our Allies effectively ... I have no definite idea of General Joffre's general plan; its general result is the advance of the Germans and the retreat of the Allies.
>
> We will advance into the front line tomorrow and do our utmost if you choose to order it, but I am sure that the result of this would be a grave disaster to the French troops. I could never hope to extricate them as I extricated them before.[106]

This idiosyncratic interpretation of the events of late August would probably only have confirmed Kitchener in his determination to visit Sir John. In the event, however, he had already departed, by special train from Charing Cross, by the time the telegram reached London.

The meeting between French and Kitchener took place in the British Embassy on the afternoon of September. Its circumstances could scarcely have been more inauspicious. Despite the routine politenesses of his letters to the Secretary of State, French already harboured a deep-seated distrust of Kitchener. He was aghast to see that Kitchener 'was dressed in khaki as a FM', and suspected that the Secretary of State had worn uniform in order to undermine his authority with the French and with the army.[107] It was natural enough for Kitchener to wear uniform, for, as Lieutenant-Colonel Maurice Hankey pointed out, 'he lived in uniform at the time ... and he had come away in such a hurry that it had probably never occurred to him to change into plain clothes.'[108] Nevertheless, even Hankey, who was no admirer of French, admitted that it might have been more diplomatic if Asquith himself had visited Sir John, or if Kitchener had not worn uniform.

The sight of Kitchener's uniform inflamed French from the start. Huguet, who watched the two Field-Marshals meet, noted that while Kitchener was 'calm, balanced, reflective', Sir John was 'sour, impetuous, with congested face, sullen and ill-tempered in expression'.[109] French's temper was not improved when Kitchener announced his intention of inspecting the BEF. Bertie sided with French over this issue, and the project was eventually abandoned.[110] The strategic question remained. French's Irish temper was too well known for Kitchener not to see the danger signs: realising that the interview was likely to become heated, he suggested that they should withdraw from the main body of the meeting, which included Viviani, the French Premier, and Millerand, the Minister of War, into a neighbouring room.

The only accounts of the conversation which followed are Sir John's. He wrote in his diary that 'we had rather a disagreeable time. I think K found he was making a mistake.'[111] The fuller, if less reliable, version in *1914* describes how Kitchener opened the conversation by objecting to French's tone. Sir John then reminded the Secretary of State that the responsibility for operations was his alone, and although:

> I valued highly his advice and assistance, which I would gladly accept as such ... I would not tolerate any interference with my executive command and authority so long as His Majesty's Goverment chose to retain me in my present position.
>
> I think he began to realise my difficulties, and we finally came to an amicable understanding.[112]

The nature of this understanding is revealed in a telegram sent by Kitchener to the Cabinet shortly after the meeting.

> French's troops are now engaged in the fighting line where he will remain conforming to the movements of the French army though at the same time acting with caution to avoid being in any way unsupported on his flanks.

He copied the message to French, adding:

> I feel sure that you will agree that the above represents the conclusions we came to; but in any case, until I can communicate with you further in answer

233

to anything you may wish to tell me, please consider it as an instruction.[113]

Kitchener had, in short, forbidden Sir John to pull the BEF out of the line and to withdraw behind the Seine.

The affair caused lasting resentment as far as French was concerned. Asquith encouraged Churchill to act as mediator, and on the 4th Churchill wrote to Sir John, saying that Kitchener had only intervened because:

> The Cabinet was bewildered by your telegram proposing to retire from the line ... We feared that you and Joffre might have quarrelled, or that something had happened to the army of which we had not been informed. In these circumstances telegraphing was useless, and a personal consultation was indispensable if further misunderstandings were to be avoided.[114]

French was not mollified. On 6 September he wrote:

> K's visit was really most unfortunate. He took me away from the front to visit him in Paris on a very critical day ...
>
> I do beg you, my dear Friend, to add once more to all the many and great kindnesses you have done me & *stop this interference* with field operations. Kitchener *knows nothing* about European Warfare. Of course he's a fine organiser but he never was & never will be a Commander in the field ...

He added a postscript early the following morning, admitting that the letter might have been 'rather strong', but concluding:

> To send another FM out here to lecture me (he came in FM's uniform!) seems to me a sign of distrust and it *hurts* me. Remember this if you think I should not have written like this and burn this letter PLEASE.[115]

By the 10th Sir John was in a more forgiving mood. 'I fear I was a little unreasonable about K and his visit,' he told Churchill, 'but we have been through a hard time and perhaps my temper isn't made any better by it.'[116]

Relations between French and Kitchener never recovered from the effects of the 1 September meeting. Sir John's letters to the Secretary of State remained outwardly cordial and French occasionally permitted himself a cheerful reminiscence about the good times they had shared in South Africa. Resentment spread, like a cancer, beneath the surface. French's diary contains increasingly outspoken attacks on Kitchener: by the end of the year he believed that 'the man has gone mad ... ' The same bitter sentiments were contained in letters to personal friends, and by the spring of 1915 Sir John's hatred of Kitchener, and his suspicions concerning the Secretary of State's ambitions regarding the command in France, were common knowledge at GHQ and had percolated through to GQG.[117]

The weight of the evidence in the Kitchener–French dispute is undoubtedly against Sir John. Kitchener did not behave improperly in visiting Paris, although, given his knowledge of French, it was tactless of him to wear uniform and to suggest a visit to the troops. French was, predictably, jealous of his own authority, and made dangerously insecure by what he sensed as threats to it. In *1914* he attempted to conceal the truth by suggesting that Kitchener visited Paris with the prime intention of preventing him from retreating. As John Terraine has pointed out, it was not the fact of the retreat that perturbed Kitchener, but the manner in which French intended to carry it out.[118] Kitchener's knowledge of European war was indeed sketchy, but his instinct was sounder than French's. The fate of the BEF was, for good or ill, inextricably bound up with that of Joffre's armies: a unilateral withdrawal behind the Seine was quite out of the question.

French's insistence on such a retirement was, as has already been noted, the logical consequence of his military upbringing, his experiences of inter-allied co-operation, and an honourable desire to spare his soldiers. It is hard not to sympathise with him for being summoned from his headquarters while his army was in action, although, given the limited value of GHQ's contribution to the battles of Mons and Le Cateau, a temporary absence was scarcely likely to prove fatal to the BEF.

A studious dissection of the Paris meeting and the events leading up to it does not go far enough. French was not in a position to analyse events clearly and dispassionately, nor was it in his nature to do so. He reacted emotionally to the fighting of August and to Kitchener's visit, and came to believe in the truth of his own initial assumptions. His book, *1914*, was not a mere tissue of lies: it represented, to a very great degree, Sir John's view of events. And if this view was distorted by French's passionate involvement with the events he describes, it is, none the less, invaluable. To understand why French behaved as he did it is important to grasp not only the facts themselves, but the facts as he saw them.

Before returning to GHQ, Sir John drafted a note for Millerand, recommending that a position should be prepared along the Marne, with a counter-attack force concentrated behind its left flank. If this was done he would be willing to hold his present line, but he warned that he was not prepared to place the weakened BEF 'in a situation where it might be attacked by superior forces without the certainty of its being supported and helped'.[119] Millerand forwarded the note to Joffre, adding that he found the proposal reasonable. Joffre replied the following day. In what French called 'a very friendly letter', the French Commander-in-Chief turned down the suggestion, although he agreed that the BEF had a useful part to play in the defence of Paris. This new *rapprochement* between GHQ and GQG augured well, and it was no small recompense for the Paris conference.[120]

Joffre's own plans were rapidly coalescing. On 1 September a new General Instruction sketched out a scheme for a continued withdrawal, prior to a counter-attack against the inner wing of the German armies. But no sooner had this order gone out than reports from the RFC, and information gleaned from a map found on the body of a German officer, offered enticing possibilities. Von Kluck's 1st Army, on the German right, was now marching south-east, swinging in front of Paris. Joffre decided that the time was not yet ripe for a thrust against the German flank. Paris seemed dangerously vulnerable: the government left the capital on the night of the 2nd, and General Gallieni, the city's military governor, remained understandably apprehensive even after Joffre put Maunoury's 6th Army under his command.

The BEF crossed the Marne on 3 September. To its northeast von Kluck smashed into the left flank of the 5th Army about

Château-Thierry, while to its west the 6th Army snatched its breath in the outer defences of Paris. It was the crisis of the campaign. Joffre realised that the moment for the counter-stroke was fast approaching. But cruel necessities demanded his attention before the attack was launched. Despite his affection for Lanrezac, he had come to the conclusion that the 5th Army needed a new commander, and he replaced Lanrezac with Franchet d'Esperey, soon christened 'Desperate Frankie' by the British. The news was well received at GHQ. Sir John thought that Lanrezac had been sent off, under arrest, for trial, and his Military Secretary reported to the King that the 'fat pompous political general' had been sacked.[121]

Franchet d'Esperey descended upon the staff of the 5th Army like the howitzer shell which, according to Spears, he resembled. He then sent a telegram to French, assuring him of his desire for friendly co-operation, and signing it 'Franchet d'Esperey KCVO' to show his appreciation of his British order. French spent most of 4 September with his troops. He had a long discussion with Haig, finding him:

> anxious he might be attacked and generally much depressed about the state of his troops. He was very nice about everything and just like himself but I feel strongly that all he says is justified and rest and replacement for the troops is absolutely necessary.

Smith-Dorrien then arrived, and complained that discipline was suffering as a result of the heavy casualties amongst officers. This, French agreed, was unfortunate, but it was 'a characteristic of *war*, and things may ... look better in a few days'.[122]

Few things pleased French more than to escape from his headquarters and move amongst the soldiers he loved, chatting to them in his bluff, breezy way: as his fiercest critics admitted, it was something he did supremely well. But great though its assets were, it was a custom which often cost him dear, and 4 September was no exception. On his return to GHQ at Melun he found that his staff had tentatively agreed to the BEF's participation in two plans for an offensive against the German right wing, plans which, though similar in concept, differed substantially in points of detail. Murray had been visited by Gallieni and Maunoury, and had produced orders for the implementation of one scheme: Wilson had travelled, on Sir John's behalf, to meet d'Esperey at Bray-sur-Seine, where he discussed a somewhat different project.

D'Esperey's plan became the basis for Joffre's *Instruction Générale No. 6*, the order which gave birth to the Battle of the Marne. The scheme depended upon the BEF's participation, and the misunderstandings of 4 September ensured that this was by no means guaranteed. There was, in the first place, a practical problem. Orders had been issued on the basis of Murray's agreement with Gallieni, and by the time Joffre's instructions arrived it was too late to cancel them: the BEF was therefore to start the battle some 15 miles behind the line intended for it by Joffre. A telegram from Huguet also brought Joffre bad news. Owing to the confusion, Sir John did not consider himself bound by the promises of his staff: he intended to study the question anew before coming to a decision.

Joffre reacted quickly. He sent a liaison officer to GHQ with a copy of his instructions and a clear statement of their importance. In what he described as 'agonising' uncertainty, he decided to leave no avenue unexplored, and sent a note to Millerand asking for the government to generate what pressure it could.[123] Joffre's liaison officer, Major de Galbert, returned at 9.30 a.m. on the 5th. He had given the orders to Wilson, but had not been able to see French, and was not optimistic. But Huguet phoned at almost exactly the same time. The news was good: Sir John would conform to Joffre's plan. Joffre determined to take no chances. He telephoned his thanks to GHQ, and announced that he was on his way to Melun to see French.

Joffre arrived at Sir John's quarters at the Château of Vaux-le-Pénil at 2 p.m. and went straight into the small room where the Field-Marshal was waiting with Murray and Wilson. Joffre put his cap on the table, faced French, and thanked him for taking a decision upon which the fate of Europe might depend. Then, in what Spears called his 'low, toneless, albino voice', he explained the situation. All eyes were upon French: several officers were ready to translate, but Sir John indicated that he understood. Speaking with absolute confidence, Joffre explained his plan, emphasising the importance of the next twenty-four hours. He was ready to throw his last company into battle to save France, and begged passionately for the total support of the BEF. He reached the climax of his appeal. Turning full on to Sir John, he clasped his hands so tightly as to hurt them, and said: '*Monsieur le Maréchal, c'est la France qui vous supplie.*'

Sir John had been listening attentively, and was visibly in the grip of a powerful emotion. His face reddened: tears welled up in his eyes and coursed down his cheeks. He tried to reply, wrestling with his feelings and the language, but gave up, turning to a liaison officer and exclaiming: 'Damn it, I can't explain. Tell him that all that men can do our fellows will do.' Wilson translated: 'The Field-Marshal says "yes",' he said. Murray at once stepped in, pointing out that the BEF could not start its advance as early as Joffre hoped. The French commander, exhausted by his pleas to Sir John, shrugged his shoulders. 'It cannot be helped', he said. 'Let them start as soon as they can. I have the Marshal's word, that is enough for me.'[124]

The BEF advanced on the morning of the 6th as Joffre's great counter-stroke boiled up along the valley of the Marne. Morale in the BEF rocketed: 'The happiest day of my life,' wrote Jack Seely, 'we marched towards the rising sun.' French was up with his corps commanders. While he was with Haig he realised that Joffre had chosen his time to a nicety.

> I got the first inkling that the Germans are doing exactly what I always thought they would do. They have deliberately walked into a trap which they are now trying to get out of. All their columns are marching North rapidly and have already begun to recross the Marne.

One cloud dimmed an otherwise clear sky. A wire arrived from Kitchener, telling him that the French government requested him to press the enemy hard: it was the result of Joffre's note to Millerand. Sir John was furious. 'It is a telegram which I don't in the least understand,' he wrote, 'and which I greatly resent.'[125] Joffre soon repaired the damage, apologising to French and sending a telegram to Kitchener complimenting Sir John and the BEF on their performance. But the incident revealed that the ice of Anglo-French relations was dangerously thin: it was to creak and groan ominously throughout Sir John's time in France.

The Battle of the Marne went on for four days. It was a confused, swirling struggle, with few of the traditional attributes of victory or defeat. From the BEF's point of view the fighting focused on sharp tussles with strongly-posted German rearguards as the advance gathered momentum, albeit slowly, in an air of growing optimism. In mid-September, as the Allies reached the line of the Aisne, the German resistance grew stronger. On the 14th Sir John wrote what was, in effect, the epitaph of this phase of the campaign. 'I think it is very likely,' he observed, 'that the enemy is making a determined stand on the Aisne ... '[126] The stand was to last for four long years.

Eight

The Swing of the Pendulum
September 1914–March 1915

As his infantry dug themselves into the slopes above the Aisne, French quickly realised that the whole character of the war had changed. His frequent visits to the front, which often coincided, as he noted with delight in his diary, with German shelling, rapidly convinced him that artillery was the dominant arm in trench warfare. 'Nothing but the most powerful and efficient entrenchments', he told the Duke of Connaught, 'will avail against the modern *heavy* artillery which is brought into the field.'[1] His report to the King was equally prophetic:

> I think the battle of the Aisne is very typical of what battles in the future are most likely to resemble. Siege operations will enter largely into the tactical problems – the *spade* will be as great a necessity as the rifle, and the heaviest calibres and types of artillery will be brought up in support on either side.[2]

On 23 September Sir John told his corps commanders of 'the importance of entrenching whenever they seemed inclined to make the *least stand* – the *combination* of aircraft and artillery the employment of the new howitzers and', almost as an afterthought, 'the *Role of the Cavalry*'.[3]

Reinforcements arrived to make up the losses of the retreat, and new formations appeared in the BEF's order of battle. The 4th Division was joined by the newly-arrived 6th Division in Major-General W. P. Pulteney's III Corps, and the cavalry was reorganised into two divisions. The inconclusive fighting along the Aisne, with hopes of an Allied advance one minute being followed by fears of a renewed German effort the next, was little to Sir John's taste. It was also unappealing to Wilson who looked eagerly at the open flank away to the north-west, and to Churchill, who was preoccupied with the safety of the scantily-defended Channel ports. Churchill broached the question of a move to the Channel coast on a visit to GHQ on 17 September, and the persuasive Henry Wilson pushed French in the same direction on the 24th.[4] Three days later Sir John made a formal request to Joffre, asking him 'to disengage us from our present position as soon as possible and put us on the left flank of the Allied forces'. This would, he suggested, increase the value of the lightly-gunned BEF, and allow the cavalry to operate against the German flank.[5]

Joffre found the Field-Marshal's argument 'irrefutable', although he felt that the time might not be right and, privately, had some doubts about placing the British army on the left wing without French troops between it and the Channel. His reply, however, spoke of 'the entire unanimity of views' which existed between Sir John and himself, and the only changes suggested by GQG concerned transport arrangements and timings. Joffre later came to believe, though, that the move of the BEF interrupted railway traffic to such an extent that no French troops could be moved to the left flank for ten days: the loss of Lille was, he wrote, the almost direct result of this.[6]

No sooner had Joffre agreed to the BEF's move than another crisis shook GHQ. The Belgian field army had fallen back upon Antwerp, and on 28 September German heavy howitzers opened fire against the outer ring of forts. The threat to Antwerp led to frenzied negotiations between the British and French governments concerning the possibilities of reinforcement, and on 1 October the 7th Division, which Sir John hoped to receive in the BEF, was earmarked for the task of saving Antwerp, and soon set off on that mission. On the next day Kitchener suggested to French that, if he was disengaging from the line, he should send part of his force to assist with the relief of Antwerp while the remainder moved into its new positions.[7] French was well aware of the importance of Antwerp, and feared that its loss might imperil the Allied hold on the Channel ports. Nevertheless, he was not convinced of the wisdom of the Kitchener–Churchill rescue plan. As he told Churchill, he was opposed to the concept of 'putting mobile troops *inside* a fortress', and shared Joffre's view that the 7th Division would be far more use as part of the main Allied forces in France.[8]

French's ambivalent attitude to the relief of Antwerp was further complicated by the clash of personalities. He suspected that Kitchener was once again interfering directly with the conduct of operations, and was not keeping him fully informed of British plans. Sir John was particularly irritated by the fact that Rawlinson was given what amounted to an independent command at Antwerp. French had long regarded Rawlinson with considerable suspicion, and their relationship was not improved by telegrams like this: 'I really do not understand whether you regard yourself as under my orders or not; but if you do, please be good enough to explain your situation clearly without delay ... '[9]

Rawlinson's force came under the command of French on 9 October, the day before Antwerp fell, and successfully retired to the south-west. The BEF, meanwhile, was concentrating in Flanders, its withdrawal from the Aisne phased over a fortnight to allow French troops to relieve it. In early October there was another tussle between Sir John and Joffre, over information disclosed by the latter to Poincaré, but French was soon soothed by a courteous apology from GQG and the gift of some captured German colours.[10]

GHQ moved from Fère-en-Tardenois to Abbeville on 8 October, and five days later it was established in the little town of St Omer. On his way to Abbeville French called in at Doullens to visit Foch, Joffre's representative in the north, who was shortly to be appointed commander of the *Groupe des Armées du Nord*. Foch produced a guard of honour, and gave the Field-Marshal 'a kind of tea and champagne party'. The two men had met on several occasions before the war: in August 1912 French had described Foch to Seely as 'the kind of man with whom I know I can get on'.[11] His high opinion of Foch was to be confirmed by the events of 1914, and he later told Lord Selborne that Foch was 'the best general in the world'.[12] Not all Sir John's subordinates were similarly impressed. Wully Robertson, for example, grumbled that Foch was 'rather a flat-catcher, a mere professor, and very talkative'.[13]

If Foch's loquacity dismayed the terse Robertson, it had exactly the reverse effect on French. Operating against an open flank was one of the motives which had drawn Sir John to the north. Equally potent, however, was his desire to open direct communications with England through the Channel ports, and in mid-October he thought in terms of establishing an 'entrenched camp' at Boulogne or Calais. Sir John fell a willing victim to Foch's exuberant confidence and, although the concept of an entrenched camp still lingered on in his mind, he lost no time in collaborating in Foch's plan for a general advance towards Roulers to roll up the German flank.

The German high command was also looking hard at steadily decreasing room for manoeuvre on the northern flank. As both sides stretched their forces ever closer to the coast, still feeling for the elusive open flank, the front gradually stabilised from La Bassée to Armentières and up towards Ypres. French's confidence in the offensive was as great as ever, and he chivvied his corps commanders on. As the southern end of his line ground to a halt about La Bassée, he pressed Rawlinson – his command now entitled IV Corps – to take Menin, and complained bitterly when, on the 18th, he failed to do so.[14]

GHQ continued to crack its whip on the 19th, urging Rawlinson to advance down the Ypres–Menin road, while Haig swung north-east towards Roulers. Sir John was again guilty of allowing his own belief in the offensive to override the sombre pronouncements of GHQ's intelligence staff, who estimated that there were at least $3\frac{1}{2}$ German corps north-east of Ypres.[15] His optimism was sustained by what Liddell Hart called 'the Fochian serum', often administered through the energetic intercession of Henry Wilson. Wilson, like many members of GHQ, was convinced that the Germans were as good as beaten, and he capitalised upon every ounce of influence with Sir John to persuade the Field-Marshal to press hard to the north-east and elbow his way round the German flank.

The bustling little town of Ypres lay in a saucer. To the south stood the high ground of Scherpenberg and Kemmel Hill, and a low, irregular ridge curled away to the north-east of Kemmel, pointing up towards Roulers and Thourout. Small spurs rippled down from this main ridge. Due south of Ypres,

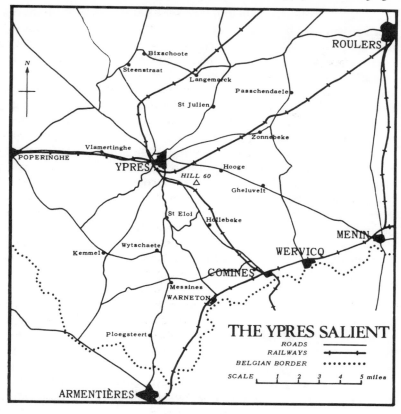

THE YPRES SALIENT

ROADS
RAILWAYS
BELGIAN BORDER

SCALE   1   2   3   4   5 miles

the Messines–Wytschaete feature jutted sharply into the low-lying country of the Lys valley, while to the north-east of Ypres fingers of high ground stretched out towards the villages of Langemarck and St Julien. The main road through Ypres ran from Poperinghe, to the west, through Vlamertinghe, and into Ypres itself. It ran out towards Menin, across the main ridge, through the villages of Hooge and Gheluvelt. In 1914 the area was scattered with woods, whose trees and undergrowth offered good cover. Thick hedges, and the many small streams which meandered through the low country under the ridges, combined to restrict movement. The area was well-suited for defence, and favoured an army whose marksmanship and fieldcraft were of a high standard.[16]

Sir John's confidence began to wane on the 21st. Information from prisoners, from intercepted wireless messages and from the ubiquitous RFC suggested that several German reserve corps were attacking the French and Belgians on the Yser north of Ypres, and were also advancing between Menin and Roulers, towards Ypres itself. Although, as French wrote, these corps 'had been hastily formed and were not composed of the best troops', the identification of no less than five fresh corps on the Menin–Ostend front was 'a veritable bolt from the blue'.[17] Sir John had already speculated that the Germans were running out of men, and the sudden appearance of large numbers of new troops was extremely discouraging.

Joffre visited GHQ on the 21st, and the discussion went well enough until Sir John's fears regarding the growing German strength on the BEF's front expressed themselves in the resurrection of the entrenched camp scheme. French asked for facilities to construct a position at Boulogne large enough to take the whole BEF. Joffre, the agonies of August fresh in his mind, feared that this would give the BEF a refuge into which it could withdraw, for subsequent evacuation by sea, if the German pressure became too great. His 'face instantly became quite square and he replied that such a thing could not be allowed for a moment'.[18] Joffre announced that he was sending another French corps to the Ypres area, and Sir John knew that the Lahore Division of the Indian Corps was concentrating West of Hazebrouck: he decided to hold his ground in front of Ypres, and at 8.30 that night GHQ's orders set the tone for the First Battle of Ypres: 'Action against enemy will be continued to-morrow on general line now held, which will be strongly entrenched.'[19]

His meeting with Joffre on the 21st, together with the BEF's fine stonewalling performance in the face of fierce attacks, raised French's spirits. He reported to Kitchener that: 'In my opinion the enemy are vigorously playing their last card, and I am confident they will fail.' Four days later he was certain that the crisis had passed, and assured Kitchener that his anxiety was over.[20] The situation did, indeed, appear to have improved considerably. Joffre had honoured his promise to reinforce the northern front and drafts from England had made good many of the BEF's losses. Inter-allied relations were better than they had been since mid-August. On the 24th Sir John visited General d'Urbal, commanding the French detachment on the BEF's left, and discovered with delight that d'Urbal was a cavalryman, 'the old Murat type of *beau sabreur*'.[21] French had a conference with Foch the following day, at the latter's new headquarters at Cassel: the meeting further diminished French's fears.

At midnight on the 25th Smith-Dorrien arrived at GHQ with altogether different news. He warned French 'that he was afraid his corps might go during the night'. 'Sir John', wrote Wilson 'was rather short with him ... '[22] French's concern was tempered by his belief that Smith-Dorrien was exaggerating the perils facing II Corps. After a short discussion, he decided that nothing could be done until morning. Sir John sent Smith-Dorrien more troops and guns on the 26th and 28th, and reiterated his intention to relieve II Corps by the Indian Corps in the near future. The incident intensified French's suspicions of Smith-Dorrien's moral fibre, and it is not unreasonable to conclude that, in this instance, Sir Horace was unduly influenced by the gloomy representations of his divisional commanders.

The German high command took stock of the situation on 27 October. Despite their superiority in men and guns, the German 4th and 6th Armies, attacking in the Flanders sector, had failed to achieve a breakthrough. Lieutenant-General Erich von Falkenhayn, who had succeeded the exhausted von Moltke in mid-September, cobbled together a new formation, Army Group Fabeck, and planned to hurl it at the British lines between Gheluvelt, on the Menin Road, and Ploegsteert Wood, between Messines and Armentières.

GHQ still thought in terms of pressing on with its own offensive. Its orders continued to specify attacks by I, IV and the Cavalry Corps, moving forward from the left to conform with the anticipated advance of d'Urbal's men. The fighting was generally inconclusive, but Sir John was sure that the Germans would shortly run out of steam and crumble before the sustained Allied pressure. Some alterations were made to the BEF's order of battle: on the 27th IV Corps was broken up, Rawlinson and his headquarters being sent home to supervise the preparation of the 8th Division for its dispatch to France.

The orders issued by GHQ on the night of the 28th again decreed a continuation of the offensive. Haig was, however, aware that all was not well to his front, and although he made some preparations for an attack, he also took steps to strengthen vulnerable points of his line.

A preliminary German attack went in shortly after dawn on the 29th. I Corps blunted the assault in a day of savage fighting on the axis of the Menin Road, though the key Gheluvelt cross-roads was lost and valuable reserve battalions were dragged into the battle. It might have been expected that the advent of what was unmistakably a major offensive would have convinced French to shelve his own offensive projects, and had he spent the day at GHQ, studying reports as they came in, this might well have been the case. However, Sir John motored over to Cassel in the afternoon, and Foch assured him that the French were making satisfactory progress between the British left and the sea. This salvo of unrealistic optimism convinced Sir John that it was essential to resume his attack to co-operate with the French to his north, and on the night of the 29th GHQ declared that operations would continue 'in accordance with previous order', which had specified attacks echeloning forward from the left.[23]

Sir John subsequently claimed that he knew perfectly well 'that it was utterly impossible for us at that time to do more than hold our own with the utmost difficulty'.[24] If he really believed this at the time, it is unlikely that he would have ordered a resumption of the offensive, and GHQ's operations orders leave no doubt that he did so. He also wired cheerfully to Kitchener that evening, noting that I Corps had launched a successful counter-attack in the afternoon, and suggesting that 'if the success can be followed up, it will lead to a decisive result'.[25] One serious worry clouded French's mind on the evening of 29 October. The consumption of artillery ammunition over the last three months had been prodigious. In the two-and-three-quarter years of the South African War some 273,000 shells had been fired: between 15 August 1914 and 15 February 1915 the BEF fired no less than one million. French had already complained to the War Office that the supply of ammunition was failing to keep pace with expenditure. On 28 September he pointed out that his 18-pounder field guns were receiving only 7 rounds per gun per day although they were firing 14, a rate of expenditure which, he stressed, was unusually low. He informed the War Office, on 10 October, that his guns were now rationed to 20 rounds per gun per day, and feared that even this modest allocation might soon have to be halved. Murray was sent to London to press the point. On 29 October, with the critical phase in the battle about to open, Sir John again told Kitchener of his anxiety concerning ammunition. Kitchener realised that this was as much a rebuke as an appeal, and assured French that he was not keeping ammunition back deliberately.

Nevertheless, the ammunition problem continued to smoulder. Sir John knew that he was desperately short of ammunition, and tended to blame the authorities at home for the shortage. It was not in his nature to make a balanced assessment of the problems of ammunition supply, or to ponder the enormous difficulties with which Kitchener was contending. Nor was he in a position to appreciate that GHQ's demands for new types of ammunition — the first 18-pounder High Explosive shells were used at Ypres in late October — would present technical problems of manufacture and supply. His soldiers were being blasted from their improvised trenches by an artillery whose weight and volume of fire far exceeded anything the BEF could produce, and in his anger and frustration Sir John had little doubt where the blame for this unsatisfactory situation lay: with Kitchener and his fellow-incompetents at the War Office.[26]

Von Fabeck's main attack rolled forward in the fog on the morning of the 30th. The Germans made slow but steady progress against the determined resistance of I Corps and the Cavalry Corps, the latter fighting dismounted with a skill which bore ample tribute to the thoroughness of its pre-war training. Sir John visited Allenby's headquarters at Kemmel late in the morning, and then went on to see Haig at the White Château, near Hellfire Corner on the Menin Road. He left the conduct of the battle to his corps commanders, contenting himself with raking together reinforcements to buttress the shuddering front. The Indian Corps was to relieve II Corps, and Sir John ordered Smith-Dorrien to send a brigade to support Allenby. General Dubois, commanding the French corps on Haig's left, had already placed his own corps reserves at Haig's disposal, in a pleasing demonstration of inter-Allied solidarity.

When Sir John retired to bed that night the situation was still unclear. GHQ was not sure of the details of the fighting, and had not yet realised the weight behind the German attack. French was not dissatisfied with the day's results, telling Kitchener that the enemy had thrown substantial forces against him, but adding that he hoped to regain the lost ground in a counter-attack.[27] Haig was indeed preparing just such a blow, although the limited fire support available made the enterprise decidedly risky. Foch received an up-to-date report of the situation from one of his staff officers at 10 p.m. The officer warned that there was a gap in the British line behind Hollebeke Château, and there were no British forces available to fill it. Foch telephoned GHQ, obtained no useful information, and departed at once for St Omer.

He arrived half an hour after midnight, and had the Field-Marshal roused from sleep. 'We are all for it', muttered Sir John when told of the gap. 'We shall see', replied Foch. 'In the meantime, hammer away, keep on hammering, and you will get there.' This advice would have been of no practical value without some concrete support, for there was little enough with which the BEF could hammer. Foch promised to support Sir John with eight battalions and three batteries, and suggested that they should be used to strengthen the line at Hollebeke Château. This made all the difference: Sir John was visibly cheered, and thanked Foch 'in the warmest terms'.[28]

The German assault continued on the morning of the 31st, with savage attacks falling on the Cavalry Corps on Messines Ridges and on I Corps astride the Menin Road. Haig's counter-attack failed to get under way, though the ammunition stockpiled to support it ripped gaps in the attacking German infantry. But the weight of German numbers and of shellfire soon told. The position about Gheluvelt began to crumble, and by midday the total collapse of Haig's centre was imminent. Just after 1 p.m. a shell hit Major-General Monro's headquarters at Hooge Château, killing and wounding a number of staff officers, including Major-General Lomax of the 1st Division, who was visiting Monro to discuss the worsening situation.

This blow inevitably disrupted plans for bolstering up the gap through which the Germans must shortly pour: only one battalion, 2nd Worcesters, was on hand to avert disaster.

French's martial instinct left him in no doubt as to the proper place for a Commander-in-Chief now, at the crisis of the battle. It was not at GHQ, watching the arrows creep steadily over maps while grim-faced staff officers listened to telephone messages from the corps, but up at the front, watching the battle as it surged and roared between Ypres and Messines. He left GHQ early, and was with Allenby as the Cavalry Corps struggled to retain Messines. At about midday he visited Gough near Hollebeke, saw that the line was firm, and drove on to see Haig. Sir John drove out of Ypres against a tide of wounded, stragglers and wagons of every description. 'It was a regular debacle', he said. 'The heavy field guns were trotting. When a heavy field gun trots you may be sure things are pretty bad.'[29] The Field-Marshal abandoned his car not far from the White Château and made his way to Haig's headquarters on foot. He found the commander of I Corps 'very white but quite calm'. 'They have broken us right in', said Haig, 'and are pouring through the gap ... '[30] Haig had already selected a fall-back position close to Ypres, but the chances of conducting a co-ordinated withdrawal seemed slim indeed. Haig, for his part, wrote that French was his usual avuncular self: 'No one could have been nicer at such a time of crisis. But he had no reinforcements to send me, and viewed the situation with the utmost gravity.'[31] After a few sharp words about the lack of French help, Sir John left the Château to seek Foch, the only man who could provide the reinforcements without which the position must surely collapse. Sir John had left Haig and was walking back to his car when Haig's aide-de-camp caught up with him. A purple-faced staff officer had just galloped up with momentous news: the Worcesters had retaken Gheluvelt and plugged the gap. French had no doubt that the Worcesters' almost incredible counter-attack had prevented a disaster: 'The Worcesters', he said, 'saved the Empire.'[32]

Defeat had been averted for the moment, but Sir John feared that the creaking front of I Corps would not hold together much longer without French help. Accordingly, he set off for Foch's headquarters at Cassel. In the village of Vlamertinghe, just outside Ypres on the Poperinghe road, his car was flagged down by a French officer: it was Major Jamet, Foch's liaison officer with I Corps, with the news that Foch himself was only a few yards away, in the Town Hall, talking to Generals d'Urbal and Dubois. French painted a gloomy picture of the battle on I Corps front. Haig's men could not survive without reinforcements, and the BEF had none available. 'I have no more reserves', announced Sir John. 'The only men I have left are the sentries at my gates. I will take them with me to where the line is broken, and the last of the English will be killed fighting.'[33]

Foch was certain that a retreat would be disastrous: any withdrawal would be likely to open up the battle, leading to the disintegration of I Corps. He assured French that he would support Haig the following day, and convinced him that, with this help, I Corps could maintain its position. Reassured, Sir John scribbled a note to Haig:

> It is of the utmost importance to hold the ground you are now on. It is useless for me to say this, because I know that you will do it if it is humanly possible.
>
> I will see if it is possible to send you any more support myself when I reach headquarters. I will then finally arrange with Foch *what* our future role is to be.

This note was accompanied by a memorandum from Foch, urging Haig to hold his ground.[34]

The hard-pressed I Corps did indeed maintain a continuous front, patched up by cooks, grooms and transport drivers. Foch's orders for a French counter-attack on both flanks of the corps went out that night, and on 1 November these attacks, despite their lack of real progress, went some way towards checking the German pressure. Messines was lost, but Sir John reported to the War Office that he was much less anxious than he had been, and told the King that, despite the heavy attacks he was 'full of hope and confidence'.[35]

Other telegrams to the War Office painted a stark picture of the awful burden being sustained by the BEF. There were only about 180 rounds per field howitzer and 320 per 18-pounder in France, a pitiful margin in view of the fact that consumption was now in the region of 80 rounds per 18-pounder per day. Officer casualties were also alarming. The 1st Royal West Kent had only three surviving officers, all subalterns; 1st Coldstream Guards, even after reinforcement, had three officers, including the Quartermaster, and a Gurkha battalion had lost 10 of its 13 British officers.[36] The loss of British officers had a serious effect upon the Indian Corps, whose CGS was soon appealing for support.[37]

November 2 was another trying day for the BEF, but at its conclusion French again wired confidently to the War Office. He nevertheless stressed the need for reinforcements, particularly regular infantry battalions. In two Special Orders of the Day he thanked the troops for their efforts and urged them to stand fast. He also told them of Russian successes in the east, victories which would, he declared, force the Germans to shift troops to the Eastern Front or accept the invasion of their eastern provinces.[38] Sir John's confidence in the Russian steam-roller remained unshaken despite the Russian defeat at Tannenberg in late August. Indeed, over the next two weeks, as the fighting in front of Ypres went on, French began to suspect that a decision on the Western Front might prove impossible. 'The fact is,' he told Lord Stamfordham, 'that everything now *depends on Russia* — we can hold on here without much difficulty but are not strong enough ... to take a vigorous offensive.'[39]

The Germans kept up their pressure on I Corps during the first two weeks of November, and although there were times of acute crisis, particularly on 11 November, the line held. Sir John agreed with Foch that French troops would relieve I Corps at Ypres, enabling the whole BEF to concentrate further south, between Kemmel and the La Bassée Canal, without any French formations interleaved between its corps. The reorganisation was completed by the 22nd.

French's relationship with Joffre and Foch had undergone another of its periodic transformations. On 1 November Kitchener had met Joffre, Foch, Millerand and other French officials at Dunkirk. Sir John, who was to have attended the meeting, felt unable to leave his army with the battle at its peak, and sent his Military Secretary and an aide-de-camp to represent him. The discussion centred upon the employment of the New Armies, composed of the volunteers who had responded so enthusiastically to Kitchener's call to arms. Kitchener guaranteed to have one million soldiers on French soil within 18 months, but Joffre replied that he would prefer fewer men to arrive sooner. The Secretary of State, however, made it clear that the BEF could not expect any substantial reinforcements until the spring of 1915.

At some stage in the proceedings, Kitchener offered to replace Sir John with Ian Hamilton. Joffre declined the proposal, saying that he worked 'well and cordially' with French, and pointing out that a change of command at such a stage in the campaign would have a bad effect upon the BEF's morale. Four days later Foch told Wilson of Kitchener's offer and suggested that Sir John should be informed.[40] The result was predictable. French was horrified by what he regarded as Kitchener's unspeakable duplicity, and sent an aide-de-camp, Captain Freddy Guest, to complain to the Prime Minister. Asquith believed that there was not 'a word of truth or even a shadow of foundation for the story', but he wrote a reassuring letter to Sir John and Churchill did likewise.[41] Churchill assured French that 'you are our man and we are going to stand by you', and begged him not to let 'these mischief makers build a barrier between you and Kitchener.'[42] Sir John refused to believe Churchill's assertion that there was no truth in the story. He became increasingly insecure, and his distrust of Kitchener came close to attaining the proportions of real paranoia.

Kitchener's behaviour had the effect of driving Sir John, for the time at least, into the arms of Foch and Joffre. On 6 November he drove to Cassel with Henry Wilson, and thanked Foch personally, 'and in the warmest terms for his comradeship and loyalty. They shook hands on it. Sir John told Foch that he proposed to go and see Joffre to thank him also.'[43] The incident did nothing to ensure permanent good relations between the British and French high commands, but it lent a new edge to the four-way relationship between GHQ, GQG and the British and French governments. There were times when Sir John was prepared to side with GQG against his own government, agreeing with Joffre that the Cabinet was *affolé* – a word which Wilson obligingly translated to mean 'mad, frantic, distracted, bewildered, flighty, flickering, deranged'.[44] At other times the Field-Marshal was out of sympathy with GQG, and complained that Joffre was once more making unreasonable demands upon the BEF. The swirls and eddies of inter-Allied politics swept French along like driftwood in a torrent. Commanding an army was difficult enough in itself, but coping with the centrifugal tendencies of two governments and an Allied headquarters was all but impossible.

Sir John's growing fears and suspicions made him increasingly dependent upon the men he trusted. His staff included Billy Lambton as Military Secretary, Brinsley Fitzgerald as Private Secretary, and Fitz Watt and Freddy Guest among his aides-de-camp. They lived in the Field-Marshal's quarters in the comfortable but flamboyantly-decorated notary's house in the Rue St Bertin in St Omer, ran his errands and knew most of his secrets. Few others shared the Field-Marshal's high regard for his personal staff. Margot Asquith, never one to mince her words, told him:

> I wish ... you had clever men in your immediate surroundings. I know your kind heart and susceptibility to affection. Freddy and Brinsley are both very stupid. Billy Lambton is a far better type and he is no genius but sound and straight.

She warned him that Guest and Fitzgerald went 'backward and forward making mischief like old women between you and K and all the generals'. Fitzgerald was her particular *bête noire*: he was, she wrote, 'wonderfully unclever'.[45] Esher also told French that 'your "War Cabinet" requires strengthening', and noted that the King regarded the Commander-in-Chief's advisers as trouble-makers.[46]

The events of the first three months of the war had drawn Sir John even closer to Henry Wilson than he had been in March 1914. Wilson acted as CGS when Murray visited the War Office in late October, and French decided to appoint him to Murray's post when the opportunity arose. Wilson took care not to appear to undermine Murray's position, for he realised that Sir John liked Murray but found his performance as CGS unsatisfactory.[47]

The strain of command began to tell upon French's health.

Athough remarkably fit for his age, Sir John was sixty-one, and was living an energetic life with comparatively little sleep. On 21 November Haig lunched with him at St Omer, and noticed that he looked 'rather pulled down'. French thought that he might have had a heart attack, and told Haig that his doctors had ordered him to rest.[48]

This was easier said than done. A number of urgent problems confronted the Field-Marshal in the lull that followed First Ypres. The most pressing concerned repair of the damage done to the BEF by the fighting of October and November, during which it had lost over 58,000 officers and men. Casualties since the outbreak of war now totalled some 90,000. These statistics may not be as terrible as those of the Battle of the Somme in 1916 or Passchendaele in 1917, but the burden had fallen most heavily on the infantry of the first seven divisions, which had originally numbered only 84,000. The old army was gone for ever: in the battalions which fought on the Marne and at Ypres, there remained on average only one officer and thirty men who had landed in August.[49] There was a crippling lack of trained officers and NCOs, and Sir John himself believed that the shortage was most marked at the level of infantry company commander, a post which he regarded as increasingly important.[50] It is small wonder that he was reluctant to send experienced men home to help train the New Armies.

The Territorials helped. The London Scottish, the first Territorial battalion in action, gave an excellent account of itself at Messines, and there were twenty-two Territorial battalions and six Yeomanry regiments in France by mid-December. Sir John, always more pro-Territorial than the majority of his regular army colleagues, thought that he could not have held the line without them.[51] Useful though the Territorials were, however, they were no real solution to the manpower problem, and French soon found himself looking eagerly towards the New Armies, still training in Britain.

Not only was the BEF hungry for trained drafts, but it was also developing a voracious appetite for all the paraphernalia of trench warfare. As the army's trenches improved, so demands for sandbags, duckboards, barbed wire, picks, shovels and telephone cable grew. The new style of fighting created a need for new weapons, and a variety of experimental mortars, hand-grenades and catapults, some of them alarmingly impartial in their action, appeared in the British trenches. The Germans had a clear lead in such weapons: the first British flare pistols were so few in number and limited in effect that their firing drew derisive applause from the enemy trenches. French found the BEF's shortcomings in trench-warfare weapons extremely frustrating. He took a great personal interest in the experiments carried out on mortars and grenades, and urged the War Office to expedite the manufacture of these weapons. As long as he commanded the army, however, more mortar bombs and grenades were produced in the BEF's own workshops than were received from England.[52] Sir John was also convinced of the utter inadequacy of the existing scale of issue of machine-guns. In mid-December he estimated that a battalion required at least six or seven guns, and he had already told Robertson that he would willingly accept the new-fangled Lewis guns rather than wait for the production of sufficient Vickers guns.[53]

The supply of artillery ammunition continued to cause Sir John acute anxiety. In late November II and III Corps had little more than enough for one day's battle, and I Corps had even less.[54] Complaints about the shortage of ammunition became increasingly frequent in Sir John's diary and in his letters to the War Office. It was not merely that the shells flowed in slowly, but that they often failed to arrive in the numbers predicted by the War Office. In January 1915, for example, Robertson pointed out to Major-General Sir Stanley von Donop, Master-General of the Ordnance, that a shortfall of 8,000 rounds of 4·5 howitzer ammunition was rather a blow: uncertainties regarding the arrival of ammunition made it very difficult to plan operations with any confidence.[55]

The fighting on the Aisne had already convinced French of the importance of heavy artillery, and the experience of First Ypres, where German artillery superiority was revealed in its awful glory, confirmed him in his desire to get as many heavy guns as possible into line as quickly as he could. He was delighted with the effect produced by the first of the 9·2 howitzers to arrive in France, and gave Kitchener a graphic description of the destruction of the old fort at Condé on the Aisne with these weapons.[56] In early December he told the Secretary of State: 'The fact is that Krupp is our most formidable enemy at present, and we must find means to get on terms with the enemy's heavy artillery before any advance can be very speedy or vigorous.'[57] Heavy guns and howitzers trickled into France in such pitiful numbers that the fate of a single gun could generate a lengthy correspondence between St Omer and Whitehall.[58]

The much-vexed question of the supply of weapons and ammunition to the army in France sharpened the conflict between French and Kitchener. Sir John's sense of proportion was never his most notable quality, and he was disinclined to consider the problems faced by Kitchener and von Donop while his own troops were being shelled out of their trenches in the freezing misery of a Flanders winter. Robertson took a rather wider view, but even he could not resist telling von Donop that it was a pity that his department had provided guns capable of firing ten rounds per minute if the factories could only produce those rounds in twenty-four hours' work.[59] The fact that all the combatant armies, even the German, were experiencing difficulties in producing an adequate supply of ammunition was scant comfort to French and his staff when the evidence suggested that both the French and the Germans were coping far better than the British.

Other, less serious, problems also made inroads into French's time. A stream of visitors arrived at GHQ. Lord Roberts came out on 11 November and visited his beloved Indians the following day. He saw Foch at Cassell on the 13th, contracted a chill while inspecting some more Indian troops, and died on the evening of the 14th. French had not always seen eye-to-eye with Roberts, but the old man's death upset him.[60] The King visited France between 30 November and 5 December. Sir John thought that:

> He is very pessimistic about the war, and greatly fears invasion. He thinks that the Germans have 250,000 men put by and ready for the express purpose of invasion!! He says that we must absolutely bust up the German Empire and they must give up all their fleet!! ... I don't believe a word of all this. I think Fisher is spreading some of the rumours.

The King became more cheerful after meeting Poincaré, Viviani and Joffre, and the next evening French recorded that: 'HM has been induced to take a more optimistic view of things in general since he has been here'.[61] The crowds who descended on St Omer made short work of the Field-Marshal's entertainment allowance. His appointment as Commander-in-Chief of the BEF carried with it an annual salary of £5,000, in addition to certain field allowances, but by early 1915 Sir John was feeling the pinch. Brinsley Fitzgerald asked the War Office to give Sir John some more 'table money', but Sir Reginald Brade replied that, eager though he was to help, somebody would have to make an official application.[62]

By far the most difficult of the problems facing French in the early winter of 1914 concerned Allied strategy for the early part of the coming year. His faith in an Allied offensive wavered considerably in November, but he grew more sanguine in December as reports reached him of Russian successes in Poland and Galicia and of the declining quality of German troops. On 27 November he wrote: 'In view of their heavy defeats in Poland it seems almost incredible that the Germans can afford to keep many troops on this side. I strongly suspect that they are engaged at *bluffing* us: a game at which they are adept.'[63] At a conference three days later d'Urbal reported the disappearance from his front of two German corps, and on 4 December Sir John received a message from the British ambassador at St Petersburg, drawing attention to the strengthening of German forces in the east. The Russians, wrote the Ambassador, were pressing the Western Allies to launch an offensive of their own, a demand echoed by the Russian liaison officer at GQG.[64] Sir John discussed the Russian situation with Foch on 5 December, and at another meeting three days later Foch formally requested British help in his coming attack. Sir John agreed, not without considerable haggling, to co-operate, but when he briefed his commanders on 12 December he emphasised the need for caution. Instead of a simultaneous and determined assault, he specified a gradual attack in which 'everyone was to wait for the man on his left'.[65] The affair was singularly half-hearted, a fact explained as much by Sir John's own uninspiring orders as by the atrocious weather. Another attack, launched a few days later in response to Joffre's appeal for assistance in his own offensive round Arras, was similarly irresolute.

French's motives for pulling his punches bear witness to the tangled state of relations between Sir John, the French, and Kitchener. Sir John feared that if he turned down French requests for assistance the matter would be reported to Kitchener, and the events of 1 September left little doubt as to what his attitude would be. Moreover, his affection for Foch impelled him to do something to help. On the other hand, the terrible weather, the state of the ground, and the shortage of ammunition all combined to persuade him that the offensive was doomed before it started. He visited Smith-Dorrien's lines in mid-December, and wrote glumly that: 'The weather was terrible and the ground only a quagmire. The rain, the cold, and the awful *holding* ground seemed to damp down my energy.'[66] He finished with the worst of both worlds, sporadic attacks which added to the butcher's bill to no real purpose. Worse still, the Germans lost no time in retaliating. On 20 December they fell upon the shivering Indians with such a sharp blow that the Corps had to be pulled back into reserve.

The greatest single reason for French's uninspired contribution to the December offensive was probably his growing conviction that better prospects glimmered elsewhere. Sir John had been in close touch with Winston Churchill since the outbreak of war. Although friction between the War Office and the Admiralty over naval units serving in France — the 'Dunkirk Circus', or Churchill's 'freaks' — resulted in ill-tempered letters from Kitchener to French, Sir John's friendship with Churchill survived unscathed.[67] On 26 October Churchill impressed upon Sir John the 'damnable' consequences of the German presence on the Channel coast. 'We must have him off the Belgian coast', he maintained, 'even if we cannot recover Antwerp.'[68] Churchill visited GHQ in early December and discussed the possibility of an offensive up the Flanders coast to recover Ostend and Zeebrugge. French found the concept attractive. He had not altered his opinion as to the desirability of the BEF's operating on the extreme left of the Allied line, without any French units between it and the coast, and had already written to Churchill about operating with the Belgians on the northern flank.[69]

The scheme gained momentum. On 9 December the Foreign Office formally asked the French government for the British army to be moved to the coast, where it could work in conjunction with the fleet and the Belgians. Churchill wrote enthusiastically of the plan, and urged Sir John to press it hard 'both here at home and on the French generals'.[70] Millerand at once referred the scheme to Joffre, who regarded it as a '*mouvement eccentrique*', of little relevance to the main struggle.[71] Sir John was in two minds about the plan. He warned Kitchener and Churchill that it could not be carried out until the projected French offensive, in which he had agreed to participate, was over. He also felt duty bound to send Wilson to tell Foch 'of all that had happened so that he might not think that I was working "behind" him'.[72] Foch treated the official British proposals, which he received from Wilson on the 11th, 'with the greatest contempt', and immediately accompanied Wilson to GHQ, where Sir John seemed to be decidedly lukewarm about the plan.[73]

On 27 December French drove over to Chantilly for a conference with Joffre. The discussion was wide-ranging: contingency plans to meet a German offensive, the relative merits of high explosive and shrapnel, and the situation in Russia, were all examined. French felt that he and Joffre 'arrived at a complete understanding as to future plans'. Joffre, at his most affable and persuasive, spoke expansively of his ideas for a two-pronged offensive in the Arras and Rheims areas in the spring. He agreed that Sir John should take over the line between La Bassée and the coast, but only gradually, as reinforcements arrived, and he also approved of French's plan to collaborate with the Belgian army.[74]

The conference did little for the Flanders coast project. If the British army was only to extend its left to the sea as reinforcements arrived, taking over miles of French trenches in the process, it would not be in a position to attack along the coast in the foreseeable future. This may have been acceptable to French, but it was certainly not what Churchill had in mind: on 13 December, for example, he had warned Sir John that his naval force, upon whose fire support the attack would depend, could not 'hang about day after day amid these perils'.[75] Furthermore, Sir John's scheme for collaboration with the

Belgians, to which Joffre had given his approval, involved nothing less than the incorporation of the Belgian army in the British. French believed that this would enable him 'to take over the line within the next two or three weeks and find a sufficient reserve to enter energetically upon a land advance'.[76] If the amalgamation scheme foundered, as Joffre must have suspected it would, then Sir John had two alternatives: to abandon the coastal offensive altogether, or to procure elsewhere the troops required for the operation.

On 2 January, Tom Bridges, now liaison officer with the Belgians, brought bad news: the King of the Belgians had vetoed the amalgamation scheme. Sir John at once decided to press on with the coastal offensive and to ask for the New Armies. These had been formed and trained in regionally-recruited divisions, but Sir John was certain that to employ raw troops with partly-trained corps, divisional and brigade staffs was to court disaster. He therefore suggested that the New Armies should be sent out 'in small units either battalions or brigades and to gradually get experience by mixture with the seasoned units'.[77] French himself was in favour of 'uniting three battalions into a regiment on the continental army principle. It would still be quite possible to unite three regiments into a brigade.'[78] Sir John's senior commanders all agreed that it was folly to send out the New Armies in formed divisions and corps. The matter soon became yet another bone of contention between French and Kitchener, and the latter successfully resisted all attempts to have the New Army divisions broken up.

GHQ was formulating its request for reinforcements in the wake of the Belgian refusal when another piece of bad news crashed on to Sir John's desk. Churchill, Hankey and Lloyd George had all maintained, in papers written in late December, that there was stalemate on the Western Front, and suggested that the time had come to seek other theatres of operations. On 2 January 1915 Kitchener sent what Sir John angrily called 'another incomprehensible letter', telling him that:

> The feeling here is gaining ground that, although it is essential to defend the line we now hold, troops over and above what is necessary for that service

could better be employed elsewhere. The question *where* anything effective could be accomplished opens a large field and requires a good deal of study. What are the views of your staff?[79]

Kitchener's letter changed the dimensions of the debate about the coastal offensive. If another theatre of operations was opened up, in the Near East or elsewhere, then the Western Front might become a mere sideshow. But if offensive operations in the west earmarked the New Armies for France, then the primacy of the Western Front was assured. In his reply to Kitchener, Sir John assured the Secretary of State that, given sufficient men and munitions, the German front could be broken by direct assault. To attack Turkey would be 'to play the German game and to bring about the end which Germany had in mind when she induced Turkey to join in the war — namely, to draw off troops from the decisive spot, which is Germany herself'. If the government insisted on a Second Front, wrote French, he preferred an advance into Serbia from Salonika or, better still, a combination with the fleet to attack Zeebrugge and Ostend. He also took the opportunity to warn Kitchener that if the Russians collapsed every British soldier would be required to resist the Germans in France. Either way, the Western theatre was the only one in which decisive results could be achieved.[80]

Murray, sent to England to press GHQ's case, delivered a copy of this memorandum directly to the Prime Minister. Kitchener was not at all pleased, and informed Sir John that Asquith did not want any change made in the rule that official communications from him to the government should pass through Kitchener as Secretary of State.[81] French promptly apologised, assuring Kitchener, not without a hint of sarcasm, that:

> I had no idea that you would possibly object to such a course of proceedings as the Prime Minister has been throughout so closely associated with my deliberations ...
>
> As to your postscript about the latter not being sealed, of course it should have been and I am sorry

it was not. Such details are apt to be overlooked when one's mind is engaged with the command of ¼ million men in war.[82]

Sir John's formal proposals, which included a demand for 50 Territorial or New Army battalions and sufficient ammunition to provide his field guns with 50 rounds per day for 10 or 20 days, were discussed by the War Council on 7 and 8 January. Churchill, whose encouragement had played such a large part in persuading French of the merits of the coastal offensive, did not support the proposals with much conviction, and Kitchener was, as Hankey observed, 'definitely hostile'.[83] The plan was eventually rejected; 'further consideration' would be given to Sir John's remarks on the New Armies and, while the Western Front was accorded primacy for the time being, other prospects would be studied. Kitchener's dispatch, telling French of the War Council's decision, caused consternation at GHQ, although it was somewhat softened by a letter from Churchill in which he assured French that Kitchener had given his views a fair airing.[84]

French did not regard the decision as final. He sent Wilson and Murray to England to whip up support, and on 12 January he arrived in London himself, accompanied by Macdonogh. On the following day he presented his case to the War Council. He was optimistic about ammunition, which he was successfully stockpiling, and about casualties, anticipating only 5,000–8,000 for the whole operation. He informed the War Council that the Germans were running short of copper for the driving-bands of shells: moreover, Germany was exhausting her manpower reserves and would have reached the end of her resources by October or November. These statements, 'but above all French's personality and confidence', began to sway the Council. The Field-Marshal believed that, if the weather improved, Joffre had a fair chance of breaking through at Arras and Rheims, and his own attack should clear the coast to the Dutch frontier. In the last analysis, however, he did not think that a decision could be reached in the West, and 'relied on the Russians to finish the business'.[85]

Kitchener had announced his agreement to French's proposals, and the meeting seemed to be nearing its close, when

Churchill revealed his ideas for a naval attack upon the Dardanelles. He spoke well and lucidly, and persuaded the Council that the plan was worth trying. The meeting's conclusions pleased almost everybody. French was to receive two Territorial divisions by the middle of February and a decision on the offensive would be made early that month; the Admiralty was to prepare for an attack on the Gallipoli Peninsula, and a sub-committee of the CID would consider the question of alternative theatres of war in case the Western Front became a stalemate.[86]

This decision proved to be the high-water mark of the plan's success. Joffre failed to share French's jubilation when the Field-Marshal told him of the Council's conclusions. He renewed his requests for the BEF to take over large sectors of the French line, and Millerand visited England, assuring Kitchener and his colleagues of France's opposition to the scheme. On 28 January Kitchener told the War Council that French army withdrawals from the north meant that 'our army would have its work cut out to render the line secure', and the Flanders coast offensive was, for all practical purposes, a dead duck. Its chances of success, given the flat and inhospitable terrain over which the attack was to be launched, were never good, and Sir John's estimates of likely casualties were, in view of the losses sustained even in the modest efforts of mid-December, unduly optimistic. But its demise left something of a planning vacuum at GHQ, a vacuum which would have to be filled if the Western Front was not to be upstaged by developments elsewhere.[87]

The BEF had undergone substantial internal changes between the time when the Flanders plan was first mooted in October 1914 and the project's eventual demise at the end of January 1915. With effect from the evening of 25 December the force was reorganised into two armies, First Army, under Haig, comprising I, IV and the Indian Corps, and Second Army, commanded by Smith-Dorrien, containing II Corps, III Corps and the 27th Division. Allenby's Cavalry Corps and Major-General Rimington's Indian Cavalry Corps came directly under GHQ.

If this reorganisation was accomplished with comparatively little heartache, the same cannot be said of certain other changes. French had been considering putting Wilson in Murray's place since late October, and on 20 December he discussed the matter with Asquith and Kitchener during a brief meeting at Walmer Castle. Neither Asquith nor Kitchener had much time for Wilson. Asquith thought that he was 'voluble, impetuous and an indefatigable intriguer', and regarded him as the author of many of the government's woes in March 1914.[88] Kitchener, for his part, feared that Wilson's appointment would infuriate the many senior officers who disliked him. Although Sir John had given Wilson the impression that he was prepared to make a resignation issue of the appointment, he gave way before the combined pressure of Asquith and Kitchener.

But he did not abandon the idea altogether. On 2 January he advised Wilson to ingratiate himself with the Prime Minister. 'You are such a brute,' said Sir John, 'you will never be nice to people you don't like. Now I am going to get Asquith out here, why don't you make love to him?'[89] It was a wasted plea. Asquith realised that the pressure for Murray's removal was substantial, and came from Joffre's GQG as well as from GHQ, but he noted on 31 December that he agreed with Kitchener that Robertson was the right man to replace him. Churchill favoured Haig, but Asquith believed that it would be almost impossible to find an army commander to take over from him.[90]

French's handling of Murray's replacement was characteristic. The impending change had been freely discussed amongst senior officers for some time, and on 24 January a medical report which stated that Murray would be off duty for a month gave Sir John his opening. He sent Murray a note regretting the collapse of his health, but telling him that he would have to relinquish his post. Murray replied that he was by no means as unfit as the doctors suggested, and would be back at work within a few days. French wrote back immediately, insisting that Murray should go home.[91] Although it was abundantly clear to all cognoscenti that Sir John had been dissatisfied with Murray's performance for some months, the Field-Marshal did his best to make it seem that it was only the breakdown of Murray's health which had brought about his removal. He emphasised this point in a telegram to Kitchener, assuring the

Secretary of State that this was 'the *sole* reason why I have suggested any alteration in the post of CGS'.[92] A sore throat, possibly diplomatic in origin, prevented French from seeing Murray off when the latter left France on the 29th, but he sent the dejected Murray a letter saying that he hoped to see him back as an army commander before long.[93]

It was typical of French to try to soften the blow by finding a pretext for the dismissal of Murray, but equally typical for the attempt to miscarry. Haig summed up the feelings of many senior officers when he wrote: 'Murray was a kindly fellow but not a practical man in the field. Most of us commanders felt that French had done right to remove him, though we did not like the way it was done.'[94] Whatever Sir John may have told Kitchener or Murray, there is no doubt that Murray's short-comings as CGS were the real reason for his downfall. Not only had his removal been discussed at GHQ for a considerable time, but on 24 January, before the question of Murray's replacement had been finally settled, French told Haig and Smith-Dorrien that Murray was ill and would be going home, 'but he did not intend to have him back again'.[95]

Wully Robertson took over as CGS. He did so reluctantly, because he knew that French would rather have had Wilson, and also because, as he told Wilson: 'He could not manage Johnnie, who was sure to come to grief and carry him along with him.'[96] GQG had backed Wilson so heavily that even French, who would have been delighted to see Wilson as CGS had it not been for Asquith's pressure, grumbled to Foch about it. Foch told Joffre: 'The Field-Marshal is asking why we cannot busy ourselves with our own affairs and leave his alone.'[97] The French government had formed the impression that Wilson would succeed Murray, and there were rumblings on the diplomatic front when the post went to Robertson. Wilson was shunted off as chief liaison officer to GQG with the local rank of Lieutenant-General. When French told Wilson of the appointment, the latter pointed out that the Field-Marshal had no authority to make such a promotion. Sir John was undismayed. 'He said he would put me in Orders', wrote Wilson, 'and then, if the WO or the Cabinet objected, we would go home together.'[98]

Robertson's appointment was generally welcomed by the

army, although there were some dissidents who muttered that Wilson had been deprived of the post by political chicanery. French was on reasonably good terms with Robertson, though their relationship had little sparkle, for he found Wully's dour efficiency far less attractive than Wilson's chatty enthusiasm. Nevertheless, he was soon writing of the 'sense and soundness' of Robertson's advice, and he recognised that Wully's methodical approach had imparted a new and businesslike air to GHQ.[99]

Discussions concerning the spring offensive went on against a background of constant trench warfare, with messy little actions at Cuinchy, Givenchy and St Eloi as reminders that, if the Germans were now concentrating their major effort in the east, they remained formidable foes in the west. Joffre proposed to exploit the reduction of German strength in the west by launching an offensive as soon as the weather improved. He planned to strike hard, in Artois and Champagne, against the shoulders of the great German salient which bulged like a malignant bubble between Amiens and Rheims. Once these attacks had broken the German line and brought about a retreat, he would unleash another attack from the Verdun–Nancy area, with the aim of cutting German lines of retreat across the Rhine.

Sir John was eager to help. Although he remained convinced that the war would be decided on the Eastern Front, and saw the Russian withdrawals in February as 'only a strategic move' deliberately designed to over-extend the Germans, he believed that it was essential to maintain the pressure in the West.[100] He also felt that his army's morale had suffered as a result of a long winter in the trenches, and thought that the troops would be cheered by going on to the offensive: on 8 February he issued a memorandum to his army commanders in which he spoke of the possibility of launching an attack. A week later, after considering a number of options, Sir John ordered Haig to plan an attack with the La Bassée–Aubers Ridge as its objective. This seemed to him to offer better prospects than a move against the almost equally inviting Messines–Wytschaete Ridge. Moreover, the latter feature was on 2nd Army's front, while Aubers Ridge lay opposite 1st Army. This clinched the matter. Sir John told Haig that he had decided upon the

Aubers Ridge because 'he could never be sure of getting satisfactory results from SD, and ... because my troops were better'.[101]

On 16 February a memorandum from GQG lent new impetus to the work of Haig's staff. Joffre told Sir John that he proposed to launch General de Maud'huy's 10th Army against Vimy Ridge, and suggested that the British should co-operate by seizing Aubers Ridge to its north. The operation entrusted to Haig now became more than an isolated British effort: it was an essential component of a large-scale Allied operation designed to secure a suitable jumping-off point for a subsequent drive into the plain of Douai.

The offensive depended, in Joffre's view, upon the relief by the British of two French corps north of Ypres, and on 21 January Sir John had agreed to carry out the relief as soon as reinforcements arrived. On 9 February Sir John attended a meeting of the War Council, listening to 'the usual amount of somewhat vapid talking', and discovering, to his chagrin, that the 29th Division, which he expected in France, was likely to be sent to Salonika instead.[102]

Joffre reacted sharply to suggestions that the British might not be able to carry out the relief as agreed. On 19 February he modified his demands, but emphasised that: 'The relief of the IX Corps is ... the *necessary condition* of the offensive in which you have asked me to participate.' He went on to suggest that the British could afford to take over more front, for they had almost twice as many men per kilometre as the French.[103] Sir John was extremely cross. 'I sent for Huguet', he wrote, 'and directed him to inform the French generals that I objected very strongly to the tone adopted by them.' He described the letter as 'grossly incorrect, very embarrassing, and ... making ridiculous and impossible demands'.[104] Joffre's assertion that Sir John had asked the French to participate in the offensive was profoundly galling, as was the comparison of strengths per kilometre of front.

The storm quickly passed. No sooner had he expended his ire on the unfortunate Huguet than Sir John sent Robertson and Wilson to say that he hoped to co-operate as requested. 'I fancy Joffre hardly saw this letter', he remarked, 'and it was probably written by some young upstart French staff officer.'[105]

On 23 February Sir John's polite but firm formal reply was sent to Joffre. French reminded Joffre that the relief had always been conditional upon the receipt of reinforcements and, in view of the fact that the 29th Division was being sent to Salonika, it was now impossible. Useful deductions were, he suggested, not possible from mere comparison of numbers and length of front: terrain and the tactical value of the sector should also be considered.[106]

Joffre was as annoyed by this letter as Sir John had been by Joffre's missive of the 19th. French had admitted that the 46th (North Midland Territorial) Division was being sent to France in place of the 29th. This being so, Joffre expected French to honour his obligations and take over more of the line. Sir John's refusal to do so was, from GQG's viewpoint, evidence that the British were as little in earnest in February 1915 as they had been in December 1914. On 7 March Joffre informed GHQ that, owing to British failure to relieve French formations in the line, the projected offensive was now postponed.

This news came as no surprise to Sir John. On 28 February Haig had visited de Maud'huy and discovered that, unless the relief operation went ahead as planned, the 10th Army would offer only limited artillery support to Haig's attack. 'The net result of this information,' Haig told French, 'is that our proposed offensive action must be considered an entirely independent operation.'[107] Sir John was not downcast by this news: he had been prepared to launch the attack before he knew that it conformed with Joffre's offensive, and now, with the French advance postponed, he remained determined to press on.

As Haig's plans neared completion, a backwash of bitterness and distrust rolled over GQG and the French War Ministry. Millerand sent a private letter to Kitchener, bewailing the lack of unity of command and enclosing a complaint from Joffre. On 3 March Kitchener forwarded both notes to French, and added, for good measure, a covering letter of his own, noting that 'having received reinforcements you are not prepared to carry out what Joffre requires of you', and regretting that Sir John appeared to have a low opinion of the Territorials.[108]

French received the letter on his return to St Omer from a tour of the front. He wrote:

> When I returned I found one of Kitchener's usual worrying letters. They might be written by an old woman ... Anyone but Kitchener would have seen the [illegible] of the whole thing and would have refrained from worrying a commander in the field with such silly trash.[109]

His irritation was, for once, amply justified. It was Kitchener who had told him, only a few days previously, that the 29th Division would not be available in time for the operation. In other words, having deprived Sir John of the means of carrying out his agreement with Joffre, Kitchener was now blaming him for breaking faith with the French. French valued the Territorials highly, but it was obviously impossible, as he told Kitchener, to 'carry out, with a Territorial Division, what I had proposed with a regular one'. Sir John assured Kitchener that his relations with Joffre were 'of the most cordial nature', and added that although slight differences of opinion were bound to arise, 'we never quarrel and I have no idea how it ever came to be supposed that we did'.[110]

This was stretching the truth to breaking-point, for relations between GHQ and GQG had, from time to time, been anything but cordial, and they continued to be characterised by sweeping fluctuations. Sir John summed things up when he commented in his diary on Joffre's letter announcing the postponement of the French offensive: 'the whole tone of his letter shows that he is dissatisfied. However he wrote in a kindly spirit. The French are a very curious people to deal with.'[111] Having written off any hope of French assistance, Sir John then turned his attention to tying up the loose ends of what was to prove the first systematic British attack since the commencement of trench warfare: the Battle of Neuve Chapelle.

Nine

Changing the Bowler
March–December 1915

At 7.30 on the damp and misty morning of 10 March, 276 field guns and howitzers and 66 heavy guns drenched the German positions around Neuve Chapelle with a fire whose violent intensity surpassed anything yet experienced on the Western Front.[1] Thirty-five minutes later the leading waves of Haig's 48 assaulting battalions left their trenches and plodded towards the debris-strewn German lines as fast as the heavy mud would allow. By nightfall the Indian and IV Corps had overrun the German defences on a front of 4,000 yards, penetrating to a maximum depth of 1,200 yards. But that was as far as success went. Neither renewed British assaults nor a German counter-attack made much progress over the next few days, and on the night of the 12th Haig ordered his commanders to entrench and wire the line they currently held.[2]

Neuve Chapelle was, predictably enough, hailed as a British victory, and Sir John's official dispatch spoke in glowing terms of 'the defeat of the enemy and the capture of his position'.[3] Yet the battle went only a short way towards fulfilling the aspirations of its authors. Sir John had been particularly sanguine. His motives for embarking upon the offensive were numerous: he hoped, amongst other things, to show the French that he was in deadly earnest and to demonstrate to the sceptical Kitchener that a breakthrough could indeed be achieved on the Western Front.

Sir John saw the battle, however, as a great deal more than a publicity stunt on a grand scale: he was genuinely confident of achieving a breakthrough. It was only to be expected of him to assure the Prime Minister that he anticipated making 'good progress', but he was almost equally optimistic concerning the forthcoming 'great event' in his letters to Winifred Bennett, to whom he usually wrote with remarkable frankness.[4] At the tactical level, he was content to rubber-stamp Haig's plans, which enshrined his own belief in the supremacy of firepower, a conviction born of the experience of the Aisne and Ypres. In strategic terms, Sir John saw the assault on Neuve Chapelle as merely the curtain-raiser to a lengthy 'Battle of Lille' which would drive the Germans from the Lille–Douai plain.[5]

It was a measure of Sir John's confidence that he took pains to brief the commanders of his exploitation force, Allenby of the Cavalry Corps and Rimington of the Indian Cavalry Corps, personally. His intention of pushing cavalry through the gap ripped by Haig's attack was by no means inconsistent with his high regard for firepower, nor was it the archaic fumbling of an old hussar who was intoxicated by the holy odour of the horse. One of the many tactical problems posed by the deadlock of trench warfare concerned the exploitation of a breakthrough. It was not until after the development of the tank that this particular problem was solved: in the spring of 1915 cavalry, whatever its limitations, seemed to be the only arm whose mobility gave it a chance of moving through the enemy's broken line and dislocating his position before reserves could arrive.

In practice, the difficulties of communication and movement on the battlefield itself, coupled with the inherent vulnerability of the horse, made cavalry almost useless as a weapon of exploitation. But in March 1915 the evidence available to commanders was by no means conclusive and, moreover, no satisfactory alternative to cavalry existed. Sir John was sure that his cavalry could, if properly handled, set the seal on the victory he expected Haig's infantry to win. It is, however, ironic that French, who had been so concerned with training for shock action before the war, should admit that the radically changed nature of the battlefield rendered any form of mounted action in contact with the enemy a decidedly hazardous business. On 8 March he saw Rimington: 'I cautioned him against risking his troops mounted too close to the enemy. He is not experienced in this kind of warfare and thinks he may be able to do some dashing cavalry work.'[6] It was a poignant comment from the hero of Klip Drift.

Sir John left St Omer on the morning of the attack and moved to a forward command post at Hazebrouck, 15 miles behind the battle zone. He preferred Hazebrouck to St Omer: he was nearer his army commanders, and his quarters had a small walled garden in which he could walk undisturbed.[7] He paid daily visits to Haig's headquarters and was generally cheerful about the progress of the battle although he soon found fault with the diversionary attacks launched by Smith-Dorrien, noting that: 'a certain *lack of determination in command and execution* characterises the work of the 2nd Army'.[8]

On 13 March Haig drove over to Hazebrouck and told French of his intention to attack another point in the German line once preparations were complete and the weather was

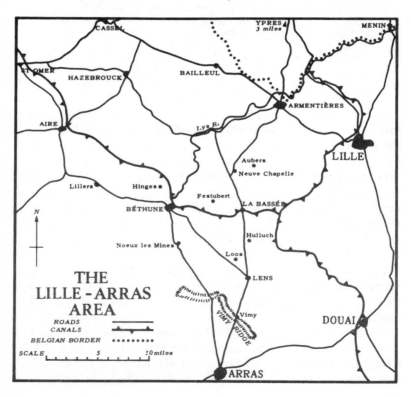

THE
LILLE - ARRAS
AREA

ROADS
CANALS
BELGIAN BORDER
SCALE   5   10 miles

favourable: 22 March was provisionally selected for the operation. Sir John at once wired to Kitchener: 'Cessation of the forward movement is necessitated to-day by the fatigue of the troops, and, above all, by the want of ammunition ... Further plans are being matured for a vigorous offensive.'[9] On the following day Robertson's successor as QMG, Lieutenant-General R. C. Maxwell, arrived from St Omer with news which made short work of Sir John's concept of a continuing Battle of Lille. Ammunition stocks were now so low that even if operations were postponed for several days another attack could be launched with only half the artillery support which had been available at Neuve Chapelle. Worse still, Major-General J. P. du Cane, French's artillery adviser, announced that defective fuses for the 4·5 guns had resulted in five of the weapons bursting.[10]

Four days later Sir John informed the War Office that:

> If the supply of ammunition cannot be maintained on a considerably increased scale it follows that the offensive efforts of the army must be spasmodic and separated by a considerable interval of time. They cannot, therefore, lead to decisive results.[11]

The shell shortage has been hailed as 'the perfect excuse for failure' as far as French was concerned, enabling him to shift the blame from his own shoulders on to those of Kitchener and his Cabinet colleagues.[12] Although there is some substance in this allegation, the truth is infinitely more complex. Sir John was indeed suspicious of Kitchener, fearing that he intended to bring the New Armies out to France himself, and was anxious to preserve not only his own position as Commander-in-Chief, but also his army's status as Britain's major instrument in the war. This made him reluctant to tell the War Office of the real reasons for the failure at Neuve Chapelle, although, as he soon recognised, there had been shortcomings in the planning and execution of First Army's attack which had nothing to do with ammunition.[13]

As far as Neuve Chapelle itself was concerned, then, the ammunition shortage was something of an excuse. But Neuve Chapelle was only a component of the Battle of Lille, and it was this operation, in which Sir John had substantial if misplaced confidence, which was brought to a halt by a shortage of shells. French may justly be accused of failing to appreciate that he had insufficient ammunition available for a sustained offensive of this sort. In this context his lack of staff training, complete dependence upon specialist advisers who were themselves learning new lessons in a hard school, and fondness for getting away from GHQ where detailed statistics were most readily available, all contributed to Sir John's difficulties.

Nor was this all. French had always been a deeply emotional man with a mercurial personality, and even in August 1914 he had tended to over-identify with his soldiers. By the spring of 1915 the pressures of high command were clouding his mind. He found it hard to forget that almost any action he took as Commander-in-Chief resulted, to a greater or lesser degree, in British casualties. His diaries and letters to personal friends reflect the anguish that the growing casualty lists caused him. In early September he wrote of 'this awful sum total' of losses, and he was similarly stunned by the butcher's bill for Neuve Chapelle.[14]

French's unconventional religious beliefs lent a curious twist to the impact of casualties on his judgement. His views were well summed up in a letter he wrote in the autumn of 1915.

> The earthly bodies we know here are only a kind of model in clay of what our real spiritual bodies are — and we only *resume* these real and everlasting shapes when the great change comes.

Mortal bodies were shackled to the earth, but spirits were free to wander in 'star-swept fields'.[15] Churchill commented on Sir John's

> firm belief in the immortality of the soul.
>
> If you looked over the parapet, he thought, and got a bullet through your head, all that happened was that you could no longer communicate with your fellows and comrades; there you would be; knowing ... all that went on; forming your ideas and wishes but totally unable to communicate. This would be a worry to you, so long as you were interested in earthly affairs. After a while your centre

of interest would shift. He was sure that a new light would dawn; better and brighter at last for all. If, however, you looked over the parapet on purpose, you would start very ill in the next world.[16]

When Johnnie Gough was killed in February 1915 Sir John felt that his room at St Omer was '*thick* with the spirits of my dead friends'. Even before Neuve Chapelle he told Winifred Bennett how:

> I sometimes people my room with these glorious friends (all boys compared to me!), who have gone over. That 'Silent Army'. Alas, alas! The room is getting small to hold even my intimate friends. Dear old 'Bobs' was with us in that same room the night before he died — perfectly well and enraptured by being amongst us.[17]

The sheer misery of the war in human terms contended in French's mind with the pleasure he experienced in commanding men in action. As the war went on, the weight of casualties dulled the glow of battle:

> I spoke to one battalion (2 Shropshire LI) which lost 20 officers — 8 of them killed! It seems horrible butchery. I talked with a young subaltern whose voice got quite husky when he spoke of it. It is rather an awful thing to miss *so many comrades* so suddenly. Poor boy, he *felt* it.[18]

Death snatched at his friends and relatives all around him.

> Two of my young cousins (brothers) were killed on the 9th. They were in the same regiment, poor boys: and their poor old mother wrote to me about three months ago ... They've had a bad setback in the Dardanelles and I hear poor Jack Milbanke is killed! He was my ADC in South Africa ... [19]

Esher visited GHQ on the eve of Neuve Chapelle, and recorded how:

> The FM said today 'It is a solemn thought that at my signal all these fine young fellows go to their death.'

This tenderness does Sir John infinite credit, for warriors are commonly made of sterner stuff; yet he is a warrior.[20]

When Sir John searched for a reason for the failure of his Battle of Lille, he was not merely attempting to stave off criticism from London, although this was, of course, one of his motives. He was more concerned with justifying his actions to himself, so much so that he came to believe passionately in the truth of his own assertions. There was more than a measure of truth in his lamentations over the failure of ammunition supply, and before long the ammunition question came to dominate all other considerations in French's mind. He could convince himself that he was not responsible for it: the spirits of his dead friends, even more than the stony-eyed spectre of Kitchener, demanded reasons, not excuses.

Even though he managed to persuade himself that it was not his own errors that were decimating the army, Sir John still found the burden of command almost unbearably heavy. He was strengthened by the last, and probably the greatest, love affair of his life. Winifred Youelle, one of the three daughters of a British businessman living in Roumania, was a tall, stately woman who had married Percy Bennett, a diplomat. 'Pompous Percy', as Winifred called him, was preoccupied with his own career and failed to understand his wife's deep-seated need for an intensely romantic relationship. By 1914 she had found solace in the arms of a more flamboyant figure, Captain the Honourable Arthur 'Jack' Annesley, of the 10th Hussars, and her involvement was one of the open secrets of London society. Sir John was on nodding terms with Annesley, and had met Mrs Bennett in 1913. When Annesley was killed near Ypres on 15 November, Sir John sent Mrs Bennett a short note of condolence for the death of her lover.[21]

The friendship blossomed. Winifred called on French at Lancaster Gate during the Field-Marshal's visit to London in January, and the tone of their correspondence changed rapidly. Although their relationship undoubtedly had its sexual side, for the onset of years had not extinguished Sir John's ardour, it was above all the deeply romantic union of 'two shipwrecked souls who have found one another'.[22] French, who had had a succession of mistresses, and one particularly painful affair, in the years before the war, assured Winifred that his experience of women made him love her all the more. 'I can say before God', he wrote, 'that I have never a thought for any woman in the world but you – and now I feel I never shall.'[23] He told her:

> You don't know how constantly and truly I can love. It is only when women you love and worship do things which are debasing and degrading – when they *lie* and *cheat* and *pretend* – it is then that love is stretched to breaking point – in fact it goes.[24]

There is something charming, if faintly ridiculous, in the prospect of an elderly Field-Marshal signing himself 'Peter Pan' and announcing, on the eve of Neuve Chapelle, that: 'Tomorrow I shall go forward with my War Cry of "Winifred".'[25] French drew great strength from his relationship with Winifred Bennett, while her emotional needs were gratified by the highly-charged romantic content of their affair. Sir John wrote to Winifred almost daily during 1915, ensuring that the letters contained no precise details of forthcoming operations and sending them to England by a trusted courier, often one of his *aides*. Nevertheless, his letters display a wealth of information on his personal feelings, and give a unique insight into the Commander-in-Chief's mind.

Four dominant themes characterise Sir John's correspondence with Mrs Bennett. Mention has already been made of his frequent references to the losses suffered by his army, and the depressing effect of the deaths of so many of his friends. The letters also reveal the intensity of French's hatred of Kitchener and the War Office. 'I have more trouble with the War Office than I do with the Germans', he complained.[26]

> While they are fiddling Rome is burning. What we want is more and more High Explosive ammunition and they do nothing but squabble amongst themselves. I devoutly wish we could get rid of Kitchener at the War Office – I'm sure nothing will go right whilst he is there. It is so hard to have enemies *in front* and *behind*.[27]

He also made frequent reference to his ambivalent feelings towards the French, although it was telling comment on his own relationship with London when he expressed sympathy with Joffre over his political difficulties: 'We are both hampered by our respective governments. They are the greatest "thorn in the side" a general in the field can suffer from.'[28]

Finally, Sir John's letters trace the development of his views on Allied strategy. He watched anxiously events in the East, and remained confident that the Germans would never succeed in destroying the Russian army, and unless they did so they were 'as far removed as ever from any decisive conclusions'.[29] As the Central Powers' 1915 offensive rolled into Russia, he acknowledged that the enemy were 'quite right for it is really the only chance they have. I am sure of it, but I am equally sure they won't succeed.'[30] His hopes that the war would end in the summer of 1915, or later, the spring of 1916, were jarred by the news of Russian reverses, but he was certain the Germans could not sustain a war on two fronts indefinitely, and, if only the Allies would continue to 'worry them well' final victory was assured.[31]

As long as he commanded in France Sir John was convinced that the Western Front was the crucial theatre of war as far as Britain was concerned. Nevertheless, he initially found the concept of attacking Turkey attractive: 'I hope the Navy will get on quickly with that Dardanelles business. It will make an enormous difference and settle old Constantinople for good and all.'[32] His view changed radically, however, once it appeared that the Dardanelles project would consume troops and ammunition which might otherwise be used in France. In mid-May he declared that: 'We have certainly made a hideous mistake in getting mixed up there at all. I was *dead against it* but they wouldn't listen to me.'[33] A month later he was even more convinced that:

> We were absolutely mad to embark on the infernal Dardanelles expedition. It is the very thing the Germans would have wished us to do. Certainly if we win this war it will not be on account of our Great Strategic combinations.[34]

French's comments on the war were interspersed with social

chit-chat, much of it concerning his American friend, George Moore, who paid frequent visits to France, advising Sir John on America's attitude to the war and helping with the experiments on grenades and trench-mortars. He was far from popular, even amongst French's personal staff, who resented his influence upon the Field-Marshal. But French was not Moore's only powerful friend: Moore was also highly regarded by the press baron Lord Northcliffe.[35]

On 15 September 1915 Sir John wrote of an incident which, while it has nothing to do with the progress of the war, throws interesting light upon his social attitudes and, indeed, upon those of many of his contemporaries. He told Mrs Bennett of a couple he knew:

> The husband is a very well known man — a rich man — and the wife very good looking. They've been married some 17 or 18 years. A few years ago they found out the same old story that they weren't *meant* to be in love with one another — so each went his and her way but they remained together and are the best of friends. The wife found what she thought was her '*alter ego*' in a Guardsman who is serving out here. About a year or two ago he gave her up and *married*. The husband then wrote to him and told him he had behaved like a cad to his wife and that he should always cut him in future and he has always done so.
>
> Now I call that husband a real good fellow. Don't you? He saw no reason why his wife shouldn't be made happy simply because she happened to be his wife.[36]

But we must return to what Sassoon was to call 'the real War, that big bullying bogey'.[37] Joffre resumed negotiations for a general offensive on 24 March, suggesting that an attack would only succeed if sufficient reserves of men and ammunition were accumulated. He asked for French's co-operation and, as a preliminary measure, requested the relief of the two French corps north of Ypres.[38] Sir John replied that he hoped to complete the relief by 20 April, and by the end of the month First Army should be available for an attack.[39] The opening of the Gallipoli campaign, and the possibility that the Western

Front might be eclipsed by the new theatre of war, made comprehensive planning for Allied action in the West difficult. There were, as the *Official History* admits 'no signs of substantial reinforcements, and during the month of March the Commander-in-Chief could obtain no information as to when the New Army divisions would be sent, or even if they were to be sent at all'.[40] Undeterred, First Army began to prepare for the combined offensive. But before its preparations were complete, the Germans lashed out in an attack of their own.

During the first weeks of April Second Army took over almost five miles of French front, extending the British left to the Poelcappelle–St Julien road north-east of Ypres. It was an uncomfortable sector, for many of the French trenches were in 'deplorable condition', and an unusually large number of unburied corpses lent an acrid smell of death to the air.[41] A second line of defences, known to the British as GHQ line, lay between the front line and Ypres itself, and was well dug and wired, but the area was in general extremely vulnerable. Not only did the Germans possess artillery superiority, but three Allied contingents, British, French and Belgian, with no unified command, held the northern part of the salient.

It was upon precisely this fragile sector that the German blow fell. Late on the afternoon of 22 April greenish-yellow clouds were seen drifting towards French positions around Langemarck, and soon afterwards panic-stricken African troops began streaming through the rear areas of Plumer's V Corps. At 7 p.m., two hours after the attack had started, the 75s of the French divisional artillery, which had previously been firing steadily, fell ominously silent. Many of the retreating French coughed and pointed to their throats, and at V Corps report centre, some five miles from Langemarck, a peculiar smell was noticed, accompanied by an unpleasant sensation in the nose and throat. The Germans had used poison gas, and had done so with devastating effect.

Plumer's divisional commanders acted quickly to shore up the threatened flank, moving reserves to support the Canadian Division, whose flank had been left in the air by the French collapse. Smith-Dorrien did his best to co-ordinate the defence, and at 9 p.m. he arrived at GHQ with what Sir John called 'a bolt from the blue'. French's attention had been fixed on the fighting around Hill 60, on the southern end of the salient, and the news of the German attack and more particularly, of the manner of its delivery, came as a ghastly surprise.[42]

Second Ypres was a broken-backed battle. The information arriving at GHQ was confusing and often contradictory, and French's handling of the battle bore witness to a crisis of confidence. On the one hand he agreed with Foch that it was essential to recover the lost ground, and spurred Smith-Dorrien on into launching a series of costly counter-attacks in an effort to achieve this. On the other hand, however, his confidence in the French high command was fast disappearing. He believed that the French had made 'a horrible mistake' in holding the northern sector so thinly, and wrote angrily that 'Joffre ... really deceived me'. Being allied to the French once in a lifetime was, he remarked ruefully, more than enough.[43]

During the last days of May Sir John swayed between the two extremes, encouraged to counter-attack by Joffre and Foch, but riddled with doubts as to his chances of success. Smith-Dorrien, in a well-argued appreciation of the situation, suggested to Robertson that a withdrawal on GHQ line was likely to be the only satisfactory option: given the small numbers of British troops available, and the strictly limited nature of French support, the counter-attack policy was unlikely to work.[44]

It is a cruel irony that this suggestion might have borne immediate fruit if it had come from almost any other senior commander, for Sir John already suspected that withdrawal might be the only answer. Coming from Smith-Dorrien, however, it was like a red rag to a bull. French's opinion of Smith-Dorrien had not improved as winter thawed into spring. In February he confided to Haig that Smith-Dorrien was 'a weak spot', and he told Kitchener of his serious misgivings in March.[45]

Smith-Dorrien, for his part, wrote approvingly of Sir John's ability in letters which make strange reading in view of the strained relations between the two men. In November he told the King's assistant private secretary that:

> Sir John has been very bold in his handling of us and
> has earned the complete confidence of everyone ... I

don't believe there is another man in the army who could have steered us as Sir John has done — over and over situations arise bad enough to create panic in most breasts, but Sir John is unmoved and invariably does the right thing.[46]

Two months later he assured Wigram that he would not hesitate 'to warn my chief if I think it necessary to save him from a pitfall'.[47]

In March, however, it was Sir John who was doing the warning. He was concerned that the rate of sickness in Second Army was running at three times that in the First, and felt that some of the minor reverses suffered by Smith-Dorrien's men might have been averted by firmer leadership.[48] On 19 March Billy Lambton informed the King that:

I am afraid Sir H. Smith-Dorrien's position is not very secure. He will worry about details, passes his commanders and does not get good work out of them. I am sure Sir John will keep him if possible, and he had an interview and plain talk to him a few days ago.[49]

On 27 April Sir John decided to act. He declared that Smith-Dorrien had 'failed to get a real "grasp" of the situation', his messages were all 'wordy, "windy" and unintelligible', while his 'pessimistic attitude has the worst effect on his commanders and their troops'.[50] He made Plumer responsible for the operations around Ypres, and, on 6 May, Sir Horace was formally relieved of the command of Second Army. Whatever the truth of Sir John's accusations of weakness against Smith-Dorrien during the spring of 1915 — and the sickness statistics do appear to support French — there can be no doubt that the pretext for Sir Horace's dismissal was thin indeed. Smith-Dorrien had done his best to co-operate with the French under difficult circumstances, and his recommendation of withdrawal was a realistic assessment of the facts rather than a triumph of pessimism. Plumer, who took over from Smith-Dorrien, shared his predecessor's view of the situation in front of Ypres, and Sir John himself eventually agreed that a retirement to a shorter line was desirable. The truth was that Sir

John had finally lost what little confidence he had ever had in Smith-Dorrien. He spoke in glowing terms of the 'confidence and *order*' which prevailed at V Corps headquarters, and was sure that Plumer was the man for Second Army.[51]

Although the fighting at Ypres, which rumbled on throughout May, caused Sir John considerable concern, his main preoccupation was with First Army's offensive. For dangerous though the German attack on Ypres was, far more perilous consequences would be likely to result from the failure of an Allied offensive. On 31 March French had breakfasted with Kitchener, and had been left in no doubt as to the Secretary of State's opinion:

> He told me that he considered Joffre and I were 'on our trial' – that if we showed within the next month or 5 weeks that we really could make 'substantial advances' and 'break the German Line' he would – so far as he was concerned – always back us up with all the troops he could send. But if we failed it would be essential that the government should look for some other theatre of operations ... I told him that I thought he had put the matter very fairly and I was content to accept what he said.[52]

This left Sir John writhing on the horns of a dilemma. If he failed to launch a successful attack, he risked seeing the troops and ammunition which, he believed, should be sent to the Western Front, being dispatched elsewhere. There was also the question of his own position. Sir John was well aware that there were many who regarded his performance with less than satisfaction, and his personal staff were not slow to suggest – probably without foundation – that Kitchener himself coveted the command in France.[53]

Sir John undoubtedly thought that a successful attack was indeed possible, provided that he had adequate ammunition available. On 4 April GHQ issued a memorandum on the tactical lessons of Neuve Chapelle, a document which laid great emphasis upon thorough preparation and the accurate registration of enemy positions by the artillery.[54] On 14 April French and Kitchener had a lengthy discussion on ammunition, and Sir John was somewhat reassured by the conversation. Nevertheless, the imperative need to launch an offensive, and the risks involved in failing to do so, bulked so large in French's mind that he was already well on the way to convincing himself that Haig's men would attack in co-operation with the French, whatever the state of the ammunition supply. On 2 May Sir John assured Kitchener that 'the ammunition will be all right', a declaration which Kitchener passed on to the Prime Minister.[55]

Learning the lessons of Neuve Chapelle was a game that two could play, and on 9 May First Army assaulted a much stronger German position than that into which it had bitten so deeply two months before. The Battle of Aubers Ridge cost the British 11,500 officers and men — much to Sir John's anguish — for a negligible gain. Both French and Haig speedily realised that a short, relatively heavy bombardment, was no answer to the problems posed by well-sited defensive positions. Sir John wrote:

> They've dug themselves in their entrenchments so deeply and so well that our shrapnel can't get at them, and owing to the bungling and want of foresight at our fine War Office we only have a very insufficient quantity of 'High Explosive' ... it's simple murder to send infantry against these powerfully fortified entrenchments until they've been heavily hammered.[56]

Sir John's assessment of the reasons for the attack's failure is supported by the *Official History*, which speaks of:

> the strength of the German defences and ... the lack ... of sufficient shells of large calibre to deal with such defences — and thirdly the inferior quality of much of the ammunition supplied and the difficulties of ranging ... [57]

The fact that there was too little ammunition available to destroy the German positions was a bitter blow to French and Haig, both of whom had pinned their hopes on a repeat of the Neuve Chapelle style lightning bombardment. But while it was merely a costly tactical setback as far as Haig was concerned, First Army's bloody repulse at Aubers Ridge was infinitely more serious from French's viewpoint. Not only had he failed to show Kitchener that a 'substantial advance' could be achieved, but he had been watching the battle from a ruined church, and had seen his infantry cut to pieces by German machine-guns.

Sir John was in a black mood when he returned to his headquarters on 10 May. His temper was not improved by a telegram from the War Office ordering him to send 2,000 rounds of 4·5 inch howitzer ammunition and 20,000 rounds of 18-pounder ammunition to Marseilles for shipment to the Dardanelles. He immediately protested, but, on receipt of a promise that the ammuntion would be replaced at once, reluctantly complied. The 18-pounder shells were replaced immediately, although it took several days for the 4·5 ammunition to arrive.[58]

Others shared Sir John's gloom at the results of the attack. Repington of *The Times* had also watched the operation, and was particularly hurt by the casualties suffered by his old battalion of the Rifle Brigade. On 12 May he sent a telegram to his paper saying that the 'want of an unlimited supply of high explosive shells was a fatal bar to our success'. The telegram was heavily censored by Macdonogh, but was eventually released after Brinsley Fitzgerald had assured him that the Field-Marshal would approve.[59] Repington denied that French had any prior knowledge of the telegram, but Sir John later admitted that he had provided Repington with all the information he required on the question of ammunition.[60]

He did not stop there. Brinsley Fitzgerald and Freddy Guest were sent to England with the same documents which had been shown to Repington, with instructions to lay them before Lloyd George, a cabinet minister who was far from satisfied with Asquith's leadership, and the opposition leaders Balfour and Bonar Law. Sir John later claimed that he embarked upon this highly irregular course in order to 'destroy the apathy of a Government which had brought the Empire to the brink of disaster', in the full knowledge that the consequences were likely to be serious.[61]

Repington's article appeared in *The Times* on 14 May under the dramatic headline: 'Need for shells: British attacks checked: Limited supply the cause: A Lesson from France.'

The article was of considerable political significance for, in a speech at Newcastle on 20 April, Asquith had stated that the supply of ammunition was equal to the army's needs, and had done so on the basis of an assurance from Kitchener. The Repington article, therefore, cast doubt on the wisdom and honesty of both the Prime Minister and the Secretary of State for War.

The government would have weathered the storm had the shells scandal been the only crisis confronting it in mid-May 1915. Lord Fisher had, however, just resigned as First Sea Lord, and rumours of his resignation were discussed alongside Repington's alarming revelations. When the opposition leaders visited Asquith three days later, on Monday 17 May, they had already been in possession of the papers distributed by Fitzgerald and Guest for some days, and it was the crisis at the Admiralty, rather than that over ammunition, which prompted their visit. As a result of this meeting Asquith sent a note to all members of his Cabinet, asking for their resignations. A covering letter explained that:

> The resignation of Lord Fisher, which I have done my best part to avert, and the more than plausible parliamentary case in regard to the alleged deficiency of high-explosive shells, would, if duly exploited ... in the House of Commons at this moment, have had the most disastrous effect upon the general political and strategic situation ... [62]

A coalition government was duly formed: Asquith remained Prime Minister, but Lloyd George became Minister of Munitions and Reginald McKenna replaced Churchill at the Admiralty. Lord Kitchener stayed on at the War Office.

The Northcliffe press continued its attacks on Kitchener. On 21 May the *Daily Mail* told its readers of 'The Shells Scandal: Lord Kitchener's Tragic Blunder', and suggested that Kitchener should go. Northcliffe was overplaying his hand, for there was great public sympathy for Kitchener, who remained a popular hero despite the efforts of Northcliffe's journalists. Indeed, so great was the wave of reaction in Kitchener's favour that Lloyd George, who was no friend of the Secretary of State, felt obliged to warn Northcliffe that the campaign was proving counter-productive.[63]

Kitchener reacted to these attacks with remarkable calm. On 14 May he told French that he did not consider that Repington should be allowed out with the army, and received the unhelpful reply:

> Repington is an old friend of mine and has constantly stayed with me for the last 10 or 12 years. He was here for a day or two in an entirely private capacity. I really have no time to attend to these matters.[64]

Sir John's role in the shells scandal became a topic of bitter debate. Although gossip in London society hinted that French was behind the attacks, many public figures — including Asquith himself — refused to believe that Sir John would carry his feud with Kitchener to such extremes. It is difficult to assess accurately the level of Sir John's involvement. He certainly supplied Repington with information, and would have been well pleased if the press campaign had swept Kitchener from office. But Sir John had never been astute in his handling of the press, and it seems likely that the affair rapidly got out of hand.

There was considerable sympathy between French and Northcliffe. Both were violently anti-Kitchener, and Northcliffe's hostility had been deepened by the recent death in action of his young nephew, a tragedy for which he held Kitchener responsible. Both agreed that war correspondents, accredited to GHQ, should be allowed in France, a policy which was anathema to the journalist-hating Kitchener. And both considered that the Western Front was the only theatre to which British troops should be sent. French wrote:

> I rejoice to hear the view which you take in regard to the dividing of our forces. I entirely agree with what you say, and I earnestly hope you will do your utmost in your powerful control of the Press to insist upon concentration of all available forces in this theatre.[65]

French was already well aware that the press was a powerful, if double-edged, weapon. In late March he had granted an interview to the Havas press agency, warned that the war would be protracted and had emphasised the need for munitions. The King was far from pleased, and Northcliffe told French that it was dangerous to speak of a protracted war, for this would only encourage the slackers.[66] Sir John repaired the damage by a *Times* interview in which he stated that:

> The protraction of the war depends entirely upon the supply of men and munitions. Should these be unsatisfactory, the war will be accordingly prolonged. I dwelt emphatically upon the need for munitions in the interview to which you refer.[67]

There is, then, a clear link between French and Northcliffe as regards the munitions crisis, and Sir John's own admissions in *1914* revealed his disclosures to Repington and the opposition leaders. But there can be no doubt that the press campaign was given extra momentum by factors outside French's control: Northcliffe's fierce hostility towards Kitchener accounts, in itself, for much of the violence of the attacks. There were also suggestions that the campaign was being hurried along by French's friends, who believed that they were acting in the Field-Marshal's best interests. Lord Selborne suggested to Fitzgerald that George Moore was whipping up the attacks, and Fitzgerald agreed, noting that Moore was 'a curious fellow ... He is a mad enthusiast about French, and equally mad in his bitterness against Kitchener, and being an American wouldn't have the same ideas about the Press as you or I have.'[68] Esher thought that the campaign was being orchestrated by 'a small knot of people who believe themselves to be friends of Sir John', while Margot Asquith felt that George Moore and Lloyd George were largely responsible for the scandal.[69] Whether they would have said this after Sir John's revelations in *1914* is a matter of considerable doubt.

It is impossible to establish the degree to which Moore acted with Sir John's tacit approval, or the extent to which Fitzgerald, who was more deeply involved in the campaign than he admitted to Selborne, used the already unpopular Moore as a whipping-boy. If French did instigate the majority of the attacks – and the balance of probabilities suggests that this was so – then one crucial question emerges. It is often maintained that Sir John used the ammunition issue as a mere smoke-screen to cover his own failure. But it is surely improbable that he would have risked a scandal over ammunition unless he had been certain that Kitchener would be unable to refute his arguments. Far from defending himself on points of detail, Kitchener was eager to let the matter drop. This is no doubt a tribute to his public-spirited attitude, but it may also reflect an unwillingness to challenge GHQ's case. When von Donop, Master-General of the Ordnance, who had himself come in for a good deal of abuse, demanded an inquiry to clear his name, Kitchener prevailed upon him to withdraw the request, saying that such an investigation would result in the immediate recall of French.[70] Such regard for French's position is curious in view of the fact that, on 18 March, Kitchener had told Asquith that French 'is not a really scientific soldier; a good capable leader in the field, but without adequate equipment and expert knowledge for the huge task of commanding 450,000 men.'[71]

Sir John certainly hoped that the shells scandal would bring Kitchener down, and he may even have suspected that Asquith himself would fail to survive it. In *1914* he claimed to have brought down the Liberal government, although, as Asquith pointed out, the shells crisis was at most a contributory cause to the change of government.[72] During the crisis itself, however, French and Asquith continued to correspond most warmly, and on 20 May Sir John sent a fulsome letter to the Prime Minister:

> I am sure in the whole history of war no General in the field has ever been helped in a difficult task by the head of his government as I have been supported and strengthened by your unfailing sympathy and encouragement.

French then went on to address the Prime Minister 'privately and as a friend', telling him that Kitchener had been '*overbearing* and *unfair*', and had sent an insulting message via Allenby, saying that the troops lacked 'go' and 'dash', and should be able to take trenches without artillery if they were properly led. He concluded by saying that the presence of Kitchener at the War

Office was 'most detrimental to the successful conduct of operations so long as I remain in command'.[73]

Asquith's most recent biographer has asked why, if French really was fighting a single-handed war against a lethargic government, as he claimed in *1914*, he wrote such a cordial letter to the man he was attempting to destroy.[74] The truth is, for once, relatively simple. By the time he wrote *1914* French regarded Asquith as the man who had forced him out of France. His papers betray little evidence of hostility towards Asquith until after his dismissal in December 1915. Indeed, Sir John told Freddy Guest, from whom he had few secrets, that he had absolute confidence in Asquith:

> and moreover I am deeply grateful ... for all the generous and kindly support he has rendered me. No general in the field has ever had such reason to be thankful to a Prime Minister ... But it is impossible for me to put to him in writing my inmost feelings and sentiments towards Kitchener. You know them ... [75]

By 1918 Sir John saw Asquith in an entirely different light. He told Esher of his deep and lasting resentment about the events of December 1915, when:

> I was driven out of France by Asquith at the instigation of Haig ... I had lived all my life for 'Service in the field', and I had tried to prepare myself for it: and I was taken away from it for no adequate reason. Nothing that can ever happen to me could compensate for the loss of 1916 and 1917 and half of 1918 *in the field*.[76]

Kitchener, rather than Asquith, was the real target for French and his supporters in 1915: Sir John's assertions in *1914* were both a means of justifying his own dismissal, blaming it on political malice aroused by his disclosures to the press, and a gratifying stab at a man he had come to hate.

May was a difficult month for Sir John. He was under pressure from the French high command to resume offensive operations against Aubers Ridge; the fighting at Ypres went on; the ammunition continued to be in short supply, and the new divisions upon which his co-operation with the French depended failed to appear, despite Kitchener's assurances that reinforcements would arrive.[77] The Secretary of State was far from sanguine at Allied prospects. The Russians were in full retreat, and it might soon be possible for the Germans to transfer troops to the Western Front. Kitchener feared that the Germans would soon attempt an invasion of England, and on 14 May he told the War Council that he was not prepared to send the New Armies overseas. He sent two divisions to France at the end of the month, but only to satisfy Joffre, not because he believed that a breakthrough was possible.[78]

Sir John, too, had serious doubts about the wisdom of attacking. The Battle of Aubers Ridge seemed to have disproved the lessons of Neuve Chapelle. The French had achieved better results at Vimy than the British at Aubers Ridge by a longer, more methodical bombardment, and on 10 May Sir John wondered whether 'we ought not to stand altogether on the defensive until an adequate supply of HE is available'.[79] Joffre, however, insisted that the British must attack in order to attract German reserves which might otherwise oppose the Tenth Army, and Sir John, after much soul-searching, agreed to co-operate in the attack, and to take over a sector of the French front to free more of Joffre's troops for the offensive.

Opinion was hardening at both GHQ and First Army Headquarters concerning the artillery preparation for the next phase of the attack. On 11 May Haig wrote that a '*long methodical bombardment*' was the only way of smashing German machine-gun nests, and GHQ's orders of 11 and 14 May spoke of:

> a deliberate and persistent attack. The enemy should never be given a complete rest by day or by night, but be gradually and relentlessly worn down by exhaustion and loss until his defence collapses. As the element of surprise is now absent [owing to the length of the artillery preparation] it is probable that your progress will not be rapid ... [80]

Such progress as there was was anything but rapid. Poor

visibility and defective ammunition hampered the preliminary bombardment, and the infantry battle began on the night of 15–16 May and ceased, with the consolidation on the new British line, on the 27th. The results of the Battle of Festubert were, though, far more encouraging than those of Aubers Ridge. Although casualties totalled over 16,500 officers and men, some ground had been gained—a maximum of some 1,000 yards on a front of 3,000 yards—and all available German reserves had been rushed to the threatened sector. Just as Neuve Chapelle seemed to offer the tantalising prospect of success, so Festubert too raised hopes. Sir John regarded the battle as ample proof that, if only high explosive arrived in the requisite quantities, he could:

> break thro' this tremendous *crust* of defence which has been forming and consolidating throughout the winter: once we have done it I think we may get the Devils on the run. How I should love to have a real good 'go' at them in the open with lots of cavalry and horse artillery and run them to earth. Well! It may come.[81]

The fighting at Ypres and Festubert died away at the end of May, and although there were small actions between then and the autumn, the summer of 1915 was in the main a period of planning and preparation. GHQ and GQG continued to jockey for position, and the great bone of contention was, as usual, the matter of relative lengths of front. Joffre was not prepared to see British troops on the Channel coast, arguing that 'Dunkirk must be defended by Frenchmen', and Sir John agreed to extend his front to the south as reinforcements arrived.[82] During August the British took over a large sector south of the French Tenth Army, holding the ground with the newly-formed Third Army.

Haggle though they might over the details of British relief of French troops, Joffre and Sir John were, broadly speaking, agreed as to the outline of future operations. At Chantilly on 24 June they rejected a passive defence in the West, arguing that it was 'bad strategy, unfair to Russia, Serbia and Italy, and therefore wholly inadmissible'. They were equally united in their opposition to the Dardanelles project, and agreed to badger their respective governments in order to ensure that all available British troops were sent to France. 'Aggressive, though local, enterprises' were to be carried out, pending the completion of arrangements for a major offensive in August.[83]

The growing air of solidarity was enhanced by a series of meetings in July. There was a long Anglo-French conference at Calais on the 6th. Its conclusions represented a compromise between the views of Kitchener, who opposed 'a too vigorous offensive', and Joffre, who advocated 'the strongest possible offensive'. The war of attrition was to be continued and there were to be 'local offensives on a considerable scale'. Kitchener dictated a memorandum on the arrival in France of the New Army divisions, and French noted with approval that this was an eminently satisfactory result, though he was less pleased by the fact that Joffre and Kitchener had had a long private discussion before the meeting started.[84]

An inter-Allied conference, attended by French, British, Belgian, Russian, Serbian and Italian members, took place at Chantilly the next day. Joffre told the assembled representatives that a co-ordinated offensive, on all fronts, against the Central Powers offered the best prospects of success, but he admitted that it was rather too early to plan such an operation. French agreed that the general strategic situation demanded that the Allies should assume the offensive, and he pledged himself to support Joffre to the best of his ability. Sir John found Asquith and Kitchener at St Omer when he returned home that evening. He asked Asquith 'if he had any idea in his mind that I had in any sense misled him on the ammunition question'. Asquith assured him that all was well on this point, and went on to express his confidence in Sir John's judgement.[85]

Joffre's plans for offensive action in the West had not greatly changed since the spring of 1915. He proposed to strike at the shoulders of the great German salient whose apex was near Noyon, with the BEF and the French Tenth Army attacking into the Douai Plain, while other French formations thrust north and north-east from the area of Rheims. Cavalry supported by infantry in motor-buses were to exploit the breakthrough, with the line Mons-Namur, beyond the Belgian frontier, as their final objective.

Sir John was once again in two minds about the offensive. He had pledged himself to support Joffre, and agreed with the French Commander-in-Chief as to the necessity for offensive action. But he was less than happy about the form this action should take. His worries focused on two major issues. The old question of ammunition reared its ugly head, and Sir John, in a lengthy memorandum summing up GHQ's case, reiterated his opinion that a successful advance depended primarily upon the availability of artillery ammunition, and gave 17 rounds per gun per day as the minimum rate of supply if a joint offensive was to be undertaken. The Field-Marshal was, though, anxious to keep his options open, and added a *caveat* to the effect that some sort of attack might be possible even if this level was not attained.[86]

The question of the ground over which the attack was to be launched was closely related to that of ammunition. In mid-June, long before plans for the offensive gained full momentum, French agreed with Foch that the most useful area for a British attack was on First Army's extreme right, south of the Bethune Canal. A British offensive in this sector, carried out at the same time as a French attack on Vimy Ridge, would have the desirable effect of presenting the Germans with a very broad attack sector. Sir John ordered Haig to investigate the possibilities, and on 23 June Haig arrived at St Omer with his verdict. He considered the sector manifestly unsuitable. The German defences were exceptionally strong, and the slag-heaps and rows of miners' cottages which littered the area of Loos made the ground exceptionally difficult from the attacker's point of view, particularly as so little artillery ammunition was available. French was not convinced. He suspected that Haig was exaggerating the difficulties, and decided to see for himself.[87]

On 12 July Sir John peered down from Notre Dame de Lorette across the gloomy industrial squalor of the Lens–Loos area. He acknowledged that 'the actual terrain of the attack is no doubt difficult, as it is covered with all the features of a closely inhabited flourishing mining district — factories — slag heaps — shafts — long rows of houses — etc., etc.' Yet he considered that the sector did offer some possibilities, especially in view of the fact that the high ground in British hands offered excellent observation for the preliminary bombardment.[88] On mature reflection, however, Sir John decided that Haig was right. On 20 July he told Clive, liaison officer with French headquarters, to inform GQG that ammunition shortages would only permit him to launch strong 'holding' attacks, and five days later he announced that he had altogether given up the idea of attacking the Loos area. The combined pressure of Haig and Robertson undoubtedly helped bring about this decision. Robertson bluntly told Clive that 'we should not be helping the French by throwing away thousands of lives in knocking our heads against a brick wall'.[89]

This left Sir John in an unenviable position. He had promised to support Joffre, and it was Joffre himself who had drawn French's attention to the Loos–La Bassée area, suggesting that it offered 'particularly favourable ground' for an attack.[90] Not only did Sir John not consider the ground favourable, but he considered that 'to have any prospect of success such an attack would have to be supported by an almost unlimited expenditure of artillery ammunition, and our present receipts do not provide an adequate supply for this purpose'.[91] Moreover, he suspected that the French did not intend to launch 'any *decisive* attack' at Arras, and therefore British attacks should be directed against points which offered greater tactical advantages than did the slag-heaps of Loos.[92]

But despite all his well-founded misgivings, Sir John eventually decided that he must leave the final decision in Joffre's hands. On 28 July, the day after an unsatisfactory meeting with Foch, he wrote a personal letter to Joffre, having discarded the General Staff's draft, and sent it to GQG via Clive. He wrote in his diary:

> I have decided that in the end it is necessary to leave the direction of affairs in the hands of the Generalissimo … I have asked the C-in-C to give due weight and consideration to the points I have just put forward and then to tell me what he wishes me to do and I *will do it*.[93]

If Joffre felt that an attack on Loos was vital to the Allied cause, then Sir John was prepared to carry it out, but he made it abundantly clear that he disagreed with the project, and thought that there were more promising sectors.

Joffre was well pleased with the tone of French's letter. He tried to reassure Clive, telling him 'this is going to be an artillery, not an infantry, battle', but the mood of GHQ remained gloomy. Sir John, for his part, warned Clive that the attack would be 'very half hearted; for everybody who knows the ground is sure success is impossible'.[94]

Why did French consent to attack the Loos sector when all his military instincts, and the opinions of his most trusted advisers, were steadfastly opposed to it? He shared Joffre's view as to the necessity of an offensive in the West, and had reluctantly come to the conclusion that strategic responsibility for the Western Front must ultimately rest with GQG. There were reports that the French government was becoming increasingly disenchanted with the support it was receiving from Britain. 'They think', remarked Sir John, 'that we should organise much better against bad recruiting and *strikes*. They complain that we don't have conscription.' Unless Britain gave some positive sign of her continuing commitment, he feared that France might break away from the alliance and conclude a separate peace.[95]

Sir John was also concerned about his own position as Commander-in-Chief. He had already discovered that Joffre, for all his geniality, was quite prepared to complain to the British government, some of whose members needed little convincing that the BEF's ills could be laid at the Field-Marshal's door. A growing body of influential men, both within the army and outside it, favoured a change of command in France. Robertson set about undercutting French's position early in the summer: on 1 June he told Hankey that Sir John was 'always wanting to do reckless and impossible things', and he made similar remarks to Kitchener a month later.[96] Kitchener had already informed Asquith of his misgivings regarding French, and on 26 June the Prime Minister had a lengthy discussion as to the desirability of French being superseded by Haig: similar discussions were not unknown at First Army headquarters. Haig himself knew that Kitchener found Sir John difficult to manage, and on 14 July he discovered that the King too had 'lost confidence in Field-Marshal French'.[97]

The King's loss of confidence was scarcely surprising. News from France flooded into Buckingham Palace in an unceasing flow as an astonishingly large number of officers wrote to the King's private secretaries on one pretext or another. Haig, Robertson and Smith-Dorrien were in regular contact with the Palace, and some corps commanders – and even the occasional divisional commander – did not hesitate to add their loyal pennyworth when the mood took them. The King had never been one of Sir John's warmest admirers, and on 1 July, after a long talk with Robertson, he noted that 'it would be better for all concerned if the C-in-C were changed'.[98]

French's cronies gave him some idea of the stories which flew round London, although they probably saw no more than the tip of the iceberg. Even Henry Wilson, who had no love for Haig, thought him too good a fellow to go behind French's back. He would no doubt have been surprised to discover that Haig was corresponding secretly with Kitchener, who, in Haig's words, 'would treat my letters as secret, and would not reply, but I would see my proposals given effect to and must profess ignorance when that happened'.[99] Whatever the merits of the case, this was no way for the government to go about its business. Sir John, already possessed of an obsessive dislike of Kitchener, became increasingly neurotic as new rumours of dismissal arrived at St Omer. It was not a state of mind which made for clear, rational decisions.

Sir John was not alone in changing his mind, albeit reluctantly, as to the wisdom of Joffre's plans. At the Calais conference of 6 July Kitchener had spoken against the projected offensive, but in mid-August events persuaded him that an attack was indeed necessary. On 16 August he travelled to France for lengthy discussions with Joffre and Millerand. It was evident to all that the Germans were making good progress in the East. Warsaw had fallen on the 4th, and the French leaders feared that the Russians might sue for peace unless the Western Allies took resolute action. Wilson believed that the French government would fall unless the offensive was launched, and thought it possible that France herself might seek peace. Kitchener had little confidence in Joffre's projects, but he was now convinced that a large-scale joint offensive in the West was essential in view of the situation in

Russia and the depressing news from the Dardanelles. He accordingly ordered Sir John to do his utmost to assist the French, 'even though, by doing so, we suffered very heavy losses indeed'. [100]

GHQ responded to Kitchener's order with surprising cheerfulness. Clive visited St Omer on 25 August, and found French and his staff 'quite happy about the point of attack; now that it is settled, they are getting quite optimistic'. [101] During the next month the staffs at GHQ and First Army went through a curious process of self-deception. They had been united in their opposition to an attack in the Loos area, largely because of the unfavourable nature of the ground. Once the attack had been decided upon, and the decision imposed on GHQ by Joffre and Kitchener, French and his subordinates began to persuade themselves that the assault would succeed. This was, no doubt, partly due to a natural enough desire to avoid the conclusion that they were sending large numbers of men to certain death. But there were other reasons: Loos was psychologically acceptable to French and Haig only if they could convince themselves that their appreciations of June and July had somehow been overtaken by changed circumstances.

Gas helped. Sir John had been horrified by the German use of gas at Second Ypres, saying that it was 'a very dirty "low down" game to play shooting out that damnable "gas" ... '[102] He immediately demanded a retaliatory capability, and railed angrily that: 'All the chemists and scientists have been wrangling and talking and contradicting one another and *nothing* seems to be settled.'[103] By July both French and Haig were thinking in terms of using gas in an attack on Aubers Ridge, and by early September there was widespread confidence that gas, if 'lavishly used', would be 'effective up to two miles, and it is practically certain that it will be quite effective in many places if not along the whole line attacked'. [104]

Agree though they might about gas, French and Haig disagreed profoundly concerning another aspect of the coming battle. The initial assault was to be carried out by the six divisions of I and IV Corps of First Army, while the army's other two corps made subsidiary attacks. Sir John decided to keep a strong force under his hand to exploit a breakthrough, or to meet any emergency which arose on another part of the front. This general reserve comprised the Cavalry Corps, the Indian Cavalry Corps, and Lieutenant-General R. C. B. Haking's newly-formed XI Corps. Two of Haking's divisions, 21st and 24th, were inexperienced New Army formations, which had only just arrived in France: Haking's corps headquarters was also new, and included a number of officers who had previously neither worked together nor served on a corps staff. [105]

French believed that XI Corps would be the ideal instrument for his purpose. Its troops were enthusiastic, and had not acquired the sedentary habits of trench warfare. Archie Murray, now Deputy CIGS, had told French of their virtues at some length, and suggested that their single best characteristic was the ability to carry out long marches in the post-breakthrough phase. [106] They were likely to prove less suitable for taking over a section of the front. Murray admitted that the shooting of their artillery was 'an unknown quantity', and Robertson had already suggested that they should not go straight into the line, but should relieve units exhausted by the offensive, thus minimising their need for integral artillery support. [107]

Using XI Corps as part of the general reserve was, then, not as eccentric as French's detractors subsequently suggested. It was in the positioning of the reserve that French's judgement can more reasonably be challenged. Sir John thought that the second day of the attack would be crucial, and it was at this stage that he would inject XI Corps into the battle. The reserve would, therefore, be positioned well behind First Army's front on the day of the assault. Haig disagreed profoundly. On 19 September he pointed out that all First Army's available troops were being employed in the attack, and: 'The whole plan of operations of the First Army is based on the assumption that the troops of the General Reserve will be close at hand ... '[108] GHQ agreed to position the reserve closer to the front than it had originally intended, but French still clung to the view that the reserve would be used on the second day of the operation, leading Haig to comment crossly that: 'It seems impossible to discuss military problems with an unreasoning brain of this kind.'[109]

The question of the deployment of the general reserve was to become the central issue of the Battle of Loos, and it was this that shattered French's friendship with Haig and proved the last straw as far as Sir John's position in France was concerned. French was undoubtedly wrong in leaving XI Corps over five miles from First Army's start-line: Foch and Haig believed that 2,000 metres would have been more appropriate. This deployment was, in part, the result of French's fundamental misunderstanding of the nature of the fighting: he underestimated the difficulties of getting fresh troops through the wilderness of trenches and shell-holes behind an attacking army.

Yet the deployment was not dictated solely by French's misconceptions. For although Haig had now persuaded himself that the attack would succeed at relatively little cost if the wind favoured the use of gas, French's earlier doubts still flickered alarmingly. He spoke of using reserves 'in case we are fortunate enough' to break the German line, a comment which lacked the ring of certainty. He was more specific in a letter to Winifred Bennett:

> I have little fear of defeat or disaster, but it might be little better or no better than previous attempts. Whatever may happen I shall have to bear the brunt of it and in cricket language they may 'change the bowler' ... We shall of course have some terrific losses but – alas! – we are getting accustomed to that now. War is really a very brutal way of settling differences and the more I see of it the more I hate it ... [110]

The commander of XI Corps had the reputation of being a fighting general: in the words of one authority, 'loyalty to and consideration for his troops did not appear to have been characteristics of Haking ... '[111] If his Corps was put at Haig's disposal from the start, and was positioned close behind the assaulting formations, French had little doubt what would happen: it would be thrown into the battle at the earliest possible moment. And this was exactly what Sir John, who feared that Haig's men might not make much progress, wanted to avoid.

Sir John left St Omer on 24 September, the eve of the battle, and drove up to a forward command post near Lilliers, less than 20 miles behind First Army's front. His ability to influence the battle from this point was decidedly limited. He was connected to Robertson's room at GHQ by telephone, but there was no direct phone link with First Army headquarters at Hinges. Moreover, Sir John took with him only a couple of his personal staff, leaving all the bustling apparatus of GHQ far behind him. He did not regard this as a disadvantage: he had approved Haig's plans, and now intended to let him get on with fighting the battle.

As dawn came up on the 26th Haig and his staff watched the wind anxiously, and at 5.15 Haig gave the order to launch the gas as planned. Thirty-five minutes later, as a heavy bombardment pounded the German front trenches, a yellowish-white cloud rolled slowly out across no-man's-land. The infantry went forward at 6.30, heavily laden with grenades, picks, shovels and extra rations, their advance made more than usually nightmarish by their primitive gas masks. Despite the fact that the artillery preparation had failed to destroy many German strong-points, and had left masses of wire uncut, several of the attacking divisions made good progress, but suffered heavy casualties in the process.

The bitter, close-quarter fighting in the smoke and gas around Loos and Hulluch consumed First Army's troops at an alarming rate. At about 7 a.m., after receiving news of the satisfactory advance of the leading waves, Haig sent an officer by car to Lilliers to report on the initial success and to urge that XI Corps should be ready to move at once. About an hour and a half later he informed GHQ that all his reserves were committed, and asked that XI Corps should be put at his disposal immediately. It was not until 10.02 that he heard that the two divisions were to move forward 'when the situation requires and admits', coming under his orders when they reached the old front line. The remaining formation in XI Corps, the Guards Division, was to stay in reserve.

Sir John visited Haig between 11.00 and 11.30, and, having satisfied himself that Haig was indeed in earnest, at last agreed to put the divisions at his disposal. But instead of doing so by telephone, he drove off to Haking's headquarters at Noeux-les-Mines and issued his orders personally at about 12.30. At 1.20 Haig received from Haking the welcome news that XI Corps, less the Guards Division, was under his command, and was moving forward in accordance with the anticipatory orders issued by First Army during the morning. Haking added, however, that there were serious delays on the road.[112]

The 21st and 24th Divisions had had a trying time on their approach march, and the latter stages of their journey, on the afternoon of the 25th and the night of the 25th–26th, were exceptionally harrowing. The rain came down in torrents, and the advancing troops picked their way with difficulty through the debris of the battlefield to the positions from which they were to assault the German second position south of Hulluch.

French was once again about to get the worst of both worlds. He had successfully resisted demands that XI Corps should be put at Haig's disposal before the battle, and had only released it when the available information seemed to indicate that a clean break had been made in the German line. He therefore hoped that the corps would not only exploit the breakthrough, but would do so without suffering too heavily in the process. But Sir John's desire to save XI Corps excessive casualties was to bring about the very situation he feared. If the corps was to have had any chance of success – and this remains a highly debatable point – it should have been on hand, behind the assaulting divisions, by mid-morning on the 25th. Committing it to Haig's command in the afternoon, with several miles of crowded and dangerous earth separating it from the most fragile points of the German line, was to ensure that it would be launched against a strengthened German position the following morning, without the artillery support which alone could have given it even the slimmest prospect of victory.

Sir Henry Rawlinson gave Lord Stamfordham a graphic account of the fate of Haking's two divisions. He wrote:

> From what I can ascertain, some of the divisions did actually reach the enemy's trenches, for their bodies can now be seen on the barbed wire. Hostile artillery and MG fire were, however, turned on to them from the flanks as they advanced, the effect of which upon troops in action for the first time turned out to be disastrous. The whole of the two divisions, spread out as they were over open plain and sub-

jected to considerable punishment from the enemy's
artillery, turned and retired in one huge mass to our
original line ... [113]

The twelve attacking battalions, just under 10,000 strong
when they moved down the slope into Loos valley, lost over
8,000 officers and men in under four hours. It was a rough way
to learn the trade of soldiering.

On the 26th Joffre sent a warm letter of thanks and encouragement to Sir John in an effort to ensure that he kept up
the attacks. Clive sensed that Joffre had no real confidence in
the British operation, and regarded it as simply a useful diver-
sion. 'He does not think we shall get through in Artois', wrote
Clive, 'but wishes the Germans kept in fear that we may get
through, until he has done the trick in Champagne.'[114] Sir John
was not easily mollified, and complained that the French
Tenth Army was making 'very slow and decidedly disappoint-
ing' progress. He threatened to pull back to his original line
unless the French took some of the weight off the British right,
and on 29 September Foch agreed to take over part of the
British front around Loos itself.[115]

It was Sir John's last major battle, and he fought it in his old
style, riding around behind the lines, watching the 24th Division filing through Bethune and noting that 'they seemed a fine
workmanlike looking lot'.[116] One officer saw him 'riding quite
alone through the sheltered villages behind the line and thanking all he met ... wearing his familiar khaki stock around his
neck and his soft gor' blimey general's hat'.[117] He spent two
hours of the morning of the 26th going round the casualty
collecting stations: 'Dead, dying and badly wounded all mixed
up together. Poor dear fellows they bear their pain gloriously
and many of them gave me a smile of recognition.'[118] On the
27th he wrote sadly that:

> Poor General Capper died of his wounds this morn-
> ing and another Divisional General (Thesiger) was
> killed this afternoon ... My *Darling Darling*, we've
> had such terrible losses which make me very de-
> pressed and sad – over 900 officers and 35,000 men
> up to this morning.

A few days later he told Mrs Bennett of 'another great loss ...
General Wing, a very great friend of mine ... was killed by a
shell.'[119]

He oscillated between hope and despair. On the 28th he saw
Foch, and:

> I told him that if I was in the position of C-in-C of the
> whole Western Allied Front I should put every
> available man in just N of Hill 70 and 'rush' a gap in
> the enemy's line. I should feel quite confident of
> success.

Foch tactfully dodged the issue, saying that it would be difficult to co-ordinate such an attack.[120] During the first days of
October, Sir John tried hard to string together a 'shoulder to
shoulder' offensive with the French, but Haig reported, to his
'surprise and regret', that First Army could do little for the time
being.[121] The strain and the disappointment told heavily upon
French, who had been ill, probably with flu, for several days
before the attack. 'Sir John French is played out', wrote Major
Charteris of Haig's staff. 'The show is too big for him and he is
despondent.'[122] Even Brinsley Fitzgerald, himself depressed by
the results of the battle, found Sir John unusually snappish, in
one of his 'weird and marvellous' moods.[123]

After the battle came the recriminations. On 9 October
Haldane warned Sir John that 'responsible members of the
Cabinet' were complaining about his handling of the reserves,
and two days later Kitchener wrote, pressing him for an
explanation.[124] Although Sir John believed that the accusations
were all 'false and stupid', the clamour against him grew. Haig
told Haldane that Sir John's handling of the reserves had led to
the loss of the battle, adding it would be difficult to win the war
if existing conditions continued.[125]

On 9 November French's policies were sharply assailed in
the House of Lords, leading the harassed Field-Marshal to
observe that: 'The only thing that surprises me is that the
British Empire finds any men to fight for her ... '[126] In another
debate later the same month Lord St Davids launched a violent
attack on GHQ, accusing it of idleness and incompetence. He
also spoke of late-night bridge parties, and complained of 'the
presence of ladies at the Great Headquarters'.[127] Charteris

noted that First Army headquarters was amused by St Davids's effort, and GHQ had become very touchy on the subject: 'Of course', he admitted, 'it is all utter nonsense.'[128] St Davids's accusations raised Sir John to new heights of fury, and he wrote angrily that:

> it does seem rather hard that an institution like the House of Lords can allow people to tell such bare-face lies within its precincts about soldiers serving in the field. Well, I only wish they *would* send someone to take my place for I'm tired to death of this kind of life. The *Germans* are *nothing* compared to our people. [129]

The real damage was done not by well-publicised attacks in Parliament but by astute hatchet-work behind the scenes. Robertson went to London, ostensibly to assist the General Staff, in early October, and while there he discussed the question of French's replacement with the King and with Archie Murray, who was now CIGS. On his return he told Haig of the results of his interviews, and Haig recorded in his diary that:

> I had been more than loyal to French and did my best to stop all criticism of him or his methods. Now, at last, in view of what had happened in the recent battle over the reserves, I had come to the conclusion that it was not fair to the Empire to retain French in command. Moreover, none of my officers commanding corps had a high opinion of Sir John's military ability or military views; in fact, they *had no confidence in him*. Robertson quite agreed, and left me saying 'he knew how to act, and would report to Stamfordham'. [130]

On 21 October the King arrived in France to sample opinion for himself. Sir John was not best pleased, having earlier grumbled that 'the King wants to come out here again. I'm very sorry to hear it … It's an awful nuisance and a great responsibility having him.'[131] Sir John met him at Boulogne, but was summoned to England, for meetings with Kitchener and the Dardanelles Committee, two days later. By the time he returned to France the damage had been done.

Gough and Haking visited the King in his quarters at Aire after tea on the 24th, and agreed that 'everyone has lost confidence in the C-in-C'. At dinner that evening Haig 'entirely corroborated what the other two had said, but went much further and said that the C-in-C was a source of great weakness to the army, and no one had any confidence in him any more'. Haig added, perhaps a shade superfluously, that he was personally ready to do his duty in any capacity.[132]

The King's stay in France was marred by an accident on the 29th, when he was badly shaken by a fall from his horse while inspecting a detachment of the RFC. French was worried about 'these damned Germans making attempts to "bomb" him with aircraft'; he sent an extra section of anti-aircraft guns to Aire, and ensured that the château was watched by RFC patrols. Sir John may, however, have gauged royal opinion accurately when he heard that the King, when told that French was anxious for him to leave the country as soon as possible, had replied: 'Tell Sir John to go to hell.'[133]

The political waters grew progressively murkier in November. Brinsley Fitzgerald scuttled to and fro, whipping up support and keeping Sir John informed of the state of the odds. Lord Edmund Talbot, an old friend from the Boer War, told Fitzgerald that Asquith's attitude was uncertain, although he was likely to back French: Bonar Law would, however, be 'on the wrong side' if it came to a vote in the Cabinet.[134] Wilson announced confidently that Sir John's strongest card was his 'cordial relations with, and appreciation for, the French', and joined Fitzgerald in putting pressure on Carson in an effort to counteract the influence of Bonar Law.[135] Lord Selborne felt that there was change in the air, and considered that Sir John's position was 'certainly serious', but Walter Long, a junior minister and an old friend of French's, told Fitzgerald that he had not heard of any change of command being discussed by the War Council. It was certainly discussed in a variety of other places: Charles Callwell heard Asquith, Lloyd George and Grey debating French's replacement in the restaurant car of a train, much to the interest of the waiters.[136]

Sir John was laid up with a severe cough towards the middle of the month, and spent several days in long discussions with Esher and Fitzgerald as to his best course of action. Kitchener had departed for the Mediterranean on a fact-finding mission, leaving Asquith as caretaker at the War Office. French thought that 'there may be a row between me and the government', but believed that, with Kitchener off the scene, his 'good friends in the Cabinet' would defend him. The prospect of dismissal did not disturb him unduly. He wrote:

> Such a fate has befallen much better and greater men than I am and I am only thankful to be able to know in my heart that the army I have commanded has really saved the country from dire disaster. One never does look for much gratitude in this world.[137]

Meanwhile, the bickering between GHQ and First Army assumed the proportions of an epidemic. GHQ suggested that XI Corps had, according to Haking's own report, been subjected to 'avoidable delay' in its approach march, and complained of 'the futility of pushing reserves through a narrow gap'.[138] Haig denied that there had been any avoidable delay. Haking conveniently changed his mind, and in a second report attributed the slowness of his divisions' march to their inexperience and lack of march discipline.[139] The dispute gained fresh momentum with the publication, on 2 November of Sir John's dispatch on the battle, in which he stated, *inter alia*, that the reserves had been released to First Army at 9.30. Haig was sure that French was trying to shift the blame, and considered that the dispatch was 'full of lies'.[140] His demand that it should be amended initiated another round of backbiting, which ended only after a highly unsatisfactory interview between French and Haig.

French was completely outmanoeuvred. The dispute revolved around the pre-battle deployment of Haking's divisions and the hour at which they were released. The equally pertinent question of why Haig launched them into a battle when he believed that it was already too late was never asked; nor did GHQ systematically examine Haig's assertion that a fresh division, arriving on the battlefield between 9.00 and 11.00, could have pushed through 'with little opposition'.[141] The battle was soon being cited as evidence to support the concentration of reserves close behind the attacking troops, but First Army was never entirely convinced by its own propaganda:

Charteris, for example, doubted whether the two divisions would have been much use even if they had been closer to the start line.[142]

Haig lost no opportunity to press his point. He sent copies of the relevant orders, together with a well-argued attack on GHQ's policy for the battle, to his wife: she gave the documents to Stamfordham, who sent them back after the King had seen them.[143] GHQ's own statement of its case, with a formal General Staff critique of Haig's handling of the action, wafted off to the DMO at the War Office on 1 December. By this time it was too late, for the crucial decision had already been taken. French was less than well served by his General Staff during November: this is not surprising in view of the fact that Robertson had long since decided that his primary objective was, as he told Haig on 15 November, 'to get you in command'.[144]

Asquith had made his mind up by 23 November. He discussed the matter with the King and Kitchener, both of whom agreed that Sir John was no longer up to his task, although the latter — surprisingly, in view of what French thought of him — felt that it was not the right time for a change.[145] Asquith summoned Esher, and asked him to take a message to French. He believed that the Field-Marshal's health was not up to the strain of continued command, and added that 'recent events', by which he meant, in part at least, Loos and its aftermath, made the Field-Marshal's replacement essential. Esher reminded the Prime Minister that Sir John was not financially well off and that he might have expected a substantial cash grant if he had remained in command until the end of the war. Asquith agreed to bear this point in mind, and emphasised that he was anxious to make things as easy as possible for French, offering him a peerage and command of the Home Forces. Esher, who knew his man well, set off for the continent fearing a Frenchian outburst, and praying for 'the illumination of his spirit when the blow falls'.[146]

French initially took the news remarkably well, exhibiting what Esher called 'perfect simplicity of character', and quipping that he might take the title 'Lord Sent-Homer'. His mood changed with the arrival of Fitzgerald, but Esher believed that although French insisted upon seeing the Prime Minister, he would relinquish his command with the minimum of fuss. Asquith had made it clear to Esher that Sir John had no choice in the matter: it was a decision rather than a suggestion, and was passed on as such to the Field-Marshal.[147]

Esher's confidence that French would do exactly as the Prime Minister wished proved sadly misplaced. Sir John had an interview with Asquith on the 29th, and Fitzgerald, who – significantly enough – had accompanied French to England, recorded that it had gone well. French understood Asquith to have said:

> I wish you clearly to understand that unless you yourself take the first step, I will take no action. Your case is quite different from some of the others. They were recalled and given no option. You are in no sense recalled.[148]

Asquith's attempt at handling the matter delicately miscarried badly. French seized his opportunity and, shortly before returning to France, thanked the Prime Minister for his kindness, and acknowledged that there was much to be said for his suggestions. He feared, however, that there would be friction between a Commander-in-Chief of Home Forces and the Secretary of State for War unless a civilian Secretary of State was appointed. He was sure that Kitchener would take the point, and he awaited the Prime Minister's decision on the matter.[149]

Sir John returned to France on the 3rd, feeling that he had at least bought time, and had probably struck a fatal blow at the already insecure Kitchener, implying that the latter's removal was a precondition for his own acceptance of the Home Forces command. But Asquith, though briefly outmanoeuvred, still held all the cards. Wully Robertson thought that French's arrival in London had sparked off various intrigues, as a result of which 'Mr Asquith wavered'.[150] Asquith was well aware that he could not go on wavering: the pressure for French's removal remained as great as ever, and Haig had already been tentatively informed that he would take over from Sir John. Stamfordham assured Asquith that the King thought that French had been shown 'every consideration', and agreed that the issue should now be pressed.[151] The Prime Minister replied that, as Sir John had quite failed to take the hint, he would send him a 'plain spoken reply'.[152]

This time the task of administering the blow was entrusted to Walter Long. On 4 December he told French over the phone that he had just seen the Prime Minister, and there was no alternative to immediate resignation. He declined to say exactly why this was, but 'said this action in his opinion was imperative, and we must trust his judgement. After long deliberation between the general, Esher and self [Fitzgerald] the letter was written.'[153]

French's formal letter of resignation reached Downing Street on the morning of 6 December. In it the Field-Marshal recommended Robertson as his successor, and thanked Asquith for his 'kindness and consideration'.[154] The news became public property with announcements in the press on 17 December, and the change of command took effect from noon on the 18th. Despite French's suggestion that Robertson should take over, it was clear, as Wully himself acknowledged, that Haig was the only serious candidate. Robertson had, in any case, been earmarked for the post of CIGS, in an effort to revive the moribund General Staff at the War Office.

Sir John dragged himself painfully away from France. He spent mid-December making his farewells, visiting Paris, Chantilly and the corps commanders. He had by now realised what had been going on behind the scenes, and when he met Haig on the 18th the conversation was painfully formal. French was eager that Churchill, who had left office following the Dardanelles fiasco and was now serving at the front, should be given command of a battalion, and Haig promised to consider this. Brinsley Fitzgerald noted that Haig 'never for one moment unbent', and another officer had already observed that Sir John was 'very bitter against Haig'.[155] The friendship forged in the trim world of Aldershot and amidst the dust and sunshine of the veldt was gone for ever, and its place was taken by a deep and lasting mutual contempt.

French spent his last evening in the country as he had his first, dining alone at the Ritz with Brinsley Fitzgerald. The conversation was anything but sparkling, and both men were engulfed in a rising tide of emotion. Some of the farewells had already been highly charged: Foch had cried, and Joffre had lamented: 'If they do things like that, how can we hope to win the war?'[156] The road outside Lilliers had been lined for miles by cheering troops who had come to see the Field-Marshal off: Fitzgerald thought it a wonderful sight, but, looking back at events since August 1914, admitted sadly that it was all like a strange dream. The 19th Hussars had the last word. They were drawn up at Boulogne when Sir John walked up the gang-plank and cheered themselves hoarse. French was profoundly moved, but remained master of himself: Fitzgerald wept silently.[157]

Ten

Home Service
January 1916–April 1918

Sir John's elevation to the peerage – he took his seat in the Lords as Viscount French of Ypres on 29 February – did little to make the process of readjustment to his new life any less difficult or painful. He spent much of January visiting hospitals around London, and wrote that it was:

> horribly sad and very pathetic to see how good and cheery and patient the dear fellows are. I love going round and talking to them ... What a lot of these poor fellows have lost a limb or are injured for life ... I hate it all so! I'm getting that horrid feeling I had after the SA war. Such horrible sadness and depression sometimes. I do so want to hear the guns again! I wonder if I was a fool not to arrange so as to stay out on French soil for ever! It would have been so easy.[1]

His mood was not improved by the 'political intrigues, lies and squabbles', which made for a 'damnable atmosphere', in London.[2]

It was clear from the outset that his newly-created post of Commander-in-Chief Home Forces was to be no sinecure. *The Times* had observed that French was 'not exchanging heavy responsibilities for a life of leisured ease', and there was widespread agreement amongst civil and military authorities that such an appointment was long overdue.[3] Robertson, who was busy establishing the parameters of his own job as CIGS, had already stated that it was essential for a single central authority to control the seven regional commands within the United Kingdom, so that the CIGS could deal with one man rather than a committee. He added, as a cautionary note, that French should not be 'C-in-C on the old lines', and must not have a seat on the War Council.[4]

French's new responsibilities were wide, and included defence against invasion — soon widened to include defence against air attack — military training, and military aid to the civil power throughout Great Britain and Ireland. The new command absorbed the War Office directorates of Home Defence and Military Training, whose officers moved across to French's headquarters in Horse Guards in January. The headquarters initially contained no Adjutant-General's or Quartermaster-General's branches, but French soon prevailed upon Robertson, who agreed that things were in 'a rare muddle', to disgorge more staff officers.[5]

Home defence had only been set up three months before, and plans were, French grumbled, 'In a state of absolute chaos ... I really think that if we were to be attacked tonight no-one would know what to do.'[6] He was not convinced that there was a significant threat of German invasion which, he told Repington, was just as well in view of the 'motley crew' at his disposal and the lack of co-ordinated plans.[7] Others were rather more worried. In January an inter-service committee agreed that a raid by up to 170,000 was possible, and Lord Selborne suggested that the longer the war went on the more likely the Germans were to 'try a great coup on London'.[8]

The official estimate of the size of a possible raid changed with the ebb and flow of inter-service politics and the fluctuations of Britain's military and naval fortunes. French's own opinion remained constant: the Germans were, he believed, unlikely to attempt an invasion or a large-scale raid unless they had already beaten the British army on the Western Front. In February 1916 the Admiralty announced its inability to interfere in a hostile disembarkation for a considerable time. French commented that:

> Rightly or wrongly I don't attach a great deal of importance to this. The Navy have had periodical 'scares' throughout the war. Personally I hold the

same views as I have always held on the subject. If I believed invasion at the present juncture of affairs anything but a very remote possibility I should feel far from happy because we are certainly not adequately prepared to meet a landing on our shores.[9]

Small though he believed the possibility of invasion was, French lost no time in disentangling the ravelled threads of home defence. He disagreed with the existing concept of a central force, which would march to oppose the invader once he had landed, and took steps to strengthen coastal defences in order to bring the invader to battle on the beach.[10] In March 1918, when German successes on the Western Front led to more gloomy speculation about the possibility of invasion, French told the Secretary of State of his plans:

> My scheme of defence for the United Kingdom is based on the principle of fighting the enemy on the coast and preventing his landing, or should he succeed in doing so, of holding him as near to the coast as possible and delaying this advance until the various mobile formations at my disposal could be brought up as reinforcements.[11]

Alongside a thorough revision of the defence plans went command reshuffles and a far-reaching series of inspections of coastal defences. French was initially refused the services of Arthur Paget and Bruce Hamilton, whom he had selected for the two major home defence commands. He immediately complained to Asquith, with the gratifying result that the War Office approved the appointments within the week.[12] In his inspections of coastal fortifications French revealed that he had lost none of his old energy: he stumped about the place muttering about poorly-concealed machine-guns here and an exposed battery there. He was, however, seriously handicapped by a shortage of good-quality troops and a lack of weapons. In May 1916 he saw a large number of 'unarmed and unfit' men in East Anglia and on the south coast, and in March 1917 he informed the War Office that his force would soon be rendered 'absolutely immobile' if any more horses went to the front.[13] Home forces reached rock bottom in the spring of 1918:

in March French heard that even soldiers with the medical grade of BI were to be sent to France, bringing his forces 'down to vanishing point'.[14]

Although French habitually complained when new drafts for the front sapped the strength of his command still further, he did so with mixed feelings. His protests were inspired, at least in part, by the frustrating feeling that he was commanding what was in effect a gigantic transit camp. As soon as troops were fit and trained, they were snatched from his grasp and sent off to fuel Haig's offensives, operations in which French had markedly little confidence. Yet he usually tempered his objections with admissions that the level of risk remained acceptable, and in public he maintained that 'not one man who can serve in the trenches should be left at home'.[15] Even in March 1918, when his forces were at their weakest and he felt obliged to warn the War Cabinet that such reductions were '*their* risk, not ours', French still admitted privately that he considered invasion unlikely as long as the Western Front held firm.[16]

The threat posed by aerial bombardment was, French believed, infinitely more serious than that of invasion. While commanding in France he had vigorously advocated the use of the RFC in interdiction missions against targets in the German rear, and had pressed for the development of gas bombs. By early 1916 his interest in air power was well-developed, and it owed much to his long-standing relationship with Lieutenant-General Sir David Henderson, Director-General of Military Aeronautics.[17]

Although the first German bomb had fallen on English soil on Christmas Eve 1914, and the raids of 1915 had killed and wounded 922 people – almost half as many as were to be killed by air attacks during the whole war – responsibility for air defence continued to be untidily divided between the Admiralty and the War Office. French assumed responsibility for the defence of London on 16 February 1916 and for the rest of the United Kingdom a few days later. Repington foresaw that it was 'a *damnosa hereditas*' which would bring French nothing but obloquy. The Field-Marshal agreed, but was convinced that centralised control was the only answer, and was not prepared to shirk the duty.[18]

Repington's assessment proved uncomfortably accurate. French was faced with the twin tasks of defending the United Kingdom against attack by aircraft and Zeppelins, and of passing timely and accurate warning to the population. Despite steady improvements in tactics and organisation, his job was anything but easy, and the consequences of failure were immediate and well-publicised. Shortly before he officially took responsibility for air defence, a vocal deputation from Birmingham arrived to complain about the lack of adequate air-raid warning. The visit gave him a cheerless foretaste of what was to come: over the next two years a procession of mayors, mine-owners and munitions workers trooped into his office at Horse Guards to bewail the failings of the air defence staff.[19]

As far as air defence was concerned, French was in very much the same position as a Commander-in-Chief in any other theatre of operations: his staff made plans, and requested resources of men and equipment from the War Office. The difficulty was, of course, that the resources demanded by French were also eagerly sought by other commanders. The system of anti-aircraft guns operating in increasingly sophisticated zones and barrage lines was impeded by a shortage of weapons. In January 1917 the War Cabinet decided that the submarine menace was so serious that the 186 3-inch and eleven 2·95-inch guns still required to make up the United Kingdom's anti-aircraft establishment should be re-allocated to the navy for use as anti-submarine guns.[20]

The conflict of priorities over aircraft was even sharper than that over guns. A Home Defence Wing was formed in June 1916 with six squadrons under its command. There were twelve squadrons in the country by the end of the year, but most of them were equipped with elderly BE aircraft, which were no match for the Zeppelins. Moreover, the demands of the Western Front imposed a constant drain on trained pilots: in the spring of 1917 the commander of the Home Defence Wing protested that the formation of new squadrons for service in France would leave him with only 107 pilots out of an establishment of 198.[21] French forwarded this complaint to the War Office with his own covering letter, in which he stated that:

I cannot too strongly impress on the Army Council my opinion that the means placed at my disposal for aeroplane defence are now inadequate and that a continuation of the present policy may have disastrous results.[22]

After a heavy daylight raid by Gotha bombers on 13 June, the Cabinet ordered Haig to detach two of his squadrons for home defence, but agreed that he could have them back in two weeks' time. French prophesied that their departure would leave him with 'wholly inadequate forces with which to meet an attack on London', and wrote a forceful letter to Robertson to place his 'most emphatic opinion on record'.[23]

French's worst fears were realised. On 7 July a force of Gothas attacked London and Margate, killing 57 people and wounding 193. There was a great public outcry, and the War Cabinet met in emergency session that afternoon. Robertson reported to Haig:

I could not get a word in edgeways. French was there and gave a long story as to his insufficient forces and made a great protest because the two squadrons you had lent him were taken away ... There is no doubt that French has not got a very good force. It is mainly made up of oddments, and of course oddments will not do.[24]

French was summoned to another meeting two days later, and noted that there was:

a disposition on the part of the War Office to say that I had not given them sufficient warning of the danger incurred by taking away the 2 squadrons on the 5th and 6th. Fortunately I was able to refute this completely by showing a copy of a letter I sent to the WO on the 2nd.[25]

It transpired that neither Robertson nor the Secretary of State had seen the letter: because it contained a minor point for the attention of the Director-General of Military Aeronautics it had been sent straight to his department. The War Cabinet can nevertheless have been in no doubt as to French's fears: his warnings on the parlous state of air defence were repeated with almost monotonous frequency.[26]

Two days later a sub-committee of the War Cabinet was set up to consider defence against air raids and air organisation in general. The Prime Minister was chairman, but the work was effectively entrusted to French's old Boer War adversary, Lieutenant-General J. C. Smuts. Smuts and French met on the 19th, and the Field-Marshal declared that:

> the time had now arrived when the air should be regarded as a separate service like the Navy and there should be a 'Minister of Air.' Failing such a possibility I didn't think much more could be done than at present and any rearrangements of command would not improve the defence. Sufficient superiority *in the air* can alone do this.[27]

The committee's first report recommended that 'a senior officer of first-rate ability and practical air experience' should be appointed to command the air defences of London under French's general authority; 'special endeavours' should be made to procure adequate guns, and no more fighter squadrons should be sent to France until the defence of London was 'reasonably secure'.[28] French was well pleased with the recommendations, and worked closely with Brigadier-General E. B. Ashmore, who was appointed to command the London Air Defence Area on 5 August.

Ashmore's appointment did not solve the air defence problem overnight. The moonlight raids of September 1917, coupled with the growing difficulties caused by barrel-wear in the anti-aircraft guns, caused French considerable anxiety. Nevertheless, it was no longer an uphill struggle. Equipment and techniques improved: the first night fighters flew on 3 September, and two days later Ashmore launched his scheme for defending London with 'aprons' of barrage balloons.

French also had the satisfaction of seeing his advice to Smuts bear fruit. He remained one of the few senior officers who favoured the creation of an independent air service, and the Air Council, with its own Secretary of State, was at last formed in January 1918. The Field-Marshal remained responsible for home defence, but there was now a single authority to direct air affairs and put forward its collective judgement.[29] The air battle was all but won when French left Horse Guards in the spring of 1918. Ashmore recorded his sorrow at French's departure:

> His sympathies made the work easier. When we failed, he was always anxious to take the responsibility; when we had a success, he wanted us to have all the credit. It was a pity he couldn't stay another fortnight to see our final victory.[30]

One of the most pressing problems to confront French during his time as Commander-in-Chief Home Forces came from a familiar quarter. The Irish Home Rule Act had gone on to the statute book in October 1914, but it had been accompanied by an act suspending its operation until after the war, and assurances were given that the Act would be amended in respect of Ulster. The frozen enactment of Home Rule damaged the Irish Nationalists, who steadily lost ground within their own country. They supported Britain in her struggle against Germany, a stance which further weakened their position: an index of their failure was the dismal performance of the army's recruiters in Ireland, despite the backing of leading Home Rulers.[31] The militant Sinn Feiners began to fill the vacuum: they were not in the least interested in old-style Home Rule, but demanded complete Irish independence.

The government of Ireland was a sphere in which constitutional theory differed sharply from practical politics. Although in theory the Lord Lieutenant and his council governed the country, in practice real power was in the hands of the Chief Secretary, nominally Chief Secretary to the Lord Lieutenant. The Chief Secretary was a politician with a seat in the Cabinet, and his political duties naturally kept him in London for much of the time: considerable executive authority devolved, therefore, upon the Under Secretary, who operated from what was unkindly called that 'sink of jobbery and corruption', Dublin Castle. R. Barry O'Brien summed up the arrangement with a nautical analogy: 'the Lord Lieutenant wore the insignia of command and signed the log, but the Chief Secretary was really the Captain of the ship, while the Under Secretary was the man at the wheel'.[32]

Early in 1916 the Lord Lieutenant, Lord Wimborne, and the Chief Secretary, Augustine Birrell, were generally optimistic concerning the state of Ireland. Major-General L. B. Friend, GOC Ireland, was more gloomy and, having failed to persuade Birrell to proclaim the Irish Volunteers an illegal organisation, he passed his worries on to French. The Field-Marshal visited Birrell at the Irish Office on 12 February. Birrell assured him that he did not think that the Volunteers posed much of a threat, but he would be glad to see them 'get a real good "knock"'. He believed that Cork and Dublin were the most dangerous areas, but considered that there was more likelihood of urban bombings than of an armed uprising. Birrell suggested that troops could be best employed by making as much display as possible, and he recommended that they should march about behind their bands. The Irish constabulary were, he lamented, 'rather lazy and inert and quite useless from a "detection" point of view'.[33]

French told Friend and Robertson of his discussion with Birrell. He asked the former to suggest what reinforcements he would require if he was to be called upon to assist the police, but added that he had no field troops available for the task: a brigade of cavalry was the best that he could offer. As far as he was concerned the ball was still in the government's court, and unless the government changed its assessment of the threat there was little more that could be done.[34]

After a shooting incident on 20 March French summarised the Royal Irish Constabulary's reports for the Adjutant-General, and concluded that 'certain parts of Ireland were in a very disturbed state, and that insurrection had been openly suggested in the public press'. He wondered if Birrell might now have changed his mind, drew attention to the damaging effects of even a minor rising in Ireland, and recommended that trial by court-martial be introduced in certain cases.[35]

On the 23rd French discussed the 'state of preparedness in case of a sudden rebellion' with Wimborne and Friend at Horse Guards. There was general agreement that 'somehow or other, more troops should be got into the country', and French suggested to the War Office that a reserve infantry brigade might usefully be stationed in Ireland. He had no objection from the home defence point of view, though he admitted that it would interrupt training and make draft-finding more difficult.[36] The Adjutant-General passed this information on to Friend, saying that he should make official application for the brigade if he required it. Friend replied, on 7 April, that he did not propose to do so, as the security situation had, in his opinion, improved. The Adjutant-General forwarded a copy of this letter to French with the comment that no further action was now required by Home Forces. Both Birrell and the Under Secretary, Sir Matthew Nathan, continued to believe that an insurrection was unlikely, and the military authorities in London saw no reason to alter their own position in view of the assurances from Ireland.[37]

At about noon on 24 April, Easter Monday, French received what he called 'unexpected and serious news'. Parties of rebels had seized various points in the centre of Dublin, and seemed to be digging themselves in. French at once sent two infantry brigades to Ireland and put other formations on standby. The situation soon looked even more menacing: the Admiralty told him that the German fleet was out, and warned that a bombardment of the east coast was likely: there was also a possibility of Zeppelin raids.[38]

French was woken at 4.00 on the morning of the 25th with the news that Lowestoft was being shelled. He told the commanders of his two home defence armies to prepare for action, and ordered two divisions in reserve in the Midlands to be prepared to move to the coast. An intelligence report from Ireland four days previously had warned of collaboration between the Irish and the Germans, and although French had muttered 'I don't believe a word of it', for a few hours on the morning of the 25th he had a disturbing suspicion that the rising in Ireland might be part of some co-ordinated German plan.[39]

French's worst fears soon passed, and he felt confident enough to drive down to Aldershot to visit troops in training. On his return he found a message from the War Office informing him that Sir Nevil Macready had been deputed to handle the War Office's part in the suppression of the rising, and requesting that Macready should be kept fully informed of the progress of events. French then went off to see Kitchener, who was of the opinion that French should proceed to Ireland that evening, to take command personally. French disagreed, and immediately visited the Prime Minister, who agreed that London was the proper place for him. The Field-Marshal lost no time in taking the glad tidings to Kitchener, noting with astonishment that he 'expressed no annoyance at my visit to the PM!' The news from Dublin was encouraging: it seemed that the rebels had little popular support, and the military authorities reported that they had the situation well in hand.[40]

Next morning French saw the King, and found him rather pessimistic about the Irish situation. The King suggested that he should see the Nationalist leader John Redmond, and French duly met Redmond that afternoon. The latter had previously struck Asquith as being 'strongly pro-French and anti-Haig', and he gave the Field-Marshal a long and helpful account of the state of Ireland as he saw it, emphasising that Sinn Fein was strong only in Dublin, and had little grass roots support in the country as a whole. He added that the army should take great care to employ only the minimum force necessary to restore order, so as to avoid swinging public opinion in favour of the rebels.

French had a busy evening. After dining at Lancaster Gate with the commanders and staff of the Northern home defence army he heard that the government had decided to send out a new general to take command in Ireland. Offered a choice between Major-Generals Sir William Campbell and Sir John Maxwell, French selected the latter, a tough highlander whose wide experience had included a tour of duty as military governor of Pretoria. At about 11 p.m. a note arrived from Downing Street, enclosing a letter from Lord Midleton – none other than our old friend St John Brodrick, who had succeeded to his father's viscountcy in 1907. Midleton warned that the South of Ireland was inadequately garrisoned, and cast doubt upon the loyalty of the Irish regiments. French had already told Asquith that although he had ordered the 60th Division to be ready to move, he did not intend to dispatch it until he had consulted the General Staff.[41]

Maxwell reported for briefing the following morning, and, having given him his instructions, French crossed Whitehall to visit Robertson at noon. They agreed that, 'we should only be playing the German game, too many troops. We both thought there were enough there already.'[42] Not everybody concurred. Midleton called on French, on the Prime Minister's instructions, on the 28th, and persuaded the Field-Marshal to send a battalion to the South. Carson arrived that afternoon and confirmed Midleton's warnings, leading French to send the two more battalions. Maxwell then requested the Aldershot cavalry brigade, and French agreed to send that too. Although Maxwell had little detailed information, his messages were increasingly hopeful, and he confidently predicted the imminent collapse of the rebellion.[43]

The news was even better on the 29th. The Irish provisional government asked for terms and was offered only unconditional surrender. Maxwell reported that rebels were surrendering 'freely' in Dublin, and devoutly hoped that 'the movement is dead'.[44] On the afternoon of 1 May French had a long discussion with Asquith. The Prime Minister was inclined to blame Nathan rather than Friend for the initial setbacks, but it soon became evident that the War Office was less than pleased by Friend's lack of pre-planning, and was collecting reports on his behaviour.[45]

French's perspectives had not broadened since he had hanged the Cape Colony Boers: if Maxwell's court-martial sentenced the rebel leaders to death, he saw this as no more than their just deserts, though others were less certain. On 3 May Asquith's private secretary told French that the Prime Minister was 'a little surprised and perturbed by the drastic action of shooting so many of the rebel leaders'.[46] Asquith put his fears in writing, suggesting that 'any wholesale punishment by death might easily cause a revulsion of feeling in this country and lay up a store of future trouble in Ireland'. French passed the warning on to Maxwell, but added the telling reservation that he had no intention of interfering with Maxwell's freedom of action. Maxwell regarded this as *carte blanche* to continue with his policy of executing convicted rebel leaders, and French must bear a share of the blame for the counter-productive effects of Maxwell's firing parties.[47]

Maxwell soon recognised that his hopes of the early demise of Sinn Fein were groundless. As early as 13 May he prophesied that 'the younger generation is likely to be more revolutionary than their predecessors', and in mid-June he announced that 'sedition and discontent' were rampant.[48] In October the government tried to undo some of the damage done by Maxwell's stern measures. Maxwell was replaced by what the Prime Minister called 'a popular Irishman', General Sir Bryan Mahon.[49] But neither Mahon's appointment nor the government's repeated attempts to find a political solution through negotiation could arrest the long slide into chaos.

Things would have been difficult enough for H. E. Duke, the Unionist lawyer who took over as Chief Secretary in July 1916, without the added problem of conscription. Conscription was introduced in Britain in the spring of 1916, and there was much talk of its extension into Ireland. A man-hungry War Office cast jaundiced glances at the manpower available in Ireland, and as the burden of casualties increased so English clamour for conscription in Ireland grew. French acknowledged that it would be very difficult to keep the Irish regiments up to strength by voluntary recruiting alone, and in March 1918, he observed that opinion was about evenly divided on the question of conscription in Ireland.[50] There were some suggestions that recruiting might improve if it was put in the hands of a committee composed of prominent Irishmen, and if recruits were guaranteed service in Irish divisions making up an Irish army. Not only did the War Office oppose such a scheme but, in the worsening climate which followed the Easter Rising, it was probably impractical in any case.[51]

The threat of conscription concentrated Irish opinion wonderfully. It helped drive Irishmen into the arms of Sinn Fein, and provided a topic upon which most nationalist groups and the Roman Catholic church could agree. Sinn Fein steadily gained ground, and by the spring of 1918 much of Ireland was ungovernable. Many officials believed that the spectre of conscription had helped to produce this state of affairs. One reported that: 'Without in any way discounting the very live National Feeling in Ireland today, the fear of conscription is the ordinary elementary fear of the average healthy human being of being tortured and killed.' Dr O'Dea, the Bishop of Galway, put it even more succinctly: 'If the Pope himself came over to this country and told the boys to enlist,' he said, 'they wouldn't go.'[52]

French visited Ireland on a number of occasions, and

formed his own views of the state of the country. In July 1917 he recorded with delight that the women of Cork had been '*vociferous* in their welcome', but he was less favourably impressed by Dublin, recording that 'the state of Dublin is much worse than Cork'. Galway was even more depressing. 'The Galway people turned out in great numbers', he wrote, 'but showed no enthusiasm. We might have been French or Russian troops.'[53]

French was by now a convinced Home Ruler in the pre-war sense. He hoped that Ireland would be given Home Rule after the war as soon as the internal violence subsided, and continued to doubt whether Sinn Fein enjoyed much genuine popular support. He was confident enough in a peaceful solution to the Irish question to purchase property in Ireland: in 1917 he bought an attractive, smallish, country house at Drumdoe in Roscommon. Like so many of his investments, it proved to be unwise. He was rarely able to visit the house, and as the security situation deteriorated so his visits became increasingly perilous.

French's fortunes had reached their nadir with his replacement as Commander-in-Chief in France in December 1915. Although his difficulties over air defence and the Easter Rising led to some public and parliamentary criticism, his position grew stronger in 1916–17, and by the spring of 1918 he had re-established himself as one of the government's leading military advisers. His resurgence was facilitated by a combination of military and political circumstances. In June 1916 his old rival Kitchener, whose own position had become markedly insecure, was lost at sea when HMS *Hampshire*, which was carrying him on a liaison mission to Russia, struck a mine off the Orkneys and sank with only a few survivors. He was succeeded at the War Office by Lloyd George who, six months later, became Prime Minister when Asquith was at last forced to resign.

Even Haig was not fireproof. French's office at Horse Guards became a clearing-house for gossip from France as Generals, most of them with their own axes to grind, passed through London. In June 1916 Henry Lawson and B. Doran arrived with tales of woe, and two months later Robertson warned Haig that 'Winston, French and various "degommed people" are trying to make mischief'.[54] The King told Haig that 'a regular "cabal" ' of dismissed Generals was criticising the actions of GHQ, and on 25 November he summoned French to Buckingham Palace and warned him to stop undermining Haig's authority.[55]

French paid little heed to this advice. Time had not healed the scars of December 1915: moreover, the results of the Battle of the Somme convinced him that Haig's methods were bound to fail. He attacked Haig's choice of commander for the Somme battle and wrote acidly that: 'The command of so big an operation should have been entrusted to a man who enjoyed the confidence of officers and men. No-one really trusts or believes in Rawlinson.'[56] He grew more outspoken as time went on: in April 1918 he urged on the Secretary of State for War, Lord Milner, the importance of 'overhauling carefully the chief and other commands at the front—and told him firmly that I thought most culpable and inexcusable mistakes had been made'.[57]

Yet even this was moderate by comparison with a document written by French the same month, probably for use by Lloyd George in an attack on Haig. French indicted Haig for 'undermining my power and authority by ... criticising everything to his juniors, as well as to the King, the PM, the SofS and people at home'. Haig had conspired with Robertson to 'get superior military power and override the government', and 'shattered the morale of the army' by an 'unscrupulous waste of *life*, *energy* and *material* in ill-planned and impossible adventures'. He concluded by asking if still more British soldiers were 'to be sacrificed on the altar of incompetence, jealousy, self-seeking ambition and intrigue?'[58]

French's feelings of bitterness towards Haig undoubtedly contributed to his views on the conduct of the war generally. From the spring of 1916 onwards he grew increasingly despondent about Allied offensives on the Western Front. In May he told Sir George Riddell that the German defences were very strong, and gloomily agreed that the war would go on for at least another year: he was even more dejected after the Battle of the Somme.[59] The Field-Marshal's swing away from Western strategy made him a useful ally for other opponents of the Haig–Robertson strategic line. On 4 October 1916 Lloyd

George summoned him for a discussion on the shortcomings of the artillery in France, recent criticisms in the *Morning Post*, and the army's discipline.[60] As a result of this meeting French was sent to France for a series of meetings with senior French Generals, and on his return he reported directly to Lloyd George, rather than to the CIGS.

Haig was furious. He complained that 'French's visit to Joffre can do no good to anyone, but only tend to make discord.'[61] He correctly discerned that the real reason for French's visit was to provide Lloyd George with evidence which he could use to attack GHQ. Foch told Henry Wilson a few days later that French had been trying to find out why the British had lost so many men on the Somme and had made so little progress. Foch added that he had declined to discuss British Generals with the Field-Marshal: he agreed with Wilson that the mission was ill-conceived, though both admitted that Haig's methods invited criticism.[62] Haig refused to see French. He sent a senior aide-de-camp, Lieutenant-Colonel Alan Fletcher, to meet him. 'Fletcher was told by me privately', wrote Haig, 'that I would not receive Viscount French in my house. I despise him too much personally for that, but he would receive every attention due to a British Field-Marshal.'[63]

Haig reported to the King that he doubted if French would succeed in doing much harm, although he shared Robertson's fear that Lloyd George might try to oust Robertson and replace him as CIGS by French.[64] Relations continued to be chilly in 1917: in mid-January Lord Derby invited French to dinner to meet Haig, and French asked Derby for an interview in order to explain why he felt unable to accept.[65] But both men were under pressure, from the King among others, to re-establish cordial relations if only for the good of the army. A meeting was arranged for 22 June, and Haig called in at Horse Guards at midday. 'He was just like his old self', thought French, 'and brought the happy days of the past vividly to my memory.' Haig recorded that:

> He was very pleased to see me and said that the order to give up his command in France came as a great blow to him, and that he was so upset that he

> knew he thought and said things then which he was
> ashamed of now. He felt that it was the best thing for
> the country that he had given up his command
> because he was then in bad health ... I shook him by
> the hand and congratulated him on speaking out like
> a man.

Both officers noted in their respective diaries that 'we parted the best of friends'.[66]

The rapprochement, however sincere it may have been, proved sadly short-lived. French's resentment was rekindled by the continuing flow of reports of what he regarded as mismanagement in France, and particularly by the casualty lists of that most ghastly of all British offensives, Passchendaele. At the same time he drew ever closer to Lloyd George, and at the end of July he asked the Prime Minister for closer access to the War Cabinet.

> I said that it was quite wrong and irregular that
> Robertson should be a 'go-between' and commented
> on his present position and status with reference to
> the commanders of armies ... I know the PM feels as
> I do about it and I think something may be done.[67]

This was exactly what Robertson had attempted to prevent when drawing up his terms of reference in December 1915. He saw the post of CIGS as the sole avenue by which military advice should reach the Cabinet: given the existing structure, it was French's not Robertson's actions which were irregular.

Lloyd George was unimpressed by Robertson's logic. Before coming to a final decision as to what course of action he should recommend to the Cabinet and the Allies, he asked for Haig's comments on the progress of the battle. Haig reported that all was going well: his troops were 'elated and confident', and the Allies were justified in proceeding with offensives in the West. Robertson's response was similar: he stressed, with ponderous predictability, the importance of concentrating the major effort in the main theatre of war, which he regarded as the Western Front.[68] Lloyd George had entertained French and Wilson to lunch at Great Walstead in August. He had a long conversation with them after the meal, and later remarked that

'French is the biggest soldier we have yet produced in the war. Not an organiser, but a soldier.'[69] In early October, having received opinions of Haig and Robertson, he decided to follow the precedent of Asquith's August 1914 Council of War and seek alternative advice, and it was to French and Wilson that he turned.

On 11 October French and Wilson attended the War Cabinet and were formally requested to comment on the alternative strategies discussed. These were four in number: firstly, single-minded concentration on the Western Front; secondly, emphasis on the Western Front, with the maintenance of forces in other theatres at their current levels; thirdly, defensive strategy on all fronts until American troops were able to intervene in strength – the Cabinet termed this 'The Pétain Solution' – and finally, concentration on some other theatre of operations. On the next day Hankey sent French a note reminding him that his paper should be submitted to the CIGS rather than to the War Cabinet direct, but French either managed to get this instruction rescinded or simply took no notice of it, for his completed report went straight to the War Cabinet.[70]

The first part of French's memorandum embodied a savage attack on the principles and details contained in Haig's report on the progress of the war. French suggested that it was quite wrong to see the German army as Germany's prime instrument for fighting the war: in view of recent events, her U-Boats and air force could not be ignored. He challenged GHQ's statistics, pointing out that there was a marked difference between the figures produced by GHQ and those emanating from the War Office. Haig's confidence was, he declared, not justified by the facts. Between 1 July 1916 and 1 October 1917 the British army had taken 200 square miles at the cost of over one million casualties: there was no firm evidence to suggest that German losses had been commensurate. Another offensive on the Western Front 'has become more of a "gamble" than anything else we have undertaken': he earnestly begged that 'every statement, every estimate and every forecast made by the Commander-in-Chief in France should be put to the most crucial test'.

In the second part of his paper French considered the four options. He rejected the first and second – total or partial

331

concentration on the Western Front—out of hand, examined the fourth in some detail, and concluded that 'The Pétain Solution' was the only feasible one. He added that some form of Supreme Allied War Council was essential for the superior direction of the war: he recommended that it should meet at once to appreciate the general situation and to formulate plans.[71]

Wilson's memorandum argued somewhat differently. Its author admitted that he was still a Westerner, because it was along the Western Front that 'the bulk of the forces of our principal enemy' were deployed. He then went on to make a strong case for a small War Cabinet and for 'an intelligent, effective and powerful superior direction'.[72] Although French and Wilson disagreed on the question of the Western Front, there had been a measure of collaboration in the production of their papers. Wilson had toned down some of the more outspoken comments in French's memorandum, and the draft copy in French's papers bears amendments in Wilson's hand.

Hankey met French and Wilson on 24 October in an effort to persuade them to change their minds. He feared that Haig and Robertson would resign rather than carry out a policy with which they disagreed, and if they went, the Conservative ministers might follow, bringing about the fall of the government. French flatly refused, saying that Haig was 'always making the same mistake'. He made no secret of his desire to bring down Robertson: 'We shall do no good,' he assured Hankey, 'until we break down the Haig–Robertson ring.' Hankey suggested that French's views were determined by more than merely military judgement. 'There was envy, hatred and malice in the old boy's heart as he spoke', he wrote. He eventually managed to prevail upon French to make some alterations in his paper, and the finished version, still firmly anti-Haig in tone, was handed to Lord Derby, the Secretary of State for War, on the 25th.[73]

Haig regarded French's paper as simply 'the outcome of a jealous and disappointed mind'.[74] Although French's opinion was partially moulded by his feelings towards Haig and Robertson, the memorandum reflected his increasingly gloomy outlook on the war in general. He had never fully recovered from hearing of the severe losses on the first days of the Battle of the Somme: in mid-July 1916 he asked Repington if he thought the game was really worth the candle.[75] By the autumn of 1917 he was even more dejected, and his morale was not improved by his frequent visits to hospitals where he saw the human consequences of the failure of Allied strategy.[76]

French gained some satisfaction from the fall of Robertson. The latter's position became increasingly insecure during 1917, as he continued to push Haig's demands for troops to feed the fighting on the Western Front in the face of Lloyd George's growing conviction that other, more profitable, theatres of operations should be found. With the constitution of the Supreme War Council in November 1917 his days as CIGS were definitely numbered, and he eventually resigned, after a lengthy squabble with Lloyd George, in mid-February 1918. Derby contemplated resigning in sympathy, but decided to stay on. He did not survive for long, however, and was soon shunted off to be Ambassador to France. Lord Milner went to the War Office in what French called 'a beautiful and most salutary change'.[77]

With Robertson gone, French redoubled his efforts to bring about the recall of Haig. He was thrown into a frenzy of grief and despair by news of German successes in March. On the 23rd he regretted that the enemy had inflicted 'a heavy blow' on the army in France, and, while walking back from a Cabinet meeting with Lloyd George and Bonar Law:

> expressed myself very strongly as to the necessity for an immediate investigation into the question of *adequate command* ... As regards the Chief Command I expressed the strong conviction that *Haig* should be replaced by *Plumer*.[78]

Two days later he was out riding in Richmond Park when he was summoned to a meeting of the War Cabinet. He spoke in favour of unified command on the Western Front, but feared that it might already be too late to preserve the unity of the Allied armies. If the Germans managed to achieve a clean breakthrough, which seemed not improbable, he suggested that the British army might either fall back to cover the Channel ports on the line Abbeville–Dunkirk, or withdraw into Normandy to screen Cherbourg. The Cabinet came to no conclusion on the subject, but French expressed himself well pleased that it had at least discussed 'the terrible and urgent decisions they may be called upon to consider and take within a week or 10 days'.[79] French's opposition to the concept of a joint retirement with the French rang with the hollow echoes of late August 1914, and revealed that, whatever he might say about inter-Allied relations of the unity of command, he was at heart unable to accept that the fates of the British and French armies on the Western Front were inextricably entwined.

Even when he relinquished his Home Forces command in May 1918 French let fly a last Parthian shot at Haig, suggesting to Wilson, who had succeeded Robertson as CIGS, that Haig should take over as Commander-in-Chief Home Forces. 'Henry rather jumped at the idea', observed French, 'and said that he would put it before Milner'.[80] Haig's well-informed wife warned him what was afoot, but nothing came of the move: even Lloyd George recognised that it was a dangerous moment to change horses, and there was no generally acceptable successor to Haig, although the names of Plumer and Lord Cavan were often mentioned in this context.

It is tempting to see Lloyd George's use of French as an alternative to the CIGS as a source of strategic advice as nothing more than the skilful manipulation of a man he knew to be bitterly hostile to Haig. The events of late April and early May 1918, however, suggest that Lloyd George was telling at least part of the truth when he wrote so effusively of French's abilities in his *War Memoirs*. The worsening situation in Ireland, coupled with the likelihood of the extension of conscription to that already troubled land, persuaded Lloyd George that a radical change in the Irish government was urgently required. On 29 April he informed French that the Lord Lieutenant had resigned and that Duke had been replaced as Chief Secretary by Edward Shortt. He intended to replace the Lord Lieutenant with three Lord Justices: James Campbell, the Unionist Lord Chief Justice of Ireland, was one; Midleton was another, and French himself was the third.[81]

French spent the 30th discussing the situation in Ireland with Midleton and Campbell. The former declared himself in favour of '*strong action*' to establish order, and the immediate introduction of conscription to provide drafts for France.

Campbell believed that conscription could not be made to work, and thought that the government recognised this. French's own views were perfectly clear.

> Martial Law should be declared at once for the whole of Ireland. The ordinary law must be held in abeyance and the Law Courts must be closed. 'Home Rule' must be abandoned and the Lord Justices must be charged with the fullest powers to use every means at their disposal to administer the law of conscription throughout Ireland.

The three men drew up and signed a memorandum on the powers of the Lord Justices, and went to Downing Street with it. When the government declined to accept the terms, Campbell announced that he could no longer associate himself with the project.[82]

Midleton also had serious doubts. At a Cabinet meeting on 2 May he declared that the Lord Justices should advise on policy as well as implement instructions from Westminster: unless this was the case they would arrive in Ireland 'branded with the odium of coming to enforce two most obnoxious measures' — conscription and Home Rule. French sympathised with Midleton, but he was prepared 'to act in any way the government desired provided they gave us full powers and full support'. The Prime Minister eventually decided that he could accept the services of neither Midleton nor Mr Justice Ross, an alternative to Campbell. On Sunday 5 May Milner offered the Lord Lieutenancy to French in the Prime Minister's name. French replied that:

> in ordinary circumstances or in peace time such a position would be impossible for me but that on the understanding that I was to go to Ireland for the purpose of *military order* and combating German intrigue; as a *Military Viceroy* at the head of a *Quasi-Military Government* I would consider it my duty to obey what I regard as a distinct *order* or direction to me by HM govt.

French then went to the War Office to talk things over with Wilson. He arranged for Sir Frederick Shaw, his CGS at Horse

Guards, to take over from Mahon as Commander-in-Chief Ireland, and for Ireland to be removed from the authority of Home Forces and to come directly under the War Office. He left for Ireland on the mail boat on the evening of the 10th, to face one of the greatest challenges of his career.[83]

French took with him his personal staff, and made no provision for Lady French to follow him. His relationship with his wife had reached the point where a meeting between them merited a slightly surprised entry in French's diary, but it was to be some time before Mrs Bennett could visit Viceregal Lodge. French's affair with Winifred had continued unabated during 1916–17, with what might best be called 'afternoon delights' at Lancaster Gate breaking up the humdrum routine of French's appointments.

Although the passionate affair between French and Winifred Bennett was no secret to many of those who moved in the same circle, there was never any open scandal. It was, ironically, George Moore who dragged French into court. Moore had been viciously attacked by an article in the *World* which suggested that he was pro-German and that his influence upon French was a source of danger, and the article was copied in the *Manchester Chronicle*. French gave evidence for Moore in March 1916, and, although Moore eventually obtained apologies from both newspapers, the business did French no good. Fitz Watt suspected that the articles were really aimed at French rather than Moore, and the attention drawn to the Field-Marshal's close friendship with this rich and raffish American was exactly the sort of publicity French would most have liked to avoid.[84]

French was sixty-five when he set off to be Lord-Lieutenant of Ireland. His health seemed to have recovered from the rigours of France, although he had put on weight and looked unusually florid. A private in the Civil Service Rifles saw him at an inspection in May 1917, and commented with more accuracy than respect that: 'He looked quite short, and his moustache looked very white against his very red face ... I did not like the look of him very much. He looked cross and cantankerous.'[85]

The Field-Marshal's popularity had recovered from the depths of December 1915: compared with the casualties of

Ypres and Passchendaele, the losses of Loos looked almost nostalgically trivial. French's political power-base was as strong as ever: he enjoyed the confidence of the Prime Minister, and his old friend Walter Long was a man of great and growing influence. French was nevertheless a strange choice for Lord Lieutenant, especially in view of the fact that his appointment reversed the established relationship between Lord Lieutenant and Chief Secretary. His touch had never been light or deft where matters of internal security were concerned, and his own deep sense of Irishness did nothing to help him see the Irish problem in anything but the starkest of blacks and whites. The very fact that Lloyd George chose to appoint him gives a clear indication of the fact that the government was fast running out of options.

Eleven

Lord Lieutenant
May 1918–May 1921

French was sworn in as Lord Lieutenant of Ireland at Dublin Castle at noon on Saturday 11 May. He took with him a very definite view of his own position and of his immediate course of action. He had already told Lloyd George that he understood that the government proposed to introduce Home Rule and to link it to the extension of conscription into Ireland. He warned:

> The condition of Ireland is such that neither policy can in my opinion, be carried out until the authority of the government has been re-established, and, in particular, an end has been put to the relations which now exist between the Germans and the rebels in Ireland.
>
> I understand that in order to deal with such a situation that it is proposed to set up a quasi-military government in Ireland with a soldier Lord Lieutenant.[1]

His immediate aim was, therefore, to destroy Sinn Fein in order to create an environment in which Home Rule could safely be granted.

French's opinion of Sinn Fein had not changed materially over the past two years. He believed that it was essentially a violent and extremist organisation which enjoyed little support amongst the people, and throughout his stay in Ireland he consistently underestimated the movement's growing power and popularity. He cherished two fatal misconceptions: firstly, that his own deep personal commitment to Ireland gave him a special insight into the country's problems, and secondly that Sinn Fein survived only by terrorising the population. He told Lord Esher:

> I have loved this country and these people all my life and I would do anything or sacrifice anything for them. They are so infernally emotional. If they could only be got to realise the true character of such leaders as De Valera ... I feel sure the Irish would cast them out like the swine they are. My first great effort is to stamp out the German intrigue – Many who are implicated in it have been absolutely terrorised by their leaders.[2]

He had no doubt that his task would be difficult, and drew up a memorandum on counter-measures to be put into effect if a strike was called after the arrest of the Sinn Fein leaders. He was concerned to establish the full extent to his own powers, to ascertain the limitations of the Defence of the Realm Act (DORA), and to discover the circumstances in which he could proclaim martial law in all or part of Ireland.[3]

To help him proceed with his task, French enjoyed a position quite dissimilar to that of any Lord Lieutenant within living memory. In September 1918 he put Shortt firmly in his place, reminding him that:

> I accepted the office of Lord Lieutenant upon the recommendation of the Prime Minister, on the clear understanding that I was to be the *de facto* as well as the *de jure* Governor of Ireland, and indeed I may remind you that the Prime Minister went so far as to say in the Cabinet, on more than one occasion, that I was to be responsible for the Government *in Ireland* while you were to represent the Irish Government in the House of Commons ... I cannot admit that there is any equality in our positions ... To do so would be to make my position impossible and I feel sure that, on reflection, you will see the force of what I am saying.[4]

Shortt at once replied that he had only claimed equality out of 'duty to the dignity of the office I hold', and stressed that this 'implies in no possible degree any disloyalty to you personally or to your great office, or any lack of appreciation of the kindness with which you have always treated me'.[5]

French told Brinsley Fitzgerald that Shortt was 'a good fellow but wants reminding of his place occasionally'.[6] Relations between the two men worsened, however, and in October French informed Lloyd George that: 'unless Mr Shortt can be induced to change his methods, I do not consider it will be to the general advantage that he and I should any longer be associated together in the government of Ireland'. He went on to stress that he had only accepted office on the understanding that he was 'to exercise the full functions of a Governor General *de facto* and *de jure*'. The Prime Minister backed French.[7] When Lloyd George formed a new government in January 1919 Shortt was replaced by the more pliable Ian Macpherson, and French regarded this as something of a victory.[8]

The new importance of the Lord Lieutenant was underlined by the fact that he was formally appointed to the Cabinet, and kept in contact with the Cabinet when in Ireland not through the Chief Secretary, which would have been usual, but through a special liaison officer, Walter Long, who was now Colonial Secretary. Long was a Conservative MP with large estates in Wiltshire. He had commanded the Wiltshire Yeomanry in 1898, and his eldest son Toby, a cavalry officer, had been killed at the head of a brigade in France. French and Long were birds of a feather: their robust friendship was cemented by a mutual interest in horseflesh, and it survived even the trials of Ireland.[9]

French's attack on Sinn Fein had all the subtlety of a cavalry charge. On the night of 17/18 May the majority of its leaders were arrested, and large quantities of documents were seized. French wrote jubilantly of the success of 'the great coup'. He reaffirmed his conviction that 'the people are not "in" with Sinn Fein *really*', and was confident that the captured documents would provide firm evidence of links between Sinn Fein and the Germans.[10] The evidence, such as it was, was published on the 25th. French reluctantly admitted that the Irish seemed to be unconvinced: 'with the Irish temperament of trying to believe what they want to believe they endeavour to justify themselves, their leaders and their cause'.[11]

Nor were the Irish in a minority. Repington found the official explanation of the arrests 'very lame', Mahon complained that the plot was not proven, and even Macready admitted that the 'supposed German plot ... was not substantiated by very convincing evidence'.[12] The arrests failed to achieve the desired results. Two of the more extreme Sinn Feiners, Michael Collins and Cathal Brugha, escaped arrest, and their influence grew in the vacuum created by the absence of the moderates. There was also the practical problem of securing the prisoners, and French soon found himself dragged into endless squabbles about the status of the prisoners and the legality of the clauses of DORA under which they were detained. It was not a debate in which an elderly Field-Marshal, with no grounding in the law, was likely to excel.[13]

If his attempt to destroy the Sinn Fein leadership was something of a botched shot, French was more successful in other, less dramatic, respects. He had been appalled on his arrival by what he termed:

> the extraordinary lack of method of co-ordination in thought and in act by which the Viceroy, the Chief Secretary and the Heads of Departments could exercise authority and reach decisions which would represent their united will and opinion.

He immediately set up an Executive Council, whose members were the Lord Lieutenant, the Chief Secretary and the Commander-in-Chief, which discussed, at least in the early period of French's regime, 'all questions of importance relating to the Government of Ireland'. A Military Council was established slightly later, and had its first meeting on 2 July 1918. It comprised the Lord Lieutenant, Lieutenant-General Sir Frederick Shaw, the Commander-in-Chief, together with his CGS and Major-General in charge of administration, and was intended to be 'a more technical advisory and consultative body'. Senior police officers—the Chief Constable of the Dublin Metropolitan Police (DMP) and the Inspector-General of the Royal Irish Constabulary (RIC)—were occasionally co-opted on to both committees. The establishment of these committees represented a considerable advance in terms of organisation, and French may be credited with establishing a command framework which foreshadowed developments in subsequent counter-insurgency campaigns. [14]

Thus far French was operating within a sphere he understood. His attempt to extend the committee system by creating a Viceroy's Advisory Council, which would give him 'direct means of seeking information and advice from reliable residents as to local conditions in different provincial districts in Ireland', took him on to the quicksand of politics. [15] For whatever French said in public about the Advisory Council, he envisaged it as a good deal more than merely an advisory body. In August 1918 Mr Justice Ross advised him to use 'the primary power which is his by right' to circumvent 'jobbers and plotters' such as Shortt. [16] French considered using the Council as an executive body, and Long was 'all in favour' of using it as 'a "temporary government" to replace the Castle bureaucracy'. [17] In the autumn of 1918 it looked briefly as if the Council might gather momentum. Haldane suggested that it would gain prestige if it included Sinn Fein members. [18] Carson approved of it, arguing that it should be given another Ulsterman and at least two Nationalists: he suggested fusing it with the Executive Council to give it real executive responsibility. [19] The King regarded the Council as 'a wise step', and was ready to approve the appointment of such Irish Privy Councillors as French proposed to make. [20]

But the Council contained a fatal flaw. Much as Long might eulogise its representative character, all the Council's members were well-connected, wealthy men: they were, as a sharp *Times* article pointed out, representative only of Dublin's exclusive Kildare Street Club. [21] Haldane's pious hope that Sinn Feiners might serve was little more than a chimera. At the other extreme, most of the Irish law officers and Castle officials were united in their opposition to the Council: the Irish Lord Chancellor informed French that it was constitutionally impossible for it to exercise executive power, and the Chief Secretary was steadfastly opposed to anything other than a purely advisory body. [22]

Under fire from both flanks, the Council staggered on, but it never attained any executive status and from April 1919 it no longer met regularly. When Sir Thomas Stafford resigned from it in August 1920 French told him he was quite right to have done so, for 'the so-called Viceroy's Advisory Council has gone into complete abeyance by reason of the dislike displayed towards that Body by certain people ... '[23] Given the nature of its composition, the Council's failure was inevitable. Several of its members shared French's misconceptions regarding the strength of Sinn Fein, and most of them thought in terms of pre-1914 Home Rule. Their genuine concern for Ireland was undoubted, but by 1918 the Ireland they thought they understood had undergone irreversible change.

Yet the Council was not entirely sterile. It did offer French useful advice on commercial and industrial questions, and gave serious consideration to the problems of dealing with discharged soldiers after the war. Some of its members, notably Stafford and Sir Henry Robinson, had an important influence on the Lord Lieutenant, and encouraged him to believe that Home Rule based on a Federal System was both possible and desirable. French warmly advocated a Federal solution in the summer of 1918, and for the remainder of his time in Ireland he regarded the division of the country into two federated states, North and South, as the most feasible solution to its problem. He believed that these states should enjoy wide powers, but favoured the reservation of certain matters, notably defence, to the United Kingdom Parliament at Westminster.[24]

Whatever his confidence in the ultimate success of Home Rule, French was convinced that unrest should be quelled before any measure of self-government could safely be introduced. For the first six months of his viceroyalty the Cabinet was considering the introduction of both conscription and Home Rule. French regretted that the government had undertaken to bring in Home Rule, before order had been restored, but looked upon conscription as a means of bringing about 'the complete removal of useless and idle youths and men between 18 and 24 or 25'. With this 'turbulent element of the population' usefully employed in France, he thought that the security problem would prove easier to solve.[25] He had little doubt that the voluntary recruiting campaign would fail to reach its target, and told the King that 'any hesitation or avoidable delay in carrying out the conscription policy would be fatal to the future of the country'.[26] He was confident that the enforcement of conscription would 'not involve much bloodshed, although there will, undoubtedly, be a good deal of opposition'.[27] Military plans for the implementation of conscription were finalised in early October, and work began on an Order in Council to extend conscription to Ireland. But no sooner had the Commander-in-Chief Ireland received his orders than the Prime Minister suggested that the question could be ignored in view of the improving military situation in France. French was thus spared the numerous and grave difficulties which would have arisen had conscription been enforced: it is probable that his confidence in the authorities' ability to inflict conscription on an increasingly recalcitrant population was sadly misplaced.

The conscription crisis over, French was immediately forced to contend with the troubles which arrived with demobilisation. On the one hand, the forces at Shaw's disposal shrank steadily. In August 1918, Shaw reported that he regarded fifteen 800-man infantry battalions and twenty-four 450-man cyclist units as the minimum satisfactory military force level in Ireland: this strength was not, in fact, attained until the summer of 1920, and many of the troops sent to Ireland were, in any case, inexperienced and at best partly-trained.[28]

At the same time as demobilisation whittled down the fighting strength of the army, discharged Irish soldiers returned home from the front. The Viceroy's Advisory Council was swift to point out that unless these men could be resettled with the minimum of fuss they would fall easy prey to Sinn Fein propaganda. French was well aware of the risk, and also believed that the government had a powerful moral responsibility towards Irishmen who had volunteered for service. He suggested that a new ex-serviceman's organisation, 'Comrades of the Great War (Ireland)', should be set up to counteract the Sinn Fein dominated 'Soldier's Federation'. He also recommended that ex-soldiers should be given practical assistance by cash and land grants, and floated a scheme for the establishment of 'soldiers' colonies', in various parts of Ireland.[29] His attempts to ensure that discharged Irish soldiers were kept loyal to the government were thwarted as much by inter-departmental friction and financial stringency as they were by Sinn Fein propaganda. There was a lengthy dispute over the structure and responsibilities of a resettlement committee, and endless squabbles over money.[30] If French's concern for the welfare of Irish ex-soldiers was not entirely altruistic, it was nevertheless sincere and heartfelt: it merited better success than it achieved.

During his first six months in office the Field-Marshal took increasingly severe steps towards the outlawing of Sinn Fein. On 3 July the Irish Volunteers and Sinn Fein with all its associated clubs were proclaimed as dangerous organisations, in certain areas, and the military authorities immediately issued orders under DORA banning all meetings and fairs in these places except by permit. West Cork was made a Special Military Area in late September, and the results in this case seemed good, but by October it was clear from RIC reports that the increase of repression had not reduced disaffection.[31]

French blamed the police for their failure to combat the growth of Sinn Fein, during this early period and, indeed, throughout his time in Ireland. No sooner had he arrived than he addressed himself to the task of improving the 'status, numbers and pay of the DMP and IC'. He put the case for a pay rise forcefully before Lloyd George and Long, and was rewarded by the immediate grant of a bonus which produced a good effect on both forces.[32] Not only did he continue to press for increases in police pay, but he also took pains to ensure that the Irish police received its fair share of decorations.[33]

A good deal of stick accompanied these morsels of carrot. The Chief Constable of the DMP and the Inspector-General of the RIC soon became first-hand experts on Frenchian outbursts. In early August 1918 the DMP launched one of its customarily fruitless searches for stolen explosives, as a result of which: 'I read the riot act pretty firmly to them all and directed Col Johnson to tell his Divisional Inspector that I consider the whole incident reflects much discredit on the Dublin police.'[34] Eight months later Walter Long warned him that:

> I firmly believe that the Head of the Police has lost his nerve ... I believe that there are other men in Dublin connected with the RIC in responsible positions who are either worn out or are incompetent. I

am satisfied that there are County Inspectors who are past their work, and are responsible for difficult and dangerous counties.

Long was preaching to the converted. French thought that the DMP was beyond hope: it was 'quite useless' to expect any improvement under its existing management.[35]

Brigadier-General Sir Joseph Byrne, Inspector-General of the RIC, became French's particular *bête noire*. In December 1919 French sent him on leave 'for the good of his health', but made it clear to Ian Macpherson that he regarded Byrne's dismissal as a resignation issue. He told Long that he was 'one of the greatest impediments we have had in Ireland to the cause of law and order', and Byrne was eventually prised out of office.[36] The astute Macready advised Byrne to refuse the appointment in the first place, warning him that he would be 'thrown to the wolves' in Ireland, but Byrne was more than capable of looking after himself, and put up such a stiff rear-guard action that the government had to send him off to the first of a series of comfortable colonial governorships.[37]

French's dissatisfaction with the performance of senior police officers was paralleled by his lack of confidence in the Dublin Castle administration. It was this that persuaded him to attempt to give his Advisory Council executive authority and to make some changes within the Castle itself. Largely in an effort to placate Catholic opinion, French appointed James MacMahon Under-Secretary on the retirement of Sir William Byrne in the summer of 1918. MacMahon had acted as French's contact with the Roman Catholic hierarchy, and French was initially delighted with his performance, writing approvingly of his 'ability, grasp of the situation, and sound sense', and describing him as 'a most excellent and trustworthy colleague and friend'.[38] Walter Long had serious doubts about the appointment, and hoped that it would not lead to 'the active participation of the Roman Catholic hierarchy in government', and French himself admitted that MacMahon was 'simply the mouth piece for the most rabid of the Irish priests'.[39]

French's attempt to boost Catholic confidence in the Castle administration by the appointment of MacMahon proved unsuccessful. MacMahon was not trusted by Macpherson and his associates, and was soon excluded from any important duties. His functions were taken over by the Assistant Under-Secretary, Sir John Taylor, whose passion for centralisation led to the creation of an administrative bottleneck serious even by the labyrinthine standards of the Castle. French continued to warn the Cabinet that the Castle required reorganisation, but it was not until the spring of 1920 that a team under Sir Warren Fisher was at last appoined to investigate it. No sooner had Fisher reported than Sir John Anderson was appointed joint Under-Secretary with MacMahon, while Andy Cope became Assistant Under-Secretary. Matters soon improved but, as far as French was concerned, it was two years too late.[40]

The Lord Lieutenant's efforts to improve the police and the Castle administration took place in a deteriorating security situation. His initial hope that the arrest of the Sinn Fein leaders had struck a fatal blow at the organisation proved misplaced, and on 8 October 1918 he informed the War Cabinet that struggle against Sinn Fein could not be thought of in terms of strategies: it would be necessary to bring about 'a radical change' in Irish sentiment before the country could be trusted with Home Rule.[41] Although French did not believe that there was such a thing as a military solution, pure and simple, to the problems of Ireland, he was convinced that the reform of the Castle, the resettlement of demobilised soldiers and the injection of English money into the Irish economy should be accompanied by a military offensive against the 'physical force' elements of Sinn Fein. He believed that such men were in a minority amongst the 'Constitutional Home Rulers' and 'Theoretical Republicans' who, he believed, made up the bulk of Sinn Fein. French recognised that the 'physical force' men were 'most aggressive, actively disruptive, and dangerous in the highest degree', and it was against them that the security forces should concentrate their efforts.[42]

In his recognition that the struggle against Sinn Fein was a complex operation which should be pursued on economic and social, as well as purely military, levels, French displayed a far greater perception than might have been expected. But in his approach to the fight against the 'physical force' men, he showed a desire for clear-cut definitions and the elimination of uncertainty that was more typical of the professional soldier of his generation. He was a firm believer in the introduction of martial law. It would, he hoped, cut through the hotch-potch of regulations and orders which were applied, at one time or another, to different parts of the country, and establish a centralised command system in which the unreliable police would be subordinated to the more reliable army. Finally, French's unhappy ventures into the quagmire of the Irish judicature persuaded him that the existing legal system was quite unable to sustain the stresses imposed upon it.

French had argued in favour of martial law in April 1918, and events of late 1918 and 1919 only confirmed him in his belief that martial law was essential. Sinn Fein won a landslide victory in the General Election of December 1918, and the following month those Sinn Fein MPs not in prison met in the Mansion House in Dublin as the first Dáil. Two of French's agents, one of them none other than George Moore, attended the proceedings, and reported that they were 'perfectly orderly'. Moore went further and suggested that the Dáil represented 'the general feeling in the country'.[43] French did not agree. He told Long that he was sure that 'these seventy-three devils will soon go bag and baggage over to Westminster', and Long agreed that the Sinn Fein MPs would troop off to Westminster as soon as they discovered that they could not draw their salaries in Dublin.[44] Both men were, once again, guilty of fatally underestimating the strength and resilience of their opponents: this underestimation was all the more serious because French and Long both backed it with the unshakeable conviction that they fully and deeply understood the Irish problem.

Shortly before the Dáil met in Dublin, Haldane arrived at Viceregal Lodge to discuss the possibility of negotiating with the Sinn Fein leaders. On the afternoon of the 17th Haldane visited 'some very important people of *the other side*', and French reported to Long that he was pursuing negotiations through Haldane while at the same time considering a more 'drastic and extensive' solution which could be employed if the talks failed.[45] Long replied that he had heard of Haldane's mission 'with no little dismay', and warned that Haldane was unpopular and distrusted in England.[46]

Long need not have worried. The peace plan, whatever its

chances might have been, was killed off from another quarter. On 21 January Sean Treacy and a detachment of the Tipperary Volunteers ambushed a cartload of gelignite bound for the quarry at Soloheadbeg, and shot both the RIC men guarding it. The attack was a deliberate act of violence by the 'physical force' party, and it produced a disproportionate effect upon French. He wrote sharply to Haldane, telling him that it was 'useless for us to think of going any further' with his scheme, going on to lament the 'brutal murder' of the policemen, and complaining that 'this horrible outrage occurred on the very day when we had reason to hope that secret influences would have been brought to bear to prevent anything of the kind'.[47] Haldane apparently believed that his peace plan had been thwarted by Long's opposition, but as far as French was concerned it was the Soloheadbeg murders that made negotiations impossible.[48]

Macpherson arrived in Ireland in late January, and French was initially delighted with him. He confided to Long that Macpherson 'will be amenable to advice and a certain amount of direction ... and I think he also has a very charming personality'.[49] There was a fair measure of agreement between French and his new Chief Secretary. Both believed that some conciliation was possible, and agreed that it was an appropriate moment for the release of the Sinn Fein leaders arrested in the spring of 1918. Macpherson hoped to move on towards old-style Home Rule, but he shared French's alarm at incidents like Soloheadbeg, and admitted that Home Rule was impossible until the violence had been ended.

French caught influenza on 8 February, and ten days later he contracted pneumonia. The illness kept him out of Ireland for nearly two months, and it was not until 7 April that he was able to resume regular office work. He was still rather shaky, and Long feared that he might have gone back to work too soon.[50] Some observers suggested that French's absence during the early stages of Macpherson's administration had a serious effect. The lawyer A. M. Sullivan told French that 'the mean Government betrayed everything when you were dying', and it is possible that the exclusion of MacMahon from his duties at the Castle might not have happened had French not been on sick leave.[51]

In general terms, however, French agreed with Macpherson that Sinn Fein and its associated organisations should be declared illegal throughout Ireland, although Long pointed out that such a proclamation would be useless because the government lacked the means to enforce it.[52] During the spring and early summer of 1919 the Lord Lieutenant continued to press for the proscription of Sinn Fein, but some Cabinet members were reluctant to embark upon such a step while Lloyd George was in Paris discussing what was to become the Treaty of Versailles.[53] French told the Prime Minister that 'we have taken strong measures and may have to take stronger', and was confident that he could overcome the militants if only he was given a free hand to do so.[54]

Just as the Soloheadbeg murders had affronted French in January, so the shooting of District Inspector Hunt in broad daylight in Thurles on 23 June spurred him into fresh demands for firm action. He told the Cabinet that the Sinn Feiners in Tipperary were 'an organised club for the murder of police', and suggested that the time had come to proclaim Sinn Fein illegal in that area.[55] His formal proposal to the Cabinet, however, suggested the wholesale proscription of the organisation throughout Ireland, and the Cabinet eventually consented on the condition that the Irish government was unanimous in its support for the declaration. On 5 July Sinn Fein and its associated organisations were declared illegal, and by the end of the year they were banned throughout Ireland.[56] It may be doubted whether the Irish government was, in fact, as unanimous as French suggested: by this stage his patience was exhausted and he was doing his best to hustle things along.

By early autumn French had come to the conclusion that the police, hampered as they were by a steady fall in numbers, were unable to cope, and in October he suggested that martial law should be temporarily imposed throughout the country to enable the police to carry out a 'clean up' with the army's assistance.[57] Early the following month, after a long discussion with General Shaw and the police chiefs, he told Macpherson that:

There is a consensus of opinion here that the declaration of martial law is not the best way of attaining our object. I do not mean to say that I agree in this, because I do not agree. But if we are to have martial law at all I feel strongly that it must be administered by people who thoroughly believe in its power and efficacy.[58]

A week later he begged Macpherson to press the Cabinet for a decision, and to extend article 14B of DORA or to impose martial law. 'This kind of hesitation and indecision', he grumbled, 'will end in completely demoralising the police forces in this country.'[59]

The Cabinet, reluctant to alienate its more liberal members or to authorise any action which might prejudice an eventual political solution, continued to vacillate. In December French assured Macpherson that the extremists were 'getting stronger and more arrogant in every direction and that it would be most dangerous to delay our action a moment longer than we can possibly help'.[60] He was frankly aghast at the Government's lack of support, and protested bitterly against the recent decision of the Disposal Board not to release army surplus vehicles to the RIC, but to request the RIC to compete for the vehicles on the open market:

I cannot see how we can possibly go on governing Ireland if we are continually handicapped in this senseless idiotic manner ... We are literally asked to make bricks without straw, and our situation is exactly analogous to a pugilist who is asked to commence and fight with one arm tied up. I am getting really rather sick of it.[61]

Early the next month he warned that 'a large number of men must be arrested and deported; *or else we must have martial law*', and he protested that the activities of what was now generally identified as the IRA were 'nothing more or less than acts of war, and we absolutely must meet the situation firmly'.[62]

French was well aware that the lack of trained troops in Ireland made the sort of firm action he envisaged somewhat difficult to achieve. He had his own ideas as to how this shortage could best be offset. On 14 April 1918 he had decided that aircraft could be used with good effect in Ireland: he decided to set up 'Entrenched Air Camps' from which the country could be policed, and he ordered Shaw to carry out a feasibility study. Shaw's staff reported that the effective operating radius of fighter aircraft would permit the aerial policing of Ireland if one squadron was deployed in each province. This would require the dispatch of three more squadrons to Ireland to join the one already there.[63]

The use of aircraft against the insurgents was discussed at the first meeting of the Military Council, and in August 1918 French asked the General Staff in Ireland 'to formulate some scheme by which aeroplanes and armed motors may be used to economise the numbers of men which will suffice to maintain order'.[64] The scheme was fraught with difficulties. While the war was in progress the demands of the Western Front precluded the dispatch of extra squadrons to Ireland, and after the war the RAF, in the throes of demobilisation, was unable to provide the aircraft required in Shaw's original estimate. There was, moreover, the question of what aircraft could actually do against insurgents. Bombing and machine-gunning from the air were only practicable in extreme cases: they were hardly satisfactory ways of preventing illegal cattle-driving or drilling. French was eventually driven to conclude that aerial policing could best be used in specified areas from which the civilian population had been removed. He compared this with the policy of concentration camps and flying columns in South Africa, and one can recognise in French's last desperate suggestions on the use of air power in Ireland the ugly phenomenon of the free-fire zone.[65]

Hopes that technology would fill the gap left by a lack of manpower proved delusive and throughout French's time in Ireland the army was hampered by an acute shortage of trained soldiers. Shaw had serious doubts about the legal foundation of martial law, and even if the legal difficulties were overcome he doubted the ability of the security forces effectively to control large and populous areas such as Dublin and Cork.[66] In November 1919 Irish Command put its minimum infantry requirement at 25,000 men, and although there were 37,259 soldiers in Ireland at the time, their bayonet strength was below this minimum and was, furthermore, declining. At least

36 battalions were required, and even in January 1920, after substantial reinforcement, there were only 34 available, and six of these were due for disbandment. This was largely symptomatic of the state of the post-war army as a whole: Henry Wilson, CIGS, was worried that his bayonet strength in England was also dangerously low.[67]

Nor was the RIC in a more satisfactory state. Rebel attacks on the RIC, coupled with the intimidation of policemen and their relatives, weakened the structure of the police: the drying-up of traditional sources of information was particularly damaging to their effectiveness. Long was keen on the recruitment of non-Irishmen into the RIC, and French agreed that English ex-soldiers would be useful: Byrne's resistance to the introduction of English volunteers was a contributory cause of his dismissal. RIC recruiting offices were set up in England in late 1919, and soon the first non-Irish recruits, called 'Black and Tans' from their black berets and khaki army uniforms, appeared in Ireland. The recruitment of Englishmen was taken a stage further in July 1920, when the Auxiliary Division of the RIC was inaugurated. Recruited from ex-officers who had served in the Great War, members of the Auxiliary Division were designated as Temporary Cadets in the RIC and enjoyed the status of police sergeants. The Black and Tans and the Auxies provided a useful increase to the RIC's strength, but their attitude and discipline often left much to be desired, and their excesses came to occupy a prominent place in IRA mythology.[68]

French had long recognised that his position was likely to make him the object of assassination attempts. In January 1919 he told Long that he received threatening messages 'from supposed "Hidden Channels" ', and added that he always welcomed such threats 'as the best proofs we can have that our action is being severely felt'.[69] French was a target of obvious propaganda value. The IRA leader Dan Breen stressed that there was no personal animosity against him, but: 'His name was known throughout the civilised world [and] we knew that his death would arouse all peoples to take notice of our fight for freedom.'[70]

On 19 December 1919 the IRA came within measurable distance of killing French. He had spent a few days at Drumdoe, and returned to Dublin by train, arriving at Ashtown Gate station at about 1 p.m. French's party left the station in four cars, with the Field-Marshal himself riding in the first vehicle. As the convoy approached Kelly's Corner, near the entrance to Phoenix Park, a party of IRA men opened fire and threw grenades. The attack was foiled as much by the quick thinking of French's driver, Sergeant Anthony, as by confusion amongst the attackers as to the position of French's car in the convoy. The second car, which was believed to contain the Field-Marshal, was very badly damaged: one grenade burst on the back seat, and French would almost certainly have been killed had he been in the vehicle. As it was, he was lucky to escape unscathed. His personal detective, Detective-Sergeant Halley, who was sitting beside his driver, was wounded by small-arms fire, and other bullets penetrated his car.[71]

Letters congratulating the Lord Lieutenant on his escape poured into Viceregal Lodge. Ian Macpherson was particularly shocked by the attempt, and was nettled by Lloyd George's laconic comment: 'They are bad shots.'[72] The ambush helped to persuade Chief Secretary and Cabinet that firmer measures were required. Long had already drawn up a memorandum which stated that the Irish government could impose martial law whenever it pleased, without reference to the Cabinet, and on 30 December Lloyd George informed French that this 'fairly represents our attitude'.[73]

January 1920 saw the extension of the army's involvement in the struggle. Military authorities now took over responsibility for initiating action against insurgents, and interning suspects under DORA 14B on warrants signed by the Chief Secretary. French capitalised on Macpherson's horror at the assassination attempt to press him for as many internment warrants as he could get, and he assured the Chief Secretary that there would be no reaction from the Cabinet, 'so long as we refrain from arresting people like Arthur Griffiths and others simply for making seditious speeches'.[74]

French's hopes that the army's increased participation in the campaign would produce quick results proved illusory. Both he and Shaw overemphasised Sinn Fein's dependence on its leaders, and the army's intelligence was too sketchy to permit it to operate effectively against opponents who were themselves winning the hearts and minds of the Irish people. French also reckoned without the Cabinet's havering. It was one thing for the Lord Lieutenant to demand what amounted to a free hand to take military action against Sinn Fein, but quite another for Lloyd George, whose aim remained a political settlement, to support his militant viceroy in policies which might make a settlement more difficult to achieve.

Nowhere was the divergence of policies better demonstrated than in the case of hunger-strikers amongst the Sinn Fein prisoners. French was opposed to temporary release under the 'Cat-and-Mouse' Act — the Prisoners (Temporary Discharge for ill-health) Act of 1913 — and recommended that the government should 'boldly proclaim that after proper food has been provided people will simply be allowed to die'.[75] The arrests of January 1920 produced a new wave of hunger-strikes, and French came under pressure, in Bonar Law's words, 'to try and save the government's face ... '[76] On the morning of 14 April French had a lengthy conference with his advisers, and eventually decided to release the prisoners on parole: he resented the fact that the government had favoured conciliation rather than coercion, and later complained to Long that this 'surrender to hunger-strikers' had raised Sinn Fein morale.[77]

In April 1920 the Cabinet decided upon changes of policy which were to have far-reaching effects as far as French's position was concerned. Macpherson, whose fragile health was unequal to the strain of fighting the current Home Rule Bill through its committee stages, resigned and was replaced by Sir Hamar Greenwood, a tough Canadian Liberal, well summed up as being 'a man of one idea at a time'. Sir Nevil Macready, who had foresaken khaki for dark blue to become Commissioner of the Metropolitan Police in the autumn of 1918, was offered the post of GOC Ireland in place of Shaw, on the grounds that his unique mixture of military and police experience would prove invaluable. He accepted with reluctance, and maintained that it was only French's appeal which persuaded him to serve in a country he hated.[78] French regarded Macready's appointment with mixed feelings. He recognised that the latter's police experience would indeed be useful, but he felt that Shaw was being shabbily treated, and did his best to ensure that he received full recompense for his time in Ireland.[79] There had been some talk of Robertson being appointed to the post, but French made no secret of the fact that he would rather not have him. Robertson was eventually compensated with a Field-Marshal's baton on retirement, a promotion which struck Henry Wilson as 'very disgusting'.[80]

The appointment of Greenwood heralded the end of the Lord Lieutenant's supremacy, and it soon became clear that the relationship between Lord Lieutenant and Chief Secretary had reverted to its pre-1918 pattern. In July Walter Long tactfully explained to French that 'there has been a change in arrangements as compared with what was laid down when Your Excellency first went to Ireland'.[81] Although French denied that he was aware of any such change, he went on to assure Long that:

> I have always regarded the Chief Secretary as the responsible Minister ... I am rather at a loss to understand why you should think I want to take action without the sanction of the Chief Secretary. I have taken no active part in political matters for the last two months; and I think it is much better that I should not do so now.[82]

The old Field-Marshal was quite definitely eclipsed, but he was almost past caring. When Liberal H. A. L. Fisher met him in late July he recorded that he was only 'a shadow of his former self and quite useless'.[83]

Reduced to the status of little more than a figurehead, French continued to offer advice to the government and to use what powers he still possessed in what he saw as the interests of Ireland. He was more than ever convinced that 'drastic measures' should be adopted, suggesting that the Ulster Volunteers should be called upon to assist with the preservation of order, and that martial law should be declared throughout the country:

> We should take up the war-like challenge which the Sinn Feiners have sent us and declare war against them. With fifty or sixty thousand British troops, reinforced by the Ulster Volunteers, I think there is no doubt whatever as to the result.[84]

He wrote bitterly of Greenwood's conciliatory policy. 'I suppose you have heard of a well-known member of the Irish Privy Council called Frank Brooke?' he asked Churchill.

> He was shot dead in his office at Westland Row this morning. Yesterday night three military patrols were overcome in the centre of Dublin ... And yet on top of this somebody writes from Dublin Castle and says that 'the political atmosphere' is much improved ... In my mind I am convinced that 'force' is the only power that will ever solve the Irish question; and I am equally convinced that if applied at once and efficiently it would solve the question in a very short space of time.[85]

He lamented to the King that Irish affairs showed no ray of light: there was only 'a long and painful story of murder, intrigue and outrage'. Although he welcomed the Restoration of Order in Ireland Act, designed by Greenwood as a modification of DORA, he feared that it did not go far enough.[86]

Macready, who had initially not been in favour of martial law eventually came close to sharing French's view of the subject. On 4 October French recorded that the Commander-in-Chief 'is in fact coming round to my opinion as to the necessity for much more drastic measures and has written a memo to that effect'.[87] In the memorandum Macready suggested that the government should either impose martial law throughout Ireland, or acknowledge that a state of insurrection existed, and would require similar measures to martial law.[88] On 1 December the Cabinet authorised the Chief Secretary to apply martial law in those areas where he considered it appropriate, and the first proclamations were signed ten days later. But obstacles still remained. There was legal confusion over the status and implications of martial law, and the system was never applied uniformly throughout Ireland. And although Macready had more troops than Shaw – there were 51 battalions in the country in early 1921 – he too was handicapped by the low numbers of most units and the large quantity of young soldiers. The police were also labouring under numerous difficulties. The appointment of a police co-ordinator had failed to improve police discipline, and the recruitment of large numbers of non-Irishmen, who had little interest in police work properly speaking, led to a decline in standards.[89]

In the early part of 1921 the Cabinet came to the conclusion that, as Macready put it, 'there was no half-way house between complete Home Rule and permanent military occupation'.[90] The cost of the campaign was too great, and a political settlement became regarded as a means of achieving peace, rather than a measure which would follow the restoration of order.[91] With elections under the Government of Ireland Act in the offing, French was an uncomfortable reminder of the past. On 23 March he saw Greenwood at the House of Commons, and realised that he would probably have to give up the Lord Lieutenancy 'in a very few weeks'.[92]

On the 30th a special message from the Prime Minister arrived by aircraft. French was to relinquish his post at the end of April, and was to be succeeded by Lord Edmund Talbot, who, as a Catholic, would be more acceptable to Irish opinion. Lloyd George congratulated him on his 'resolution and fearlessness', and told him that he would be advanced a step in the peerage.[93] French was 68, and had aged appreciably over the past year, but he did not find the prospect of retirement altogether appealing. 'I was grieved at first', he wrote, 'by this sudden wrench from work but on the whole I am glad. It is delightful to be succeeded by so old and tried a friend as E. T.'[94]

It is perhaps surprising that French had survived at Vice-regal Lodge for as long as he had. Wilson and Macready had agreed that he was likely to be replaced in the spring of 1920. 'I think Johnny French won't last much longer', wrote Wilson on 1 April. 'Poor little man he is so weak and pliable and then has such inconsequential gusts of illogical passion. He is an Imperialist, a Democrat, a Home Ruler all at the same time. Poor man.'[95] But whatever French's limitations from Wilson's standpoint, he was not without his uses even after April 1920. He remained committed to the creation of a peaceful Ireland, and made no secret of his own intention to live in the country after independence. He was, as Wilson was the first to admit, 'brave as a lion', and he enjoyed a substantial personal following even amongst those who disagreed with his policies.

French was, though, something of an expensive luxury. His

private life remained colourful even by the vivid standards of the day. Mrs Bennett visited Viceregal Lodge on a number of occasions and when the Field-Marshal departed to the South of France on leave from Ireland, he shared the delights of Cannes with Winifred.[96]

And it was not only French's private life that gave the Cabinet cause for concern. In February 1917 two attacks had been made on French's conduct of the retreat from Mons. Smith-Dorrien gave the *Weekly Dispatch* an interview which emerged as 'How the Old British Army Died', and a special reserve gunner, Major A. Corbett-Smith, published *The Retreat From Mons*. It was Corbett-Smith's misfortune to find himself commanding a battery in England, and therefore under French's command, when his book appeared. French drew his Adjutant-General's attention to Corbett-Smith's offering, and the ensuing investigation revealed that Smith-Dorrien had worked on the proofs. French regarded this as evidence that Sir Horace 'had personally inspired the whole book', and he determined to reply in kind.[97]

Lovat Fraser, a well-established *Times* journalist who had edited the *Times of India* until his return to England in 1906, was the chosen instrument. French spent a great deal of time with Fraser during 1917, and the result, which was to be *1914*, was very much of a co-production. Early in 1919 Edmonds, the official historian of the war, was approached by 'a clean and tidy widow' who was helping Fraser. 'I gathered from officers of French's staff', wrote Edmonds, 'that the field-marshal sat in an armchair and talked to his ghost and was questioned by him, a shorthand writer taking down what was said.'[98] Edmonds was perhaps overstating the case, for the French Papers contain parts of *1914* in French's hand. But they also reveal the extent of Fraser's collaboration, for there is a note attached to some papers which declares: 'This is written just as though you had dictated it in a conversational way (as indeed you did). LF.'

1914 first appeared in serial form in the *Daily Telegraph* in April and May 1919. It brought French more brickbats than bouquets. Stamfordham informed him that the King was 'much concerned' about the articles, and there was a chilly interview after which the unrepentant author admitted that 'I don't think I made things much better'.[99] The politicians then joined in. Summoned by Bonar Law, acting as Prime Minister in Lloyd George's absence, French was warned that if his action 'was debated in the H of C he could not undertake to *defend* it: but he would do his best for me and the government would not ask me to resign unless a vote of the House compelled them to do so'.[100] Lord Bertie pointed out some errors in French's account of the 1 September 1914 meeting, and Midleton begged French not to become involved in more literary disputes without submitting his work to some independent authority for vetting.[101]

French justified his action by claiming that he was not employed in his capacity as Field-Marshal when the articles appeared, and he pointed out that Field-Marshals Wolseley, Roberts and Wood had all ventured into print. 'If I have erred', he concluded, 'I can only plead inexperience of Government official life and express my deep regret.'[102] Others also expressed regret at the appearance of the articles and their subsequent publication in book form. Asquith defended himself with vigour, and Smith-Dorrien was only dissuaded from doing so by the Army Council. In October Sir John Fortescue examined *1914* in the *Quarterly Review*. Pronouncing it 'one of the most unfortunate books that was ever written', he accused its author of 'misstatements and misrepresentations of the clumsiest and most ludicrous kind'. Fortescue finished with an outspoken tirade against French. 'No accumulation of titles, batons, grants, orders or decorations', he declaimed, 'can ever fit him to stand in the company of such men as Ralph Abercromby, John Moore, Rowland Hill and Thomas Graham.'[103] The viciousness of Fortescue's attack, which was, it was suggested, not unconnected with the Field-Marshal's dismissal of Fortescue's brother from his command of a brigade in France, swung opinion in the Field-Marshal's favour, and a second edition of the book rectified some of the more serious errors.[104]

There can be no doubt that *1914* was designed as a piece of propaganda and that perhaps not all its errors were accidental. The process of partial ghosting introduced other mistakes, and French's fears that Smith-Dorrien's supporters were sharpening their quills for new endeavours did not encourage moderation. But much of the book undoubtedly contained what

French genuinely believed to be the truth. He sent the proofs of the first chapters to Spears, for whom he had a high regard, inviting comment, an action he would hardly have taken had he consciously twisted the facts. [105] For the most part *1914* was an account of events as French remembered them: by the time the book was written, however, French's memory and objective history were not necessarily the same thing.

Epilogue

Kingstown Quay to Ripple Church
April 1921–May 1925

On 29 April 1921 French took his leave of the generals and staff of Irish Command in the great hall of the Royal Hospital, Dublin. Next morning Macready drove down to Kingstown Quay with him: the Field-Marshal, wearing the uniform of Colonel of the Irish Guards – his predecessors in the post had been Roberts and Kitchener – inspected a guard of honour found by the Wiltshire Regiment, bade Macready an emotional farewell, and stepped aboard the mail boat that took him out of official life for ever.[1]

The congratulatory letters which descended upon French in an avalanche paid tribute to his courage and tenacity in Ireland, and revealed that he still exercised that curious charm which many of those who knew his failings all too well still found irresistible. Macready told him that 'your approbation is more to me than I think that of any other person I have come across in my professional career', and admitted that 'your safety was the greatest anxiety ... that I had upon my shoulders'.[2] George Macdonogh, now a Lieutenant-General, asked for a photograph of 'the best chief I ever had the good fortune to serve', and a host of other eminent men, civilians and soldiers, congratulated French on his safe return.[3]

French's retirement was busy. He was much in demand as a speaker at ex-servicemen's gatherings, and in 1922 and 1923 he paid long visits to the battlefields of Flanders and Northern France. When the 19th Hussars were threatened with disbandment in the spring of 1921 he fought hard for his old regiment, begging Wilson 'as my good friend to do all you can to help me in this matter'.[4] The regiment survived, albeit at the price of amalgamation with the 15th to form the 15th/19th The King's Royal Hussars. The Royal Irish Regiment, of which French was Colonel-in-Chief, was less fortunate: it was disbanded, along with the other four Southern Irish regiments, in 1922.

The Field-Marshal initially lived in London, but hoped to return to Ireland to end his days. He purchased another country house, Hollybrook near Boyle, but soon discovered that conditions in Ireland were far too disturbed to permit him to live either there or at Drumdoe. In March 1922 Edmund Talbot told him frankly that there was no possibility of his moving to Ireland in the immediate future. The Lord Lieutenant warned him:

> Now I consider that your presence in Ireland would now be a disturbing factor ... the very fact of the presence of an ex Viceroy would be a real temptation to these gentlemen ...
>
> If I am wrong and the Republicans win, then there is a bust up and neither you nor I nor any of our friends can stay here.

Even if French slipped across to Viceregal Lodge, he was on no account to risk the journey up to Roscommon.[5]

Worse was to follow. Early in 1923 Drumdoe was raided by a party of armed men, who carried off most of the furniture, pictures and cutlery in horse-drawn carts. T. M. Healy, Governor-General of the Free State, commiserated with French over the attack, and assured him that 'a proper guard will be posted in future'. He ended with the hope that it would soon be possible 'for your Lordship to feel free to take up residence and your further enjoyments in this country'.[6]

French found himself in the unenviable position of having two country houses in Ireland and being unable to live in either. The troubles had made such properties a drug on the market, and French had insufficient capital to purchase a suitable residence in England. It was, alas, all too typical of French's financial acumen that, at the end of a successful and lucrative career, he found himself short of money. The very act of becoming an Earl was far from cheap: French protested vigorously at having to pay stamp duty on his letters patent, and became Earl of Ypres with rather a bad grace.[7] Parliament had granted him £50,000 in 1916, and he continued to receive Field-Marshal's half-pay, but he eventually left only £8,450 net in his will. While some of the money was spent on his Irish properties, large sums were swallowed up by an expensive life-style, which included lengthy stays at the Hotel Crillon, Paris, which was scarcely an appropriate establishment for old gentlemen in financial straits.

French's friendship with George Moore seems to have ended during his time in Ireland, possibly as a result of political disagreements. It was Moore who had financed 94 Lancaster Gate, and with Moore's return to America French found himself without a permanent residence in England. In August 1923 Lord Beauchamp, Lord Warden of the Cinque Ports, offered French the appointment of Captain of Deal Castle. The post was purely honorary, but it gave the Field-Marshal the right of residing in the castle, and he at once set about having his surviving furniture moved over from Drumdoe. It was hardly a bijou residence: Allenby, French's successor there, found it difficult to furnish and impossible to keep warm, but it did provide French with a *pied à terre* to which he could return when the Crillon and its bills grew wearing.[8]

Lady French had not followed her husband to Ireland – the official excuse was that it was too dangerous – and she saw little of him after his return. French had been estranged from his family for several years, but in 1922 he re-established contact with his second son Gerald, who had won a DSO during the war and was currently deputy governor of Dartmoor Prison. Gerald grew close to his father during the last years of his life, and it was he, rather than French's eldest son Dick, who defended his father's reputation with dogged tenacity until his own death in 1970. Dick, who was to succeed as second Earl of Ypres, was a quiet and likeable man whose military career had been cut short by a riding accident. He was a talented artist, a fact which did not endear him to the Field-Marshal, who would have preferred enterprise of a more martial kind. Dick's military pictures were particularly good, but they were small compensation to the old Field-Marshal. French's affair with Winifred Bennett had diminished in intensity. Perhaps he was now too old for such a passionate relationship, or perhaps he had tired of the beautiful Winifred as he had of so many mistresses in the past. But the old man's zest for life was as strong as ever. He enjoyed a lively social round in Paris, and wintered on the Riviera, staying with Lady Wavertree at the Villa Edelweiss at Cannes.

Late in 1924, French began to experience persistent abdominal pain while he was in France, and a surgeon there carried out an operation which appeared to be successful. The trouble recurred in March 1925, and another operation took place, this time in England. French was optimistic, and on 18 March he told Gerald: 'they are going to cut me open tomorrow, but I don't think it is anything serious.'[9] The operation, carried out by Sir John Atkins, was long and complex, and although French was confident about its result, announcing 'thank God I've got over it', his condition worsened, and newspapers spoke euphemistically of 'a grave internal malady'. George V was more frank. On 13 May he recorded: 'I paid poor Ypres (French) a visit in Nursing Home in Vincent Square. I fear he can't live long, he has cancer in the bladder, he looks very ill.'[10]

Four days later French was moved down to Deal Castle, ostensibly for a change of air, but really because he had asked to be taken home to die. He rallied on arrival at Deal, and, propped up in bed near a window, returned the salutes of old soldiers who had gathered to wait for news. The rally proved short-lived. French lapsed into semi-consciousness on the 21st, and died on the evening of the 22nd. He had fought his final battle with characteristic courage, and his last coherent words were a declaration that he felt 'much better'.[11]

French had expressed the wish to be cremated and, after cremation at Golders Green, his ashes were placed in an oak coffin which lay in state in the Guards Chapel, Wellington Barracks. An estimated seven thousand people, most of them old soldiers, filed past the coffin during the first two hours of the lying-in-state. Journalists recorded some of their comments. 'I didn't mind living on biscuits for six weeks for him', remarked a bus conductor who had been wounded at Mons. 'It meant a stiff tramp back,' said another veteran, who had marched in from the suburbs, 'but we had to say good-bye to the general'.[12]

On 26 May a funeral service was held at Westminster Abbey, after which the coffin was carried on a gun carriage to Victoria Station for its journey to Ripple. It was the first funeral of a major First World War leader, and the ceremonial was lavish. Old Joffre was there, looking unusually slim in his old age, and Haig, Robertson, Ian Hamilton and the Duke of Connaught were amongst the pall-bearers. Smith-Dorrien was also a pall-bearer, and it was a measure of his magnanimity that he travelled from France to attend the funeral of a man with whom he had so often clashed.[13] The cortège wound its way between crammed pavements. Spectators stood twelve deep outside the Abbey, and the whole route was thickly lined with those who had come to pay their last respects. The majority of them were men, who stood stiff and hatless as the coffin passed. Some wept unashamedly: not so much for their old chief, perhaps, as for their own youths and for a past which now seemed as remote as the long aching summer of '14.

French's military reputation was already under fire even before his coffin was lowered into the Kentish soil at Ripple on 27 May 1925. The appearance of Edmonds's *Official History* did nothing to enhance it; Duff Cooper's creditable *Haig* revealed the full dimensions of the French–Haig controversy; and Alan Clark's *The Donkeys* completed the process of destruction begun by Corbett-Smith over forty years before. Gerald French's attempts to defend his father were gallant but ill-considered, and although some recent monographs have paid glancing tribute to French's activities in the period between the Boer War and the First World War, he nevertheless remains a discredited man.

History has dealt too harshly with French. His manifest failings have received more than their fair share of attention, while his achievements have sunk into obscurity. As a cavalry leader he was, as John Terraine rightly points out, the most distinguished Englishman since Cromwell.[14] French's work at Aldershot Command and as Inspector-General of the Forces was of genuine and lasting importance, and his attempt to solve the problems of the Ireland he loved had at least the merits of absolute sincerity and self-denial.

If victory is the most reasonable criterion of military success, then French must be acknowledged a failure on the Western

Front in 1914–15. Indeed, it may well be argued that French's temperament and experience made him totally unsuited for command of the BEF. But even in this sphere his achievements were not unremarkable. Whatever French's failings as Commander-in-Chief in August and September 1914, it was his personality that animated the BEF in its hour of trial; Robertson, much as he admired Haig, was compelled to admit that no other general could have held the army together as French did. And the problems faced by French were far harder than those which confronted his successor: it was French who sustained the first onslaught, in new and strange conditions, when the BEF was at its weakest and the enemy at his strongest.[15]

French was not a great general. He was a brave man and a good cavalry leader, and cared deeply about his profession. But in many respects he never transcended the nineteenth century, and his attempts to solve the tactical and strategic conundrums of 1914–15 were fatally marred by his undisciplined intellect and mercurial personality. Yet he should not be allowed to sink, disdained, into oblivion. Even those who knew him warts and all agreed that, whatever his shortcomings as tactician, strategist, or indeed, politician, 'French, in the sacred fire of leadership, was unsurpassed ... '[16]

Notes

Introduction

1 Edmonds Papers 111/8 and 111/10, Liddell Hart Centre for Military Archives, King's College, London.
2 Gough to an unknown staff officer, 29 January 1916, Imperial War Museum.
3 Robert Blake (ed.), *The Private Papers of Douglas Haig 1914–19* (London, 1952), pp. 93–4, 105.
4 Ibid., p. 170.
5 Chetwode to Lord Wigram, regarding Duff Cooper's *Haig*, 29 August 1935, Royal Archives GV P564/54.
6 Macready to Macpherson, 11 January 1919, Strathcarron Papers, Bodleian Library MS Eng Hist C490.
7 Colonel J. W. B. Parkin to French, 29 September 1906, French Papers.
8 Seely to French, 19 November 1915, ibid.
9 Haldane to French, 16 December 1916, ibid.
10 M. V. Brett (ed.), *The Journals and Letters of Reginald Viscount Esher* (London, 1934: 4 vols), I, p. 380.
11 Ibid., II, pp. 58, 70–1.
12 Ibid., III, p. 293.
13 Ibid., IV, p. 49.
14 Asquith to French, 21 May 1915, French Papers.
15 H. H. Asquith, *The Great Shell Story: Mr. Asquith's reply to Lord French* (London, 1919), pp. 9–10.
16 D. Lloyd George, *The War Memoirs of David Lloyd George* (London, 1938: 2 vols) II, pp. 1419, 2031.
17 Churchill to French, 1 January 1915, French Papers.
18 Churchill to French, 12 December 1915, ibid.
19 Churchill to French, 6 May 1921, ibid.
20 Winston S. Churchill, *Great Contemporaries* (London, 1937), p. 84.
21 J. W. Fortescue, 'Review of Field-Marshal Lord French's *1914*', *Quarterly Review*, October, 1919, p. 363.
22 A. J. Smithers, *The Man who Disobeyed: Sir Horace Smith-Dorrien and His Enemies* (London, 1970).

23 Lord Crewe to Seely, 5 September 1913, Mottistone Papers, Nuffield College Oxford MSS 17/224.
24 See George Cassar, *Kitchener: Architect of Victory* (London, 1977), and John Terraine, *Douglas Haig: The Educated Soldier* (London, 1963), especially pp. 160–7.
25 Alan Clark, *The Donkeys* (London, 1961), p. 20.
26 Survey compiled by Mr Keith Simpson, Department of War Studies, RMA Sandhurst.
27 Norman Dixon, *On the Psychology of Military Incompetence* (London, 1976), p. 172.
28 Brian Bond, *The Victorian Army and The Staff College* (London, 1972), pp. 301, 313.

Prologue

1 A manuscript copy of the order, in Haig's hand, is in *Diary of the Operations of the Cavalry in Natal, 20 October–2 November 1899*, Haig Papers, National Library of Scotland Acc 3155/35.
2 For general accounts of the action see L. S. Amery (ed), *The Times History of the War in South Africa* (London, 1900–9: 7 vols), II, pp. 175–95, Major-General Sir F. Maurice and Captain H. M. Grant, *Official History of the War in South Africa* (London, 1906–10: 4 vols of text, 4 of maps), I, pp. 157–71, and Thomas Pakenham, *The Boer War* (London, 1979), pp. 132–41. See also G. W. Steevens, *From Cape Town to Ladysmith* (London, 1900), pp. 56–65, Anon., *Pen Picture of the War* (London, 1900), pp. 54–66, and *The Times* 13 December 1899.
3 General Sir N. Macready, *Annals of an Active Life* (London, 1924: 2 vols), p. 79.
4 French *Diary* 21 October 1899, quoted in Gerald French (ed.) *Some War Diaries, Addresses and Correspondence* ... (London, 1937), p. 13. French's extant manuscript diaries, in the Imperial War Museum, do not begin until March 1900.
5 French to Mrs Bennett, 21 October 1915, French Papers.

Chapter 1   Light Cavalry, 1852–99

1 I am indebted to Major Antony Mallaby for information on French's ancestry. See also John D'Alton, *Memoir of the Family of French* (Dublin, 1847), and *Burke's Peerage* (London, 1963), p. 2642.
2 See Andrö Linklater, *An Unhusbanded Life* (London, 1980).

3 An account of her funeral is to be found in the *Daily Sketch*, 24 March 1917.

4 See Mary Colum, *Life and The Dream* (London, 1947), for recollections concerning Lottie Despard and Maud Gonne. Her story that the latter had been French's mistress lacks firm foundation.

5 French started an autobiography which never got beyond his early career. The original draft is in the French Papers, and frequent quotations are made by Major the Hon. Gerald French in *The Life of Field-Marshal Sir John French, First Earl of Ypres* (hereafter referred to as French, *Life*) (London, 1931), p. 5.

6 Ibid.

7 Ibid., pp. 8–9.

8 Ibid., p. 10.

9 Ibid., p. 14.

10 Ibid., p. 18.

11 Cecil Chisholm, *Sir John French: An Authentic Biography* (London, 1915), p. 5.

12 The Marquess of Anglesey, *A History of the British Cavalry, 1816–1919* (London, 1973–5: two vols published, one in preparation). II, p. 330.

13 French, *Life*, p. 20.

14 Anglesey, op. cit., II, p. 366.

15 Ibid., p. 370, and Field-Marshal Sir Evelyn Wood, 'British Cavalry 1853–1903', *Cavalry Journal*, I, 1906, p. 153.

16 Chisholm, op. cit., p. 6.

17 See particularly French to Sir Charles Boxall, 20 October 1901, Watt Papers; and French to Buller, 15 July 1902, quoted by Major the Hon. Gerald French in *Some War Diaries ...* , p. 95. (Hereafter referred to as *War Diaries*).

18 The Central Register Office at Somerset House furnished certified transcripts of French's Marriage Certificate and Decree Absolute. Major Antony Mallaby and Mr Edward Lydall provided information concerning French's relations with his brother-in-law. See also the latter's *Lydall of Uxmore* (London, 1980).

19 French, *Life*, pp. 20–1.

20 Chisholm, op. cit., p. 8.

21 General Sir E. B. Hamley, *The Operations of War* (London, 1866). Hamley's work was essentially in the Jominian tradition, seeking to illustrate permanently valid principles from the study of past operations. See Brian Bond, *The Victorian Army and the Staff College* (London, 1972), p. 87.

22 Interview with the late Lady Essex French 25 July 1977. See also French, *Life*, p. 37.
23 I am indebted to the Marquess of Anglesey for information on the September 1877 mutiny in the 19th.
24 See Colonel John Biddulph, *The Nineteenth and their Times* (London, 1899), pp. 291–9.
25 French, *Life*, p. 21.
26 Ibid., pp. 24–5.
27 Quoted, ibid., p. 23.
28 French to Mrs Edith Watts, 26 December 1882; letter in the possession of Lady Patricia Kingsbury.
29 See Biddulph, op. cit., pp. 233–46.
30 Bond, op. cit., p. 95.
31 General Sir Ian Hamilton, in Major A. Farrar-Hockley (ed.), *The Commander* (London, 1957), p. 50.
32 Bond, op. cit., pp. 97, 107.
33 Field-Marshal Sir William Robertson, *From Private to Field-Marshal* (London, 1921), pp. 88–90.
34 Biddulph, op. cit., p. 247.
35 Count Gleichen, *With the Camel Corps up the Nile* (London, 1888), p. 64.
36 Ibid., pp. 72–3.
37 Sir Charles Wilson, *From Korti to Khartoum* (London, 1886), p. 97.
38 For a notable exception see T. Pakenham, *The Boer War*, pp. xvii, 457–8.
39 M. V. Brett (ed.), *Journals and Letters of Reginald Viscount Esher* (London, 1934: 4 vols), I, p. 245.
40 Field-Marshal Viscount Wolseley, *The Story of a Soldier's Life* (London, 1903: 2 vols), II, p. 279.
41 French to Buller, 15 July 1902, in French, *War Diaries*, p. 95.
42 French, *Life*, p. 35.
43 Field-Marshal Sir Evelyn Wood, *From Midshipman to Field-Marshal* (London, 1906: 2 vols) II, p. 177.
44 Quoted in Biddulph, op. cit., p. 256.
45 Lieutenant-Colonel the Hon. E. G. French, *Goodbye to Boot and Saddle* (London, 1951), p. 18.
46 Ibid., p. 23 and French, *Life*, p. 38.
47 General Sir Hubert Gough, *Soldiering On* (London, 1954), p. 36.
48 Sir Evelyn Wood, op. cit., II, p. 208.
49 Sir William Robertson, op. cit., p. 38.
50 Sir George Barrow, *The Fire of Life* (London, nd), p. 34.

51 Sir Hubert Gough, op. cit., p. 43.
52 Inspector-General of Cavalry, India, to Adjutant-General, India, 7 February 1893, in India Office Records, L/MIL/7/1534.
53 Field-Marshal Lord Birdwood, *Khaki and Gown* (London, 1941), p. 68.
54 Frewen to Haldane, 1 October 1907, in Haldane Papers, National Library of Scotland MSS 5905.
55 See Moreton Frewen, *Melton Mowbray and Other Memories* (London, nd), and Anita Leslie's more stimulating *Mr. Frewen of England* (London, 1966). The latter book notes the Frewen–French controversy, and Stephen Frewen's pamphlet, *The Case of Stephen Frewen and the War Office*, but makes no mention of Frewen's attempt to blackmail Haldane.
56 There was also a dark but unsubstantiated rumour connecting French with the daughter of an Anglo-Indian railway official, as well as a suggestion that French, while a junior officer, had an affair with his own Commanding Officer's wife: for the latter see Rayne Kruger, *Good-bye Dolly Gray* (London, 1964), p. 81. These may simply have been canards put about by French's enemies, but there is no doubt whatever concerning his involvement in the Indian divorce.
57 French, *Life*, pp. 47–8.
58 *Pall Mall Budget: Special Cavalry Number*, 11 October 1894.
59 Chisholm, op. cit., pp. 26–7.
60 On balance, it seems likely that Luck's influence was, in this instance, more significant than Buller's. Buller had been Adjutant-General since 1890, whereas French's appointment coincided with Luck's arrival as Inspector-General of Cavalry.
61 Major E. W. Shephard, *The Ninth Queen's Royal Lancers 1715–1936* (Aldershot, 1939).
62 See Duff Cooper, *Haig* (London, 1935: 2 vols), I, pp. 43–6.
63 Interview with the late Lady Essex French, 25 July 1977, and French, *Life*, p. 51.
64 R. Blake (ed.), *The Private Papers of Douglas Haig 1914–19* (London, 1952), p. 37.
65 Cooper, op. cit., vol. I, pp. 99–100.

Chapter 2 Carving a Reputation: South Africa, 1899

1 Haig, *Diary*, 23 September 1899, Haig Papers, National Library of Scotland, Acc 3155.
2 See T. Pakenham, *The Boer War*, pp. 96–7, and R. Kruger,

Good-bye Dolly Gray, pp. 51, 73. For the uncertainty surrounding French's appointment see Haig, Diary, 10–11 October 1899.

3 Pakenham, op. cit., p. 5.
4 Quoted, ibid., p. 64.
5 Ibid., p. 97.
6 Major-General Sir F. Maurice and Captain H. M. Grant, *Official History of the War in South Africa* (hereafter referred to as *Official History*), I, pp. 457–9. L. S. Amery (ed.), *The Times History of the War in South Africa* (hereafter referred to as *Times History*), II, p. 88 gives a mobilisation total of 37,000–40,000 men and an all-up figure of 60,000–65,000.
7 *Official History*, I, pp. 91–5.
8 Ibid., p. 90.
9 See Colonel J. K. Dunlop, *The Development of the British Army 1899–1914* (London, 1938), Part I. Although outdated in some respects, Dunlop's study of the period leading up to the Boer War remains the best general account of the British Army at this time.
10 *Official History*, I, p. 90.
11 See Dunlop, op. cit., Part I, *passim*, and Bond, *The Victorian Army*, p. 146.
12 See a concise account in Correlli Barnett, *Britain and Her Army* (London, 1970), pp. 353–4.
13 Haig, Diary, 10 October 1899.
14 Ibid., 11 October 1899.
15 Pakenham, op. cit., p. 126.
16 French to Chief of Staff, Natal Field Force, 1 p.m. 20 October 1899, in *Diary of the Operations of the Cavalry in Natal*, Haig Papers, National Library of Scotland, Acc 3155.
17 Chief of Staff to French, 1.20 p.m. 20 October 1899, ibid.
18 *Official History*, I, p. 159.
19 Ibid., p. 160.
20 *Diary of the Operations*, 21 October 1899, Haig Papers; *Official History*, I, p. 160.
21 French to Chief of Staff, 7.10 a.m., 21 October 1899, *Diary of the Operations*, Haig Papers.
22 French to Chief of Staff, 9 a.m., ibid.
23 French to Chief of Staff, 12.15 p.m., ibid.
24 French to Chief of Staff, 1 p.m., ibid.
25 *Times History*, II, p. 179.
26 For accounts of Elandslaagte generally see *Official History*, I, pp. 157–71. *Times History*, II, pp. 175–95 and Pakenham, op. cit., pp. 132–41. It is difficult to disentangle precise details of the arrival of the various elements of French's force: where possible,

the evidence of *Diary of the Operations*, Haig Papers, has been used to illuminate the matter.

27 *Official History*, I, p. 164.
28 French to Gore, *Diary of the Operations*, Haig Papers.
29 *Times History*, II, p. 188.
30 *Official History*, I, p. 464, *Times History*, II, pp. 194–5.
31 Erskine Childers, *War and the Arme Blanche* (London, 1910), p. 67.
32 *Official History*, I, p. 185.
33 Cooper, *Haig*, I, p. 74.
34 Ibid., I, pp. 381–2.
35 *Official History*, I, p. 200–3.
36 Ibid., p. 277.
37 Ibid., pp. 278–9.
38 Ibid., p. 278 and *Times History*, II, p. 123.
39 Telegrams, Buller to Forestier-Walker, 26 and 27 November 1899, in *Official History*, I, p. 279, and Haig, Diary, 27 November 1899.
40 French, *War Diaries*, pp. 14–15.
41 *Official History*, I, p. 282.
42 Ibid., pp. 282–3.
43 Ibid., p. 283.
44 Pakenham, op. cit., pp. 242–3.
45 *Official History*, I, p. 389.
46 See C. S. Goldman, *With General French and the Cavalry in South Africa* (London, 1903), panoramas of Colesberg facing page 68.
47 *Times History*, II, p. 142.
48 Quoted in French, *Life*, p. 65.

Chapter 3   Cavalry Division: South Africa, 1900–2

1 *Cavalry Division Diary*, 10 February 1900, Haig Papers.
2 *Official History*, I, pp. 412–13.
3 Ibid., pp. 415–25, *Times History*, II, pp. 437–54.
4 *Official History*, II, pp. 428–33.
5 Ibid., pp. 436, footnote.
6 French Diary, 22 March 1900, French Papers.
7 T. Pakenham, *The Boer War*, pp. 318–20.
8 Haig, Diary 4 December 1899, Haig Papers.
9 Haig to his sister Henrietta, 16 March 1900, Haig Papers.
10 French to Kitchener 18 January 1900, quoted in Cooper, *Haig*,

I, p. 79. French seems to have by-passed Erroll almost completely. It was Haig who kept the Divisional War Diary, and all the orders for the Kimberley operation are signed by him.

11 *Official History*, I, pp. 436–7, *Times History*, III, pp. 369–70.
12 French, *Life*, pp. 69–70.
13 C. S. Goldman, *With General French and the Cavalry in South Africa*, p. 85.
14 *Official History*, II, pp. 18–20, *Times History*, III, pp. 382–3.
15 Cooper, *Haig*, I, p. 80.
16 Ibid., p. 81, *Official History*, II, p. 384.
17 Cooper, op. cit., p. 81.
18 Order of 13 February 1900, *Cavalry Division Diary*, Haig Papers.
19 French, *War Diaries*, 12 February 1900.
20 *Cavalry Division Diary*, 13 February 1900, Haig Papers.
21 *Official History*, II, pp. 26–7, *Times History*, III, p. 388.
22 *Times History*, III, p. 388.
23 *Cavalry Division Diary*, 15 February 1900, Haig Papers.
24 Sources differ as to the precise distance between files. Five yards is the distance given in the *Cavalry Division Diary* but Erskine Childers in *War and the Arme Blanche* (London, 1910) p. 100, suggests that there were eight yards between files. The difference is not without significance, for Childers was seeking to demonstrate that the cavalry's very open deployment was a prime ingredient of success.
25 *Times History*, III, pp. 394–5.
26 Childers, op. cit., p. 100.
27 Quoted, ibid., p. 107.
28 *Official History*, II, p. 36.
29 Goldman, op. cit., pp. 410–11.
30 The whole question of the *arme blanche* is more fully discussed in the following chapter.
31 Pakenham, op. cit., p. 328.
32 *Cavalry Division Diary*, 17 February 1900, Haig Papers.
33 *Official History*, II, pp. 88, 95, *Times History*, III, p. 408.
34 *Times History*, III, p. 413.
35 Official History, II, p. 88, 95, *Times History*, III, p. 408.
36 Kitchener to French, 16 February 1900, French Papers. Punctuation as in original.
37 *Times History*, III, pp. 416–17.
38 Ibid., p. 418.
39 Roberts to Kitchener, 17 February 1900, quoted in *Official History*, II, p. 104.

40 Philip Magnus, *Kitchener: Portrait of an Imperialist* (London, 1961), p. 164.
41 Ibid., p. 165.
42 French's message was carried to Kitchener by Major Lord Edmund Talbot, who was to succeed French as Lord-Lieutenant of Ireland in April 1921. See French, *Life*, pp. 87, 371.
43 *Official History*, II, pp. 143–4.
44 French to Kitchener, 18 February 1900, quoted in *Official History*, II, p. 122.
45 *Official History*, II, p. 178. The figure does not include African servants, or Boers who håd already dribbled into British lines to surrender.
46 Ibid., pp. 140–2.
47 *Report of His Majesty's Commissioners ... War in South Africa* (Elgin Commission) Cd 1789, 1903, French's evidence in *Minutes*, II, p. 304.
48 Ibid., pp. 304–5.
49 L. S. Amery, *My Political Life* (London, 1954: 3 vols) I, p. 299.
50 David James, *Lord Roberts* (London, 1954), p. 299.
51 *Official History*, II, p. 192, and D. S. MacDiarmid, *The Life of Lieutenant-General Sir James Moncrieff Grierson* (London, 1923), p. 154.
52 *Official History*, II, p. 197.
53 The argument is summarised in Childers, op. cit., pp. 134–48.
54 *Official History*, II, p. 207.
55 See particularly Major-General F. Smith, *Veterinary History of the War in South Africa* (London, 1919); *Army (Remounts) Reports ...* Cd 963, 1902; and *Proceedings of a Court of Enquiry on the Administration of the Army Remount Department ...* Cd 993, 1902.
56 Childers, op. cit., p. 141.
57 Haig to his sister Henrietta, 16 March 1900, Haig Papers.
58 Pakenham, op. cit., pp. 381–3.
59 French, Diary, 5 and 6 April 1900.
60 French, Diary, 13 April 1900.
61 Ibid., 5 April 1900.
62 Ibid., 14 April 1900.
63 *Times History*, IV, p. 112.
64 Ibid.
65 Goldman, op. cit., p. 221.
66 *Times History*, IV, p. 122.
67 Ibid., pp. 124–5.

68 Hamilton to Erskine Childers, 30 October 1910, Hamilton Papers, Liddell Hart Centre for Military Archives, King's College, London, 7/3/15.
69 *Times History*, IV, p. 126.
70 Pakenham, op. cit., pp. 424–5.
71 French, Diary, 17 May 1900.
72 Pakenham, op. cit., p. 381.
73 *Official History*, III, pp. 204–25.
74 French, Diary, 12 July 1900.
75 Ibid., 20 July 1900.
76 *Times History*, IV, p. 405.
77 French, *Diary*, 25 July 1900.
78 Ibid., 30 July, 1 August and 4 August 1900.
79 Ibid., 13 and 14 August 1900.
80 Ibid., 24 August 1900.
81 Ibid., 13 September 1900.
82 Macready, *Annals of an Active Life*, I, p. 93.
83 French, Diary, 13 September 1900.
84 Ibid., 10 November 1900.
85 Ibid., 11 November 1900.
86 Kitchener to Roberts, nd, quoted in Sir George Arthur, *Lord Kitchener* (London, 1920: 3 vols), III, p. 24, and Sir Harold Nicolson, *King George V* (London, 1953), p. 71.
87 French, Diary 4 and 6 February 1901.
88 Ibid., 8 June 1901.
89 Pakenham, op. cit., p. 514.
90 French, Diary, 8 June 1901, Haig's view was every bit as rigid as French's: see Haig to Brinsley Fitzgerald, 25 October 1901, in the Fitzgerald Papers, Imperial War Museum.
91 Milner to French, 30 December 1899, French Papers.
92 French, Diary, 8 July 1901.
93 Ibid., 10 July 1901.
94 Ibid., 28 July 1901.
95 Haig to Fitzgerald, 25 October 1901, Fitzgerald Papers, Imperial War Museum.
96 Ibid., 12 August 1901.
97 Ibid., 3 November 1901.
98 French to Roberts, 22 September 1901, Roberts Papers, National Army Museum 7101–23–30.
99 Kitchener to Roberts, 6 September 1901, Roberts Papers, National Army Museum 7101–23–33.
100 Kitchener to Roberts, 17 January 1902, ibid.
101 Kitchener to Roberts, 14 February 1902, ibid.

102 French to Fitzgerald, 14 march 1902, Fitzgerald Papers.
103 Hamilton, in Farrar-Hockley (ed.), *The Commander*, pp. 109, 133.
104 French, Diary, 1 and 2 June 1902.
105 Ibid., 20 June 1902.
106 French to Roberts, 27 October 1901, quoted in French *War Diaries*, p. 77.
107 French to Buller, 23 November 1901, quoted ibid., p. 81.
108 French to Sir Charles Boxall, 20 October 1901, Watt Papers, Lt-Col J. J. F. Scott.
109 French, Diary, 23 May 1902.

Chapter 4 The Dangerous Years, 1902–13

1 Lieutenant-Colonel the Hon. Gerald French, *The Kitchener–French Dispute: A Last Word* (Glasgow, 1960), pp. 18–19.
2 Sir Frederick Ponsonby, *Recollections of Three Reigns* (London, 1951), p. 319.
3 French, Diary, 13 June 1902.
4 P. Magnus, *Kitchener: Portrait of an Imperialist* (London, 1961), p. 136.
5 Sir George Arthur, *Lord Kitchener* (London, 1920), III, p. 22.
6 C. Chisholm, *Sir John French* (London, 1915), pp. 95–6.
7 Esher to Edward VII, 27 February 1903, RA W38/80.
8 John Gooch, *The Plans of War: the General Staff and British Military Strategy* (London, 1974), pp. 38–40.
9 Wilson, Diary, 10 and 11 February 1904, Wilson Papers, Imperial War Museum.
10 See David James, *Lord Roberts* (London, 1954), pp. 398–404.
11 *Richard Burton Haldane: An Autobiography* (London, 1924), pp. 180–4.
12 See Gooch, op. cit., and Nicholas D'Ombrain, *War Machinery and High Policy* (Oxford, 1973).
13 J. K. Dunlop, *The Development of the British Army 1899–1914* (London, 1938), pp. 253–87.
14 *Invasion of the British Isles* ... 22 October 1908, Public Record Office, CAB 2/2.
15 French to Fitzgerald, 10 May and 30 October 1901, Fitzgerald Papers.
16 French, *Life*, pp. 135–6.
17 French's notes on Major-General Stopford's memorandum, 24 January 1904, in RA W25/42.

18 French to Esher, 19 August 1904, French Papers.
19 M. V. Brett to French, 21 August 1904, French, *War Diaries*, p. 102.
20 French to Esher, 20 September 1904, ibid., pp. 103–4.
21 French to Esher, 23 November 1904, ibid., p. 104.
22 Haldane to French, on French's paper 'The New System versus the Old', 3 August 1906, French Papers.
23 Esher to Edward VII, 1 April 1906. M. V. Brett (ed.), *The Journals and Letters of Reginald Viscount Esher*, II, p. 150.
24 Quoted in Gooch, op. cit., pp. 48–9.
25 French, *Life*, p. 137.
26 French to Esher, 24 February 1904, French, *War Diaries*, p. 103.
27 French to Esher, 5 December 1904, French Papers.
28 French to Esher, 8 September 1904, French, *War Diaries*, p. 102.
29 Esher to French, 29 November 1904, French Papers.
30 French to Esher, 18 December 1904, French, *War Diaries*, p. 105.
31 Esher to French, 23 December 1904, French Papers.
32 French to Esher, 11 February 1905, French, *War Diaries*, pp. 105–6.
33 See French's undated report on the Household Cavalry, RA W21/101, and French to Ponsonby 23 June 1908, RA X34/433.
34 French to Esher, 7 September 1918, French Papers.
35 Esher to French, 23 August 1906, ibid.
36 Esher to French, 28 September 1906, ibid.
37 French to Esher, 29 September 1906, Brett (ed.), op. cit., II, p. 187.
38 Davidson to French, 18 September 1907, French Papers.
39 Esher's Journal, 2 January 1908, Brett (ed.), op. cit., II, p. 272.
40 *Memorandum on the Inspector-General's Department*, undated, but based on the War Office memorandum of 18 December 1907, War Office Library.
41 Gough, *Soldiering On*, p. 192.
42 Ibid.
43 French to Knollys, 10 September 1908, RA W28/56, 57. There is also a copy in the Haldane Papers: French was clearly trying to counterbalance the criticism which his action had raised in certain social circles.
44 *Annual Report of the Inspector-General of the Forces*, 1908, 1909, War Office Library.
45 Ibid., 1908.

46 Ibid., 1909.
47 Ibid., 1911.
48 *Report on the Canadian Forces and Defences*, 5 July 1910, War Office Library.
49 *Annual Report*, 1910, 1911, and French, *Life*, p. 178.
50 Lieutenant-General Sir Tom Bridges, *Alarms and Excursions* (London, 1938), p. 80, Gough, op. cit., p. 94.
51 French's nephew L. C. Jones, an Indian Army officer serving in France in 1914, overheard a ferocious exchange allegedly culminating in the memorable phrase: 'Too many whores around your headquarters, Field-Marshal!' Information from Major Antony Mallaby, to whom Major-General Jones told the story.
52 General Sir Horace Smith-Dorrien, *Memories of Forty-Eight Years Service* (London, 1925), pp. 355–7.
53 Ibid., p. 359.
54 Esher's Journal, 28 January 1908, Brett (ed.), op. cit., II, p. 278.
55 General Sir George Barrow, *The Fire of Life*, p. 87.
56 Crewe to Seely, 5 September 1913, Mottistone Papers, Nuffield College, Oxford.
57 Major-General Sir Charles Callwell, *Experience of a Dug-Out* (London, 1920), p. 57.
58 French, *Life*, p. 177.
59 French to Watt, 22 December 1904, Watt Papers.
60 French to Fitzgerald, 23 August 1910, Fitzgerald Papers.
61 Wilson, Diary, 18 September 1913.
62 Scrap-books in the possession of Lady Patricia Kingsbury.
63 Gooch, op. cit., p. 257.
64 French to Arnold-Forster, 16 July 1905, French, *War Diaries*, p. 108, French to Knollys, 6 August 1905, RA W26/52.
65 French to Esher, 2 June 1906, French, *War Diaries*, p. 111.
66 French to Esher, 21 January 1912, ibid., p. 131.
67 Ibid., pp. 133–4.
68 Wilson, Diary, 16 March 1912.
69 Stamfordham to Seely, nd (November 1913), Mottistone Papers.
70 French to Seely, 31 July 1913, ibid.
71 Secretary, War Office, to Seely's Private Secretary, 4 September 1913, ibid.
72 French to Seely, 8 September 1913, ibid.
73 *Pay of the Army Officer*, January 1913, ibid.
74 Notes on an audience, 16 December 1913, ibid.
75 Notes on an audience, 7 April 1913, ibid.
76 French to Winifred Bennett, 21 September and 19 March 1915, French Papers.

77 D. S. MacDiarmid, *The Life of Lt-Gen. Sir James Moncrieff Grierson*, p. 216, and Esher to French 26 September 1906, French Papers.
78 Major-General Sir Charles Callwell, *Field-Marshal Sir Henry Wilson* (London, 1927: 2 vols), I, p. 157. The point is open to dispute.
79 *Report on the Bosphorous and Dardanelles*, October 1904, RA W45/29.
80 See, for example, *Remarks* ... by Sir John French, 28 June 1906, PRO, CAB 3/1.
81 *Report on Army Manoeuvres*, 1904, War Office Library, and H. R. Moon, 'The Invasion of the United Kingdom: Public Controversy and Official Planning', (unpublished London PhD thesis, 1968), pp. 253–7.
82 'General French on Invasion', *Daily Mail*, 12 May 1906.
83 *Notes of a Conference* ... 19 December 1905, PRO, CAB 18/24.
84 *Notes of a Conference* ... 6 January 1906, ibid.
85 Lieutenant-Colonel Charles A'Court Repington, *The First World War 1914–18* (London, 1920), pp. 2–11.
86 *Notes of a Conference* ... 12 January 1906, CAB 18/24.
87 *Notes of a Conference* ... 19 January 1906, ibid.
88 Repington, op. cit., p. 12.
89 French to Esher, 25 December 1905, French, War Diaries, p. 110.
90 French to Esher, 18 January 1906, ibid.
91 MacDiarmid, op. cit., pp. 216–17.
92 French to Fitzgerald, 21 June 1906, Fitzgerald Papers.
93 Report 11 September 1906, RA W27/37.
94 MacDiarmid, op. cit., p. 222.
95 French, *Life*, p. 167.
96 Interview with Lieutenant-Colonel Watt's daughter, Mrs Geraldine Scott, 28 July 1977.
97 Charles Harding to Knollys, 17 December 1906, RA W50/110.
98 French to Esher, 20 June 1907, French, *War Diaries*, p. 113, and interview with Lady Essex French, 25 July 1977.
99 *Military Needs of the Empire*, 24 July 1909, CAB 4/3/109B.
100 Esher's Journal, 24 November 1907, Brett (ed.), op. cit., II, p. 262.
101 Quoted Moon, op. cit., p. 357.
102 *Invasion of the British Isles* ... 22 October 1908, CAB 2/2.
103 General V. Huguet, *Britain and the War* (London, 1928), p. 7.
104 *History of the Growth of the Scheme*, WO 106/49A/1.
105 Esher to Roberts, 5 October 1906, Brett (ed.), op. cit.

106 Fisher to Reginald McKenna, 20 August 1911, quoted in Arthur J. Marder, *Fear God and Dread Nought* (London, 1952–9: 3 vols), II, p. 380.
107 French, *War Diaries*, pp. 129–30.
108 Lord Hankey, *The Supreme Command 1914–18* (London, 1961: 2 vols), I, pp. 79–82, The balder *Action to be taken in the event of Intervention in a European War*, is in CAB 2/2.
109 MacDiarmid, op. cit., pp. 241–2.
110 *Les Armées françaises dans la Grande Guerre* (Paris, 1923–4: 10 tomes, 34 vols in all, *tome premier, premier volume*, pp. 9–15.
111 *Directive Générale*, 7 February 1914, ibid., tome I, 1st volume, Annexes, p. 21.
112 Ibid., tome I, 1st volume, p. 19.
113 See S. R. Williamson, 'Joffre reshapes French Strategy', in P. M. Kennedy (ed.), *War Plans of the Great Powers* (London, 1979), and A. J. P. Taylor, *The Struggle for Mastery in Europe* (Oxford, 1960), footnote p. 487.
114 French, *Life*, p. 182, and Winston S. Churchill, *Great Contemporaries* (London, 1937), p. 82. Although both authors are clearly describing the same incident, they differ on details: I have taken Gerald French's dating and Churchill's form of words.
115 Wilson, Diary, 8 and 12 November 1912.
116 Ibid., 17 November, 1912.
117 Ibid., 21 November 1912.
118 Ibid., 2 December 1912.
119 *Invasion of the British Isles* ... 15 April 1914, CAB 3/2/5/62A.
120 Wilson, Diary, 8 August 1913.
121 See Gooch, op. cit., pp. 292–3.
122 Edmonds, Unpublished Autobiography, Chapter XXII, p. 12, Edmonds Papers, Liddell Hart Centre for Military Archives, King's College, London.
123 Wilson, Diary, 25 September 1913.
124 French to Esher, 1 October 1913, French, *War Diaries*, p. 136.
125 Wilson, Diary, 26 September 1913.
126 Edmonds, Unpublished Autobiography, Chapter XXIII, p. 25, Edmonds Papers.
127 Ibid., Chapter XXII, p. 15.

Chapter 5   The Tactical Debate, 1902–14

1 The constraints imposed by a biography prevent a full examination of the cavalry tactics question. For useful studies of the topic

see particularly Edward M. Spiers, 'The British Cavalry 1902–14', *Journal of the Society for Army Historical Research*, vol. LVIII, no. 30 (Summer, 1979), Brian Bond, 'Doctrine and Training in the British Cavalry', in Michael Howard (ed.), *The Theory and Practice of War* (London, 1965), and William L. Taylor's more general 'The Debate over changing Cavalry Tactics and Weapons', *Military Affairs*, XXVIII (Winter, 1965).

2 Erskine Childers, *War and the Arme Blanche*, p. 261.

3 Ibid., p. 291.

4 Ibid., p. 8.

5 See for example, A. J. Smithers, *The Man who Disobeyed*, p. 131.

6 French, Diary, 5 April 1900, French Papers.

7 French to Lonsdale Hale, 12 April 1900, Staff College Library, Camberley.

8 French to Roberts, 15 September 1901, National Army Museum 7101–23–30.

9 *Report on the Organisation and Equipment of Cavalry*, 8 November 1901, WO 33/38.

10 French to Roberts, 10 November 1901, National Army Museum 7101–23–30.

11 French to Hutton, 21 February 1902, British Library Add MSS 50086.

12 *Report of His Majesty's Commissioners* (Elgin Commission), Minutes, II, pp. 300–6.

13 Hutton to French, 1 April 1903, British Library Add MSS 50086.

14 French to Winifred Bennett, 13 May 1915, French Papers.

15 *Report of His Majesty's Commissioners*, Minutes, II, p. 308.

16 Roberts to Kitchener, 28 January 1904, National Army Museum 7101–23–124–4.

17 Circular Memorandum, 10 March 1903, WO 32/6782.

18 Haig, Diary, 25 September 1903, Haig Papers.

19 *Cavalry Training (Provisional), 1904*, pp. iii–iv.

20 French to Secretary of the Army Council, 7 March 1904, WO 32/6782. There is a copy in RA XI/65b, an indication of French's desire to keep the King informed.

21 Kitchener to Roberts, 12 May 1904, National Army Museum 7101–23–33.

22 Roberts to French, 4 March 1904, RA XI/64.

23 French to Roberts, 6 March 1904, National Army Museum 7101–23–30.

24 Roberts to Douglas, 12 April 1904, WO 32/6782.
25 Baden-Powell memorandum, 10 March 1904, ibid.
26 Grenfell to Lyttelton, 12 April 1904, ibid.
27 Wood to Lyttelton, 29 March 1904, ibid.
28 Lyttelton to Wood, 29 March 1904, ibid.
29 Army Council Minute, 2 February 1905.
30 *Cavalry Training 1907*, p. 187.
31 Lieutenant-General Frederick von Bernhardi, *Cavalry in Future Wars* (London, 1906), p. xxii.
32 Ibid., p. xxiii.
33 *The Russo–Japanese War: Reports from British Officers* (London, 1908: 3 vols), III, p. 262.
34 Lieutenant-General Sir Ian Hamilton, 'The Training of Troops during 1906', *Journal of the Royal United Services Institute*, December 1906, pp. 1516–17.
35 Brigadier-General E. C. Bethune, 'The Uses of Cavalry and Mounted Infantry in Modern Warfare', ibid., February 1906, pp. 619–36.
36 There is an extensive correspondence between Childers and Roberts in National Army Museum 7101–23–223–1, and between Childers and Hamilton in the Hamilton Papers, Liddell Hart Centre for Military Archives, King's College, London.
37 French to Seely, 20 September 1913, Mottistone Papers.
38 Haig, Diary, 11 September 1908.
39 *Annual Report*, 1909, War Office Library.
40 Erskine Childers, *The German Influence on British Cavalry* (London, 1911), p. 17.
41 French to Esher, November 1904, French, *Life*, pp. 144–5.
42 *Annual Report*, 1907, War Office Library.
43 Dominick Graham, 'The Development of the Tactics and Weapons of the British Expeditionary Force, 1907–1914', unpublished seminar paper.
44 Major-General Sir Charles Callwell, *Stray Recollections* (London, 1923: 2 vols), II, p. 246.
45 Lieutenant-General Sir Tom Bridges, *Alarms and Excursions*, p. 73.

Chapter 6   Irish Imbroglio: The Curragh, 1914

1 A. T. Q. Stewart, *The Ulster Crisis* (London, 1967), p. 19.
2 Quoted in A. P. Ryan, *Mutiny at the Curragh* (London, 1956), p. 52.

3 Margot Asquith, *The Autobiography of Margot Asquith* (London, 1962), p. 399.

4 J. E. B. Seely, *Adventure* (London, 1933), p. 156. Although an invaluable insight into Seely's personality, this work is by no means reliable on matters of fact.

5 Sir Harold Nicolson, *King George V* (London, 1952), p. 226.

6 French to Stamfordham, 25 September 1913, RA GV K2553.

7 French's Memorandum, *Position of the Army with regard to the situation in Ulster*, December 1913, Mottistone Papers.

8 Paget to French, 19 October 1913, ibid.

9 Seely to Asquith, 24 October 1913, ibid.

10 General Sir Nevil Macready, *Annals of an Active Life*, I, p. 171.

11 Wilson, Diary, 4 and 6 November 1914, Wilson Papers.

12 Ibid., 9 November 1914.

13 Ibid., 20 April 1913.

14 V. Bonham-Carter, *Soldier True* (London, 1963), p. 78.

15 Nicolson, op. cit., p. 238.

16 Paget to French, 10 October 1906, French Papers.

17 See a memorandum sent by French's Military Secretary to the King, 8 June 1915, in RA GC 832/230. This is at variance with Sir James Fergusson, *The Curragh Incident* (London, 1964), p. 198.

18 This is not the view taken by General Sir Anthony Farrar-Hockley in his admirable *Goughie* (London, 1975).

19 General Sir Hubert Gough, *Soldiering On*, p. 107.

20 *Correspondence Relating to Recent Events in the Irish Command*, Cd. 7318, 1914.

21 Macready, op. cit., I, p. 157.

22 Ruan, op. cit., p. 116.

23 Ibid., p. 119.

24 B. B. Cubitt to Paget, 14 March 1914, Mottistone Papers.

25 Paget to Seely, ibid.

26 See Fergusson, op. cit., p. 48.

27 Wilson, Diary, 18 March 1914, Wilson Papers.

28 Ibid.

29 Field-Marshal Sir William Robertson, *From Private to Field-Marshal* (London, 1921), p. 194.

30 Paget to Friend, 18 March 1914, Mottistone Papers.

31 French to H. A. Gwynne, editor of the *Morning Post*, April 1914, quoted in Robert Blake, *The Unknown Prime Minister* (London, 1955), p. 187.

32 This meeting is described by both Ryan and Fergusson. The most useful account, to which they appear not to have had

access, is that of Seely's Private Secretary in the Mottistone Papers.

33 Blake, op. cit., p. 187.
34 Wilson, Diary, 19 March 1914.
35 Blake, op. cit., p. 187.
36 Seely to French, 20 March 1914, French Papers.
37 Paget's own account is quoted, ibid., pp. 224–9, Fergusson's ibid., pp. 67–9, and Gough's in *Soldiering On*, pp. 101–2.
38 Quoted in Roy Jenkins, *Asquith* (London, 1964), p. 307.
39 Wilson, Diary, 20 March 1914.
40 Paget to Adjutant-General, 20 March 1914, in *Correspondence Relating to ...* , Cd 7318.
41 Seely to Paget, 20 March 1914, ibid.
42 Paget to Adjutant-General, ibid. The total was, in fact, sixty officers plus Gough himself. The figure of 57 is inexplicable.
43 Lieutenant-Colonel R. W. Breeks RHA, quoted in Fergusson, op. cit., p. 115.
44 Wilson, Diary, 21 March 1914.
45 French to Roberts, 19 March, 1914 National Army Museum 7101–23–202.
46 MS Note in the French Papers: a similar account is to be found in the Royal Archives, RA GV F674/15.
47 Lord Roberts, *Ulster and the Army*, Roberts Papers, National Army Museum 7101–23–202, p. 4.
48 David James, *Lord Roberts* (London, 1954), p. 467.
49 Nicolson, op. cit., p. 238.
50 Roberts, *Ulster and the Army*, Roberts Papers, pp. 5–6.
51 General Sir Archibald Wavell, *Allenby: A Study in Greatness* (London, 1940), p. 123.
52 Nicolson, op. cit., p. 238.
53 Quoted in Fergusson, op. cit., pp. 132–3.
54 Quoted in Farrar-Hockley, op. cit., p. 106.
55 Major-General Sir Frederick Maurice, *Haldane 1856–1915* (London, 1937), p. 342.
56 Fergusson, op. cit., p. 136.
57 *The Times*, 23 March 1914.
58 Brigadier-General John Charteris, *Field-Marshal Earl Haig* (London, 1929), pp. 72–3.
59 See Fergusson, op. cit., p. 148. Macready had, in fact, already arrived in Belfast.
60 For accounts of this meeting see ibid., pp. 146–9, Ryan, op. cit., pp. 152–3 and Gough, op. cit., pp. 107–8. Seely's version, in *Adventure*, p. 168, seems somewhat improbable.

61 *Correspondence Relating to* ... , Cd 7318, p. 4.
62 Ibid.
63 Ibid.
64 See Haig, Diary, 23 March 1914.
65 French, *Life* p. 194. There is an almost illegible transcript of the peccant paragraphs and this interpretation, in French's hand, in the French Papers.
66 Quoted in Fergusson, op. cit., pp. 153–4.
67 Wilson, Diary, 25 March 1914.
68 Ibid., 24 March 1914.
69 Roberts to French, 22 March 1914, French Papers.
70 French to Roberts, 24 March, 1914, ibid.
71 Jenkins, op. cit., p. 313.
72 Wilson, Diary, 26 March 1914.
73 Ibid.
74 MS Statement, initialled by French and Haldane, 27 March 1914, Watt Papers.
75 Quoted in Fergusson, op. cit., p. 165.
76 Wilson, Diary, 28 March 1914.
77 Ibid.
78 Quoted in Jenkins, op. cit., pp. 213–14.
79 Wilson, Diary, 29 March 1914.
80 French to Asquith, nd, in Haldane's hand but with MS alterations by French, French Papers.
81 Wilson, Diary, 29 March 1914.
82 Asquith to Haldane, 30 March 1914, in Maurice, op. cit., pp. 344–5.
83 Wilson, Diary, 30 March 1914.
84 Esher to L. B(rett), 22 March 1914, Brett (ed.), *The Journals and Letters of Reginald Viscount Esher,* III, p. 159.
85 Esher to Stamfordham, 30 March 1914, ibid., p. 160.
86 Gwynne to Watt, 30 March 1914, Watt Papers.
87 Locker-Lampson to Watt, 2 April, ibid.
88 Quoted in Jenkins, op. cit., p. 314.
89 Ibid., p. 313.
90 Asquith to French, 25 July 1914, in French, *Life,* p. 198.
91 Winston S. Churchill, *Great Contemporaries* (London, 1937), p. 83.
92 See Fergusson, op. cit., pp. 211–16.
93 G. M. Trevelyan, *Grey of Falloden* (New York, 1948), p. 175.
94 Robert Blake, 'Great Britain' in Michael Howard (ed.), *Soldiers and Governments* (London, 1957), p. 36.

Chapter 7 Mons and the Marne, August–September 1914

1 Lord Riddell, *Lord Riddell's War Diary* (London, 1933), p. 6; see also Lord Hankey, *The Supreme Command 1914–18* (London, 1961: 2 vols), I, p. 162.
2 Field-Marshal Viscount French, *1914* (London, 1919), p. 3.
3 Asquith (Earl of Oxford and), *Memories and Reflections* (London, 1928: 2 vols), II, p. 25.
4 Ibid., p. 24.
5 See John Terraine, *Douglas Haig: The Educated Soldier* (London, 1963), p. 72.
6 *Secretary's Notes* ... in PRO, CAB 22/1.
7 Wilson, Diary, 5 August 1914, Wilson Papers.
8 Ibid., 7 August 1914.
9 Ibid., 12 August 1914.
10 French's copy of these instructions is to be found in the Imperial War Museum: the instructions are quoted in full in Edmonds, *History of the Great War ... Military Operations, France and Belgium, 1914* (hereafter referred to as Edmonds, *Military Operations*) (London, 1923–5, 2 vols), I, pp. 444–5.
11 John Terraine, *Mons: The Retreat to Victory* (London, 1960), p. 37.
12 Esher to French, 3 April 1915, French Papers.
13 French, Diary, 30 September 1914, French Papers.
14 French to Kitchener, 15 November 1914, quoted in Philip Magnus, *Kitchener: Portrait of an Imperialist* (London, 1961), p. 290.
15 See French, Diary, 21 February 1915.
16 Ibid., 2 January 1915.
17 French to Mrs Bennett, 7 March 1915, French Papers.
18 French to Mrs Bennett, 27 May 1915, ibid.
19 *The Times*, 3 August 1914.
20 General V. Huguet, *Britain and the War* (London, 1928), p. 38.
21 Field-Marshal Sir William Robertson, *Soldiers and Statesmen* (London, 1926: 2 vols), I, p. 71.
22 C. D. Baker-Carr, *From Chauffeur to Brigadier-General* (London, 1930), p. 27.
23 Haig, Diary, 11 August 1914, Haig Papers.
24 Brigadier-General John Charteris, *At GHQ* (London, 1931), pp. 10–11.
25 Haig, Diary, 22 February 1915.

26 French, Diary, 14 August 1914.
27 Ibid., 15 August 1914.
28 R. Poincaré, *The Memoirs of Raymond Poincaré* (London, 1929), p. 51.
29 French, Diary, 15 August 1914.
30 J. J. Joffre, *The Memoirs of Marshal Joffre* (London, 1932: 2 vols), I, p. 161.
31 French, *1914*, p. 31.
32 Brigadier-General E. L. Spears, *Liaison, 1914* (London, 1930), p. 70.
33 B. H. Liddell Hart, *The Real War* (London, 1930), p. 61.
34 Huguet, op. cit., p. 51.
35 Spears, op. cit., p. 74.
36 Huguet, op. cit., pp. 51–2. For Lanrezac's own account of the meeting see General Lanrezac, *Le Plan de campagne français* (Paris, 1920), pp. 91–3.
37 French, Diary, 17 August 1914.
38 See ibid., and Smith-Dorrien, *Memories of Forty-Eight Years Service* (London, 1925), p. 375.
39 French, Diary, 18 August 1914.
40 Ibid., 20 August 1914.
41 Ibid., 18 August 1914.
42 Ibid., 20 August 1914.
43 See A. J. Smithers, *The Man who Disobeyed* (London, 1970), p. 164.
44 See French to Kitchener, 22 and 25 August 1914, French Papers, and Wilson, Diary, 23 August 1914.
45 Robertson, *From Private to Field-Marshal*, p. 205.
46 See Spears, op. cit., pp. 134–5 and French, Diary, 22 August 1914.
47 French, Diary, 22 August 1914.
48 Spears, op. cit., pp. 148–9.
49 Ibid.
50 French, *1914*, p. 58.
51 French, Diary, 22 August 1914.
52 Edmonds, *Military Operations*, 1914, I, p. 63. French's Diary, 23 August, times his arrival at Sars-la-Bruyère at 6.30.
53 French, *1914*, p. 60.
54 'General Sir Horace Smith-Dorrien's statement with regard to the first edition of Lord French's book "1914"', British Library Add Mss 52776, p. 5.
55 Smith-Dorrien, op. cit., p. 3.
56 French, Diary, 23 August 1914.

57 Edmonds, *Military Operations*, 1914, I, p. 63.
58 French, Diary, 23 August 1914.
59 Quoted in Spears, op. cit., p. 162. In *1914*, p. 59, French dates this message 24 hours earlier, but Spears's evidence is conclusive.
60 Wilson, Diary, 23 August 1914.
61 French, Diary, 23 August 1914.
62 Spears, op. cit., p. 174.
63 Ibid., p. 172 and French, *1914*, p. 64.
64 Spears, op. cit., p. 188.
65 Joffre, op. cit., I, p. 183.
66 French to Joffre, 24 August 1914, French Papers.
67 French, Diary, 24 August 1914.
68 French, *1914*, pp. 67–8.
69 Ibid., p. 70.
70 Diary of Lieutenant-General Sir Archibald Murray, 24 August 1914, Murray Papers, Imperial War Museum.
71 French, *1914*, p. 71, and Spears, op. cit., pp. 191–2.
72 Diary of Major G. S. Clive, 25 August 1914, in the papers of Lieutenant-General Sir George Clive, Liddell Hart Centre for Military Archives, King's College, London.
73 French, Diary, 25 August 1914.
74 Wilson to Smith-Dorrien, 3.45 p.m. 25 August 1914, quoted in Edmonds, *Military Operations*, 1914, I, p. 461.
75 French, Diary, 26 August 1914.
76 Ibid.
77 Edmonds, *Military Operations*, 1914, I, p. 136.
78 French, Diary, 26 August 1914.
79 Wilson, Diary, 26 August 1914: see also Smith-Dorrien, op. cit., p. 405.
80 French, *The Despatches of Lord French* (London, 1917), pp. 10–11.
81 French, *1914*, pp. 79–80.
82 Smith-Dorrien, *Statement*, pp. 8–9, Smith-Dorrien Papers, Imperial War Museum.
83 Haig, Diary, 30 April 1915, 4 September 1914.
84 Murray to Jasper (surname unknown), 28 December 1933, Murray Papers.
85 Terraine, *Mons*, p. 143.
86 Murray to Jasper (surname unknown), 28 December 1933, Murray Papers.
87 This assessment of French's character is Spears's, in *Liaison*, p. 73.

88 Huguet, op. cit., p. 67.
89 Spears, op. cit., pp. 233–8.
90 Ibid., p. 240.
91 Joffre, op. cit., I, pp. 199–200.
92 French, Diary, 28 August 1914.
93 See Spears, op. cit., p. 254 and Edmonds, *Military Operations,* 1914, I, p. 465.
94 Spears, op. cit., pp. 266–8. Lanrezac, in *Plan de campagne,* writes of French's 'bad humour and cowardice'.
95 French, Diary, 29 August 1914.
96 Joffre, op. cit., I, p. 214.
97 French, Diary, 29 August 1914.
98 Spears, op. cit., p. 288.
99 Ibid., pp. 295–6.
100 French to Kitchener, 30 August 1914, in Edmonds, *Military Operations,* 1914, I, p. 475.
101 French to Kitchener, 30 August 1914, French Papers.
102 Kitchener to French, 31 August 1914, in Edmonds, *Military Operations,* 1914, I, p. 475.
103 French, Diary, 31 August 1914.
104 Ibid.
105 French to Kitchener, 31 August 1914, Edmonds, *Military Operations,* 1914, I, p. 476.
106 French to Kitchener, 1 September 1914, ibid., pp. 476–7.
107 French, Diary, 1 September 1914.
108 Hankey, *Supreme Command,* I, p. 191.
109 Huguet, op. cit., p. 84.
110 Lord Bertie, *The Diary of Lord Bertie 1914–18* (London, 1924: 2 vols), II, pp. 25–6.
111 French, Diary, 1 September 1914.
112 French, *1914,* p. 100.
113 Kitchener to French, 1 September 1914, French Papers.
114 Churchill to French, 4 September 1914, ibid. Martin Gilbert in *Winston S. Churchill,* vol. III, 1914–16, dates this letter 2 September 1914.
115 French to Churchill, 6 September 1914, in Gilbert op. cit., III, pp. 61–2. Gilbert dates the latter 3 September, but Churchill himself, in *World Crisis,* I, p 234, dates it 6 September. The question of dating is not of pivotal importance: this letter was clearly written in reply to that above.
116 French to Churchill, 10 September 1914, in Churchill, *World Crisis,* I, p. 234.
117 See French to Kitchener, 10 October 1914, in Sir George Arthur,

Lord Kitchener, III, p. 70, and French, Diary, 11 December 1914.

118 Terraine, *Mons*, p. 189.

119 Spears, op. cit., p. 259.

120 Joffre to French, 2 September 1914, French Papers: Sir John's favourable comment on the letter is in his Diary, 3 September 1914.

121 French, Diary, 4 September 1914, and Brigadier-General the Hon. W. Lambton to the King, 7–8 September 1914, in RA GV Q832/202.

122 French, Diary, 4 September 1914.

123 Joffre, op. cit., I, p. 252.

124 The best account of the meeting is in Spears, op. cit., pp. 415–18. See also Joffre, op. cit., I, pp. 254–5 and Clive, Diary, 5 September 1914, Liddell Hart Centre for Military Archives.

125 French, Diary, 6 September 1914.

126 Ibid., 14 September 1914.

Chapter 8 The Swing of the Pendulum, September 1914–March 1915

1 French to Connaught, 25 September 1914, in RA Add A15/6527.

2 French to George V, 2 October 1914, in RA GV Q832/72.

3 French, Diary, 23 September 1914, French Papers.

4 Winston S. Churchill, *World Crisis*, I, p. 236 and Wilson, Diary, 24 September 1914, Wilson Papers.

5 French, Diary, 27 September 1914. See also Clive, Diary, 27 September 1914, Clive Papers, Liddell Hart Centre for Military Archives.

6 See Joffre, *Memoirs*, I, pp. 300, 303–4, and Joffre to French, 1 October 1914, French Papers.

7 Kitchener to French, 2 October 1914, French Papers.

8 See French to Churchill, 5 October 1914, in Churchill, *World Crisis*, II, p. 330.

9 French to Rawlinson, 11 October 1914, in French, *1914*, p. 179.

10 GQG to French, 6 October 1914, French Papers, and Huguet, *Britain and the War*, pp. 124–5.

11 J. E. B. Seely, *Adventure*, p. 180.

12 Typescript recording details of Selborne's visit to French, February 1915, in Bod. Lib. MSS Selborne 93.
13 Robertson to Stamfordham, 28 September 1915, in RA GV Q832/282.
14 French, Diary, 19 October 1914.
15 Captain B. H. Liddell Hart, *Foch: Man of Orleans* (London, 1931), p. 134.
16 Edmonds, *Military Operations*, 1914, II, pp. 128–31.
17 French, *1914*, pp. 227–8.
18 Wilson, Diary, 21 October 1914.
19 Edmonds, *Military Operations*, 1914, II, p. 168.
20 French to Kitchener, 21 and 25 October 1914, French Papers.
21 French, *1914*, p. 234.
22 Wilson, Diary, 25 October 1914.
23 Edmonds, *Military Operations*, 1914, II, p. 522.
24 French, *1914*, p. 242.
25 French to Kitchener, 29 October 1914, French Papers.
26 The two most important sources for the whole question of ammunition supply are Major-General Sir Stanley von Donop, 'The Supply of Munitions to the Army', Von Donop Papers, Imperial War Museum, and French's 'Memorandum on the Supply of artillery ammunition to the Army in the Field', 17 June 1914, WO 32/5155.
27 French to Kitchener, 30 October 1914, French Papers.
28 For accounts of this meeting see French, *1914*, p. 245, Foch, *Memoirs*, p. 176, and Liddell Hart, *Foch*, pp. 140–1.
29 Riddell, *War Diary*, p. 281.
30 Selborne typescript in Bod. Lib. MSS Selborne 93.
31 Haig, Diary, 31 October 1914, Haig Papers.
32 Selborne typescript in Bod. Lib. MSS Selborne 93.
33 Quoted in Spears, *Liaison*, p. 13.
34 Edmonds, *Military Operations*, 1914, II, p. 342.
35 French to George V, 1 November 1914, RA GV Q832/75.
36 Edmonds, *Military Operations*, 1914, II, pp. 360-1.
37 French, *1914*, pp. 265–6.
38 Orders of the Day, 2 November 1914, quoted in French, *1914*, pp. 266–70.
39 French to Stamfordham, 15 November 1914, RA GV Q705/7.
40 Wilson, Diary, 5 November 1914.
41 Asquith, *Memories and Reflections*, pp. 48–9.
42 Churchill to French, 6 November 1914, French Papers.
43 Wilson, Diary, 5 November 1914.

44 Minutes of the Chantilly conference, 27 December 1914, with annotations in Wilson's hand, French Papers.
45 Margot Asquith to French, 2 July 1915, French Papers.
46 Esher to French, 26 June 1914, ibid., and Brett (ed.), *Journals*, III, pp. 247–8.
47 See Basil Collier, *Brasshat: A Biography of Field-Marshal Sir Henry Wilson* (London, 1961), pp. 203–4.
48 Haig, Diary, 21 November 1914.
49 Edmonds, *Military Operations*, 1914, II, pp. 465–7.
50 French, Diary, 24 September 1914, 23 May 1915.
51 French, *1914*, p. 294.
52 Edmonds, *Military Operations*, 1915, I, pp. 7–9.
53 French, Diary, 13 December 1914, Robertson to von Donop, 28 November 1914, Robertson Papers, 1/4/8, Liddell Hart Centre for Military Archives, King's College, London.
54 Edmonds, *Military Operations*, 1915, I, p. 9.
55 Robertson to von Donop, 23 January 1915, Robertson Papers 1/4/19.
56 French to Kitchener, 24 September 1914, French Papers.
57 French to Kitchener, 4 December 1914, ibid.
58 See, for example, Churchill to French, 27 August 1914, 3 February, 6 April and 9 April 1915, French Papers.
59 Robertson to von Donop, 24 November 1914, Robertson Papers. 1/4/7.
60 French, Diary, 14 and 15 November 1914.
61 Ibid., 30 November, 1 December 1914.
62 Brade to Fitzgerald, 6 February 1915, Fitzgerald Papers.
63 French, Diary, 27 November 1914.
64 Ibid., 30 November, 4 December 1914.
65 Edmonds, *Military Operations*, 1915, I, p. 19.
66 French, Diary, 15 December 1915.
67 See Kitchener to French, 11 December 1914, French Papers.
68 Churchill to French, 26 October 1914, ibid.
69 French to Churchill, 25 October 1914, in Gilbert, *Winston Churchill*, III, p. 218, and French, Diary, 7 November 1914.
70 French, Diary, 10 December 1914, Churchill to French, 8 December 1914, French Papers.
71 Edmonds, *Military Operations*, 1915, I, p. 15.
72 French, Diary, 10 December 1914.
73 Wilson, Diary, 11 December 1914.
74 See French, Diary, 27 December 1914, and minutes of the conference, French Papers.
75 Churchill to French, 13 December 1914, French Papers.

76 French to Churchill, 31 December 1914, in Gilbert, op. cit., III, p. 342.
77 Lambton to George V, 13 January 1915, RA GV Q832/18.
78 French, Diary, 7 January 1915.
79 Kitchener to French, 2 January 1915, French Papers.
80 French to Kitchener, 3 January 1915, ibid.
81 Kitchener to French, 6 January 1915, ibid.
82 French to Kitchener, 8 January 1915, ibid.
83 Hankey, *The Supreme Command 1914–18*, I, p. 262.
84 Kitchener to French, 9 January 1915, Churchill to French, 8 January 1915, French Papers.
85 Hankey, op. cit., I, p. 264.
86 Ibid., I, pp. 266–7.
87 French, Diary, 17 and 18 January 1915, Hankey, op. cit., I, p. 269.
88 Asquith, *Memories and Reflections*, II, pp. 154–5. See also Lord Edmund Talbot to Brinsley Fitzgerald, 14 February 1915, Fitzgerald Papers.
89 Wilson, Diary, 2 January 1915.
90 Asquith, op. cit., II, p. 53.
91 Two letters from French to Murray, and one from Murray to French, all 25 January 1915, Murray Papers.
92 French to Kitchener, 25 January 1915, RA GV F1058/2.
93 French to Murray, 29 January 1915, Murray Papers.
94 Haig, Diary, 26 January 1915.
95 Ibid., 24 January 1915.
96 Wilson, Diary, 17 January 1915.
97 Foch to Joffre, 5 January 1915, in Liddell Hart, *Foch*, p. 162.
98 Wilson, Diary, 31 January 1915.
99 See French, Diary, 15 March 1915.
100 Ibid., 13 February 1915.
101 Haig, Diary, 13 February 1915.
102 French, Diary, 9 February 1915.
103 Joffre to French, 19 February 1915, French Papers.
104 French, Diary, 21 February 1915.
105 Ibid.
106 French to Joffre, 23 February 1915, French Papers.
107 Quoted in Edmonds, *Military Operations*, 1915, I, p. 73.
108 Kitchener to French, 3 March 1915, French Papers. The letter is dated 1916, but it is abundantly clear from the context that is an error.
109 French, Diary, 6 March 1915.
110 French to Kitchener, 7 March 1915, French Papers.

Chapter 9 Changing the Bowler: March–December 1915

1 Captain G. C. Wynne, *If Germany Attacks: The Battle in Depth in the West* (London, 1940), p. 25.
2 See Edmonds, *Military Operations*, 1915, I, pp. 89–148.
3 French, *The Despatches of Lord French*, p. 23.
4 French to Asquith, 7 March 1915, Asquith Papers 26, French to Winifred Bennett, 2 March 1915, French Papers.
5 French, Diary, 10 March 1915, French Papers.
6 Ibid., 8 March 1915.
7 M. V. Brett (ed.), *The Journals and Letters of Reginald Viscount Esher*, III, p. 24.
8 French, Diary, 13 March 1915.
9 French to Kitchener, 13 March 1915, French Papers.
10 French, Diary, 14 March 1915.
11 French to Kitchener, 18 March 1915, French Papers.
12 David French, 'The Military Background to the "Shell Crisis" of May 1915', *Journal of Strategic Studies*, September 1979, p. 200.
13 French, Diary, 16–17 March 1915.
14 Ibid., 3 September 1914, 15 March 1915.
15 French to Winifred Bennett, 12 and 23 November 1915, French Papers.
16 Winston S. Churchill, *Great Contemporaries*, pp. 90–1.
17 French to Winifred Bennett, 5 March 1915, French Papers.
18 French to Winifred Bennett, 12 August 1915, ibid.
19 French to Winifred Bennett, 12 May and 28 August 1915, ibid.
20 Brett (ed.), op. cit., III, p. 219.
21 French to Winifred Bennett, 19 November 1915, French Papers.
22 French to Winifred Bennett, 18 February 1915, ibid.
23 French to Winifred Bennett, 24 February 1915, ibid.
24 French to Winifred Bennett, 6 April 1915, ibid.
25 French to Winifred Bennett, 9 March 1915, ibid.
26 French to Winifred Bennett, 27 February 1915, ibid.
27 French to Winifred Bennett, 21 May, 1915, ibid.
28 French to Winifred Bennett, 24 June 1915, ibid.
29 French to Winifred Bennett, 21 June 1915, ibid.
30 French to Winifred Bennett, 6–8 August, 1915, ibid.
31 French to Winifred Bennett, 8 November 1915, ibid.
32 French to Winifred Bennett, 25 February 1915, ibid.

33 French to Winifred Bennett, 18 May 1915, ibid.
34 French to Winifred Bennett, 10 June 1915, ibid.
35 Lady Cynthia Asquith, *Diaries 1915–18* (London, 1968), p. 24.
36 French to Winifred Bennett, 15 September 1915, French Papers.
37 Siegfried Sassoon, *Memoirs of a Foxhunting Man* (London, 1971), p. 254.
38 Joffre to French, 24 March 1915, French Papers.
39 French to Joffre, 1 April 1915, ibid.
40 Edmonds, *Military Operations*, 1915, I, p. 155.
41 Ibid., pp. 160–1.
42 French, Diary, 22 April 1915.
43 Ibid., 24 April 1915, French to Winifred Bennett, 28 April 1915, French Papers.
44 Smith-Dorrien to Robertson, 26 April 1915, in Smithers, *The Man Who Disobeyed*, pp. 252–5.
45 Haig, Diary, 5 February 1915, French, Diary, 28 March 1915.
46 Smith-Dorrien to Wigram, 6 and 9 November 1914, RA GV Q832/338/339.
47 Smith-Dorrien to Wigram, 18 January 1915, ibid., /348.
48 See French, Diary, 3 March 1915.
49 Lambton to George V, 19 March 1915, RA GV 832/224.
50 French, Diary, 27 April 1915.
51 Ibid., 26 April 1915.
52 Ibid., 31 March 1915.
53 Some senior French officials also believed this: see the account of a conversation between Northcliffe and Tardieu in Valentine Williams to Brinsley Fitzgerald, 6 April 1915, Fitzgerald Papers.
54 Edmonds, *Military Operations*, 1915, II, p. 13.
55 Kitchener to Asquith, 14 April 1915, in Bod. Lib., MSS Asquith 14.
56 French to Winifred Bennett, 1 and 11 May 1915, French Papers.
57 Edmonds, *Military Operations*, 1915, II, p. 41.
58 Ibid., I, p. 331.
59 Repington, *The First World War*, pp. 36–7.
60 French, *1914*, p. 357.
61 Ibid., pp. 357–61.
62 Asquith, *Memories and Reflections*, II, p. 95.
63 See Cassar, *Kitchener*, p. 355.
64 French to Kitchener, 14 May 1915, French Papers.
65 French to Northcliffe, 25 March 1915, French Papers.
66 Wigram to Lambton, 24 march 1915, RA GV Q750/6, and Northcliffe to French, 24 March 1915, French Papers.

67 *The Times*, 27 March 1915.
68 Fitzgerald to Selborne, 27 May, Fitzgerald Papers.
69 Brett (ed.), op. cit., III, p. 240, and Margot Asquith to French, 2 July 1915, French Papers.
70 Von Donop to Asquith, 27 November 1915, von Donop Papers.
71 Asquith, *Memories and Reflections*, II, p. 66.
72 See Asquith, *The Great Shell Story*, and Jenkins, *Asquith*, p. 355.
73 French to Asquith, 20 May 1915, Bod. Lib., MSS Asquith 26.
74 Jenkins, op. cit., p. 355.
75 French to Guest, undated, French Papers.
76 French to Esher, 7 September 1918, French Papers.
77 Edmonds, *Military Operations*, 1915, II, p. 45.
78 Ibid., pp. 45–6.
79 French, Diary, 10 May 1915.
80 Haig, Diary, 11 May 1915, and Edmonds, *Military Operations*, 1915, II, p. 51.
81 French to Winifred Bennett, 24 May 1915, French Papers.
82 Minutes of a conference at St Omer, 11 July 1915, French Papers.
83 Minutes of a conference at Chantilly, in French, Diary, 24 June 1915.
84 For details of the meeting, of which no formal minutes were kept, see Asquith, *Memories and Reflections*, II, pp. 106–7, French, Diary, 6 July 1915, French to Winifred Bennett, 6 July 1915, and *Note au sujet de l'arrivée … des divisions anglaises*, 6 July 1915, French Papers.
85 French, Diary, 7 July 1915, Edmonds, *Military Operations*, 1915, II, p. 88.
86 Memorandum on the supply of artillery ammunition to the army in the field, 12 June 1915, WO 32/5155.
87 French, Diary, 23 June 1915.
88 Ibid., 12 July 1915.
89 Clive, Diary, 20 and 25 July 1915, Clive Papers.
90 GQG to GHQ, 12 June 1915, French Papers.
91 French, Diary, 24 July 1915.
92 Ibid., 28 July 1915.
93 Ibid., 29 July 1915, Clive, Diary, 28 July 1915.
94 Clive, Diary, 30 July and 4 August 1915.
95 French, Diary, 29 July 1915.
96 Hankey, *The Supreme Command*, I, p. 339.
97 See ibid., p. 346, Haig, Diary, 14 July 1915, and Charteris, *At GHQ*, p. 86.

98 Diary of George V, 1 July 1915, Royal Archives.
99 Haig, Diary, 14 July 1915.
100 Ibid., 19 August 1915.
101 Clive, Diary, 25 August 1915.
102 French to Winifred Bennett, 27 April 1915, French Papers.
103 French to Winifred Bennett, 24 May 1915, ibid.
104 Minutes of First Army Conference, 6 September 1915, Papers of Lieutenant-General Sir Richard Butler, Imperial War Museum.
105 Edmonds, *Military Operations*, 1915, II, p. 140.
106 Murray to French, 3 April 1915, French Papers.
107 Robertson, *Note for Discussion* ... in PRO, WO 159/7.
108 First Army to GHQ, 19 September 1915, Butler Papers.
109 Haig, Diary, 2 October 1915.
110 French to Winifred Bennett, 18 and 21 September 1915, French Papers.
111 Philip Warner, *The Battle of Loos* (London, 1976), p. 23.
112 Copies of the relevant telegrams are to be found in the Butler Papers: see also French, Diary, 25 September 1915 and Haig, Diary, 25 September 1915.
113 Rawlinson to Stamfordham, 28 September 1915, RA GV Q832/273.
114 Clive, Diary, 26 September 1915.
115 Ibid., 29 September, and French, Diary, 27 and 29 September 1915.
116 French, Diary, 25 September 1915.
117 Account by Colonel T. M. M. Penney, Imperial War Museum.
118 French to Winifred Bennett, 27 September and 2 October 1915, French Papers.
119 French to Winifred Bennett, 30 September 1915, French Papers.
120 French, Diary, 28 September 1915.
121 Ibid., 5 October 1915.
122 Charteris, op. cit., p. 116.
123 Fitzgerald, Diary, 5 October 1915, Fitzgerald Papers.
124 French, Diary, 9 October 1915.
125 Haig, Diary, 9 October 1915.
126 French, Diary, 10 November 1915.
127 Parliamentary Debates, 5th Series, Volume XX, House of Lords, 16 November 1915, columns 359–75.
128 Charteris, op. cit., p. 123.
129 French to Winifred Bennett, 17 November 1915, French Papers.
130 Haig, Diary, 24 October 1915.

131 French to Winifred Bennett, 15 August 1915, French Papers.
132 Diary of King George V, 24 October 1915, Haig, Diary, 24 October 1915.
133 French to Winifred Bennett, 30 October 1915, French Papers.
134 Talbot to Fitzgerald, 9 November 1915, Fitzgerald Papers.
135 Wilson to Fitzgerald, 8 November 1915, Fitzgerald Papers, and Fitzgerald Diary, 5 November 1915.
136 Fitzgerald, Diary, 16–18 November 1915, and Callwell, *Experiences of a Dug-Out*, p. 233.
137 French to Winifred Bennett, 16 November 1915, French Papers.
138 CGS to First Army, 16 October 1915, Butler Papers.
139 First Army to GHQ, 28 October 1915, enclosing XI Corps report of 27 October 1915, Butler Papers.
140 Haig to Lady Haig, Haig Papers.
141 First Army to GHQ, 21 October 1915, Butler Papers.
142 Charteris, op. cit., p. 118. For the deductions drawn from Loos, see 'Lecture on the action of IV Corps at Loos', Montgomery-Massingberd 45, and Montgomery-Massingberd to Sir Frederick Maurice, 13 October 1915, Montgomery-Massingberd 42, in the papers of Field-Marshal Sir Archibald Montgomery-Massingberd, Liddell Hart Centre for Military Archives, King's College, London. See also Sir James Edmonds's apparently definitive account, 'Sir John French and the Reserves at Loos, 25 September 1915', *Journal of the Royal United Services Institute*, vol. LXXXI, Feb.–Nov. 1936.
    The case may be less open and shut than Edmonds suggests. IV Corps telephone log, Montgomery-Massingberd 42, records that at 9.41 on the morning of 25 September First Army informed IV Corps that XI Corps had now been placed under First Army's command. This slender evidence does not seriously weaken First Army's argument, but it does suggest that French's assertion that the reserves were released to First Army at 9.30 was not merely malicious fiction.
143 Stamfordham to Lady Haig, 10 November 1915, Haig Papers.
144 Haig, Diary, 15 November 1915.
145 Asquith, *Memories and Reflections*, II, p. 114.
146 Brett (ed.), op. cit., III, pp. 282–3.
147 Ibid., pp. 285–7 and Fitzgerald, Diary, 26 November 1915.
148 Brett (ed.), op. cit., III, pp. 209–10 and Fitzgerald, Diary, 29 November 1915.
149 French to Asquith, 2 December 1915, Asquith Papers, 28.
150 Robertson to Wigram, 5 December 1915, RA GV Q832/50.

151 Stamfordham to Asquith, 2 December 1915, ibid., /47.
152 Asquith to Stamfordham, 3 December 1915, ibid., /48.
153 Fitzgerald, Diary, 4 December 1915.
154 French to Asquith, 4 December 1915, Asquith Papers 28.
155 Colonel O. Fitzgerald to Wigram, 9–10 December 1915, RA GV Q838/58.
156 Fitzgerald, Diary, 19–20 December 1915.
157 Ibid., 21 December 1915.

Chapter 10   Home Service, January 1916–April 1918

1 French to Winifred Bennett, 1 and 6 January 1916, French Papers.
2 French to Winifred Bennett, 3 and 4 January 1916, ibid.
3 *The Times*, 17 December 1915.
4 Robertson to Wigram, 5 December 1915, RA GV Q835/50.
5 Repington, *The First World War, 1914–18*, pp. 116–17.
6 French to Winifred Bennett, 3 and 4 January 1916, French Papers.
7 Repington, op. cit., p. 98.
8 Selborne to French, 1 January 1916, French Papers, and H. R. Moon, 'The Invasion of the United Kingdom ... ', unpublished thesis, University of London, 1968, pp. 597–8.
9 French, Diary, 28 February 1916.
10 Repington, op. cit., p. 98.
11 French to Milner, 25 March 1918, RA GV Q855/11.
12 French, Diary, 20 March 1915.
13 Ibid., 11 and 18 May 1916, 15 March 1917.
14 Ibid., 1 April 1918.
15 *The Times*, 30 October 1916.
16 Riddell, *Lord Riddell's War Diary*, p. 323.
17 French, Diary, 10 March and 28 May 1915. Henderson had served under French when the latter was Inspector-General, and commanded the RFC in France in August–November 1914 and May–August 1915. French thought highly of him, and used him as a temporary divisional commander in November 1914. See French to Kitchener, 27 November, and 17 December 1914, French Papers.
18 Repington, op. cit., p. 128.
19 French, Diary, 14 February 1916.
20 H. A. Jones, *Official History of the War: The War in the Air* (Oxford, 1931–5: 7 vols), V, p. 5.

21 Ibid., p. 23.
22 French to the War Office, 5 June 1916, ibid., pp. 34–5.
23 French to the War Office, 2 and 6 July 1916, ibid., p. 40.
24 Robertson to Haig, 9 July 1917, Robertson, *Soldiers and Statesmen*, II, p. 17.
25 French, Diary, 9 July 1917.
26 Jones, op. cit., V, p. 41. See also War Cabinet minutes June–August 1917, CAB 23/154–226.
27 French, Diary, 19 July 1917.
28 See Jones, op. cit., V, Appendix VI.
29 Ibid., V, p. 108.
30 Major-General E. B. Ashmore, *Air Defence* (London, 1929), p. 85.
31 See David Fitzpatrick, *Politics and Irish Life 1913–21* (London, 1977), pp. 110–11.
32 Quoted in Leon Ó Broin, *Dublin Castle and the 1916 Rising* (Dublin, 1966), p. 20.
33 French, Diary, 12 February 1916.
34 Ó Broin, op. cit., p. 63.
35 French to Adjutant-General, 20 March 1915, French Papers.
36 French Diary, 23 March 1916.
37 Ó Broin, op. cit., pp. 72–3.
38 French, Diary, 24 April 1916.
39 Ibid., 21 and 25 April 1916.
40 Ibid., 25 April 1916.
41 Ibid., 26 April 1916, French to Asquith, 26 April 1916, Asquith Papers 36.
42 French, Diary, 27 April 1916.
43 Ibid., 28 April 1916.
44 Ibid., 29 April 1916.
45 Ibid., 1 and 2 May 1916.
46 Ibid., 4 May 1916.
47 Ibid., 4 May 1916.
48 Maxwell to French, 13 May 1916, Asquith Papers 44, French, Diary, 14 June 1916.
49 Lloyd George to French, 26 October 1916, French Papers.
50 French, Diary, 26 July 1916, and 27 March 1918.
51 Captain Stephen Roskill, *Hankey: Man of Secrets*, vol. I, 1877–1918 (London, 1970), pp. 517–18, Macready, *Annals of an Active Life*, II, p. 255.
52 Sir Henry Robinson to French, 30 May 1918, enclosing reports on public opinion in Ireland, French Papers.
53 French, Diary, 11, 12 and 16 July 1917.

54 Ibid., 2 and 5 June 1916, and Robertson to Haig, 5 August 1916, Haig Papers.
55 Haig, Diary, 8 August 1916; George V, Diary, 25 November 1916, Royal Archives.
56 French, Diary, 5 July 1916.
57 Ibid., 1 April 1918.
58 MS memorandum in French's hand, 2 April 1918, French Papers.
59 Riddell, op. cit., pp. 182, 201.
60 French, Diary, 4 October 1916.
61 Haig, Diary, 7 October 1916.
62 Wilson, Diary, 17 October 1916.
63 Haig, Diary, 10 October 1916.
64 Haig to George V, 18 October 1916, RA GV Q832/127, Robertson to Stamfordham, 9 November 1916, RA GV Q1200/14.
65 French, Diary, 18–19 January 1917.
66 Ibid., 22 June 1917, Haig, Diary, 22 June 1917.
67 French, Diary, 22 July 1917.
68 David Lloyd George, *War Memoirs*, pp. 1419–21.
69 Riddell, op. cit., p. 266.
70 Hankey to French, 12 October 1917, French Papers.
71 French 'Memorandum on the Military Situation in France', 20 October 1917, French Papers.
72 Lloyd George, op. cit., p. 1433.
73 Roskill, op. cit., I, p. 466.
74 Haig, Diary, 31 October 1917.
75 Repington, op. cit., p. 281.
76 See French, Diary, 14 September 1916, 19 February 1917.
77 Ibid., 18 April 1918.
78 Ibid., 23 March 1918.
79 Ibid., 25 March 1918.
80 Ibid., 5 May 1918.
81 Ibid., 29 April 1918.
82 Ibid., 30 April 1918.
83 Ibid., 5, 10 May 1918.
84 Repington, op. cit., pp. 138, 205, 245.
85 Private W. D. Tonkyn to his parents, 10 May 1917, Imperial War Museum.

Chapter 11   Lord Lieutenant, May 1918–May 1921

1 French to Lloyd George, 5 May 1918, French Papers.

2 French to Esher, 20 May 1918, ibid.
3 Undated MS memorandum, ibid. From internal evidence this document can be dated May 1918.
4 French to Shortt, 26 September 1918, ibid.
5 Shortt to French, 27 September 1918, ibid.
6 French to Fitzgerald, 21 August 1918, Fitzgerald Papers.
7 French to Lloyd George, 12 October 1918, Long to French, 15 October 1918, French Papers.
8 French, Diary, 10 and 11 January 1919.
9 See ibid., 29 January 1917 and 10 July 1918, and Long to Fitzgerald, 4 January 1915, Fitzgerald Papers.
10 French, Diary, 30 May 1915.
11 French to Lloyd George, 19 May 1918, French to George V, 18 May 1918, French Papers.
12 C. A. C. Repington, *The First World War 1914–18*, pp. 307–8, 311, and N. Macready, *Annals of an Active Life*, II, p. 426.
13 See French, Diary, January 1919 passim.
14 See French's opening address to the Viceroy's Advisory Council, 10 October 1918, French Papers. The minutes of the VAC, Executive Council and Military Council are all to be found ibid.
15 Opening address, 10 October 1918, ibid.
16 Ross to French, 16 August 1918, ibid.
17 French, Diary, 28 November 1918.
18 Ibid., 20 October 1918.
19 Ibid., 23 October 1918.
20 Stamfordham to French, 15 September 1918, French Papers.
21 *The Times*, 13 December 1918.
22 Executive Committee minutes, 14 August 1918, Shortt to the War Cabinet, 2 December 1918, French Papers.
23 French to Stafford, 17 August 1920, French Papers.
24 See French to Long, 17 June 1918, Sir William Bull to French, 12 June 1918, Stafford to the VAC, 10 December 1918, Stephen Gwynn to French, 28 January 1919, French Papers.
25 French to George V, 12 July 1918, ibid.
26 French to George V, 10 September 1918, ibid.
27 French to George V, 17 July 1918, ibid.
28 Shaw to French, 30 August 1918, ibid.
29 French, Diary, 23 January, 28 May 1919, 18 March 1920, and French to Long, 19 May 1919, French Papers.
30 See War Cabinet Minutes, 21 November 1918, Memoranda by Brooke and Stafford, and Macartney Filgate, 20 November 1918, French to Long, 2 December 1918, 10 January 1919, Long to French 9 and 10 January 1919, ibid.

31 See Charles Townshend, *The British Campaign in Ireland 1919–21* (Oxford, 1975), pp. 10–12.
32 French to Long, 2 July 1918, Long to French, 4 July 1918, French Papers.
33 French, Diary, 5 September 1918, French to Long, 13 September 1918, French to Lloyd George, 29 May 1918, French Papers.
34 French, Diary, 9 August 1918.
35 Long to French, 21 May 1919, French to Macready, 8 March 1920, French Papers.
36 French to Macpherson, 10 December 1919, 14 January 1920, ibid.
37 See Macready, op. cit., I, pp. 252–3; Long to French, 27 January 1920, French Papers.
38 French, Diary, 6 November, 12 December 1918.
39 Long to French, 4 July 1918, French to Lloyd George, 12 October 1918, French Papers.
40 See Macready, op. cit., II, pp. 448–53.
41 French to War Cabinet, 8 October 1918, French Papers.
42 French to War Cabinet, 7 October 1919, ibid.
43 French, Diary, 21 January 1919.
44 French to Long, 14 January 1919, Long to French, 16 January 1919, French Papers.
45 French, Diary, 17 January 1919, Long to French, 16 January 1919. Haldane hoped to establish a Committee of Inquiry with himself as chairman; see Haldane to French, 16 January 1919, ibid., and R. B. Haldane, *An Autobiography*, pp. 315–17.
46 Long to French, 15 January 1919, French Papers.
47 French to Haldane, 22 January 1919, ibid.
48 Thomas Jones, *Whitehall Diary* (London, 1969: 3 vols, ed. Keith Middlemass), II, p. 83.
49 French to Long, 14 January 1919, French Papers.
50 Long to French, 13 April 1919, ibid.
51 Sullivan to French, 3 April 1919, ibid.
52 Long to French, 21 May 1919, ibid.
53 Thomas Jones, op. cit., I, p. 87.
54 French to Lloyd George, 19 May 1919, French Papers.
55 French to the War Cabinet, 26 June 1919, PRO, CAB 23/15.
56 See Townshend, op. cit., pp. 10–11.
57 French to Macpherson, 20 October 1919, French Papers.
58 French to Macpherson, 4 November 1919, ibid.
59 French to Macpherson, 11 November 1919, ibid.
60 French to Macpherson, 10 December 1919, ibid.
61 French to Macpherson, 11 December 1919, ibid.

62 French to Macpherson, 7 January 1920, ibid.
63 Memorandum by CGS Home Forces, 17 April 1918, ibid.
64 French, Diary, 30 August 1918.
65 French to Long, 1 July 1920, French Papers.
66 Shaw to French, 29 October 1919, ibid.
67 Townshend, op. cit., pp. 43–4.
68 See Frank Bennett, *The Black and Tans* (London, 1959), and D. Fitzpatrick, *Politics and Irish Life 1913–21*, pp. 1–45.
69 French to Long, 23 January 1919, French Papers.
70 Quoted Townshend, op. cit., p. 48.
71 See French, *Life*, pp. 359–60 and the report of the official inquiry into the attack in PRO, CO 904/188.
72 MS note 20 December 1919, in the Strathcarron Papers, Bodleian Library MS Eng. Hist. c490.
73 Memorandum 4 December 1919, Lloyd George to French, 30 December 1919, French Papers.
74 French to Macpherson, 11 January 1920, ibid.
75 French to Macpherson, 4 November 1919, ibid.
76 Thomas Jones, op. cit., I, pp. 112–13.
77 French to Long, 1 July 1920, French Papers.
78 Macready, op. cit., II, p. 425.
79 See French to Bonar Law, 4 April 1920, French to Churchill, 4 April 1920, and assorted letters between French and Shaw, April–July 1920, French Papers.
80 French to Churchill, 1 September 1919, ibid., and Wilson, Diary, 29 March 1920.
81 Long to French, 6 July 1920, French Papers.
82 French to Long, 12 July 1920, ibid.
83 Quoted Townshend, op. cit., p. 78.
84 French to Long, 1 July 1920, French Papers.
85 French to Churchill, 30 July 1920, ibid.
86 French to George V, 2 August 1920, ibid.
87 French, Diary, 4 October 1920.
88 Macready, op. cit., II, pp. 501–2.
89 Townshend, op. cit., pp. 142–7.
90 Macready, op. cit., II, p. 530.
91 See Townshend, op. cit., p. 173.
92 French, Diary, 23 March 1921.
93 Ibid., 30 March 1921 and Lloyd George to French, 31 March 1921, French Papers. There is something of a problem over the dating of Lloyd George's letter, unless it was, perhaps, confirming a note of the 30th.
94 French, Diary, 30 March 1921.

95 Wilson, Diary, 1 April 1920.
96 See French to Winifred Bennett, 27 July 1922, French Papers.
97 French to Bonar Law (?), 10 May 1919, ibid. Correspondence between Corbett-Smith and French's Adjutant-General is also to be found ibid.
98 Edmonds, 'Unpublished Autobiography', 111/16, Edmonds Papers, Liddell Hart Centre for Military Archives.
99 Stamfordham to French, 8 May 1919, French Papers, and French, Diary, 9 May 1919.
100 French, Diary, 9 May 1919.
101 Bertie to French, 10 May 1919, and Midleton to French, 6 July 1919, French Papers.
102 French to Bonar Law (?), 10 May 1919, ibid.
103 J. W. Fortescue, 'Review of Field-Marshal Lord French's *1914*', *Quarterly Review* (October, 1919), pp. 352–63.
104 Edmonds, op. cit., 111/6.
105 Spears to French, 16 May 1919, Spears Papers, Liddell Hart Centre for Military Archives.

Epilogue

1 N. Macready, *Annals of an Active Life*, II, p. 553.
2 Macready to French, 2 May and 17 December 1921, French Papers.
3 Macdonogh to French, 2 May 1921, in French, *Life*, p. 382.
4 French to Wilson, 15 March 1921, French Papers.
5 Talbot to French, 5 March 1922, ibid. Talbot had now assumed the title Viscount Fitzalan; his previous name has been retained in the text to avoid confusion.
6 Healy to French, 31 March 1923, ibid.
7 French, *Life*, p. 381.
8 Ibid., p. 387, and Field-Marshal Lord Birdwood, *Khaki and Gown*, p. 417.
9 French, *Life*, p. 391.
10 George V, Diary, 13 May 1925, Royal Archives.
11 French, *Life*, pp. 395–6, *The Times*, 21 May 1925.
12 *Morning Post*, 25 May 1925.
13 Gerald French acknowledged Smith-Dorrien's magnanimous gesture in *Life*, p. 401.
14 John Terraine, *Mons*, p. 32.

15 Field-Marshal Sir William Robertson, *Soldiers and Statesmen,*
I, p. 71.
16 Lieutenant-Colonel C. A. C. Repington, describing a conversation with Churchill, in *The First World War 1914–18*, p. 192.

Bibliography

Documents

Bodleian Library, Oxford
   Asquith Papers
   Selborne Papers
   Strathcarron Papers
British Library
   Hutton Papers
   Documents by Sir Horace Smith-Dorrien relating to assertions
   made in Lord French's *1914*
Imperial War Museum
   Butler Papers
   Fitzgerald Papers
   French Papers and Diaries
   Murray Papers
   Smith-Dorrien Papers
   Von Donop Papers
   Wilson Papers
India Office
   Records L/MIL/7/1534
Lady Patricia Kingsbury
   French correspondence and ephemera
Liddell Hart Centre for Military Archives, King's College, London
   Clive Papers
   Edmonds Papers
   Hamilton Papers
   Montgomery-Massingberd Papers
   Robertson Papers
   Spears Papers
National Army Museum
   Roberts Papers
National Library of Scotland
   Haig Papers
   Haldane Papers
Nuffield College, Oxford
   Mottistone Papers

Bibliography

Public Record Office
Cabinet Papers CAB 1/26, 2/2, 3/1, 3/2, 4/3, 18/24, 22/1, 23/1 et
seq., 24/1
War Office Papers WO 32, 33, 106
Royal Archives
Lt-Col J. F. Scott
Watt Papers
Staff College, Camberley
Correspondence between French and Colonel Lonsdale Hale

Official Reports and Pamphlets

Annual Reports of the Inspector-General of the Forces, War Office
Library
Army (Remounts) Reports ... (Cd 963) 1902
Cavalry Journal, 1906–14
Cavalry Training (Provisional) 1904
Cavalry Training 1907, 1912
Correspondence Relating to Recent Events in the Irish Command,
Cd. 7318, 1914
Field Service Regulations Parts I and II, 1909
*Proceedings of a Court of Enquiry on the Administration of the
Army Remount Department* (Cd 993), 1902
Report of His Majesty's Commissioners ... *War in South Africa*
(Elgin Commission) Cd 1789, 1903
Report of a Conference of General Staff Officers, 1912, 1913, 1914
Report on Army Manoeuvres, War Office Library
The Russo–Japanese War: Reports from British Officers (HMSO,
1908)

Books and Theses

AMERY, L. S. (ed.) *The Times History of the War in South Africa*
(7 vols, London, 1900–9).
—— *My Political Life* (3 vols, London, 1954)
ANGLESEY, MARQUESS OF, *A History of the British Cavalry 1816–
1919* (2 vols, London, 1973–5: a further volume in preparation).
ANON., Pen Pictures of the War (London, 1900).
ARTHUR, Sir George, *Lord Kitchener* (3 vols, London, 1920).
ASHMORE, Maj.-Gen. E. B., *Air Defence* (London, 1929).
ASQUITH, Lady Cynthia, *Diaries 1915–18* (London, 1968).

Bibliography

ASQUITH, H. H., *The Great Shell Story* (London, 1919).
—— (Earl of Oxford and), *Memories and Reflections* (2 vols, London, 1928).
ASQUITH, Margot, *The Autobiography of Margot Asquith* (London, 1962).
BAKER-CARR, C. D., *From Chauffeur to Brigadier-General* (London, 1930).
BARNETT, Correlli, *Britain and Her Army* (London, 1970).
BARROW, Gen. Sir George, *The Fire of Life* (London, nd).
BEAVERBROOK, Lord, *Politicians and the War 1914–16* (London, 1959).
BENNETT, Frank, *The Black and Tans* (London, 1959).
BERTIE, Lord, *The Diary of Lord Bertie 1914–18* (2 vols, London, 1924).
BIDDULPH, Col J., *The Nineteenth and their Times* (London, 1899).
BIRDWOOD, Field-Marshal Lord, *Khaki and Gown* (London, 1941).
BLAKE, Robert (ed.), *The Private Papers of Douglas Haig 1914–19* (London, 1952).
—— *The Unknown Prime Minister* (London, 1955).
BLOND, Georges, *The Marne* (London, 1965).
BOND, Brian, *The Victorian Army and the Staff College* (London, 1972).
BONHAM-CARTER, V., *Soldier True* (London, 1963).
BRETT, M. V. (ed.), *The Journals and Letters of Reginald Viscount Esher* (4 vols, London, 1934).
BRIDGES, Lt-Gen. Sir Tom, *Alarms and Excursions* (London, 1938).
CALLWELL, Maj.-Gen. Sir Charles, *Experiences of a Dug-Out* (London, 1920).
—— *Stray Recollections* (2 vols, London, 1923).
—— *Field-Marshal Sir Henry Wilson* (2 vols, London, 1927).
CASSAR, George, *Kitchener: Architect of Victory* (London, 1977).
CHARTERIS, Brig.-Gen. J., *Field-Marshal Earl Haig* (London, 1929).
—— *At GHQ* (London, 1931).
CHILDERS, Erskine, *War and the Arme Blanche* (London, 1910).
—— *The German Influence on British Cavalry* (London, 1911).
CHISHOLM, Cecil, *Sir John French: An Authentic Biography* (London, 1915).
CHURCHILL, Randolph S., *Winston Churchill* (vol. II, 1901–14, London, 1967), continued by Martin Gilbert (vol. III, 1914–16, London, 1971).

Bibliography

CHURCHILL, Winston S., *Great Contemporaries* (London, 1937).
—— *World Crisis* (2 vols, London, 1938).
CLARK, Alan, *The Donkeys* (London, 1961).
COLLIER, Basil, *Brasshat: A Biography of Field-Marshal Sir Henry Wilson* (London, 1961).
COLUM, Mary, *Life and the Dream* (London, 1947).
COOPER, Lady Diana, *The Light of Common Day* (London, 1958).
—— *The Rainbow Comes and Goes* (London, 1959).
COOPER, Duff, *Haig* (2 vols, London, 1935).
D'ALTON, John, *Memoir of the Family of French* (Dublin, 1847).
DIXON, Norman, *On the Psychology of Military Incompetence* (London, 1976).
D'OMBRAIN, Nicholas, *War Machinery and High Policy* (Oxford, 1973).
DUNLOP, Col. J. K., *The Development of the British Army 1899–1914* (London, 1938).
EDMONDS, Brig.-Gen. Sir James, *History of the Great War based on Official Documents, Military Operations, France and Belgium 1914, 1915* (4 vols, London, 1922–8).
FARRAR-HOCKLEY, Maj. A. (ed.), *The Commander* (London, 1957).
—— (Sir Anthony), *Goughie* (London, 1975).
FERGUSSON, Sir James, *The Curragh Incident* (London, 1964).
FITZPATRICK, David, *Politics and Irish Life, 1913–21* (London, 1977).
FOCH, Marshal F., *The Memoirs of Marshal Foch* (London, 1931).
FORTESCUE, Sir John, *Following the Drum* (London, 1931).
FRASER, Peter, *Lord Esher: A Political Biography* (London, 1973).
FREDETTE, R. H., *The First Battle of Britain 1917–18* (London, 1966).
FRENCH, Field-Marshal Viscount, *The Despatches of Lord French* (London, 1917).
—— *1914* (London, 1919).
FRENCH, The Hon. Gerald (ed.), *The Life of Field-Marshal Sir John French* (London, 1931).
—— *Some War Diaries, Addresses and Correspondence ...* (London, 1937).
—— *Goodbye to Boot and Saddle* (London, 1951).
—— *The Kitchener–French Dispute: A Last Word* (Glasgow, 1960).
FREWEN, Moreton, *Melton Mowbray and Other Memories* (London, nd).
GILBERT, Martin, *see* Randolph Churchill.
GLEICHEN, Count, *With the Camel Corps up the Nile* (London, 1888).

Bibliography

GOLDMAN, C. S., *With General French and the Cavalry in South Africa* (London, 1903).
GOOCH, John, *The Plans of War: The General Staff and British Military Strategy* (London, 1974).
GOUGH, Gen. Sir Hubert, *Soldiering On* (London, 1954).
GUINN, Paul, *British Strategy and Politics* (Oxford, 1965).
HAIG, Maj.-Gen. Douglas, *Cavalry Studies* (London, 1901).
HALDANE, R. B., *Richard Burdon Haldane: An Autobiography* (London, 1924).
HAMLEY, Gen. Sir E. B., *The Operations of War* (London, 1866).
HANKEY, Lord, *The Supreme Command 1914–18* (2 vols, London, 1961).
HARINGTON, Gen. Sir Charles, *Plumer of Messines* (London, 1935).
HOWARD, Michael (ed.), *Soldiers and Governments* (London, 1957).
—— *The Theory and Practice of War* (ed.) (London, 1965).
—— *The Continental Commitment* (London, 1972).
HUGUET, Gen. V., *Britain and the War* (London, 1928).
JAMES, David, *Lord Roberts* (London, 1954).
JENKINS, Roy, *Asquith* (London, 1964).
JOFFRE, Marshal J. J., *The Memoirs of Marshal Joffre* (London, 1932).
JOHNSON, F. A., *Defence by Committee* (London, 1960).
JONES, H. A., *Official History of the War: The War in the Air* (7 vols, Oxford, 1931–5).
JONES, Thomas, *Whitehall Diary* (3 vols, ed. Keith Middlemass, London, 1969).
KENNEDY, P. M. (ed.), *War Plans of the Great Powers* (London, 1979).
KRUGER, Rayne, *Good-bye Dolly Gray* (London, 1964).
LANREZAC, Gen. C., *Le Plan de Campagne Français* (Paris, 1920).
—— *Les Armées françaises dans La Grande Guerre* (10 tomes, 34 vols in all, Paris, 1923–4).
LESLIE, Anita, *Mr. Frewen of England* (London, 1966).
L'ETANG, Hugh, *The Pathology of Leaderships* (London, 1969).
LIDDELL HART, Capt. B. H., *The Real War* (London, 1930).
—— *Foch: Man of Orleans* (London, 1931).
LINKLATER, Andrö, *An Unhusbanded Life* (London, 1980).
LLOYD GEORGE, David, *War Memoirs* (2 vols, London, 1938).
LONG, Viscount, *Memories* (London, 1923).
LYDALL, E., *Lydall of Uxmore* (London, 1980).
MACDIARMID, D. S., *The Life of Lieutenant-General Sir James Moncrieff Grierson* (London, 1923).

Bibliography

MACREADY, Gen. Sir Nevil, *Annals of an Active Life* (2 vols, London, 1924).

MAGNUS, Philip, *Kitchener: Portrait of an Imperialist* (London, 1961).

MANSERGH, Nicholas, *The Irish Question* (London, 1975).

MARDER, A. J., *Fear God and Dread Nought* (3 vols, London, 1952–9).

MAUDE, Lt-Col F. N., *Cavalry: Its Past and Future* (London, 1903).

MAURICE, Maj.-Gen. Sir F., *The Life of General Lord Rawlinson of Trent* (London, 1928).

—— *Haldane 1856–1915* (London, 1937).

—— and GRANT, Capt. H. M., *Official History of the War in South Africa*, (4 vols of text and 4 of maps, London, 1906–10).

MEREWETHER, Lt-Col. J. W. B. and SMITH, Sir Frederick, *The Indian Corps in France* (London, 1919).

MOON, H. R., 'The Invasion of the United Kingdom: Public Controversy and Official Planning', (unpublished PhD thesis, University of London, 1968).

NICOLSON, Sir Harold, *King George V* (London, 1952).

Ó BROIN, Leon, *Dublin Castle and the 1916 Rising* (Dublin, 1966).

PAKENHAM, Thomas, *The Boer War* (London, 1979).

POINCARÉ, R., *The Memoirs of Raymond Poincaré* (London, 1929).

PONSONBY, Sir Frederick, *Recollections of Three Reigns* (London, 1951).

REPINGTON, Lt-Col. C. A. C., *The First World War 1914–18* (London, 1920).

RIDDELL, Lord, *Lord Riddell's War Diary* (London, 1933).

RIMINGTON, Maj.-Gen. M. F., *Our Cavalry* (London, 1912).

ROBERTSON, Field-Marshal Sir William, *From Private to Field-Marshal* (London, 1921).

—— *Soldiers and Statesmen* (2 vols, London, 1926).

ROSKILL, Capt. Stephen, *Hankey: Man of Secrets, I, 1877–1918* (London, 1970).

RYAN, A. P., *Mutiny at the Curragh* (London, 1956).

SASSOON, Siegfried, *Memoirs of a Foxhunting Man, Memoirs of an Infantry Officer* (London, 1971).

SEELY, J. E. B., *Adventure* (London, 1933).

SHEPHARD, Major E. W., *The Ninth Queen's Royal Lancers 1715–1936* (Aldershot, 1939).

SMITH, Maj.-Gen. F., *Veterinary History of the War in South Africa* (London, 1919).

SMITH-DORRIEN, Gen. Sir Horace, *Memories of Forty-Eight Years Service* (London, 1925).

Bibliography

SMITHERS, A. J., *The Man who Disobeyed: Sir Horace Smith-Dorrien and His Enemies* (London, 1970).
SPEARS, Brig.-Gen. E. L., *Liaison 1914* (London, 1930).
STEEVENS, G. W., *From Cape Town to Ladysmith* (London, 1900).
STEWART, A. T. Q., *The Ulster Crisis* (London, 1967).
TAYLOR, A. J. P., *The Struggle for Mastery in Europe* (Oxford, 1960).
TERRAINE, John, *Mons: The Retreat to Victory* (London, 1960).
—— *Douglas Haig: The Educated Soldier* (London, 1963).
—— *The Western Front 1914–18* (London, 1964).
TOWNSHEND, Charles, *The British Campaign in Ireland 1919–21* (Oxford, 1975).
TREVELYAN, G. M., *Grey of Falloden* (New York, 1948).
VON BERNHARDI, Lt-Gen. F., *Cavalry in Future Wars* (London, 1906).
WARNER, Philip, *The Battle of Loos* (London, 1976).
WAVELL, Field-Marshal Lord, *Allenby: A Study in Greatness* (London, 1940).
—— *Allenby: Soldier and Statesman* (London, 1946).
WILSON, Sir Charles, *From Korti to Khartoum* (London, 1886).
WOLSELEY, Field-Marshal Viscount, *The Story of a Soldier's Life* (2 vols, London, 1903).
WOOD, Field-Marshal Sir Evelyn, *From Midshipman to Field-Marshal* (2 vols, London, 1906).
WYNNE, Capt. G. C., *If Germany Attacks: The Battle in Depth in the West* (London, 1940).

Articles

BETHUNE, Brig.-Gen. E. C., 'The Uses of Cavalry and Mounted Infantry in Modern Warfare', *Journal of the Royal United Services Institute*, February, 1906.
EDMONDS, Brig.-Gen. Sir James, 'Sir John French and the Reserves at Loos, 25 September 1915', *JRUSI*, 1936.
FORTESCUE, J. W., 'Review of Field-Marshal Lord French's *1914*', *Quarterly Review*, October, 1919.
FRENCH, David, 'The Military Background to the "Shell Crisis" of May 1915', *Journal of Strategic Studies*, September, 1979.
HAMILTON, Lt-Gen. Sir Ian, 'The Training of Troops during 1906', *JRUSI*, December, 1906.
MILLER, Roger, 'The Logistics of the British Expeditionary Force', *Military Affairs*, October, 1979.

Bibliography

MOLYNEUX, Col. E. M. J., 'The British Cavalry: Some Suggestions', *JRUSI*, 1904.

SPIERS, E. M., 'The British Cavalry 1902–14', *Journal of the Society for Army Historical Research*, Summer, 1979.

TAYLOR, William L., 'The Debate over changing Cavalry Tactics and Weapons', *Military Affairs*, Winter, 1965.

'War and the Arme Blanche: The General Staff views on Mr. Childers' Book', *JRUSI*, 1910.

WOOD, Field-Marshal Sir Evelyn, 'British Cavalry 1853–1903', *Cavalry Journal*, I, 1906.

Index

Index

Index

Index

Colony, 112–16; at Aldershot, 123–8; recommended Chief of General Staff, 126; Inspector General of the Forces, 128–9; Chief of the Imperial General Staff, 135–8, 166–92; Commander-in-Chief designate BEF, 138–50; Field Marshal, 138, 170; prewar visit to France, 143–6; to Germany, 147–8; pre-war manoeuvres, 149–50, 164; and Curragh incident, 166–94; Inspector-General, 193; Commander-in-Chief BEF, 196–313; pressure to remove him, 298–9, 306–12; Commander-in-Chief Home Forces, 314–34; and Ireland, 321–7; and views on later conduct of the War, 327–34; Lord Lieutenant of Ireland, 334–58; against Sinn Fein, 338–45, 347–50; life threatened by IRA, 353–4; writing *1914*, 359–61; retirement, 362–5; Captain, Deal Castle, 364–5
battles: Abu Klea, 36–7; advance to Nile, 37–9; retreat to Jakdul, 41; Elandslaagte, 12–14, 62–7; Lombard Kop, 68–9; Ladysmith seige, 69; Colesberg, 77–80; relief of Kimberley, 82–94; Klip Drift, 88–92; Poplar Grove, 97–101; Zand River, 103–4; Diamond Hill, 106–7; capture of Barberton, 109–10; Mons, 215–16; Marne, 240; 1st Ypres, 244–56; Neuve Chapelle, 271–3; Lille, 273, 278; 2nd Ypres, 282–5; Aubers Ridge, 286–7; Loos, 295–306
conflict with: Haig, 309–10, 312, 327–34; Kitchener, 231–6, 243, 254, 258, 262; Lanrezac, 208–9, 213, 218, 221, 225, 227–8, 230–1, 237; Smith-Dorrien, 131–3, 221–6, 283–4, 359–61;
other people on: 1–6
views on: Allied strategy, 138–42, 280; cavalry, role of, 152–63; infantry, role of, 163–4; military administration, 44; military recruitment & training, 45, 130–1, 156; military tactics, 25, 49; monarchy, 128, 138; religion, 276–7; Staff College, 33–4, 126; war casualties, 276–8, 304–6, 314
books: Cavalry Drill (1898), 36, 49, 51, 157; *1914* (1919), 4, 5, 215, 222–4, 235, 236, 290–2, 359–61; *quoted*, 214–15, 233
quoted: 19–20, 29, 40, 74, 102, 124–7, 136, 143, 157–9, 161, 186; to Mrs Bennett, 279–81, 302, 305–6; concerning Ireland, 335, 339, 341, 350–1, 356, 357; concerning the War, 203, 216, 219, 222, 226, 228–9, 231, 232, 234, 237, 239, 241, 252, 258, 263–4, 271, 275–7, 285, 286, 289–92, 294, 297, 307, 309, 311, 314–16, 318–20, 330, 333

French, John Richard Lowndes (son of J. F.), 29, 364
French, John Tracy (father of J. F.), 15, 16
French Army, 149, 200, 206, 230, 246, 247, 253, 260, 261, 265, 271, 282, 284–5, 286, 293, 295, 296; Fifth Army, 206, 211–19, 226–30, 236, 237; Grand Quartier Général (GQG), 206, 208, 210, 211, 219, 220, 223, 226, 235, 236, 242, 243, 254, 255, 259, 266, 267, 269, 270, 271, 294, 297, 298; Sixth Army, 228–9, 236, 237, 242, 251, 281
Frewen, Moreton, 47; *quoted*, 47
Frewen, Lieut-Col Stephen, 47
Friend, Maj-Gen. L. B., 176, 322, 323

Galbert, Maj. de, 238
Galliéni, Gen. Joseph-Simon, 236, 238
gas, poison, 282, 300, 302, 317
Gatacre, Lieut-Gen. Sir William, 71, 74, 80
George V, King, 111, 118, 138, 168–70, 172, 182–4, 186, 189, 204, 212,

Index

Index

Index

Index